The UK Economy
A Manual of
Applied Economics

Tenth Edition

Edited by
A. R. Prest M.A. Ph.D.
Professor of Economics, London School of Economics

and

D. J. Coppock B.A. (Econ.)
Emeritus Professor of Economics, University of Manchester

Weidenfeld and Nicolson

London

First published 1966
Second impression 1967
Third impression 1968
Second edition 1968
Second impression 1969
Third edition 1970
Second impression 1971
Fourth edition 1972
Fifth edition 1974
Sixth edition 1976
Seventh edition 1978
Eighth edition 1980
Ninth edition 1982
Tenth edition 1984

First published in Great Britain by
George Weidenfeld and Nicolson Limited
91 Clapham High St London SW4 7TA

ISBN 0 297 78518 4   cased
ISBN 0 297 78519 2   paperback

Text set in 10/11 pt IBM Press Roman, printed and bound
in Great Britain at The Pitman Press, Bath

Contents

TABLES

Chapter 4

Chapter 5

FIGURES

Chapter 1

STATISTICAL APPENDIX

ABBREVIATIONS

(1) Economic Terms

BOF	Balance for Official Financing
CAP	Common Agricultural Policy
CET	Common External Tariff
c.i.f.	Cost including Insurance and Freight
DCE	Domestic Credit Expansion
ECU	European Currency Unit
FIS	Family Income Supplement
f.o.b.	Free on Board
GDP	Gross Domestic Product
GNP	Gross National Product
MCA	Monetary Compensation Amounts
MLH	Minimum List Headings
NSA	Non Sterling Area
NS	North Sea
OSA	Overseas Sterling Area
PAYE	Pay as you Earn
PDI	Personal Disposable Income
PRT	Petroleum Revenue Tax
PSBR	Public Sector Borrowing Requirement
R and D	Research and Development
RPM	Resale Price Maintenance
SDRs	Special Drawing Rights
SIC	Standard Industrial Classification
SITC	Standard Industrial Trade Classification
TFE	Total Final Expenditure at Market Prices
VAT	Value Added Tax

(2) Organizations, etc.

BTG	British Technology Group
CBI	Confederation of British Industry
CSO	Central Statistical Office (UK)
DE	Department of Employment
DTI	Department of Trade and Industry
ECE	Economic Commission for Europe
ECSC	European Coal and Steel Community
EEA	Exchange Equalization Account
EEC	European Economic Community
EFTA	European Free Trade Area
FAO	Food and Agriculture Organization
GATT	General Agreement on Tariffs and Trade
GES	Government Economic Service
IFC	International Finance Corporation
IMF	International Monetary Fund

MC	Monopolies and Mergers Commission
NEB	National Enterprise Board
NEDC(O)	National Economic Development Council (Office)
NIESR	National Institute of Economic and Social Research
NRDC	National Research and Development Corporation
OECD	Organization for Economic Cooperation and Development
OPCS	Office of Population Census and Surveys
OPEC	Organization of Petroleum Exporting Countries
TUC	Trades Union Congress
UN	United Nations
UNCTAD	United Nations Commission for Trade and Development
WB	World Bank

(3) Journals, etc.

AAS	Annual Abstract of Statistics (HMSO)
AER	American Economic Review
BB	British Business (formerly Trade and Industry)
BEQB	Bank of England Quarterly Bulletin
BJIR	British Journal of Industrial Relations
DEG	Department of Employment Gazette (HMSO)
EC	Economica
EJ	Economic Journal
ET(AS)	Economic Trends (Annual Supplement) (HMSO)
FES	Family Expenditure Survey (HMSO)
FS	Financial Statistics (HMSO)
FSBR	Financial Statement and Budget Report (HMSO)
GHS	General Household Survey
IFS	International Financial Statistics
JIE	Journal of Industrial Economics
JPE	Journal of Political Economy
JRSS	Journal of Royal Statistical Society
LBR	Lloyds Bank Review
LCES	London and Cambridge Economic Service
MBR	Midland Bank Review
MDS	Monthly Digest of Statistics (HMSO)
MS	The Manchester School of Economic and Social Studies
NIE	National Income and Expenditure (HMSO)
NIER	National Institute Economic Review
NWBQR	National Westminster Bank Quarterly Review
OEP	Oxford Economic Papers
QJE	Quarterly Journal of Economics
RES	Review of Economic Studies
REST	Review of Economics and Statistics
SJPE	Scottish Journal of Political Economy
ST	Social Trends (HMSO)
TBR	Three Banks Review
TER	Treasury Economic Report (HMSO)
TI	Trade and Industry (HMSO)

Foreword to the Tenth Edition

In 1966, when the first edition of this book was published, the Foreword began as follows:

> The central idea behind this book is to give an account of the main features and problems of the UK economy today. The hope is that it will fulfil two functions simultaneously, in that it will be as up to date as possible and yet will not be simply a bare catalogue of facts and figures. There are many sources of information, official and otherwise, about the structure and progress of the UK economy. There are also many authors to whom one can turn for subtle analyses of the problems before us. Our effort here is based on the belief that there is both room and need for an attempt to combine the functions of chronicler and analyst in the confines of a single book.
>
> The contributors to these pages subscribe rather firmly to the belief that economists should practise, as well as preach, the principle of the division of labour. The complexity of a modern economy is such that, whether one likes it or not, it is no longer possible for any individual to be authoritative on all its aspects; so it is inevitable that the burden of producing work of this kind should be spread among a number of people, each a specialist in his or her particular field. Such a division carries with it obvious dangers of overlap and inconsistency. It is hoped that some of the worst pitfalls of this kind have been avoided and there is reasonable unity of purpose, treatment and layout. At the same time, it is wholly undesirable to impose a monolithic structure and it is just as apparent to the authors that there are differences in outlook and emphasis among them as it will be to the readers.
>
> The general intention was to base exposition on the assumption that the reader would have some elementary knowledge of economics — say a student in the latter part of a typical first year course in economics in a British university. At the same time, it is hoped that most of the text will be intelligible to those without this degree of expertise. We may not have succeeded in this; if not, we shall try to do better in the future.

Despite the usual extensive re-writing, we should still, eighteen years later, regard this as an accurate description of our intentions.

Chapter 1, 'The Economy as a Whole', is concerned with questions of applied macroeconomics: fluctuations in output and expenditure, the determinants and management of demand, inflation and economic growth. The chapter ends with a section on economic prospects and policies to 1989. Chapter 2, 'The Monetary, Financial and Fiscal Systems', starts with a brief discussion of the general theoretical background and then analyses in detail the theory and practices of monetary, financial and fiscal policies in the UK in recent years. The final section discusses the policy record and prospects, especially in the light of the revision of the Medium Term Financial Strategy in 1984, and some implications of membership of the EEC. Chapter 3, 'Foreign Trade and the Balance of Payments', deals with the importance of foreign trade and payments to the UK economy and assesses UK balance of payments performance over the last two decades or so. It then looks at current problems and policies in this field and ends with a discussion of the reform of the international monetary system and of international indebtedness problems. Chapter 4, 'Industry', starts with a summary of UK industrial performance between 1960 and 1980 and then looks briefly at agriculture. Nationalized industries and the arguments for privatization, competition policy and regional policy are examined at length. The final section is on industrial policy. Due regard is paid to the implications of EEC membership throughout. The last chapter, 'Labour', analyses employment and unemployment among the UK workforce, and then discusses problems of pay and income distribution. The final section is concerned with trade unions, industrial relations, wage inflation and related policy issues.

Whilst we try to minimize unnecessary overlapping between chapters, we quite deliberately aim at complementary treatment of some topics. Thus Chapter 1 is a more Keynesian approach to macroeconomic problems whereas Chapter 2 is more monetarist-oriented. Wage inflation is looked at from different angles in Chapters 1 and 5. Aspects of EEC membership come up in Chapters 2, 3 and 4. The implications of North Sea oil are very wide-ranging both domestically and internationally, and so receive discussion in Chapters 2, 3 and 4. Most aspects of government revenue are the province of Chapter 2, but national insurance contributions are also covered in Chapter 5. Regional policy is mainly the concern of Chapter 4, but also receives attention elsewhere.

To minimize the use of space, factual material or definitions appearing in one chapter but relevant to another are not always duplicated and so it must be understood that to this extent any one chapter may not be self-contained. We have also tried to limit the number of footnotes, to avoid undue cluttering of the text.

Each chapter is accompanied by a list of references and further reading. The Statistical Appendix has seven tables dealing with different aspects of the UK economy. There is an index as well as the detailed list of headings and sub-headings given in the Contents pages.

We acknowledge the great help given to us by all those who have rendered secretarial or computing assistance.

London School of Economics   A.R. PREST
University of Manchester   D.J. COPPOCK

April 1984

1

The economy as a whole

M.C. Kennedy

I INTRODUCTION
I.1 Methodological Approach

This chapter is an introduction to applied macroeconomics. It begins with a brief
description of the national income accounts, and goes on to discuss the multiplier,
the determination of national output and prices, and the policy problems of restoring full employment without inflation. It cannot claim to give all the answers to
the questions raised, but aims to provide the reader with a basis for further and
deeper study.

In principle there is no essential difference between applied economics and
economic theory. The object of applied economics is to explain the way in which
economic units work. It is just as much concerned with questions of causation
(such as what determines total consumption or the level of prices) as the theory
which is found in most elementary textbooks. The difference between theoretical
and applied economics is largely one of emphasis, with theory tending to stress
logical connections between assumptions and conclusions, and applied economics
the connections between theories and evidence. Applied economics does not seek
description for its own sake, but it needs facts for the light they shed on the
applicability of economic theory.

At one time it used to be thought that scientific theories were derived from
factual information by a method of inference known as *induction*.[1] Thus it was
supposed that general laws about nature could be deduced from knowledge of a
limited number of facts. From the logical point of view, however, induction is
invalid. If ten men have been observed to save one-tenth of their income it does
not follow that the next man will do the same. The conclusion may be true or
false, but it does not rest validly on the assumptions. Inductive conclusions of this
kind simply have the status of conjectures and require further empirical
investigation.

More recently it has come to be accepted that scientific method is not inductive
but *hypothetico-deductive*. A hypothesis may be proposed to explain a certain
class of event. It will generally be of the conditional form 'if p then q', from which

---

1 For an introduction to the problems of scientific method the reader is referred to P. B.
Medawar, *Induction and Intuition in Scientific Thought*, Methuen, 1969, and K.R. Popper,
The Logic of Scientific Discovery, Hutchinson, 1959, and *Conjectures and Refutations*,
Routledge and Kegan Paul, 1963. For a treatment of methodological problems in economics,
see I.M.T. Stewart, *Reasoning and Method of Economics*, McGraw–Hill, 1979; M. Blaug, *The
Methodology of Economics*, Cambridge University Press, 1980; and D.M. McCloskey, 'The
Rhetoric of Economics', *Journal of Economic Literature*, June 1983.

the inference is that any particular instance of *p* must be accompanied by an instance of *q*. Thus the hypothesis is tested by all observations of *p*, and corroborated whenever *p* and *q* are observed together. It is falsified if *p* occurs in the absence of *q*.

It will be clear that this concept of scientific inference places the role of factual information in a different light from the inductive approach. Facts, instead of being the foundation on which to build economic or scientific theories, become the basis for testing them. If a theory is able to survive a determined but unsuccessful attempt to refute it by factual evidence, it is regarded as well tested. But the discovery of evidence which is inconsistent with the theory will stimulate its modification or the development of a new theory altogether. One of the purposes of studying applied economics is to acquaint the theoretically equipped economist with the limitations of the theory he has studied. Applied economics is not an attempt to bolster up existing theory or, as its name might seem to imply, to demonstrate dogmatically that all the factual evidence is a neat application of textbook theory. Its aim is to understand the workings of the economy, and this means that it will sometimes expose the shortcomings of existing theory and go on to suggest improvements.

The discovery that a theory is falsified by factual observations need not mean that it must be rejected out of hand or relegated to total oblivion. Economists, as well as natural scientists, frequently have to work with theories that are inadequate in one way or another. Theories that explain part but not all of the evidence are often retained until some new theory is found which fits a wider range of evidence. Frequently the theory will turn out to have been incomplete rather than just wrong, and when modified by the addition of some new variable (or more careful specification of the *ceteris paribus* clause), the theory may regain its status. The reader who notices inconsistencies between theory and facts need not take the line that the theory is total nonsense, for the theory may still hold enough grains of truth to become the basis for something better.

It is often argued that our ability to test economic theories by reference to evidence is sufficient to liberate economics from value judgements, i.e. to turn it into a *positive* subject. This position has more than an element of truth in it: when there is clear evidence against a theory it stands a fair chance of being dropped even by its most bigoted adherents. Nevertheless, it would be wrong to forget that a great deal of what passes for evidence in economics is infirm in character (e.g. the statistics of gross domestic product or personal saving), so that it is often possible for evidence to be viewed more sceptically by some than by others.

The discussion of economic policy which also figures in this chapter is partly normative in scope, and partly positive. The normative content of policy discussion involves the evaluation of goals and priorities. But the means for attaining such goals derive from the positive hypotheses of economics. They involve questions of cause and effect, to which the answers are hypothetical and testable by evidence. In making recommendations for policy, however, the economist treads on thin ice. This is partly because his positive knowledge is not inevitably correct, but also because it is seldom possible for him to foresee and properly appraise all the side-effects of his recommendations, some of which have implications for other policy goals. When economists differ in their advice on policy questions it is not always clear how much the difference is due on the one hand to diagnostic disagreements, or, on the other, to differences in value judgements. Indeed it is seldom possible for an economic adviser to reveal all the normative preferences which lie behind a policy recommendation. Policy judgements have to be scrutinized carefully for hidden normative assumptions, and the reader of this chapter must be on his guard against the author's personal value judgements.

I.2   Gross Domestic Product

Most of the topics discussed in this chapter make some use of the national accounts statistics. A complete explanation of what these are and how they are put together is available elsewhere.[1] It will be useful, however, in the next few pages to introduce the reader to the main national accounting categories in so far as they affect this chapter.

Gross domestic product (GDP) represents the output of the whole economy, i.e. the production of all the enterprises resident in the UK. In principle, it can be assembled from three separate sets of data — from output, from income and from expenditure. The three totals should, in principle, be equal — a point which may seem surprising when it is recalled that spending and output are seldom equal for an individual firm. But the convention in national accounting is to count all *unsold output* as part of investment in stocks, and to regard this both as 'expenditure' and as 'income' (profits) in kind. Thus the three estimates are made to equal each other by the device of defining expenditure and income differently from their everyday meanings.

Although there are three possible ways of estimating GDP, the output method is too slow and cumbersome to be used at frequent intervals. This leaves only two estimates of current-price GDP — the expenditure- and income-based estimates — both of which are shown in table 1.1.

The expenditure-based method classifies expenditure by four types of spending unit: persons, public authorities, firms and foreign residents.[2] Purchases by persons are described as consumers' expenditure, or, more loosely, as consumption. The latter description, however, may be slightly misleading when applied to expenditure on durable goods such as motorcars and refrigerators, the services of which are consumed over several years and not solely in the year in which they are purchased. One form of personal expenditure which is not classed as such is the purchase of new houses. These are deemed to have been sold initially to 'firms' and included under the broad heading of domestic capital formation or gross fixed investment. Fixed investment represents the purchases by firms of physical assets that are not used up in current production, but which accrue as additions or replacements to the nation's capital stock. The preface 'gross' warns us that a year's gross investment does not measure the change in the size of the capital stock during the year because it does not allow for the erosion of the capital stock due to scrapping and wear and

---

1   See, for example, W. Beckerman, *An Introduction to National Income Analysis*, 3rd edition, Weidenfeld and Nicolson, 1980; S. Hays, *National Income and Expenditure in Britain and the OECD Countries*, Heinemann, 1971; R. and G. Stone, *National Income and Expenditure*, 9th edition, Bowes and Bowes, 1972; H.C. Edey and others, *National Income and Social Accounting*, 3rd edition, Hutchinson, 1967; or the official publications, *National Accounts Statistics, Sources and Methods*, HMSO, 1968, and *The National Accounts: A Short Guide*, HMSO, 1981.

2   The distinctions between types of spending units are not always clear-cut, e.g. expenditure by self-employed persons is partly consumers' expenditure and partly investment.

TABLE 1.1
GDP at Current Prices, UK, 1982

FROM EXPENDITURE

	£bn	% of TFE[1]
Consumers' expenditure	167.1	49
General government final consumption	60.1	18
Gross domestic fixed investment	42.2	12
Investment in stocks	−1.2	−0.4
Exports of goods and services	73.1	21
Total final expenditure at market prices	341.3	100
less Imports of goods and services	−67.2	
less Adjustment to factor cost	−41.6	
Gross domestic product at factor cost	232.6	

FROM INCOME

	£bn	% of domestic income[1]
Income from employment	155.1	66
Income from self-employment	20.1	9
Income from rent	16.2	7
Gross trading profits of companies	33.3	14
Gross trading surplus of public corporations and other public enterprises	9.2	4
Imputed charge for consumption of non-trading capital	2.5	1
Total domestic income	236.4	100
less Stock appreciation	−3.9	
Gross domestic product at factor cost (from income)	232.5	
Residual error	0.1	
Gross domestic product at factor cost (from expenditure)	232.6	

BY INDUSTRY (FROM INCOME)

	£bn	% of total[1]
Agriculture, forestry and fishing	5.8	2
Energy and water supply	26.0	11
Manufacturing	56.5	23
Construction	13.5	6
Distribution, hotels and catering, repairs	30.0	12
Banking, finance, insurance, business services and leasing	29.0	12
Education and health	20.9	9
Other services	63.1	26
Total (after providing for stock appreciation	244.8	100
Adjustment for financial services[2]	−12.3	
Gross domestic product at factor cost (from income)	232.5	

Source: NIE, 1983, tables 1.1, 1.2 and 1.9.

1 Details do not add to totals because of rounding.
2 Deduction of net receipts of interest by financial companies.

tear. The concept of gross capital formation is also carried through into the definition of domestic product itself, indicating that the value of *gross* domestic product makes no allowance for capital consumption. The other category of investment is investment in stocks or, as the CSO puts it, 'the value of the physical increase in stocks'. This can make no distinction between voluntary and involuntary stock changes.

The sum of exports, consumers' expenditure, government final consumption and gross investment is known as total final expenditure at market prices, or TFE for short. Each of the four components contains two elements which must be deducted before arriving at GDP at factor cost. The first is the import content of expenditure which must, of course, be classified as foreign rather than domestically produced output. The simplest way of removing imports is to take the global import total as given by the balance-of-payments accounts and subtract it from TFE, and this is the usual method. Estimates do exist, however, for the import content of the separate components of final expenditure in the input-output tables, but these are drawn up much less frequently than the national accounts.

The second element of total final expenditure which must be deducted to obtain the factor-cost value of GDP is the indirect-tax content (net of subsidies) of the various expenditures. This is present for the simple reason that the most readily available valuation of any commodity is the price at which it sells in the market. This price, however, will overstate the factor incomes earned from producing the commodity if it contains an element of indirect tax; and it will understate factor income if the price is subsidized. The deduction of indirect taxes (less subsidies) is known as the *factor-cost adjustment*, and is most conveniently made globally since it can be found from the government's records of tax proceeds and subsidy payments. Estimates of its incidence on the individual components of TFE are available annually in the National Income *Blue Book*.[1]

The income-based estimate arrives at GDP by summing up the incomes of all the residents of the UK earned in the production of goods and services in the UK during a stated period. It divides into income from employment, income from self-employment and profit, and income from rent. These are factor incomes earned in the process of production and are to be distinguished from *transfer incomes*, such as pensions and sickness benefits, which are not earned from production and which, therefore, are excluded from the total. The breakdown of factor incomes for 1982 is illustrated in table 1.1

The income breakdown of GDP contains two items which may need further explanation. The first is the 'imputed charge for consumption of non-trading capital', which is imputed rent from government property and private non-profit-making bodies. This should not be confused with capital consumption, which is the wear and tear of capital equipment. The other item is the adjustment for stock appreciation, which appears here because changes in the book value of stocks have been accredited to profits. The problem of adjustment for stock appreciation arises because the change in the book value between the beginning and end of the year may be partly due to a price change.

A firm holding stocks of wood, for example, may increase its holding from 100 tons on 1 January to 200 tons on 31 December. If the price of wood was £1.00 per ton at the beginning of the year and £1.10 at the end of the year, the increase in

---

1 *NIE*, 1983, table 1.1.

the monetary value of stocks will show up as (£1.10 x 200) – (£1.00 x 100), which equals £120. This figure is inflated by the amount of the price increase and fails, therefore, to give an adequate record of what the Central Statistical Office (CSO) calls 'the value of the physical increase in stocks'. In order to rectify this, the CSO attempts to value the physical change in stocks at the average price level prevailing during the period. If, in the example, the price averaged £1.05 over the period, then the value of the physical increase in stocks would be shown as £1.05 (200–100), which equals £105. The difference of £15 between this and the increase in monetary value is the adjustment for stock appreciation.

GDP by income can be rearranged in terms of the industries in which the incomes were earned. This breakdown is available annually and gives an up-to-date picture of the industrial composition of total output, showing, for example, that manufacturing production is less than one-quarter of the value of GDP. The industry breakdown is shown in table 1.1, but it is not an independent measure of GDP.

The expenditure and income estimates are derived from different and largely independent sets of data. They never add up to exactly the same total, and the difference between them is known as the *residual error*. The published residual error (which was quite small in 1982) is actually less than the real difference because of an allowance the CSO makes for the systematic under-reporting of incomes to the Inland Revenue.[1]

An output-based estimate of GDP can, in principle, be compiled by adding up the *net output* or *value added* of all the firms and productive units in the economy. To obtain such a total it would be necessary to find the *gross output* of each firm in the economy and to subtract from it the value of *intermediate input*, i.e. goods and services purchased from other firms. In practice this herculean task cannot be accomplished in the time-span of a single year. A Census of Production is, however, in a state of continuous collection, and data from the census are used to establish the weights in the volume indices which are used to measure constant-price GDP.

Gross domestic product is the most widely used of several aggregates, the others being GNP and National Income. The relationships between the various aggregates in 1982 were:

		£bn (current prices)
	GNP at market prices	275.8
less	Net property income from abroad	−1.6
equals	GDP at market prices	274.2
less	Factor-cost adjustment	−41.6
equals	GDP at factor cost (from expenditure)	232.6
plus	Net property income from abroad	+1.6
equals	GNP at factor cost	234.1
less	Capital consumption	−33.1
equals	National income	201.1

GNP, like GDP, may be valued at market prices or factor cost. It differs from GDP by including net interest, profits and dividends earned by UK residents from productive enterprises owned overseas. The other concept, National Income, differs from GNP by the amount of capital consumption, this being the CSO's estimate of depreciation. It is also the figure which must be subtracted from gross

---

1 K.M. Macafee, 'A glimpse of the hidden economy in the national accounts', *ET*, February 1980.

investment to find net investment. GDP and the gross concept of investment are in much more frequent use than net income and net investment because they relate directly to employment. When a machine is being produced it makes no difference to the number of workers employed whether it is to replace one already in use or whether it adds to the capital stock.

I.3   Gross Domestic Product at Constant Prices

If we wish to compare the *volume* of goods produced in different periods, we must use the estimates of GDP at constant prices, the expenditure side of which is presented in the Statistical Appendix, table A-1. These show the value of GDP for each year in terms of the prices ruling in 1980. Similar estimates are available for the output total of GDP together with its main industrial components. These are derived almost entirely from movements in quantities, the various quantities for each year being added together by means of the value weights obtaining for 1980.

There are only two direct estimates of GDP at constant prices: the expenditure- and the output-based estimates. But an income estimate may be obtained by dividing the current-price total by the implied price index (or 'deflator') for GDP. This index is simply the result of dividing GDP at current prices by GDP at constant prices (both on the expenditure basis). This means that for GDP as a whole there are, altogether, three independent estimates of the constant-price total. There are often sizeable discrepancies between the three estimates, and this implies that it is unwise to be too precise about the level of constant-price GDP. In 1982, for example, GDP in constant prices was put by the expenditure estimate at 101.2% of the 1980 level, whereas the income and output estimates made it 99.9 and 99.0 respectively. These discrepancies in the level of GDP also mean that the annual rate of change is not known unambiguously. The decline in GDP from 1979 to 1981, for example, was put at less than 4% by the expenditure and income estimates but at more than 5% by the output figure. An inspection of annual changes in GNP since 1970 shows that, on average, the spread between the highest and lowest estimates was 1.3%; in one year it was 2.2%; and in only three years was it less than 1.0%.

Gross domestic product is an important entity in its own right, and changes in its real amount are the best estimates available of changes in total UK production. Even so, it must be remembered that it leaves a good deal out of the picture by excluding practically all productive work which is not sold for money. The national income statistics neglect, for example, the activities of the housewife and do-it-yourself enthusiast, even though they must add millions of hours to UK production of goods and services. It is also important to recognize that GDP stands for the production of UK residents, not their expenditure. As an expenditure total it measures the spending of all persons, resident or foreign, on the goods and services produced by the residents of the UK. Thus if national welfare is conceived as spending by UK residents, it is incorrect to represent it by GDP. The total appropriate for this purpose is GDP *plus* imports *minus* exports. This total is referred to as total domestic expenditure, and is equal to the UK's total use of resources, which is the sum of personal consumption, government consumption and gross investment.

II   FLUCTUATIONS IN TOTAL OUTPUT AND EXPENDITURE
II.1   Fluctuations in Output and Employment

The British economy has experienced cyclical fluctuations in total output and
employment since the time of the industrial revolution. During the nineteenth century these appeared to follow a fairly uniform pattern, with a peak-to-peak
duration of seven to ten years and a tendency for 'full employment' (roughly
defined) to reappear at each cyclical peak. After the First World War this pattern
ceased, and for nearly twenty years there were well over one million unemployed.
Unemployment reached nearly 9% of the workforce in the recession of 1926 and
nearly 16% in 1932.

The period after the Second World War until the early 1970s was one of continuously high employment, with only the mildest fluctuations in GDP, employment and unemployment. The unemployment rate (UK, excluding school-leavers)
never exceeded an annual figure of 2.4%, and, during peak periods of activity, was
as little as 1 or 1½% of the employed labour force. During this period, the decline
in real GDP during cyclical downturns never exceeded 1.0%, and in most recessions
GDP simply rose at a slower-than-average rate of increase. This period of high and
stable employment was also characterized by a much lower average rate of inflation
than has been experienced since 1970.

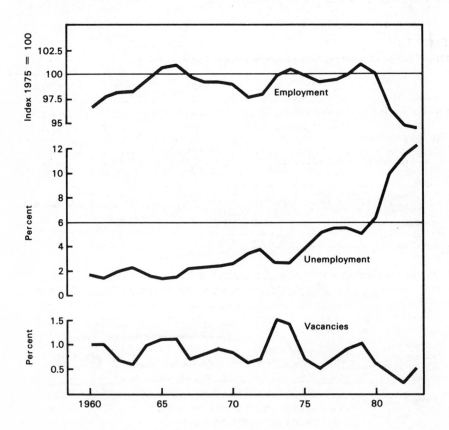

Figure 1.1   Employment, unemployment and vacancies, UK, 1960–83

It was not until the 1970s that the business cycle threatened to return on the scale of the prewar era (see figure 1.1). A mild recession in 1970-72 was followed in 1973-5 by a sharp rise in unemployment, and in 1979-81 the UK economy experienced a depression which was almost as severe as that of 1929-33. By early 1984 unemployment had reached 3 million, or about 12% of the employed labourforce, whilst the rate for young people aged between 16 and 19 was over 20%. The recession was most severe in Northern Ireland, Scotland, Wales and the industrial centres of England.

A comparison of the 1979-81 depression with that of 1929-32 is given in table 1.2, where it can be seen that unemployment in 1981 was not quite as high as it had been in 1932, but that the declines in employment, manufacturing output and estimated GDP were very similar in the two depressions. An important difference concerned the behaviour of wages and prices, which were falling in 1929-32 but increasing rapidly in 1979-81. This posed a dilemma for policy which was not present in the 1930s.

The early estimates of GDP for 1983 showed it to be 0.7 per cent above the 1979 level, and a 'recovery' was claimed to have taken place. But there was no sign of a recovery in employment and unemployment, and with 4 years of growing productivity GDP would probably have had to be about 7% above the level of 1979 for a full recovery in the labour market.

TABLE 1.2

Output and Employment in Three Recessions (percentages)

	1929-32	1973-5	1979-81
Unemployment rate: peak year	7.3	2.7	5.1
trough year	15.6	3.9	10.0
Change in employment	3.7	0.0	-4.6
Change in GDP (output estimate)	-4.8	-3.1	-5.2
Change in manufacturing production	-10.8	-8.1	-14.6
Change in prices per annum	-6.8	+22.0	+16.0

Sources: C.H. Feinstein, *National Income, Expenditure and Output in the United Kingdom, 1855-1965*, Cambridge University Press, 1972; *ET(AS)*, 1984.

II.2 Expenditures in the Cycle

Business recessions occur because of declines in total spending. In the United States' depression of 1929-32, when real GNP fell by almost one-third, the mainspring of the recession was a decline in fixed investment, which spread, through falling incomes, to personal consumption. The accompanying decline in US imports led to falling world trade and production, and thus to depression in the export industries of other countries.

In the United Kingdom in 1929-32, the decline in GDP was very largely confined to exports. These fell by 32%, which in absolute amount was enough to account for the whole of the decline in total final expenditure. There were mild declines in fixed investment and stock-building, and offsetting increases in consumers' and government expenditure (see table 1.3).

If 1929-32 was an export-led recession, those of 1973-5 and 1979-81 were predominantly stock recessions, with most of the decline in TFE being accounted for by large swings from stock accumulation to stock declines. Exports fell in 1979–81, partly because of the worldwide depression and partly because the exchange rate was allowed to rise: consumption fell in 1973–5 but held up in 1979–81. In both recessions there were sizeable declines in fixed investment, which by 1981 was running at its lowest level in 13 years.

TABLE 1.3

Expenditure in Three Recessions

	Level in 1929	Change 1929-32	Level in 1972	Change 1973-5	Level in 1979	Change 1979-81
	£bn at 1938 prices		£bn at 1980 prices		£bn at 1980 prices	
Consumers' expenditure	3.77	+0.07	127.7	−2.9	137.9	−0.8
Government consumption	0.44	+0.03	25.2	+2.3	28.6	+1.1
Fixed investment	0.46	−0.06	41.8	−1.5	41.6	−6.0
Investment in stocks	0.03	−0.03	5.0	−7.9	2.5	−5.1
Exports of goods and services	0.99	−0.32	49.5	+2.2	63.3	−1.3
TFE	5.69	−0.32	266.7	−7.2	292.8	−12.6

Sources: Feinstein, op. cit.; *ET(AS)*, 1984.

Periods of recovery have usually been led by a revival of fixed investment, but in 1975-9 the main stimuli came from exports, consumption and stockbuilding. Recovery, moreover, was somewhat incomplete with unemployment in 1979 at 1.3 million, or 5.1% of total employees. Unfilled vacancies in 1979 numbered only 241,000 compared with the 1973 peak level of 307,000. There is something in the claim, therefore, that the downturn of 1979–81 started from an initial level of activity which was already somewhat depressed. But this has to be seen against the background of an inflation rate in 1979 of 13 per cent.

II.3   The Determinants of Demand

The proximity of national output to its full-employment potential is determined by the level of total expenditure on goods and services, which, in the simplest terms, can be divided into two main categories: the 'autonomous' items, which are not affected by the current level of national income, and the 'endogenous' expenditures, which depend on current or lagged income. In the simplest textbook accounts, the former category is represented as investment, and is said to be determined by the stock of unexploited technological potential, by business expectations of the rate of return, and by the rate of interest. Consumption, on the other hand, is taken as dependent on income itself, so that the line of causation runs from investment to income to consumption, with investment acting as the principal cause of movements in total output.

This simple model of income determination is of clear relevance to the way in which GDP is determined in the 'real world'. But, as we have seen, there are complications. The autonomous component of total expenditure has to include, besides fixed investment, exports, government expenditure and investment in stocks, whilst the endogenous items must include imports as well as consumption. A large area of macroeconomics and applied econometrics is devoted to the attempt to explain in some detail how those various expenditures are determined. These explanations are essential if we are to understand economic fluctuations and to be able to forecast and control them.

II.4   Consumers' Expenditure

Consumers' expenditure is the largest single element in aggregate demand. It accounts for nearly half of TFE (see table 1.1) and, after the removal of its import and indirect-tax content, for about the same fraction of GDP at factor cost. Consumption is one of the more stable elements of demand, and it held up well in the recession of 1979–81. But its total amount is so large in relation to GDP that even quite small percentage variations in its level can have important repercussions for output and employment. An understanding of consumption behaviour, therefore, as well as an ability to predict it, are important objectives for economic analysis. A great deal of attention has been given to consumption, both in theory and statistically, although this work has been more heavily concentrated upon consumption in the US where the data are more plentiful.

The starting point for the early studies of consumer behaviour was the well-known statement by Keynes:[1] 'The fundamental psychological law upon which we are entitled to depend with great confidence both *a priori* from our knowledge of human nature and from the detailed facts of experience, is that men are disposed, as a rule and on the average, to increase their consumption as their income increases, but not by as much as the increase in their income.' Keynes was suggesting that current income was the principal, although not the only, determinant of consumers' expenditure in the short run, and that the marginal propensity to consume (the ratio of additional consumption to additional income) was positive, fractional and reasonably stable.

If we focus attention upon personal savings rather than consumption, it can be seen that the ratio of savings to personal disposable income has shown a strong upward trend over the postwar period, with deviations from trend which are associated with cyclical fluctuations (see figure 1.2). The ratio was above trend in the peak years of 1961, 1965 and 1971, and below trend in the intervening recessions. In the recession of 1973–5, however, the savings ratio was on the high side.

Cyclical movements in the savings ratio can be accounted for in various ways. One possible explanation is that consumer behaviour is partly a matter of habit and convention, so that when income declines the individual attempts to maintain his expenditure at its previous level with the consequence that the average propensity to consume (APC) rises and the savings ratio declines. A related explanation can be found in the ideas of the normal-income theorists.[2] Their main proposition is that

---

1   J.M. Keynes, *General Theory*, p. 96.

2   For an examination of these theories, see M.J. Farrell, 'The New Theories of the Consumption Function', *EJ*, December 1959 (reprinted in Klein and Gordon (eds.), *Readings in Business Cycles*, Allen and Unwin, 1966). The classic reference is F. Modigliani and R. Brumberg, 'Utility Analysis and the Consumption Function', in K. Kurihara (ed.), *Post-Keynesian Economics*, Allen and Unwin, 1955.

consumption depends not upon current income, but on *normal income*, which can
be defined either as the expected lifetime income of the consumer or, less precisely,
as his notion of average income over some future period. Thus it is changes in the
level of expected income which are likely to change consumption. If current
income increases, then it will raise consumption only in so far as it raises normal
income, and the amount by which it does so will depend upon the expected
persistence of the income change. Since cyclical changes in income are (by
definition) not persistent, it is to be expected that consumption will be high in
relation to income whenever the economy is in depression. Conversely the savings
ratio will be low in depressions and high at peaks.

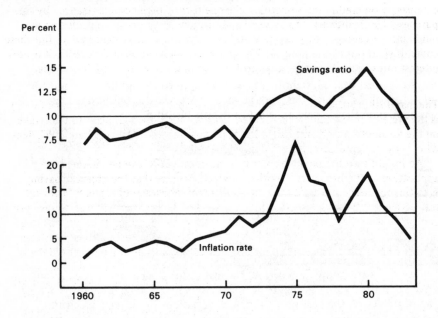

Figure 1.2   Personal savings ratio and the rate of increase in retail prices, UK, 1960–83

The rise in the savings ratio in the 1970s has been statistically associated with
the faster inflation rate, and year-to-year movements in the two variables have also
been correlated. This has led some economists to infer that changes in the inflation
rate are a major influence on the savings ratio. The theory is that inflation erodes
the purchasing power of liquid assets, and this leads people to step up their savings
rate in the attempt to restore the real value of their assets. Although the econometric estimates of the effect of inflation on the savings ratio vary a good deal
(from 0.5 to 2.5% for a 1% increase in the price level), they all point to a very
strong influence. The lowest of these estimates, for example, implies that when the
inflation rate rose by 8 percentage points in 1973–4 the induced increase in the
savings ratio was 4%. Whether the effect is really as strong as the correlation
estimates tell us, is not clear. The evidence comes mainly from a short period, and
there was no similar rise in the savings ratio in the earlier inflation of 1951. Nor
must it be forgotten that the average saver is middle-aged and has a good many

years left of working life to make up the lost purchasing power of his liquid assets. It has also been pointed out that the main non-liquid asset is house property, and this increased in real value during the 1970s. It is not impossible, therefore, that the effect of inflation on savings has been exaggerated and that some of the correlation is not causal.[1] The increase in the saving rate could also have been precautionary, reflecting fears of unemployment and of tough anti-inflationary policies.

An important influence upon consumers' expenditure is the availability and cost of credit and particularly of credit for financing purchases of durable goods.[2] These goods, which constitute 9% of total consumption, are more in the nature of capital equipment than consumption in that they yield a flow of utility over time. It is natural where income is generally rising that such goods should be bought extensively on credit, and something like one half of their total is financed by hire-purchase. HP finance used to be regulated through government controls on the minimum percentage downpayment and the maximum repayment period. But these controls went out of use in the 1970s, and were finally abolished in 1982. It is now interest rates rather than direct controls which tend to regulate HP borrowing.

The marginal propensity to consume: The marginal propensity to consume (MPC) is the increase in spending which, *ceteris paribus*, an individual plans to undertake on the assumption of a unit rise in his disposable income. The aggregate MPC, likewise, is the weighted average of all individual MPCs.

An insight into the possible size of the aggregate MPC can be obtained by application of the life-cycle hypothesis, which assumes that the object of saving is to finance consumption during retirement. An individual of representative age (say 38) who receives an increase in his income of £1 per year will plan to save just enough to maintain a constant annual addition to his spending. If he expects to go on receiving the extra income until he retires at age 65 and if he also expects to live for a further 12 years after retirement (the life expectation of a 65-year-old man), then his extra £1 will be earned for a further 27 years but will be needed for spending over a period of 39 years. These two periods are the key to his MPC, which will be $27/39 = 0.69$, whilst his marginal propensity to save will be 0.31. The calculation assumes that he disregards the interest on his savings, that the increases in income had not been previously anticipated, and that he expects it to be a permanent addition to his income. It also assumes that he is not interested in leaving any further bequests to his children, and that he is prepared to make calculations of the kind suggested. These are all rather stringent assumptions, but they do enable us to deduce that a 'representative' increase in aggregate income (i.e. one which is spread evenly across ages and income levels) might involve an MPC in the region of 0.7. This is lower than the recorded ratio of consumption to income, which was 0.89 in 1982, and well below the life-cycle theory's hypothetical APC, which is unity since individuals are assumed to consume all their life-time income.

---

1. For further information and a discussion, see K. Cuthbertson, 'The Measurement and Behaviour of the UK Savings Ratio', *NIER*, February 1982. It should be noted that figures for the savings ratio are prone to substantial revision: that for 1976 was originally put at 14.6% in 1980, but is now (*ET(AS)*, 1984) revised down to 11.7%.

2. It should be noted that the *Blue Book* definition of durable goods includes cars, motor-cycles, furniture, carpets and electrical goods, but, perhaps arbitrarily, does not include clothing, curtains, pots and pans, or books.

An empirical estimate of the MPC may be found either by econometric methods or by direct inspection of the data. Early econometric studies of consumption were in general agreement that the MPC deduced from short-term time-series data was in the region of 0.6 to 0.8.[1] These results, which related mainly to the United States, accord with the *a priori* estimates gleaned from the life-cycle hypothesis. Inspection of the data for the UK shows that the annual change in consumption, measured at current prices, has varied between 0.5 and 1.2 times the increase in disposable income over the last 30 years. Over the five years 1977–82 the figures were:

	1977-8	1978-9	1979-80	1980-1	1981-2
change in consumption (£bn)	12.9	18.8	18.5	15.3	14.9
change in personal disposable income (£bn)	16.4	22.6	24.7	13.4	13.3
estimated MPC	0.79	0.83	0.75	1.2	1.1

These show a fairly wide range, but in the calculation of the multiplier in section II.8 below we shall assume that the MPC is 0.75. There is no certainty that this is exactly the right figure, and some estimates go very much lower.[2]

II.5   Fixed Investment

Fixed investment or gross domestic fixed capital formation consists of housebuilding in both the public and private sectors of the economy, and of business investment in plant and machinery, including investment by nationalized industries. Its breakdown by industry and sector in 1982 is shown in table 1.4, where it can be seen that investment by the service industries is much larger than in manufacturing. Nevertheless, manufacturing investment is the most volatile element in the total. In the recession of 1979–81, for example, manufacturing investment fell by £2.6bn compared with a total decline in private fixed investment of £3.1bn (1980 prices). And in 1974–5 the fall in manufacturing investment of £0.6bn exceeded the decline in private fixed investment as a whole.

The explanation of investment is not without its difficulties. New capital stock is purchased and old stock replaced in the expectation of profits in the future. It is not difficult to show formally that an investment project is profitable if its marginal efficiency exceeds the rate of interest, or if its present value exceeds zero. But these calculations are based upon *forecasts* of revenues and costs which have to extend for years, or even decades, into the future. When so much depends upon vulnerable and uncertain guesses about the future, it must be expected that investment expenditure will not be as readily explicable as consumption.

1   See G. Ackley, *Macroeconomic Theory*, Macmillan, New York, 1961, and R. Ferber, 'Research on Household Behaviour', *AER*, 52, 1962, for surveys of these studies.

2   For example, the estimate of the MPC implied by the Treasury's model is not much above 0.3 for durable and non-durable goods spending. This seems to have been due to the introduction of a price variable which tends to lower the implied explanatory power of income. The variable was introduced in the attempt to account for the rise in the savings ratio in the 1970s, and is assumed to be a proxy for wealth. See H.M. Treasury, *Macroeconomic Model Equation and Variable Listing*, HMSO, 1980.

TABLE 1.4

Gross Domestic Fixed Capital Formation, UK, 1982

	Private sector	*Public sector*	*Total (£bn)*
Dwellings	3.9	2.2	6.1
Manufacturing	5.0	0.2	5.2
Energy and water supply	3.1	3.8	6.9
Distribution, hotels, catering, repairs	3.7	0.0	3.7
Banking, finance, insurance, business services, leasing	7.0	0.4	7.4
Other	7.8	5.1	12.9
Total	30.5	11.7	42.2

Source: *NIE*, 1983, p. 113; current prices.

Two of the models which are often advanced to explain investment behaviour make their own special assumptions about expected future income. The acceleration principle is sometimes justified on the assumption that the future growth of income will be equal to the past rate of growth, and on this basis it is suggested that investment is proportional to the change in income:

$$I = a\Delta Y$$

where I is investment, ΔY the change in income and a is a constant coefficient. A related model is the capital-stock-adjustment principle, which assumes that income in the next period will be equal to last period's income, so that desired investment (the change in the desired capital stock) is given as:

$$I = aY - K$$

where K is the actual level of the capital stock, and a is the assumed constant capital-output ratio.[1] Neither of these models says anything explicit about costs or interest rates, but their focus on income expectations is defensible. Another theory altogether is the view that investment can be predicted by the level of business profits, the idea being that firms simply spend what they can afford.

Whatever the merits of these models it is possible to assemble data that relate to them, and this is done in figure 1.3, where the top graph is manufacturing investment in constant prices. The figure illustrates that manufacturing investment is indeed correlated with the change in income, where this is taken as the 3-year change in real GDP at factor cost up to the previous year. (The 3-year change in manufacturing output would have given a similarly good correlation.) Figure 1.3 also shows the relationships between investment and the level of manufacturers' real profits. What we have done here is to estimate a price deflator for profits by

---

1 Because K^*, the desired capital stock, is equal to aY^* where Y^* is expected income. Hence $I = K^* - K = aY^* - K$. And if Y^* is assumed to equal current income, Y, then $I = aY - K$. It is possible to attach a coefficient to K on the assumption that investment demand in a single period is a constant fraction of $K^* - K$, i.e. $I = b(K^* - K) = abY^* - bK$. Replacement investment may also be allowed for on the assumption that is proportionate to income.

dividing manufacturing investment in current prices by manufacturing investment in constant (1980) prices. Profits are gross profits less stock appreciation. A rather less obvious correlation exists for the capital-output ratio, where the ratio shown on the graph is the capital stock at the end of the previous year divided by manufacturing output in that year (both at 1980 prices). Finally, the graph shows the long-term interest rate on government securities, and for this there is virtually no correlation whatever.

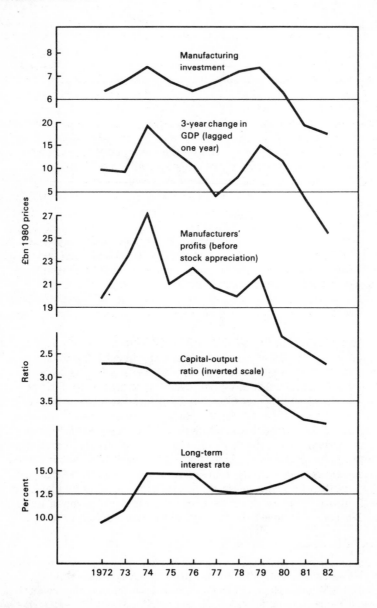

Figure 1.3   Manufacturing investment and related indicators, UK, 1972–82

The question now arises as to whether we can interpret any of these correlations as causal.[1] The best of them is the correlation with the change in income, and this might seem to give a strong case for the acceleration principle. But the argument against this conclusion is that the fastest changes in income will be those between the trough and peak of the business cycle, whilst the slower increases will be those between years either side of the peak and trough. With a cycle of 5 years' duration, a 2- or 3-year income change will tend to reach its maximum point at the same time as income *and investment* are at their peak levels. This means that investment and the income change will both reach their peaks at about the same time. Thus the correlation shown in the figure may be simply a mechanical consequence of the business cycle.

In the case of the profits hypothesis, a similar argument applies. Profits will be high when sales are high, and this will happen when autonomous spending is at its peak. Manufacturing investment is, of course, an important element in autonomous spending, so that when it peaks income will tend to be high and so will profits. So we are now arguing that it is not profits which cause investment, but investment which causes profits. But there *could* be causation in both directions.

The correlation with the lagged capital stock is not as good as the other two, and could be simply a mechanical result of low investment leading to low economic activity and, therefore, to a high ratio of capital to output. The fact that we have incorporated a lag in the correlation does not completely remove this objection, as periods of low and high economic activity tend to occur for several years at a time. There are other objections too, namely that the stock-adjustment principle makes the naive assumptions that next year's sales will be equal to this year's and that one year's sales are the relevant consideration in plant and machinery designed to last for many years. Nevertheless, we have included the correlation, and we should also note that it performed very much better in earlier years.[2]

To the question of what actually caused manufacturing investment over the period shown, we can only give a tentative answer. We doubt that the correlation with ΔY gives any real credence to the acceleration principle, even though it is the best of the four correlations. We think there is a bit of truth in both the profits and the capital-stock adjustment models, although it would not be surprising if the correlations overstated the importance of the variables. Finally, we believe on *a priori* grounds that interest rates are an influence even though here there is virtually no·correlation. It is interesting to note that the National Institute bases its forecasts of manufacturing investment on both the level of profits and the capital-output ratio, whilst the Treasury uses the acceleration principle with long distributed lags for the change in income. The Treasury also imposes, without evidence but not without reason, an influence of interest rates.[3] But at the end of the day it is still uncertain whether anybody has a robust and reliable model for explaining and forecasting manufacturing investment.

---

1 The correlation coefficient of investment with the income change is 0.81, with profits 0.78, with the capital-output ratio -0.76 and with interest rates -0.07.

2 See, for example, *The UK Economy*, 5th edition, 1974, pp. 21–3.

3 See S. Brooks and B. Henry, 'Re-estimation of the National Institute Model', *NIER*, February 1983, and H.M. Treasury, *Macroeconomic Model Equation and Variable Listing*, HMSO, 1980.

Much the same conclusion applies to other business fixed investment which, as we have seen, is not so volatile. In recent years there has been substantial investment in North Sea oil, which reached a peak in 1976 and has been falling in most years since then.

Housing investment needs to be divided between the public and private sectors and examined in relation to demand and supply influences in both sectors. The demand for public-sector building comes indirectly from population trends and directly from the policies of the public authorities. The demand for private-sector building depends both upon population characteristics (family formation and size) and also upon expected lifetime income, the cost of mortgage credit, the prices of new houses and of substitute accommodation. It is subject to the important and highly variable constraints set by the availability of mortgage credit which in turn are determined partly by general credit policy and partly by the policies of the building societies. The problem of predicting housing investment is eased, however, by the statistics of new houses started, which, with an assumption about completion times, makes it possible to forecast housing for at least a short period ahead.

II.6   Stocks and Stockbuilding

Stockbuilding or investment in stocks is the change in a level—the level of all stocks held at the beginning of the period. In any one year, stock investment can be positive or negative, whilst the change in stock investment between successive years can exert an important influence upon GDP. The increase in stock investment in 1975-7, for example, and the decline in 1979-80 were both equivalent to about 3% of GDP.

At the end of 1982 the total value of stocks held in all industries was approximately £76bn or 31% of the value of GDP in a year. Stocks held by manufacturing industry accounted for nearly £37bn, and by wholesale and retail business for £23bn.[1]

Stocks of work in progress are held because they are a technical necessity of production, whilst stocks of materials and finished goods are held mainly out of a precautionary motive. They are required as a 'buffer' between deliveries and production; or, more precisely, because firms realize that they cannot expect an exact correspondence between the amount of materials delivered each day and the amount taken into production, or between completed production and deliveries to customers.

For these reasons it seems plausible to assume that firms carry in their minds the notion of a certain optimum ratio between stocks and output. If stocks fall below the optimum ratio, they will need to be replenished; if they rise above it, they will be run down. The reasoning here is the same as that of the stock-adjustment principle which we have already mentioned in connection with fixed investment. The principle holds quite well, and is illustrated in figure 1.4 where it can be seen that peaks in stock investment generally coincided with low levels of the stock-GDP ratio.[2] This was also true in earlier years.

---

1   *NIE*, 1984, table 12.1.

2   The correlation coefficient, r, is 0.69 in figure 1.4.

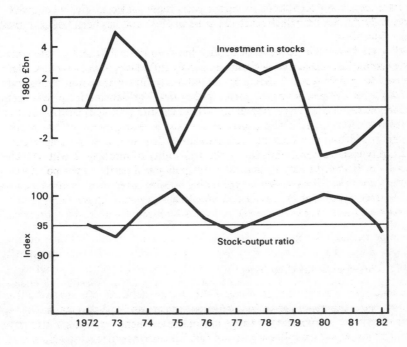

Figure 1.4   Investment in stocks and the stock-GDP ratio, UK, 1972–82

The stock-adjustment principle is only the beginning of an explanation of investment in stocks. It makes no allowance for interest rates or price expectations, both of which must be relevant to the preferred stock-output ratio. Nor can it account for unplanned movements in stocks, which for finished goods will occur when sales deviate from their expected levels.

II.7   Government Consumption, Exports, Imports and Indirect Taxes

Of the two remaining components of TFE, government consumption is primarily determined by the social and political objectives of the central and local authorities, and partly by macroeconomic and financial policy. Until 1979, it was unusual for government spending to be affected by macroeconomic policy, the preferred instrument of control being changes in tax rates. But the advent of financial targets for the PSBR and of expenditure control by cash limits represents a change of regime which could be significant. Between 1979 and 1983 government consumption increased by over 5% in real terms.

Exports of goods and services are determined by two principal factors: by the level of overseas income and by export prices, measured in terms of foreign currency. The latter are, in turn, influenced by the exchange rate for sterling. UK exports correlate quite closely with the volume of world trade in manufactures, and exports to particular countries are linked to national GNP. The influence of prices is measured by the price elasticity of demand, which according to some

TABLE 1.5

Domestic Output Content of Total Final Expenditure at Market Prices

	Percentages of market price totals				
	Consumers' expenditure	*Government consumption*	*Gross domestic fixed investment*	*Exports of goods and services*	*Total final expenditure*
Indirect taxes (less subsidies)	18	7	10	5	12
Imports of goods and services	21	11	30	26	22
Domestic output content	61	82	60	69	66

Sources: *NIE*, 1983, table 1.1; CSO, *Input-Output Tables 1979*.

econometric models is not too high: the range suggested by the National Institute, Bank of England and Treasury models is −0.6 to −0.8.[1] The 3% drop in exports during 1980, for example, was associated with a particularly sharp rise in the exchange rate and in UK export prices. Export trends are discussed in more detail in chapter 3.

TFE is the sum total of exports of goods and services, government consumption, fixed investment, stockbuilding and personal consumption. These elements are normally measured at market prices and they all contain a substantial content of imported components and materials. To proceed from TFE at market prices to GDP at factor cost it is necessary, therefore, to remove the indirect-tax and import contents of the various expenditure items. The indirect-tax content (net of subsidies) is known annually for the various expenditure items, whereas the import content is known only for TFE. Estimates of the import content for individual expenditures can be worked out by input-output methods, and are shown, together with the indirect-tax contents, in table 1.5 above.

The main determinants of imports are the level of GDP and competitive factors. It is probably this last group which is responsible for the upward trend (see chapter 3) in the ratio of imports of goods and services (at constant 1980 prices) to TFE:

1950–54	14.0%
1955–59	14.7%
1960–64	15.6%
1965–69	16.6%
1970–74	19.0%
1975–79	19.4%
1980–82	20.2%

It is possible that this trend can be broken down and explained in terms of price competitiveness, trade policy and other variables, but many forecasting equations

---

1   S. Brooks, 'Systematic Econometric Comparisons: Exports of Manufactured Goods', *NIER*, August 1981, p. 70.

for imports have simply extrapolated the trend at its recent rate of increase.

There is also some connection between the import ratio and investment in stocks. Some models used to assume that imports would rise by as much as £50m for every £100m of stockbuilding. But in recent years this influence has become smaller and less distinct.

II.8 Personal Income and the Multiplier

Any increase in GDP will normally give rise to a multiplier process. The initial rise in personal income leads to higher consumption, and thus to higher GDP. Successive rounds of higher income and consumption will lead to the eventual establishment of an 'equilibrium' level of GDP, this being the level which GDP finally settles at. The multiplier process is the succession of income changes, whilst the 'multiplier' itself is defined as the ratio of the total or cumulative increase in GDP to its initial or 'first round' increase.

In elementary models, the multiplier may be found quite simply because no distinctions are made between GDP and personal income, and because taxation, undistributed profits and the import contents of expenditure are ignored. On these lines, it can be seen that an initial increase in GDP of 100 units, combined with a marginal propensity to consume of, say, 0.5, will lead to an eventual increase in GDP of 200 units. This is because the initial rise in GDP will cause personal incomes to rise by the same amount, so that consumption will then increase (after a time-lag) by 50 units. This, in turn, raises personal incomes in the consumer-goods industries by 50 units so that consumption in the third round of the multiplier will increase by 25 units. Each increment of income leads to a rise in consumption half as large, so that the sequence of period-to-period additions to GDP will be:

$$100, 50, 25, 12.5, 6.25, 3.125, \ldots \ldots \text{etc.}$$

It is not difficult to see that if all the terms are added together they sum to 200, which is the equilibrium increase in GDP. And since this is twice the original increase, the multiplier is 2. This value may also be found from the formula:

$$\frac{\Delta Y}{\Delta I} = \frac{1}{1 - \text{MPC}} = \frac{1}{1 - 0.5} = 2$$

where ΔY is the final increase in GDP and ΔI the initial increase.[1]

The multiplier for the UK follows the same principles as the simple model. But its calculation is complicated by a number of factors, one of which is the distinction which must be drawn between GDP and personal income. This may be illustrated by a direct comparison for 1982:

---

1 The formula assumes that ΔI is a sustained increase in the level of investment expenditure. An unsustained or 'one shot' injection of new investment would lead only to a temporary rise in GDP.

GDP (£232.6bn)	equals	Income from employment and self-employment (£175.2bn)	plus	Rent, total profits and trading surpluses, and imputed charge for capital consumption (£61.2bn)	minus	Stock appreciation (£3.9bn)
Personal income (£237.9bn)	equals	Income from employment and self-employment (£175.2bn)	plus	Personal receipts of rent, dividends and interest (£26.2bn)	plus	Transfer incomes (£36.5bn)

The main point here is that personal income and GDP are similar in total, but different in composition. Their common element is employment income. But personal income includes a large transfer element—mainly pensions and social security benefits—which do not figure in GDP because they are not payments for production. Personal income from rent and profit is only a small part of total domestic rent and profit.

To arrive at an estimate of the UK multiplier we may begin by assuming an initial increase in GDP of £100m. This is the domestic-output content of a larger increase in TFE at market prices, the difference being due to the import and indirect-tax contents of the expenditure. The coefficients in table 1.5, for example, suggest that £100m of GDP would typically correspond to an increase in government expenditure of £122m or fixed investment of £167m.

A series of assumptions must now be made as to the size of various 'withdrawals' or leakages between the first- and second-round increases in GDP. The first stage in the calculation concerns the likely increase in personal income. This will depend on the way in which new GDP is divided between employment incomes and profits, on how much of the latter is distributed to the personal sector as dividend income, and also on how much transfer incomes decline as a result of lower unemployment and other national social security benefits. It can be assumed that the increase in GDP is divided between employment income and profits in its usual ratio of about 4:1, so that £80m will go directly into personal income in the form of income from employment. To this we may add about £6m for higher dividends, since most of the £20m rise in profits will find its way into undistributed profits and corporate taxes. But we also have to allow for a reduction in transfer incomes arising from lower unemployment benefits, and this would be of the order of £4m.[1] Thus the total increase in personal income will be £80 + 6 − 4 = £82 million, which gives us the first in a series of coefficients needed to derive the multiplier (see table 1.6).

The remaining stages of the calculation involve the marginal rate of direct taxation (including higher pension and national insurance payments) which is taken to be about 32%, the marginal propensity to consume, which we have already

---

1 Derived by assuming that every 1% rise in GDP leads to a 0.5% increase in employment, and from official estimates of the cost of unemployment benefit. See *Treasury Economic Progress Report*, February 1981.

estimated in section II.4 above to be about 0.75, and the marginal import and indirect-tax contents of consumption. The latter are taken from the average contents given in table 1.6 (but note that the import content of *factor cost* consumption will be higher, at 0.24, than the import content of market price consumption). It is, of course, arguable that the marginal import content is higher than the average import content but we have not allowed for this possibility.

TABLE 1.6

Stages in the Multiplier Estimate

	£m	Assumed marginal relationships
1st-round increase in GDP	100	
Increase in personal income	82	b_1 = .82
Increase in personal disposable income	56	b_2 = .68
Increase (after a time-lag) in consumers' expenditure at market prices	42	b_3 = .75
Increase in consumers' expenditure at factor cost	34	b_4 = .81
Increase in domestically produced consumption at factor cost (equals 2nd-round increase in GDP)	26	b_5 = .76

The upshot of the calculation is that the second-round increase in GDP is only £26m, or 0.26 times the initial increase. It follows that the third, fourth and later increases will all be 0.26 times the previous rise, so that the sequence of period-to-period changes in GDP can be represented as follows:

$$£100, 26, 6.8, 1.8, 0.5, 0.1 \ldots \ldots 0 \text{ million}$$

This series sums to a cumulative increase of £135m, so that the multiplier is 1.35. Its value may also be found from the expression:

$$\frac{1}{1 - 0.26} = 1.35$$

where 0.26 can be described as the marginal propensity to purchase new domestic output. It represents the five coefficients b_1, b_2, b_3, b_4 and b_5 all multiplied together.[1]

It should be noted that we have defined the multiplier as the ratio of the eventual increase in GDP to the initial increase in GDP, and not to the initial increase in market price expenditure. This is in order to keep the numerator and denominator both in terms of domestic output. The multiplier so defined applies much more directly to employment than the alternative ratio of the change in GDP to the change in the market price expenditure.[2]

These calculations help to indicate orders of magnitude only, and are not meant to be precise estimates. In practice, there are other effects of an increase in GDP besides the multiplier which also have to be taken into account. The most basic of

---

1 Thus $0.26 = \dfrac{82}{100} \cdot \dfrac{56}{82} \cdot \dfrac{42}{56} \cdot \dfrac{34}{42} \cdot \dfrac{26}{34} = b_1 b_2 b_3 b_4 b_5$ and the multiplier is

$$\frac{1}{1 - b_1 b_2 b_3 b_4 b_5}.$$

2 This discussion has followed an early estimate of the multiplier in W.A.B. Hopkin and W.A.H. Godley, 'An Analysis of Tax Changes', *NIER*, May 1965.

these is the effect on stockbuilding, since any increase in demand will be met initially from stock, so that there will be some involuntary stock decline at the start of the process, and this will be reversed later as production is stepped up to replenish stocks and to meet the higher level of demand.[1] The National Institute's econometric model, for example, shows negative stock investment in the first quarter of an increase in total final expenditure, followed by stock accumulation in the third and fourth quarters.

The main econometric models can be simulated to provide estimates of the effect of changes in expenditure on GDP quarter by quarter. According to one study, they show that the ratio of the 4th quarter rise in GDP to the initial increase is in the region of 1.1 to 1.3.[2] This is lower than our own estimate of the multiplier value of 1.35. But the econometric models attempt to estimate a variety of other relationships, the most important of which are the stock-adjustment effects on stockbuilding and fixed investment. The value of the multiplier is increased with variable exchange rates because rising imports lead to a lower exchange rate and hence to higher demand for UK exports. Any increase in wage rates due to the higher pressure of demand also raises the multiplier value, whereas rising interest rates due to pressure in the money market act in the opposite direction.

III   BUDGETARY POLICY AND DEMAND MANAGEMENT
III.1   Objectives and Instruments

The period since the Second World War has been characterized by two quite different approaches to macroeconomic policy. The first of these was the demand-management approach, whereby governments sought to influence the level of demand in the economy with the intention of maintaining or restoring an acceptable level of employment. The second approach was directed more towards the restoration of price stability, with a high level of employment taking a lower priority than hitherto. This approach reached its fullest manifestation under the Conservative government elected in 1979. It is discussed in section III.5.

The demand-management approach was inaugurated by the White Paper on *Employment Policy* (Cmd. 6527) issued in 1944 by the wartime coalition government. The White Paper stated that:

> The Government believe that, once the war has been won, we can make a fresh approach, with better chances of success than ever before, to the task of maintaining a high and stable level of employment without sacrificing the essential liberties of a free society.

The White Paper recommended that there should be a permanent staff of statisticians and economists in the Civil Service with responsibility for interpreting economic trends and advising on policy. The execution of employment policy was

---

1   In extreme cases there may be severe oscillations in GDP or even an explosive time-path. On this the classic reference is L.A. Metzler, 'The Nature and Stability of Inventory Cycles' in R.A. Gordon and L.R. Klein (eds.), *Readings in Business Cycles*.

2   See J.S.E. Laury, G.R. Lewis and P.A. Ormerod, 'Properties of Macroeconomic Models of the UK Economy: A Comparative Study', *NIER*, February 1978.

to be examined annually by Parliament in the debate on the Budget. The White Paper foresaw that high levels of employment were likely to endanger price stability, and it pointed out the need for 'moderation in wage matters by employers and employees' as the essential condition for the success of the policy.

For nearly thirty years the task of maintaining a high level of employment proved to be less difficult than had been expected. Employment levels were higher than the authors of the White Paper had hoped for, and inflation was remarkably moderate. The average rate of retail price inflation was 3% per year in the 1950s, and 4% in the 1960s.

As we observed in section II, however, the postwar economy passed through a series of fluctuations with the annual unemployment rate varying within a narrow range. Part of the reason for these fluctuations could be found in the different views taken by successive governments (or sometimes by the same government at different times) as to the most desirable pressure of demand. The aim of high employment was always in some measure of conflict with the balance of payments and price stability. A conflict with the balance of payments was also present in so far as governments were unwilling to make use of instruments of policy, such as exchange-rate devaluation or import controls, for dealing with the external balance. Thus fiscal measures which act upon the level of employment were at times directed towards the required balance of payments, with the consequence that the employment objective took second place. This conflict was particularly noticeable in two periods: from 1956 to early 1959 when the Conservative government was aiming at a long-term balance of payments surplus, and the period of eighteen months preceding the devaluation of sterling in November 1967.

The employment objective was also in conflict with that of price stability. Here there is no independent instrument of control to parallel the variability of the exchange rate. Incomes policy, in the sense of voluntary or compulsory guidelines for the rate of increase in wages and prices, was seldom found to be particularly successful and certainly not successful enough to permit nice percentage variations in the permitted rate of inflation. Thus the absence of an independent instrument for controlling inflation implied a genuine conflict of aims. This, together with the balance of payments, helps to explain why the target level of employment was not wholly stable, but tended to fluctuate according to the priorities of the government of the day.

It follows that the decision on what level of employment to aim for was normally made on the basis of a compromise with the objectives of price stability and the balance of payments. But once the employment target was settled, the problem of how to attain it became a technical issue.

One elementary point concerns the existence of time-lags between the detection of a policy problem and its remedy. This means that it is not sound strategy to wait until unemployment has reached some intolerably high figure before acting or thinking about action to correct it. The employment statistics are about a month behindhand; civil servants may take up to six months to advise the appropriate action; Parliament may take three months to enact it; and even after the policy is put into force, the full economic effects may not appear for some months afterwards. Thus a strategy based solely upon the observation of recent performance can involve a significantly long time-lag (of twelve months or longer) between the observed need for a change in policy and the effects of that change upon the level of employment.

It is partly for this reason that economic management in the UK was based upon

a strategy of looking ahead rather than on response to observed performance.
This means that the policy-maker relies heavily upon the use of economic forecasts.
If he can *correctly* foresee the emergence of a policy problem, then the problem
of the delay between the need for intervention and its effects is removed.

There is another reason, too, for relying upon forecasts. This is the need to
tailor the amount of intervention to the future size of the problem rather than to
what is currently observed. The mere observation of high unemployment or excessive inflation in no way guarantees that it will continue in the same degree of
seriousness. The problem may get worse or it may get better. Quite clearly it is
essential to form some view of what will happen in the future before deciding the
degree and the direction of policy intervention required. Failure to produce a
correct forecast of the course of employment over the next twelve to eighteen
months could result in an *inadequate* degree of corrective policy action. Or it
could be *destabilizing*,[1] in the sense that the effect of intervention is to remove
the level of output still further from target than it would have been without it.

The last four decades have seen a considerable advance in the various branches
of knowledge which bear upon the problems of forecasting and managing the
economy. The chief of these have comprised: (i) an enormous improvement,
attributable to the CSO, in economic statistics, and particularly the development
of quarterly, seasonally adjusted, constant-price, national expenditure figures;
(ii) the development of a conceptual framework and quantitative model for forecasting the levels of GDP and employment over a period of about eighteen months;
(iii) the development of a conceptual framework and quantitative model for estimating the effects on GDP of tax changes and other instruments of demand
management.

III.2   The Effects of Policy Instruments

If fiscal intervention is to achieve targets for employment and output, it is
necessary for the policy-makers to make fairly precise quantitative assessments of
the effects of their policy instruments upon the level of domestic output. In this
section we shall concentrate upon the effects of three such instruments: changes in
government expenditure on goods and services, changes in personal income tax and
changes in indirect taxation.

In the case of a change in government expenditure, the effects can be estimated
by removing the import and indirect-tax contents (see table 1.5) and applying the
multiplier estimate of 1.35 derived in table 1.6. The effects of a typical increase,
say, of £100m, will be as follows:

	£m
increase in government expenditure at market prices	+100
increase in government expenditure at factor cost	+92
initial increase in GDP	+82
multiplied increase in GDP	+111

Some expenditures, such as the purchase of foreign missiles and military aircraft,
will have a larger import content and a smaller effect on domestic output than
this.

---

1   A more accurate term would be 'perverse', since policy does not necessarily aim to
stabilize anything.

In point of fact, government expenditure was seldom used as an instrument for influencing employment during the era of demand management. This was because its level was determined by political and social objectives of a different order, and also because it was difficult to organize changes in its amount with much hope of their going precisely to schedule. The more usual instruments of demand management were changes in tax rates, particularly income and indirect taxes.[1]

The effect on GDP of a change in income tax may be illustrated by reference to a reduction of 1p in the basic rate of tax. This is estimated by the Treasury to reduce revenue by £1025m.[2] Personal disposable income would be raised by an equal amount, so that the *initial*, or multiplicand, effect upon GDP can be found using the coefficients in table 1.6:

	£m
increase in personal disposable income	+1,025
increase in consumers' expenditure at market prices	+769
increase in consumers' expenditure at factor cost	+622
initial increase in GDP	+476
multiplied increase in GDP	+642

The initial increase in GDP of £476m is simply the change in tax revenue multiplied by the marginal propensity to consume (b_3 in table 1.6), along with the coefficients b_4 and b_5 which remove the indirect-tax and import contents of the increase in consumers' expenditure. The multiplier effect raises this by 1.35 to a figure which, with current-price GDP at an estimated £270bn (in 1984), is equivalent to a gain in total output of approximately 0.2%. This is the deviation in GDP from what it would have been in the absence of the tax reduction.

In estimating the effects of changes in indirect taxes, the initial effect can be found in either of two ways. The first is to take the change in revenue and apply the relevant coefficients. As an example, we may take a reduction in VAT of 1%, which according to the Treasury would reduce tax revenue by £740m in 1984/5. Assuming that there is no initial change in either personal disposable income or consumers' expenditure at market prices, this must imply that the first effect of the tax is felt on consumers' expenditure at factor cost:

	£m
increase in consumers' expenditure at factor cost	+740
initial increase in GDP	+534
multiplied increase in GDP	+721

Here the initial change in GDP is found by applying the coefficient b_5 of table 1.5 so as to remove the import content of the change in factor-cost consumption. The multiplier effect raises the initial effect by 1.35 to give an eventual increase of about 0.3% of current-price GDP in 1984.

This method results in a larger effect on GDP for changes in expenditure taxes than for changes in income tax yielding the same initial revenue. An alternative procedure is to regard the fall in VAT as a rise in real personal disposable income.

---

1 J.C.R. Dow, *The Management of the British Economy, 1945-60*, Cambridge University Press, 1964, pp. 180–1.

2 Treasury, *Autumn Statement*, November 1983.

This will mean that the initial effect on GDP is found in the same way as for a change in income tax. If we estimate consumption and personal disposable income in 1984 at £196bn and £220bn respectively, then the reduced revenue of £740 million represents a reduction in prices of about 0.4%. Applying this to personal disposable income gives the following effects:

	£m
increase in real personal disposable income	833
increase in real consumers' expenditure at market prices	625
increase in real consumers' expenditure at factor cost	506
initial increase in GDP	387
multiplied increase in GDP	522

Here the effect of a 1% cut in VAT is to raise GDP by something like 0.2%. More particularly, it is about two-thirds as much as in the previous calculation. The difference reflects a difference of assumptions. The first method assumes that consumption and saving are determined by money income, whilst the second assumes not only that it is real income that matters, but also that consumers perceive that their real income has been changed by VAT. Our own view is that the first method is more realistic, but there is no firm evidence either way.

When discussing the effects of tax changes it is important to remember that all changes in the budget balance have to be financed either by borrowing from the public or by increasing the money supply. Strictly speaking, the effects described above must assume that the method of financing is an expansion of the money supply. This means that we have not been describing fiscal policy *per se* but a mixed policy of fiscal changes with monetary accommodation. The name does not matter since the Chancellor of the Exchequer is responsible both for fiscal and monetary policy, and is therefore able to ensure that budget deficits are financed in ways which do not subvert the objectives of the policy. It should be noted, however, that if fiscal changes are financed by borrowing from the public there will be consequential increases in interest rates which will tend to reduce (or 'crowd out') private-sector purchases of consumer durable and investment goods.

The alternative to fiscal policy is often taken to be monetary policy, although, as we have seen, fiscal expansion may be financed by an increase in the money stock. Debt management may be used to accomplish a change in interest rates without any marked alteration in the budget balance. The effects of interest changes on investment are likely to be delayed for many months and their main impact will fall outside the normal forecasting horizon of twelve to eighteen months. But the effects on consumers' expenditure through higher mortgage rates and HP payments may operate more swiftly. Monetary policy can also affect spending by altering the availability of credit.

III.3   Economic Forecasts

The Treasury's forecasts have to be published by Act of Parliament, and were originally developed as an aid to demand management. National income forecasts used to be prepared in the Treasury three times a year, with their timing geared to the Budget. They are now made to a timetable which depends on all major policy decisions, and the need, under the 1975 Industry Act, to publish at least twice a year. The published forecasts extend about 15 months ahead; that for March

1984, for example, goes forward to the first half of 1985.

One of the first problems encountered in any economic forecast is that of establishing GDP estimates for the period extending from the last known figures to the month in which the forecast is assembled. The February forecast, for example, has to be made with the benefit of quarterly GDP figures which do not go beyond September of the previous year. A GDP estimate has to be put together for the October–December quarter on the basis of monthly information which includes exports, imports, retail sales and industrial production. This can be difficult because of various gaps in coverage, and because different indicators frequently tell conflicting stories, as, for example, when the employment and industrial production figures move in different directions.

Once the base period is established, the forecast proper (i.e. the part relating to the future) can be started. The methods by which this is done need not be described in detail. But for six months to a year ahead the task is made easier by the presence of a number of forward indicators which provide fairly direct information on the prospects for particular sectors of demand. The CBI, for example, conducts regular inquiries into whether its members intend to invest more or less in the next twelve months than in the previous period. The Department of Trade and Industry has its own inquiry, in which business is asked to estimate the percentage change in prospective investment. There are new-order series for engineering, machine tools and shipbuilding, which provide a forward view of production (for investment or export) in these industries. There are also figures for new orders received by contractors for private construction work, whilst in the field of housing investment figures are collected for orders received by contractors, for new houses started, and Building Society commitments and advances on new dwellings.[1] Government current expenditure and the government component of fixed investment can be predicted from information provided by government departments and the nationalized industries. Direct information, therefore, covers a fairly significant proportion of the autonomous element in total demand, and can be processed to provide forecasts for six to twelve months ahead. Some help towards the personal income and consumption forecast is available from the knowledge of recent wage settlements which helps to establish the wage, although not the employment, dimension of total wage income; and the government will also have estimates of the pay and employment of its own employees.

For longer-term forecasts, and for the more obviously endogenous components of GDP, the forecaster must have an integrated model, in which the relationships are either estimated econometrically or arrived at in some systematic way. The Treasury has for several years had a large econometric model in which there are over 700 economic relationships at its disposal. At the risk of some simplification this may be described as a highly complex and disaggregated multiplier model, with accelerator relationships for the main investment items, and with exports linked to world production and relative prices. The model includes links between wages, prices and the exchange rate, and it also makes some use of interest rates as a determinant of investment, although here the coefficients are imposed and not estimated by regression methods. Imports are determined by GDP, stockbuilding and competitive factors.[2]

---

1 These figures are all published in *Economic Trends*.

2 A brief discussion of Treasury forecasting can be found in 'Forecasting in the Treasury', *Economic Progress Report*, June 1981, and a highly technical account in *Macroeconomic Model Equation and Variable Listing*, HMSO, 1980.

The Treasury's model is in a constant state of revision, if only because there are many different ways of formulating consumption and investment functions, and it is not an easy matter to judge which of them is best. Thus although the model is in constant use, it may be assumed that parts of it will be questioned by those responsible for getting the forecast right. The model, therefore, does not dictate the forecast to the exclusion of all argument and discussion. Furthermore, as every forecaster knows, there are always events which a model is not able to handle (strikes and fuel shortages, for example) and which necessitate judgmental estimation of their effects upon economic activity.

The main upshot of the government forecasting work is a table in considerable detail of the course of GDP and its components, quarter by quarter, over a period of two to three years. The published version of the forecast normally provides estimates by half-years.

III.4   Criticisms of Demand Management

Demand management came in for a great deal of criticism even during the period when employment was held high with comparatively little inflation. There were business objections to the frequency of tax changes, although these were heard more frequently when taxes were raised than when they were lowered. Much of the criticism came from journalists who were under contract to write regular columns in the newspapers. Opposition spokesmen in Parliament (of either main political party) were reluctant to concede the need for tax cuts because of their electoral advantage to the other side. There were complaints of 'stop-go' and, latterly, of 'too much fine-tuning' although these terms were never very carefully defined. Amidst all the clamour it was difficult to distinguish criticisms of the technical proficiency of demand management from differences about the objectives which it was seeking to attain.

The criticisms divide into four main groups: (i) that the economy fluctuated considerably despite the advocacy of 'stable' employment in the 1944 White Paper; (ii) that the technical apparatus of demand management was inadequate to its task; (iii) that economic policy was in some sense destabilizing; (iv) that errors in demand management were responsible for, or connected with, the rapid inflation of the 1970s.

(i) On the first of these points, there is no doubt that the course of the economy was not perfectly stable for most of the period when demand management was practised. (This phenomenon, which was sometimes labelled the 'stop-go' cycle, has been described in section II of this chapter.) What is not so clear, however, is the extent to which this instability reflected changes in economic objectives, or failures to achieve a constant objective. For an unstable and highly cyclical time-path for the economy may represent a series of changes of mind by successive governments about the best level of employment at which to run the economy. The conflicts or presumed conflicts between economic objectives are sufficiently obvious to make it doubtful whether the target pressure of demand was always the same. Indeed, in so far as the facts can be ascertained, the target appears to have fluctuated quite significantly.

The extent to which the targeted level of GDP fluctuated from year to year may be detected by relating the government's forecasts to the level of potential output. The forecasts represent the level of GDP which the government finds acceptable at the time they are made, and as such, they are tantamount to target levels of output. Each forecast implies a specific use of potential output, and this may be found by applying the forecast level of GDP to an estimate of productive potential. This is done in table 1.7, where productive potential is taken as representing a 1.0% unemployment rate for 1955–67 and a 0.9% vacancy rate for 1968–84. The table

TABLE 1.7

Short-term Targets and Forecast Errors, UK, 1955–84

		Target use of potential output or target pressure of demand[1] %	Forecast (and target) change in GDP from year earlier[2] %	Actual change in GDP from year earlier[3] %	Error (forecast less actual) %
1955	(years)	100	2.9	3.6	−0.7
1956	"	99	1.1	1.4	−0.3
1957	"	98	1.3	1.6	−0.3
1958	"	95	−0.4	−0.3	−0.1
1959	(4th qtr)	94	2.8	6.5	−3.7
1960	"	98	3.1	3.5	−0.4
1961	"	97	1.8	2.3	−0.5
1962	"	98	3.9	0.8	3.1
1963	"	97	4.6	6.9	−2.3
1964	"	101	5.4	3.9	1.5
1965	"	100	2.7	2.6	0.1
1966	"	99	2.0	1.3	0.7
1967	"	98	3.1	2.1	1.0
1968	(2nd half)	99	3.6	4.9	−1.3
1969	"	100	1.9	2.1	−0.2
1970	"	102	3.6	2.1	1.5
1971	"	99	1.1	1.5	−0.4
1972	"	103	5.5	3.2	2.3
1973	"	104	6.0	5.4	0.6
1974	"	99	2.6	−0.7	3.3
1975	"	99	0.0	−1.8	−1.8
1976	"	99	3.9	3.5	0.4
1977	"	98	1.5	2.2	−0.7
1978	"	100	3.0	3.2	−0.2
1979	"	97	−0.5	2.3	−2.8
1980	"	95	−3.1	−4.7	1.6
1981	"	91	−0.2	0.6	−0.8
1982	"	92	1.5	1.5	0.0
1983	"	92	2.5	2.9	−0.4
1984	"	94	3.5	−	−

Notes and Sources:

1 Potential output for 1955–67 is estimated as the level of GDP which would sustain an unemployment rate of 1.0%, and for 1968–84 as the level needed to keep the vacancy rate at 0.9 to 1.0%. The rate of growth of potential output is taken as 2.9% per annum for 1955–68 and 2.1% for 1968–84.

2 M.C. Kennedy, 'Employment Policy – What Went Wrong?', in Joan Robinson (ed.), *After Keynes*, Blackwell, 1973, and *Financial Statement and Budget Reports* (HMSO).

3 Average estimate of GDP: *ET(AS)*, 1984; *FSBR*, 1984.

shows a fall in the planned use of potential output of about 6% between 1955 and 1959, increases in 1960 and the election year of 1964, and a fairly steady target from then until 1968. The main feature in later years was the sharp increase in the intended pressure of demand between 1971 and 1973, the sharp contraction in 1975, and the acceptance of slump conditions in 1980–84, by which time demand management had been abandoned altogether.

The principal conclusion is that there were, quite definitely, fluctuations in the level of productive potential at which governments sought to run the economy. Whether these can be traced to electoral ambitions is less clear, since not all the election years were years of high targeted demand pressure. But it is, perhaps, disputable whether a government gets more votes from tax give-aways in a year of depression than it does from high employment and a neutral budget. The other explanation offered is that years of high demand led to balance-of-payments difficulties and inflation, to which the Chancellor responded with phases of demand deflation until such time as they changed their priorities once again. Whether this was really true is doubtful, but it is not established by the mere existence of fluctuations.

(ii)   As regards the technical apparatus of demand management, the key question is whether, and by how much, it failed to achieve the target levels of employment and GDP which governments were aiming for. Since the target level of GDP is equivalent to the government's forecast, this question is essentially a matter of the accuracy of forecasts.[1] If the Treasury forecasts the increase in GDP incorrectly, then it will be led into taking the wrong measures. The result will be that the target level of GDP is missed by the same amount as the forecast is in error.

The question of the accuracy of Treasury forecasts can be answered more satis-factorily for those forecasts which have been published or described with sufficient clarity to permit comparisons with the outcome. For 1968 and after, the forecasts have been published as part of the *Financial Statement and Budget Report*. But before this date the information is not always as good, and must be assembled from official documents or even from forecasts made by other bodies at the same time. Nevertheless, the task is worth attempting even though the results (see table 1.7) cannot be sacrosanct.[2]

The main point to emerge from an inspection of Treasury forecasts over the period since 1955 is that, whilst they have not been as accurate as might have been hoped, they have led policy seriously astray on only four or five occasions. There is not much doubt that the 1959 forecast, when the error was 4%, was one of the worst. It meant that an unforeseen recovery in total output was coupled with an expansionary Budget, and the result was a much higher level of employment at the end of the year than the government had actually intended. By contrast, the forecasting error in 1962 went the other way, with the result that there was a recession despite the policy aim of a roughly 4% rise in output. The error was put right in 1963, although the recovery went further than intended. The worst fore-cast of recent years appears to have been 1974, when the Treasury was much too

---

1   Forecasting accuracy is not always simple to interpret: there may be strikes or other events of an unforeseeable nature which affect the accuracy of the forecasts without necessarily discrediting the methods by which they are derived.

2   The same qualifications carry through to the series for the Target Use of Potential Output.

optimistic (by 3.7% of GDP) about the economic outlook.

Taking the whole period from 1955-81, the average error in Treasury forecasts (regardless of sign) was about 1.2% of GDP. This implies an average deviation of about 0.4% between the actual and desired unemployment rate, and is equivalent to an error between the appropriate rate of income tax and the actual rate of about 5p in the £. The size of the forecast errors must be seen, however, against the background of conflicting and by no means accurate estimates of GDP itself. There is not much evidence that the forecasts have become any more accurate with the passage of time.[1]

(iii) A number of writers have sought to show or deny that demand management has been destabilizing, which implies that policy intervention removed the economy further from target than it would have been if it had been left alone.[2] To do this it is necessary to make assumptions as to the target level of output and the level which output would have attained in the absence of discretionary intervention. Some of these assumptions have been questionable. Thus one writer has claimed that policy was destabilizing because it was demonstrable that 'policy-off' changes in GDP (i.e. after deducting the effects of changes in taxation and government spending) were less widely scattered round the average annual increase in GDP than policy-on (i.e. actual) changes in GDP.[3] It is arbitrary, however, to measure failures of policy in terms of dispersion around an average annual increase in GDP. For there is no presumption, as we can see from table 1.7, that governments were aiming each year at a constant rise in GDP; there is every reason (in times of depression or boom) to suppose that they would aim at changes in GDP of different magnitudes and sometimes of a different sign from the average annual increase.

The stabilizing effectiveness of short-term policy was also investigated in terms of the stability of GDP around its trend. It was shown by Artis[4] that for the 1958-70 period the dispersion of quarterly levels of observed GDP from their time-trend was larger than the dispersion of estimated 'policy-off' GDP. Policy-off GDP was found by deducting the cumulative effects of all tax changes introduced after a particular base year from its own (different) time-trend. The results indicated that policy was 'destabilizing' in the sense of this particular method of measurement. But, as the author made clear, there was never any presumption that trend GDP coincided with target GDP. The ambiguity was, moreover, increased by the establishment of a different time-trend for 'policy-off' than for actual GDP so that even if one of these trends had represented target GDP the other would have failed to do so.

The main conclusion seems to be that there has not, as yet, been any convincing demonstration that demand management was destabilizing. Such a demonstration

---

1 For an official assessment of forecasting errors since 1976, see 'Forecasting in the Treasury', op. cit.

2 For reviews of these and other studies of short-term policies, see G.D.N. Worswick, 'Fiscal Policy and Stabilization in Britain' in A.K. Cairncross (ed.), *Britain's Economic Progress Reconsidered* and M.C. Kennedy, ibid.

3 B. Hansen, *Fiscal Policy in Seven Countries, 1955-65*, OECD, Paris, 1969.

4 M.J. Artis, 'Fiscal Policy for Stabilization', in W. Beckerman (ed.), *The Labour Government's Economic Record, 1964-70*, Duckworth, 1972.

would have to make acceptable assumptions about both the objectives of economic
policy and the effects of policy instruments. It is not difficult to accept that policy
was destabilizing in particular years: in 1959, for example, the economy might well
have remained nearer to target if an expansionary budget had not coincided with
an investment boom which the Treasury had failed to predict. But this was an
example of exceptionally poor economic forecasting in one particular year. The
general picture was one of fairly close proximity between actual GDP and target,
with an average forecast error of only 1.2%, and this implies that *on average* the
degree to which policy might have been destabilizing (assuming that it was) would
have been very minor. It would hardly matter, for example, if the average gap
between target and policy-off GDP was, say, 1.1% when the average gap between
target and actual GDP was 1.2%. The economy would have been slightly better off
without discretionary fiscal policy, but the amount of harm done would have been
too small to worry about.

The associated criticism that there was 'too much fine-tuning' may also be
discussed briefly. If this means simply that the economy would have held very
nearly as close to target levels of output during the demand-management period
(1944–74) without the intrusion of minor alterations in tax rates, then the point
must be taken. For there is not much doubt that the effects of these tax changes
were quite small in terms of their effects on GDP. A possible objection, however,
is that the mere ritual of changing taxes up and down in response to the declared
needs of the economic situation engendered a degree of confidence in the economic
future which was beneficial for business confidence and investment. There is no
way in which this hypothesis can be satisfactorily tested, and unfortunately the
fact that the ritual of demand management coincided with the most sustained
period of high employment ever known cannot settle the issue. But it remains a
point of view to be set against the complaint that there was an excess of small-
scale intervention.

(iv) During the period of fast inflation in the 1970s, demand management came
in for some further criticisms. One of these was that the very fast expansion of
demand during 1973, together with the high pressure of demand, were responsible
for the acceleration in the rate of inflation. This criticism, however, attributes to
demand management an inflation which was mainly, although not entirely, due to
independent factors. We discuss these factors in section IV, where the main
elements in the inflation are seen as a really exceptional rise in import prices –
100% in 3 years – together with some element of wage-pushfulness.

It has also been suggested[1] that 'the whole intellectual basis of postwar
"demand management" by government is undermined if the natural unemployment
rate hypothesis is true'. The trouble with statements like this is that the authors
seldom make it clear what they mean. The least contentious part of the natural-rate
hypothesis is the view that there is some unique level of unemployment at which
the rate of inflation is zero, provided also that the expected rate of inflation is zero.
If this is what is meant by the natural-rate hypothesis then a government which is
anxious to avoid inflation would simply set target unemployment at or above the
natural rate of unemployment. It would seek to achieve its target by exactly the
same combination of forecasts and instruments which we have described. Far from

---

1   M. Friedman and D. Laidler, 'Unemployment *versus* Inflation', IEA, 1975 Occasional Paper
44, p. 45.

destroying the basis of demand management, this version of the natural-rate hypothesis simply underlines its importance.

For some economists, however, the 'natural' rate of unemployment is a full-employment situation with supply-and-demand equilibrium in all labour markets simultaneously. Unemployment is voluntary, and will only fall below the natural rate if money wages are increased ahead of the perceived or expected rise in prices.[1] Eventually, however, workers realize that their real wages have fallen, withdraw their labour, and the economy returns to full employment from what was previously a state of over-full employment. On this way of thinking, an inflating economy has to be in a continuous state of over-full employment. There is no reason to manage demand in an expansionary direction since (a) there is no involuntary unemployment, and (b) any reduction in unemployment will be subsequently reversed as workers realize that their real wages are lower than they were expected to be. To this hypothesis the obvious objection is that the economy is by no means at full employment all the time, and it is quite possible to have massive involuntary unemployment and inflation simultaneously. Most of the unemployed in the UK, for example, have either lost their jobs through being made redundant or have failed to find employment on leaving school because there are no vacancies for the kind of work they can do. The other criticism to be made of this version of the natural-rate hypothesis is that movements in total output and unemployment take place for a variety of reasons which are quite unconnected with whether the expected rate of inflation is equal to the actual rate of inflation.

III.5 Demand Management and the PSBR[2]

Demand management can, and has, been described without reference to the Budget deficit or the public-sector-borrowing requirement (PSBR), which is the combined deficit of the central government, local authorities and public corporations. This was deliberate. For if tax rates are to be decided according to the government's target level of GDP, and if the government's expenditure is set according to its social or political objectives, then the government deficit will be a *consequence* of demand management and not an independent target on its own. At given tax rates, the size of the deficit will also vary with the state of the economy, since the tax base (predominantly incomes and expenditure) will vary with the level of economic activity and prices, as will certain transfer payments, notably unemployment benefits.

To disregard the size of the Budget deficit, or the PSBR, may seem irresponsible in the present climate of opinion. But the reason for doing so is quite clear, namely that policies should be judged by their economic consequences. This is the well-known principle of 'functional finance', which was stated by its originator to be:

---

1 The hypothesis can be summarized in the statement that 'the rate of unemployment can deviate from its equilibrium in the short run but will return to its natural rate level in the long run after an adjustment for inflationary expectations' (H. Frisch, *Theories of Inflation*, Cambridge University Press, 1983, p. 4).

2 See also chapter 2, sections IV.3 and V.1.

The central idea is that government fiscal policy, its spending and taxing, its borrowing and repayment of loans, its issue of new money and its withdrawal of money, shall all be undertaken with an eye only to the *results* of these actions on the economy and not to any established traditional doctrine about what is sound or unsound.[1]

During the 1950s and 1960s it was usual, outside the Treasury, for budgetary policy to be appraised only by its results. But in recent years there has been much concern over the size of the Budget deficit and in particular of the PSBR. The latter is said to be very 'important', although the reasons for its importance are seldom, if ever, explained by those who take this view. If the PSBR is £10bn, as it was in 1983-4, then what this means is that the public authorities have to borrow this sum of money from the banking system, private residents or overseas lenders. If the money is borrowed from overseas, the interest paid will constitute a transfer of national income abroad. If it is borrowed from the private sector, it will lead to a competition for funds and a rise in interest rates. This will mean higher monthly payments for anyone buying his house with a mortgage; it also leads to falling security values, including those of ordinary shares. Thus the only alternative is to finance the deficit by the issue of new money, and this may be done without any undesirable effects on mortgage payments or property values. This last course, however, is resisted by many, including the present government, in the belief that any increase in the money stock *necessarily* involves an increase in the level of prices. This hypothesis, which is a generalization of the quantity theory of money to circumstances where real output is not necessarily fixed, is arguably false (see section IV) but very widely held in certain quarters, particularly in the City of London. Since it implies that there is no method of financing a public-sector deficit which does not have serious economic consequences, it forms the basis of a view that the PSBR should gradually be reduced.

Since 1979 the government has made the reduction of inflation the first priority of its macroeconomic policy. To achieve this goal it introduced in March 1980 a Medium Term Financial Strategy, which set target growth rates for the money stock, along with consequential limits on the PSBR—both for several years in advance. Although the limits for *future* years have been changed in successive Budgets, the PSBR figure for the current financial year has often been treated as an inflexible target (more so than the money supply). This has meant that whenever unemployment has increased by more than was allowed for in the PSBR projection, the government has felt impelled to look for cuts in expenditure, higher taxes or higher nationalized industry prices in the attempt to meet its target for the PSBR. The effect of this blind obedience to self-imposed fiscal rules has been to increase unemployment still further.

When unemployment reached alarming heights in 1980 and was predicted to rise further in 1981 the government took no preventive action. Thus the Budget forecast of 1980 pointed to a sharp decline in GDP when unemployment was already 1.4 million, and the forecast in 1981 again looked to a fall in GDP when

---

1 A.P. Lerner, 'Functional Finance and the Federal Debt', *Social Research*, Vol. 10, February 1943, pp. 38-51. Reprinted in M.G. Mueller (ed.), *Readings in Macroeconomics*, Holt, Rinehart and Winston, 1966.

by that time unemployment had reached 2.2 million. The government professed to believe that (a) demand management could lead to temporary jobs but not to any permanent improvement, and (b) that expansion could not be 'afforded' because the government did not have the money to finance public works' schemes or tax reductions. This statement that public works could not be 'afforded' made sense only on the assumption that the government's financial targets were sacrosanct. It would, however, have been quite possible to have financed increases in government expenditure by means of a higher PSBR, and to have borrowed the money either from the public (which would have raised interest rates) or from the Bank of England (which would not). Borrowing from the Bank of England would have been tantamount to the creation of new money, and although this would have breached the government's monetary targets it would have been no more inflationary than the increase in real demand which it was being used to finance. At that time, however, the government appeared to believe that every x per cent addition to the money stock led to an x per cent rise in the price level.

The other belief that seems to have inhibited government action was the view that demand expansion leads to temporary jobs but not to any permanent improvement. Aside from the quip that even temporary jobs are better than nothing, it is not clear what was meant by this position. It is possible that ministers were being briefed by advisers who accepted the more extreme version of the natural-rate hypothesis (which assumes no involuntary unemployment) and who therefore saw the situation in terms of a temporary reduction in *voluntary* unemployment to be followed, when prices have increased and real wages have fallen, by a return to the 'natural rate'. But there are a number of ideas in modern theoretical macro-economics which might have been used inappropriately to produce the same practical conclusion. The situation, however, was one of idle resources in which a permanently higher level of demand would undoubtedly have increased permanent employment—although not without some risks of additional inflation.

IV   INFLATION
IV.1   Meaning and Measurement

Inflation is defined variously as *any* increase in the general level of prices or as any *sustained* increase. In this chapter we shall use the wider definition since it enables us to include short-lived increases in the general price level, such as those of 1920, 1940 and 1951-2, within the sphere of discussion without raising the further definitional question of whether they were sufficiently 'sustained' to be called inflations.

In measuring the rate of inflation we have a choice of index numbers. The appropriate index of the prices charged for all goods produced in the UK economy is the implied deflator for GDP, so called because it is obtained by dividing the value of GDP at current prices by GDP at constant (1980) prices. The GDP deflator includes export prices. If an index is required to measure the prices of goods purchased by UK residents, the best general measure is the implied deflator for total domestic expenditure, since this is an average of the prices paid for consumption and investment goods, both privately and publicly purchased. If we are chiefly interested in the prices paid for consumer goods and services, we have a choice between the implied deflator for consumers' expenditure and the index of retail prices. The former, like all implicit indices, is not compiled directly from price data but is found by dividing the current value of consumers' expenditure by the volume estimate as measured at constant prices.[1] By contrast, the index of retail prices (the cost-of-living index) is compiled directly from price data. It registers the prices of a collection of goods and services entering a typical shopping basket. The composition of the basket has been revised from time to time so as to keep up with changes in the pattern of expenditure. Being a base-weighted index, it gradually becomes outdated in coverage. In periods of inflation, it will tend to exaggerate the increase in the cost of living because consumers will switch their expenditure patterns towards those goods which are rising less rapidly in price. Nevertheless, it is accurate enough for most purposes.

There is nothing new about inflation. The retail price index in 1980 was approximately 25 times its level at the beginning of the century. Prices fell in only 13 out of the 80 years (notably in 1920-23 and 1925-33). During the rest of the period they generally rose, with a particularly fast inflation during and immediately after the First World War (13% per annum during 1914-20). The rate of price increase was much lower in the Second World War because of widespread price controls. In the period after the war the average rate of increase was still quite low — 3% per annum in the 1950s and 4% in the 1960s — despite the high level of employment. It was not until the 1970s that inflation became really serious, with a record 24% increase in 1975 and an average rate for the whole decade of 13%.[2] In the 1980s the rate of inflation has been falling, and by 1983 the year-on-year rate of increase had fallen to 4.6% — the lowest figure for 15 years.

IV.2 A Model of Inflation

To explain inflation in an open economy like the UK it is necessary to take account of at least three independent types of impulse. These are (i) increases in world prices and UK import prices, (ii) excess demand in the home economy, and (iii) the independent influence of 'wage pushfulness'.

The influence of import prices is important because imports of goods and services account for 20% of TFE. Some imports are in competition with home production, so that if their prices are raised home buyers may switch to domestic substitutes. But the major part of UK imports cannot be made at home at all. Imports of some foods, most raw materials and many of the semi-manufactures are in this category, and as the demand for them is also highly inelastic, increases in world prices for such commodities are followed by increases in the level of UK costs and prices. UK prices will also rise if there is an increase in the world price of oil, which is the one major primary commodity it produces at home. Many of the most violent inflations in the UK can be traced to changes in the world prices of primary commodities.

The second main element in our model of inflation is the degree of excess demand (i.e. demand less supply at going prices) in the various markets for goods and labour. Wages and prices in individual markets may be expected to increase whenever demand runs ahead of supply. The rate at which they increase, moreover, will probably be related to the degree of excess demand in the market. In markets

---

1 The volume or constant-price estimates are derived from base-weighted quantity indices.

2 This is the average of annual increases. The compound rate for 1970–80 was 14%.

where there is excess supply there will be a tendency for prices to fall. In the case of wages, they may increase less rapidly than the general price level, with a consequential fall in the real wage. The balance of excess supply and excess demand in the labour market used to be measurable by the rate of unemployment or the vacancy percentage. But in the last decade or so, these two series have lost their old relationship to each other, so that there is now some uncertainty about comparisons of the pressure of demand over long periods of time. (See section IV.4 below.)

The third ingredient in our model of inflation is more controversial, and is the potentially independent force of wage-pushfulness. It seems necessary to include it as a separate force because wages are widely fixed by bargaining between the representatives of powerful groups, the union and the firm or employers' federation, each of which has the ability to influence the bargain by threatening to interrupt production and employment. Whilst there are reasons to expect that the pressure of demand for labour will normally be an influence in the bargaining process, we cannot exclude the possibility that alterations in the strength of the union, in the loyalty of its members and in its readiness to strike may act as an independent force (i.e. independent of market forces) in determining wage increases.

We can combine these three main causes of inflation into a more complete model by relating them to expected price increases and the exchange rate in the manner illustrated in figure 1.5. The model assumes that the *process* by which excess demand leads to price inflation is through the rate of increase in wages. Higher wages mean higher average costs of production and these lead, after a time-lag, to higher prices. This will happen either because business firms tend to set prices by a constant markup over variable costs or because they seek to maximize profits. Higher prices lead, again after a time-lag, to higher wages since trade unions will tend to claim compensation for increases in the cost of living, or in other words to restore the real wages of their members. Thus the central ingredient of our model is a wage-price spiral which is superimposed upon the excess demand for labour. But besides excess demand, the spiral may also be set in motion by exogenous increases in wages coming from wage-push, by increases in import prices as a consequence of movements in world commodity prices, or by exchange-rate changes induced by movements in the balance of payments.

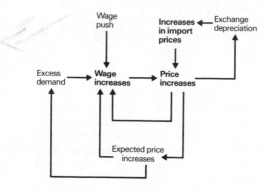

Figure 1.5   Inflationary processes

The model as it stands makes no allowance for a direct influence of excess demand upon price increases. This omission is justified for the 1960s where various investigations found no evidence for such a relationship.[1] In the 1970s, however, some correlation has been observed between profit margins and output. In the case of industrial and commercial companies, profit margins fell by about 7 percentage points in the downturn between 1973 and 1975, and they rose by 7% when demand recovered in 1975-8.[2] These are fairly small changes, and the main influence of demand pressure still seems to run through the labour market.

A second objection to the model might be that there is no reference to the quantity of money. This lack of an explicit reference, however, does not rule out monetary causation of inflation since additions to the quantity of money will lead to increases in wages through the medium of excess demand, and excess demand has a prominent place in the model. This amounts to saying that monetary inflation is a branch of demand-pull inflation. An increase in the money supply will act through interest-rate reductions or more directly through credit availability to increase the demand for goods and services, and hence create excess demand. There is no place in our model, or in economic theory in general, for an influence of money upon prices which is not transmitted through the medium of excess demand.

Besides excess demand and the wage-price spiral, figure 1.5 allows for two other possible interactions between wages and prices, both of them operating through the effect of rising prices upon expected future prices. The first of these is the possibility that expectations of future price changes, rather than compensation for past increases, may be a major factor in wage bargaining. It has been suggested by some writers[3] that the expectation of a price increase of, say, 10% in the next twelve months will induce trade unions and employers to settle for increases in nominal wages of as much as 10% more than would have occurred if prices had been expected to be stable. This hypothesis assumes a degree of sophistication in the process of wage bargaining which may not be characteristic of many trade unions. It is certainly arguable that wage claims are more likely to be based on the actual than on the expected rise in the cost of living. But the employers' side must not be neglected, and here there may be something in the idea that the propensity of firms to grant wage increases is influenced by their expectations of price increases on the part of their competitors. Price expectations, therefore, cannot be ignored in a model of the inflationary process, and they become increasingly important as people learn to live with inflation.

The second additional link between wages and prices runs from expectations of higher prices to the level of excess demand. As consumers become aware that prices are going to rise rapidly in the future they may seek to protect themselves from an erosion of the value of their money by switching out of money and financial

---

1   For example, L.A. Dicks-Mireaux, 'The Inter-Relationship between Cost and Price Changes, 1945-1959', *OEP* (NS), Vol. 13(3), reprinted in R.J. Ball and P. Doyle (eds.), *Inflation*, Penguin, 1969. The model of figure 1.5 is an extension of the relationships investigated by Dicks-Mireaux.

2   See the discussion in *NIER*, November 1982, pp. 21-2.

3   For example, M. Friedman, 'The Role of Monetary Policy', *AER*, Vol. 58(1), pp. 1-17, and *Unemployment versus Inflation*, op. cit.

assets into goods. The effects of this form of behaviour will be manifested in a tendency for the savings ratio to decline (which has not happened in the UK) and for the velocity of circulation of money to rise (which has also not happened). We have included it in the figure, along with the link between price expectations and wage bargaining, because it is a mode of behaviour which has been observed in other countries in periods of hyperinflation.[1] It is a form of behaviour which, along with expectational wage bargaining, is likely to develop as inflation gathers pace and as people learn from experience how money can lose its value. The fact that such behaviour can become general adds greatly to the danger of inflation getting out of hand and provides an extremely powerful case for stopping it as early as possible.

A third linkage in the system is that running from domestic prices through to the exchange rate and back to import prices. As domestic costs and prices rise, exporters have to increase their prices too. If the foreign demand for exports (or the home demand for imports) is elastic, this leads to a deterioration in the balance of payments which leads, in turn, to a decline in the exchange rate. When this happens the sterling price of imports increases, and domestic costs and prices go up further.

One further point which will not be clear from the scheme in figure 1.5 is that increases in the price level always tend to raise the demand for money. If the quantity of money is kept unchanged the effect will be to raise interest rates, thus lowering the levels of real output and employment, and causing a reduction in excess demand which will tend to lower the rate of inflation. This influence will be removed, however, if the central bank is aiming to hold interest rates at a steady level. It will then have to *increase* the money supply as the demand for money rises. Thus although inflationary processes may be initiated by excess demand, by wage-push or by increased import prices, they may be supported through permissive increases in the supply of money.

IV.3   Imported Inflation

Nearly every major increase or decrease in the UK price level has been associated with a major change in import prices (see table 1.8). Import prices were very volatile in the early 1920s; they rose rapidly in 1940 at the beginning of the Second World War; and again in 1951 with the Korean War. Between 1972 and 1974 they rose by 87% as a result of a very fast rise in fuel prices (260% in two years), together with price increases for basic materials (up 100%) and food, beverages and tobacco (70%). There are strong grounds for believing that this was the main factor responsible for the protracted spiral of price and wage increases in the 1970s.

The main effect of a rise in import prices is to increase costs of production which, in turn, means higher final prices. With imports comprising some 20% of TFE, it can be expected that each rise of 1% in import prices will lead to an initial rise in final prices of 0.2%; and these will be raised further by the response of wages. An additional effect occurs in the case of imports in inelastic demand such as foodstuffs and materials. Here the difficulty of substituting domestic output for

---

1   See, for example, A.J. Brown, *The Great Inflation*, London, 1955, and P. Cagan, 'The Monetary Dynamics of Hyperinflation' in M. Friedman (ed.), *Studies in the Quantity Theory of Money*, Chicago, 1956.

TABLE 1.8

Major Changes in UK Import Prices since 1920

	Change in import prices (%)	Change in retail prices (%)
1920	19	16
1921	−33	−9
1922	−20	−19
1940	39	17
1951	33	9
1973	28	9
1974	46	16
1975	14	24
1976	22	17
1977	16	16

Sources: retail prices: *BLS, DEG*; import prices 1920–40: *LCES* (average index for merchandise imports); 1951–77: *ET(AS)*, *ASS* (unit-value index).

imports means that the import bill rises and the exchange rate, assuming this to be flexible, declines. When this happens, the sterling price of imports rises further and there is an additional increase in final prices.

Imported inflation is not readily curable because there is not much prospect of offsetting the effect on final prices other than by inducing large reductions in total demand and employment. Between 1972 and 1974 the dollar prices of primary commodities in world trade rose by 130%, and this was accompanied by rapid increases in prices in all the main industrial countries: 39% in Japan and Italy, 27% in France and 13% in Germany. The UK increase, at 44%, was higher than elsewhere, but this was because of high internal demand pressure and the indexation of wages under Stage III of Mr Heath's incomes policy. The much lower inflation in Germany was partly attributable to an 18% appreciation of the Deutschmark which went some way to offset higher import prices.[1]

IV.4   Excess Demand, Unemployment and Vacancies

Whilst external influences have been responsible for most, if not all, the major inflationary episodes in UK economic history, there is not much doubt that the pressure of demand on internal resources has been an important influence too. The measurement of this pressure is not without difficulties. For many years it was taken for granted that a reasonably reliable measure of demand pressure was given by the unemployment percentage. Involuntary unemployment in a particular labour market is equal by definition to the excess of supply over demand at the going rate of pay. The degree of excess supply is measured by unemployment as a percentage of the labourforce.

It might be thought that a more direct index of excess demand is given by the number of unfilled vacant jobs. But the figures here are much less complete than those for unemployment. The unemployed have an incentive to register because, as a rule, they are entitled to unemployment benefit. Unfilled vacancies, however, are

---

1   These statistics are taken from the *National Institute Economic Review*.

recorded by employers only if they believe it worth their while to notify them. They may prefer to recruit through the local newspapers rather than through job centres. And an employer who has already notified the job centre of vacancies for a particular kind of worker will not need to register new vacancies because the original notice will be sufficient to attract applicants. Thus the vacancy statistics are bound to be incomplete, and it is officially recognized that only a part, perhaps one-third, of all new vacancies are notified to the Department of Employment.

For many years the unemployment and vacancy statistics moved in a close, consistent relationship to each other. The same unemployment percentage was always observed against the same given vacancy rate, and changes in the two percentages were the same in absolute magnitude. It was possible, therefore, to regard either measure as an index of excess demand, whilst the unemployment percentage also served as an indication of the degree of personal and social distress caused by lack of work.

In the last fifteen years, however, the measurement of excess demand has become problematical because of a major change in the relationship between the unemployment and vacancy statistics. A given level of vacancies is now associated with a much higher level of unemployment than it used to be. The extent of the change can be seen from the following comparisons:

	Unfilled vacancies, UK		Unemployment, UK	
	(000s, percentages in brackets)			
1965–6 (average)	262	(1.1)	346	(1.5)
1973–4 (average)	302	(1.3)	591	(2.5)
1979	241	(1.3)	1,229	(5.2)
1962–3 (average)	148	(0.6)	497	(2.2)
1971–2 (average)	139	(0.6)	800	(3.5)
1975–6 (average)	138	(0.6)	1,066	(4.5)
1980	143	(0.6)	1,561	(6.4)

The figures illustrate a continuing tendency for unemployment to rise relative to vacancies. Between 1962-3 and 1971-2 the unemployment rate to be associated with a given rate for unfilled vacancies increased by 300,000 (1.3%); by 1975-6 it had increased by 570,000 (2.3%); and by 1980 by over 1 million (4%).

The reasons for this change appear to be partly statistical. There has, first of all, been an increase in the ratio of recorded to actual unemployment. There has also been some rise in the ratio of recorded to actual vacancies. But the net effect of these two tendencies has been to increase recorded unemployment in relationship to recorded vacancies.

The evidence for this view comes mainly from a comparison of registered unemployment with the Census counts taken in 1966, 1971 and 1981. The population census includes the unregistered unemployed, and when these are compared with the unemployment register, it is clear that the ratio of registered to Census unemployment has increased—from 56% for male unemployment in 1966, to 71% in 1971 and around 100% in 1981. Between 1971 and 1981 the unemployment register rose by 1.7 million whilst Census unemployment rose by 1.4 million. As for vacancies, improvements in the government employment service have probably led to some rise in the ratio of recorded to actual vacancies.

In addition to the statistical reasons for the change, it has also been argued that unemployment has become less involuntary because of a rise in unemployment compensation relative to earnings. The point here is not that workers have surrendered their jobs in order to prosper on the dole, but rather that once they have been made redundant they have chosen to remain longer on the register whilst looking for the right job. They have turned down more job vacancies than in earlier years. This explanation cannot extend much beyond the early 1970s, however, since the benefit earnings ratio has been level or falling since then. But supporters of this view can point to the fact that the *U–V* shift was much more noticeable for male workers, who most generally qualify for benefit, than for female workers, who are frequently not entitled to it.

Another hypothesis is the shake-out theory, which rests on the supposition that during the 1960s employers were in the habit of holding on to labour during periods of business recession in the expectation of a quick return of boom conditions. This expectation, it is argued, has been gradually removed by the withdrawal of interest in demand management since the 1960s, so that hoarding labour has been seen as increasingly wasteful. This explanation, which originated in connection with a sharp rise in productivity in 1968, was put in question by the absence of any 'shake-in' during the boom of 1973. Unemployment declined in 1973, but not by enough to restore its previous relationship to vacancies. A further shake-out may have occurred in the recession of 1979–81.

A further hypothesis, which seems plausible but is again not too well supported by independent evidence, is that there has been a growing mismatch, in terms of skill, occupation and locality, between the demand and supply of labour.

It is not easy to make sense of what has happened. But the main statistical conclusion is that neither the unemployment rate nor the vacancy rate can be taken as consistent indicators of excess demand over long periods of years. If a single indicator has to be used, then the vacancy percentage is preferable, although it still tends to overestimate demand pressure in recent years. The 'peak' level of 1979, for example, may not have been so very different in terms of demand pressure from the trough of 1971.[1]

IV.5   Demand-pull Inflation

Whilst there is some doubt about how to measure the intensity of excess demand in recent years, there is ample evidence from earlier periods of its influence upon the rate of inflation. Numerous studies in the 1950s and 1960s showed a strong negative relationship between the level of unemployment (which is inversely related to excess demand) and the rate of change of money wage rates. One of the earlier studies of this kind, and certainly the most influential, was published in 1958 by Professor A.W. Phillips.[2] This examined the relationship between unemployment

---

1   The most recent discussion of this problem is in *NIER*, November 1983, pp. 39–41. But see also A. Evans, 'Notes on the Changing Relationship between Registered Unemployment and Notified Vacancies: 1961–1966 and 1966–1971', *Economica*, May 1977; S.J. Nickell, 'The Effect of Unemployment and Related Benefits on the Duration of Unemployment', *EJ*, March 1979; A.B. Atkinson and J.S. Flemming, 'Unemployment and Social Security and Incentives', *Midland Bank Review*, 1978, and 'The British Economy in the Medium Term', *NIER*, November 1981, pp. 9–13.

2   A.W. Phillips, 'The Relation between Unemployment and the Rate of Change of Money Wage Rates, 1861–1957', *Economica*, November 1958, although A.J. Brown, op. cit., had illustrated the same relationship.

and wage increases for nearly a century, and on the basis of data for 1861–1913 suggested that the wage increases to be associated with different rates of unemployment were as follows:

Unemployment rate	1.0	2.0	3.0	4.0	5.0
% change in wage rates	8.7	2.8	1.2	0.5	0.1

The relationship became known as the *Phillips Curve*.[1] It implies a nonlinear, marginal 'trade-off' between the rate of wage increase and unemployment. Thus the rate of wage increase declines by nearly 6% if the unemployment rate goes up from 1.0% to 2.0%, but by only 1.6% if it goes up from 2.0% to 3.0%. The trade-off suggested is a modest one at all but the highest pressure of demand for labour.

One of the more remarkable features of the Phillips Curve, and one which distinguishes it from most similar studies, was that it was found to be highly reliable in predicting increases in wages during much later periods of time than the years 1861–1913 which had been used to derive the equation. Thus Phillips was able to show a very close correspondence for 1948–57 between the wage changes implied by his relationship and those that actually took place. The Phillips Curve was also accurate in predicting wage increases over the period 1958–66, which was after the study had been published. During these eight years there was not a single error in excess of 2.5% and the mean error (regardless of sign) was only 1.1%; furthermore, the positive and negative errors tended to offset each other. These predictive successes, however, have to be seen in the light of what was an exceedingly stable level of unemployment compared with the experience from which Phillips had started. In 1861–1913 unemployment rates ranged from 1 to 11%, whereas in 1948–66 they were between 1 and 2.3%. Thus one could argue that postwar experience up to 1966 tested only a small part of the Phillips relation. Nevertheless, it passed this test fairly well.

After the mid-1960s, however, the pure Phillips Curve became increasingly unreliable as a guide to the rate of wage inflation. It under-predicted by about 4.5% per annum in 1967–9, by 10–12%, in 1970–3, and by more than 20% in 1974 and 1975. For several years there was no recognizable relationship between statistics of the unemployment percentage and the rate of wage increase. It is important, therefore, to ask whether the breakdown of the Phillips relationship can be explained, and here several factors come to mind:

(i)   Easily the most important factor is the omission from the pure Phillips equation of the causal influence of price changes. This would not have mattered so much in the early 1960s when inflation was moderate. But

---

1   The equation for the schedule was:

$$\frac{\Delta W}{W} = -0.900 + 9.638 U^{-1.394}$$

It can also be expressed in logarithmic terms as

$$\log \left\{ \frac{\Delta W}{W} + 0.9 \right\} = 0.984 - 1.394 \log U$$

Where $\frac{\Delta W}{W}$ is the percentage rate of wage change and U is the unemployment rate (Phillips, *op. cit.*).

the omission is serious with inflation at the rate experienced in the 1970s.

(ii)   A connected factor is the probability that wage increases have become much more sensitive to price increases as a result of learning to live with inflation. This is not an easy matter to establish empirically, but it is nonetheless probable that a growing number of trade-union negotiators have insisted on full compensation for price changes whilst others have sought wage negotiations at more frequent intervals. There may also have been some tendency to follow the 'expectations-augmented Phillips curve', with expected rather than actual price changes being taken as the basis for wage awards.

(iii)   A third factor is the influence of 'wage-pushfulness', which, as we discuss below, appears to have been more prevalent in the period after 1970.

(iv)   A fourth factor was the change in the relationship between unemployment and vacancies. With given rates of unemployment signalling a higher pressure of demand than previously, there was bound to be some movement in the Phillips relation.

(v)   Finally, the Phillips relationship may have been partly obscured by a number of attempts, notably in 1972–3 and 1975–8, to control wage increases by incomes policy.

These considerations are sufficient to explain why the link between wage increases and the pressure of demand became obscured after the end of the 1960s. The theoretical linkage has remained unimpaired, and since 1980 has been corroborated by the expected combination of falling rates of wage inflation and rising unemployment (see table 1.9).

IV.6   Wage-push Inflation[1]

The question of whether wages have increased as a result of unions pushing up wages independently of market forces is controversial chiefly because of the volume of historical evidence in favour of a demand-pull explanation. This evidence, however, need not preclude the possibility of sporadic outbursts of wage-push inflation. Nor is there any reason in principle why wage-bargaining procedures should respond precisely and consistently to the pressure of demand in the labour market.

The first real evidence in favour of a wage-push contribution to recent inflation came with the 'pay explosion' of 1970 when the rate of wage increase was about 12% faster than could be predicted by the pure Phillips Curve. It was also about 7% higher than could have been predicted from a relationship estimated by Artis in which price changes were included as an additional causal variable and excess demand was measured by the number of vacancies.[2] It can be argued that this was a consequence either of the relaxation of incomes policy in late 1969 or of direct wage-push on the part of the trade unions. The two types of explanation are not unconnected because the government was under strong pressure from the unions

---

1   See also chapter 5, section IV.5.

2   M.J. Artis, 'Some Aspects of the Present Inflation', *NIER*, February 1971, reprinted in H.G. Johnson and A.R. Nobay (eds.), *The Current Inflation*, Macmillan, 1971.

TABLE 1.9

Inflation and inflationary pressures 1960–83

Year	(1) Change in retail prices (%)	(2) Change in average weekly earnings (%)	(3) Unemployment percentage	(4) Unfilled vacancies percentage	(5) Days lost in industrial disputes (m)	(6) Change in import prices (%)	(7) Change in exchange rate (%)	(8) Change in money stock (£M3) (%)
1960	1	6	1.7	0.9	3	0		
1961	4	7	1.5	0.9	3	−2		
1962	4	3	2.0	0.6	6	−1		
1963	2	4	2.3	0.6	2	4		
1964	3	9	1.7	0.9	2	3		6
1965	5	8	1.4	1.0	3	1		8
1966	4	7	1.5	1.1	2	1		3
1967	2	4	2.3	0.8	3	0		10
1968	5	8	2.4	0.8	5	12	−14	7
1969	5	8	2.4	0.9	7	4		2
1970	6	12	2.6	0.8	11	4	−1	10
1971	9	11	3.4	0.6	14	5	0	14
1972	7	13	3.7	0.6	24	5	−4	25
1973	9	14	2.7	1.4	7	28	−9	26
1974	16	18	2.6	1.3	15	46	−3	10
1975	24	27	3.9	0.6	6	14	−8	7
1976	17	16	5.2	0.6	3	22	−14	10
1977	16	9	5.6	0.7	10	16	−5	10
1978	8	13	5.5	0.9	9	4	0	15
1979	13	15	5.1	1.0	29	7	7	13
1980	18	21	6.4	0.6	12	10	10	19
1981	12	13	10.0	0.4	4	8	−1	14
1982	9	9	11.7	0.2	5	9	−5	9
1983	5	9	12.4	0.5	4	10	−8	10

Sources: *ETAS*, 1984; *DEG*, February 1984 and earlier; *NIER*, February 1984; Feinstein, op. cit.; *FS*.

Notes: Col. (2) earnings in GB production industries linked to earlier indices. Col. (3) UK unemployed excluding school-leavers as percentage of employees plus *total* unemployed. Col. (6) unit value of merchandise imports on balance of payments basis. Col. (7) effective exchange rate 1969–83, parity rate 1967–8. Col. (8) end-year, unadjusted.

to bring incomes policy to an end.

In the next few years there was further evidence of wage-push inflation in terms of a tendency for money wage rates to press ahead of prices. This was certainly true of the old wage-rate index for manual workers. If this index is deflated by the retail price index to arrive at an index of real wage rates, then a very conspicuous rise in real wages appears in the early 1970s – as is shown by the following comparison of 5-year periods:

1960–65	3%
1965–70	7%
1970–75	23%
1975–80	1%

This, however, is not the story told by other indicators. The index of average weekly earnings (again deflated by the RPI) shows much the same real gain in 1970–75 as in 1965–70, and if the national accounts data of wages and salaries are deflated by prices they also fail to show a significant jump in real wages in 1970–75. This is a case of conflicting evidence. There was, however, a history of confrontation and industrial unrest in the 1970–75 period (and also in 1979) and the very sharp rise in the number of industrial disputes was at least suggestive of wage-pushfulness.

IV.7   Inflation since 1970: a Summary

In table 1.9 we have grouped together the main factors which have been suggested as causes or contributors to the rate of inflation. The main questions to be considered are why did the inflation rate rise so rapidly between the 1960s and the early 1970s? Why did it fall after 1974 and rise again in 1979 and 1980? And why did it fall so dramatically in 1980–83?

The first of these questions is the most difficult one. On the evidence available it is difficult to accept that the pressure of demand was responsible for the high rates of inflation from 1970 to 1972. In each of these years the unfilled vacancy rate was well below normal, and unemployment exceptionally high. Since import prices were also rising quite slowly it seems clear that the main factors responsible were the 'rebound effect' of the ending of incomes policy in 1970, and, as evidenced by the figures for industrial disputes, an element of trade-union pushfulness. We have seen already that on some evidence, but not all, there was a strong tendency for wages to push ahead of price increases during this period.

The next question is why did inflation rise even further in the period 1973–77? One candidate here is the pressure of demand for labour, which on the evidence of unfilled vacancies was for two years higher than it had been in any year since 1955. Combined with an exceptionally fast *increase* in demand it was clearly one element in the rapid inflation of 1973 and 1974. Nevertheless, it could hardly have been responsible for inflation rates of 16 and 24%. The main factor in this period was the huge rise in oil and other import prices. The index of import prices rose by 87% between 1972 and 1974, and with imports accounting for one-fifth of TFE, must have added 20–25% to the internal price level during these two years. An additional factor during 1974–5 was the influence of indexed incomes policies under Stage III of Mr Heath's statutory policy and the 'Social Contract'. The effect of indexing wages against the cost of living was almost certainly to increase the responsiveness of wages to prices above what it would have been in the absence of such policies.

In all of these explanations we have to bear in mind the wage-price spiral which serves to continue and prolong the effects of inflationary impulses well beyond the period of their first impact.

After 1975 there was a particularly sharp decline in the inflation rate for 3 years, and by 1978 the rate had fallen 16 points to 8%. This decline may be partly attributable to the lower pressure of demand in 1976 and 1977, but the main factor responsible was the introduction in July 1975 of an incomes policy which won the consent of the trade-union movement. Phase I of the policy set a limit of £6 a week on wage increases, whilst Phase II which began in July 1976 imposed a limit of 5%. Thus the rise in average weekly earnings fell from 27% in 1975 to 9% in 1977.

The rise in the inflation rate between 1978 and 1980 can be traced to a number of influences, of which the first was the revival of demand pressure in 1978 and 1979. Oil prices rose sharply between 1978 and 1980, with the OPEC price more than doubling between these two years. Possibly the most serious factor, however, was the withdrawal of union co-operation with incomes policy and the wage increases associated with the 1978/9 'winter of discontent'. But a further 4 percentage points were added to retail prices by the budget decision of June 1979 to raise VAT from 8 to 15%. Without this increase the task of reducing inflation in the next three years might well have proved easier.

Between 1980 and 1983 the inflation rate fell by 13 percentage points, although the decline would have been much less without the VAT increase. This decline can probably be attributed to the Phillips Curve effect of unemployment rising to the highest levels since the 1930s.

IV.8　Monetary Explanations of Inflation

The increased rate of inflation in the 1970s was accompanied by markedly faster increases in the stock of money. The money supply had been rising at about 6% a year in 1964–9, whereas in 1971–4 the rate of increase was very much faster. A number of economists, journalists and stockbrokers interpreted the connection between the rise in the rate of monetary expansion and the faster inflation rate as cause and effect. Some have attributed to money the sole blame for the inflation.[1]

It is generally accepted in economic theory that increases in the supply of money can lead to higher real output or to higher prices. But they do so by raising the aggregate demand for goods and services, thus adding to the pressure of demand. This means that if the inflation of the 1970s had been caused by the rise in the money supply it would have been accompanied by a rise in vacancies and lower unemployment. These changes, moreover, would need to have been sub-

---

1 For example, M. Parkin, 'Where is Britain's Inflation Rate Going?', *LBR*, July 1975, W. Rees-Mogg, *The Times*, 13 July 1976, and, for an American example, M. Friedman, *Money and Economic Development*, Praeger, 1973. The monetarist case against the Keynesians is put in D. Laidler, *Monetarist Perspectives*, Philip Allan, 1982, and the Keynesian case against the monetarists in N. Kaldor, *The Scourge of Monetarism*, Oxford University Press, 1982, E.H. Phelps Brown, 'A Non-Monetarist View of the Pay Explosion', *TBR*, March 1975, and M.C. Kennedy, 'Recent Inflation and Monetarists', *Applied Economics*, June 1976.

stantial to account for such a sharp rise in the inflation rate. However, as we have already explained above, there was no general or sustained increase in the pressure of demand in the 1970s. Unemployment was higher than it had been, and the vacancy rate, although high in 1973 and 1974, was lower on average in the 1970s than it had been earlier. This absence of any increase, let alone any marked increase, in the pressure of demand is fairly compelling evidence against the monetarist point of view.

This conclusion, however, does not prevent us from agreeing that *if* the money supply had not been allowed to increase so fast, then inflation in the 1970s would have been less severe. If, for example, the money stock had increased in the 1970s at its 1964-9 rate of increase of 6% a year instead of the recorded 14%, then it is reasonable to conjecture that interest rates would have been much higher and the pressure of demand would have been lower. This would have had some effect on the rate of wage increase and the exchange rate. It is difficult to believe, however, that tighter money could have cancelled out the effect of the rise in oil and other import prices.

IV.9   Inflation and Economic Policy[1]

In the period when inflation was merely creeping it was possible to regard it as a small price to pay for the benefit of high employment. A gently sloping trade-off between inflation and unemployment made the problem of political compromise minimal compared with the situation in the 1970s and 1980s. The advocacy of an incomes policy in the 1960s was associated either with those who hoped to be able to run the economy at a pressure of demand which now seems unthinkable, or else with those who sought to use it as an instrument of income redistribution.

The arrival of fast inflation in the 1970s transformed the policy problem. It meant that real incomes were rapidly eroded between wage settlements, with effects that were socially divisive and disruptive. It also transformed economic behaviour. Economic units learned how to live with inflation and sought to defend their real wages either by insisting on a full compensation for past increases in the cost of living or possibly, in a few cases, by bargaining on the basis of price forecasts. This meant that there were two main methods of bringing inflation under control. One was to deflate domestic demand to such a low pressure that the effect of unemployment upon the rate of wage increase was large enough to offset that of cost-of-living compensation and/or price expectations. Given that prices in some years were increasing at rates of over 15%, this would have necessitated either intolerably high unemployment or what was thought to be an intolerably long period of correction. The other alternative was an incomes policy under which the rate of wage increase was subjected to statutory or firm quasi-statutory control.

A statutory incomes policy was tried by the Conservative government in 1972-4 after its attempt to secure a voluntary policy had failed. The policy coincided with a major rise in import prices, and the provision in stage III of the policy for the effective indexation of wages to the cost of living had the unfortunate further effect of indexing them to the international terms of trade. But the policy collapsed, despite its statutory powers, because one strong trade union, the

---

1   See also chapter 5, section IV.5.

National Union of Mineworkers, was prepared to go slow and finally strike rather than accept the terms of policy. It was this which led to the early election of February 1974, and, it is argued, to the defeat of the Conservative Party.[1] The incoming Labour government continued the indexation provisions under the 'Social Contract' but did little further to prevent inflation until July 1975, when a voluntary incomes policy was introduced in three stages, starting with a maximum increase of £6 per week.

This was certainly the first time that an incomes policy can be said to have made a significant impact upon the rate of wage inflation. But the government was not able to obtain union agreement to a continuation of incomes policy in 1978, and it was unwilling to enforce a statutory policy.

The Conservative government which was returned in May 1979 was strongly opposed to incomes policy, and strove to contain inflation by a progressive reduction in the rate of increase in the money stock. This approach, which was formalized as a Medium Term Financial Strategy in the Budget of 1980 and reiterated in subsequent Budgets, was discussed at greater length in section III of this chapter.

V   ECONOMIC GROWTH
V.1   The Growth of Productive Potential

In ordinary language one usually speaks of any increase in GDP, however it comes about, as economic growth. In economic theory and applied economics it is best to reserve the term for increases in a country's productive potential. This means that demand-induced spurts of economic expansion, such as those occurring in cyclical recoveries, do not qualify as economic growth in the sense we have in mind. Table 1.10 shows that both the growth rates of productive potential and the underlying trend in productivity increased between the beginning of the century and the 1960s, but fell back somewhat in the 1970s.

The growth rate of productive potential can only be measured satisfactorily

TABLE 1.10

Economic Growth, UK, 1900–79 (percentage increase per annum)

	GDP (average estimate)	GDP per person	Employed labour force	Capital stock (excluding dwellings)
1900–13	1.5	0.6	0.9	1.7
1922–38	2.3	1.2	1.1	1.7
1950–60	2.6	2.2	0.4	2.8
1960–70	2.9	2.6	0.3	4.3
1970–79	2.1	1.9	0.2	3.2

Sources: 1950–79: *ET*, October 1983; *NIE*, 1983; *ET(AS)*, 1984; 1900–38: C.H. Feinstein, op. cit.

---

1   For an account of this period see M.J. Stewart, *Politics and Economic Policy in the UK since 1964*, Pergamon, 1978.

over very long intervals of time or between periods when the utilization of resources was closely similar. Thus the periods indicated in table 1.10 have been chosen because they begin and end with similar rates of unemployment. The exception is 1970–79 where unemployment was considerably higher at the end of the period, so that a full use of the labourforce (assuming that this would have been possible) might have added about 0.3% to the growth rate of GDP.

The concept of the growth rate of productive potential is not without its limitations. In the first place it says little or nothing about the causes of growth but simply describes a time-trend. An extrapolation of the growth rate for any period into the future could easily turn out wrong if the forces that determine full-employment output are going to be present in different amounts or combinations from those of the past.

A second reservation concerns the interpretation of growth *rates* generally and their relation to *levels*. In calculating growth from 1960 to 1970, for example, one takes the compound rate of increase which will transform the level of GDP in 1960 into that of 1970. This does not tell us anything about the intervening years, during which the level of GDP could have been above or below the implied time-path. Thus the average *rate* of growth is, in general, no guide to the average *level* of output over the period. An allied point is that the *level of potential output* is arbitrarily defined by the unemployment rate at which it is measured. This does not necessarily represent the most desirable level.

One of the questions which the economics of growth must try to answer is why some countries have grown so much faster than others and why, in particular, the underlying growth rate of the UK economy has been slower in the postwar period than that of most other industrial countries (see table 1.11). The answer must be sought under the more general heading of the causes of economic growth—a question which has been debated since the time of Adam Smith. Growth must depend, in the first instance, upon the increase in the quantity and quality of the factors of production and the efficiency with which they are combined. These increases may be influenced, however, by factors on the side of demand such as the pressure of demand on resources and the degree to which it fluctuates.

The supply of labour depends primarily on the evolution of the population of working age, including net migration, the secular decline in hours worked, and the increase in the length of annual and national holidays. Changes in the pressure of demand, however, affect the size of the labourforce and the number of hours worked, and, over the longer period, may influence migration.

The quality of labour must in large degree depend upon the facilities available for education and training, the opportunities taken of them, and the degree to which they match the changing demands for skills arising out of changes in technology and the structure of aggregate demand. Measurement of these influences, however, is difficult and there is little evidence to show which way, if at all, they have affected the international comparison in table 1.11. The mobility of labour from job to job and from area to area is probably an important factor in economic growth in so far as it reflects the degree to which the labourforce can adjust to economic change. It has been argued, not without evidence, that much of the relatively fast growth of the German, Italian and French economies can be attributed to the movement of labour from the agricultural to the industrial sectors.[1] But it is still not clear how much of this mobility has been a cause and

---

1   A. Maddison, *Economic Growth in the West*, Allen and Unwin, 1964.

how much a consequence of the disparity in growth rates between the agricultural and industrial sectors.

TABLE 1.11

Rates of Growth, 1970–79 (annual percentage rates)

	GDP	GDP per capita
Belgium	3.3	3.0
Denmark	2.5	2.1
France	3.9	3.3
Germany	2.9	2.8
Italy	3.0	2.4
Japan	4.9	3.6
Netherlands	3.1	2.3
Norway	4.7	4.2
Sweden	2.1	1.8
United Kingdom	2.2	2.2
Canada	4.5	3.2
United States	3.4	2.3

Source: National Accounts of OECD Countries, 1982.

One obvious influence on the growth of labour productivity is the rate of increase in the nation's stock of capital, both in quantity and in quality. Some indications of the growth of the UK capital stock are given in table 1.10, where it can be seen that the rate of increase, like that of productivity, has tended to rise during the course of this century – although it, too, fell back in the 1970s. The stock of capital, however, is extremely difficult to measure. This is because the figures of depreciation in the national accounts are based on data collected for tax purposes and cannot serve as very precise indications of the rates of scrapping and deterioration of existing capital. Moreover, the economic value of a piece of capital equipment is a subjective concept, depending on expectations of future returns and modified by problems of evaluating risk. Estimates of the capital stock, therefore, must be treated with a good deal of reserve.

The quality of the capital stock is, perhaps, even more important and even more difficult to measure. According to one widely accepted view, the quality of capital depends, by and large, upon its age structure. This view looks upon the capital stock as a series of vintages of gross investment, each new vintage containing machines of higher quality than the previous one. Scientific and technical progress are embodied in new machines, not old ones, so that the most recent capital equipment is likely to be the most efficient. This view is the basis of the 'catching-up hypothesis' which has been advanced to explain the faster growth of some countries in the early postwar period. The argument is that those countries in which the capital stock was seriously depleted by the war were in a position to replenish it with brand-new equipment, and were thus enabled to grow faster than those countries where the bombing and destruction had been less severe. The embodied view of technical progress, together with the difficulties of measuring the quantity of capital, has led a number of economists[1] to emphasize gross rather than net capital formation as the better indicator of the extent to which capital

---

1 For example, A. Maddison, ibid.

resources have been enhanced. A high rate of gross investment, even if it is entirely for replacement purposes, will reduce the age of the capital stock and increase its quality.

Turning to influences on the side of demand, two aspects of the question need to be distinguished: the average pressure of demand and the size of fluctuations around the average. It can certainly be argued that a very low average pressure of demand, such as we had during the 1930s and are experiencing again today, is inimical to innovation and investment. It hinders investment because capital equipment is under-utilized and because its continuation for any length of time is likely to set an unfavourable climate for expectations. High demand, on the other hand, will generally have the opposite effect. It has also been argued that high demand encourages managers and workers to devise new and better ways of working with existing equipment, thereby making technical progress of a variety which is not embodied in new types of machine. This effect has sometimes been described as 'learning by doing', and it fits in with the view that the scale of production problems that have to be solved is itself a stimulus to their solution. Evidence has been produced, for example, to show how the time taken to assemble a prototype airframe has progressively diminished as the workforce has gained experience of repeating the same jobs over and over again. On the other hand, it has also to be borne in mind that high demand pressure may work the other way. The presence of a sellers' market with easy profits could diminish the incentive to innovate and even lead to lazy attitudes to production. An extreme pressure of work can promote mental and physical exhaustion.

Another question is whether the amplitude of fluctuations tends to impede economic growth. It seems probable that the expectation of fluctuations will retard capital formation because profitability will be held down in periods of recession. It may also be the case that expectations of cycles lead to the installation of machinery which can be adapted to use in periods of both high and low output, whereas the prospect of steady growth could enable the introduction of machinery which would be specially designed to produce a steadier level of sales. In this case it is likely that the extra adaptability will be achieved at some cost to the efficiency of capital, and growth will be slowed down. It may be no coincidence, therefore, that three countries with some of the lowest growth rates in the 1950s—the UK, US and Belgium—suffered sharper fluctuations in unemployment than the others (Japan was the exception to this rule).

V.2   Economic Growth and Policy

Government prefers a fast rate of growth to a slow rate because it results in greater tax revenues from a given structure of tax rates, and thus permits tax reductions at full employment or a larger provision of public services (hospitals, schools and so forth) than would otherwise be possible. Fast growth may also render a policy of income redistribution less painful to the better-off than would be so if the growth of income was slow or non-existent. Thus it is not surprising that governments have sometimes announced a faster growth rate as a goal of economic policy.

What is not so clear, however, is whether the means of attaining faster growth are sufficiently well known and understood. There is considerable controversy among economists as to the effects on economic growth to be had from, say, a faster growth of the capital stock and from technical progress. Many would argue that neither are quantifiable, and that the attempts which have been made to quantify them are suspect in a number of ways. Thus it does not seem that growth policy is in the same category as, for example, demand-management policies, in which moderately fine calculations can be made as to the effects of changing the instruments of policy by known amounts. At one time it was believed by many that investment and the growth rate could be stepped up together merely by the announcement of a high growth target. This was tried in the National Plan of 1964-70 when the target growth rate was put at 4% per annum. But in the event the growth rate turned out to be only 2.6% (average estimate), and much of the public investment which had been based on the 4% assumption proved to be excessive. Probably all that can be hoped for from growth policy is the creation of an environment which is favourable to investment, innovation and enterprise. This, broadly speaking, is what the present government is trying to do with its 'supply side' policies. But whether these can succeed in a period of deep depression is, perhaps, doubtful. It is not encouraging that the Green Paper on *The Next Ten Years* (Cmnd. 9189) points to a growth rate of only 2¼% per annum from 1983/4 to 1988/9 (financial years). Although this rate may be a little higher than the growth rate of productive potential, it is a long way off what would be necessary to make any significant reduction in unemployment. The increase in GDP per employed person is put at only 1.3% per annum, which is significantly below the rates achieved in earlier years (see table 1.10).

VI ECONOMIC PROSPECTS AND POLICIES 1984-9
VI.1 The Economic Situation in 1984

Compared with two years earlier, the economic situation in the spring of 1984 could be said to have made a small, but qualified, improvement. Unemployment was not very much higher than it had been two years earlier, output was rising, and the rate of inflation in March had fallen to 5% over 12 months earlier compared with 10% in March 1982.

The qualification, of course, was that unemployment was so high. The official figures showed that unemployment in March was still 3 million (13%), whilst many others without jobs were on job opportunity programmes. About 1.2 million people had been out of work for more than a year, and the unemployment rate among 20-25 year-olds was 21%.

This situation, besides being tragic for all those concerned, was also very wasteful. With total employment some 7% below where it had been in 1979, the amount of waste could be estimated at about £19bn[1] — a figure which is somewhat in excess of the sum spent annually on education (£15bn).

In spite of the depressed state of the labour market, government ministers were claiming that the economy had 'recovered' from the recession. The statistical basis of their claim was that the latest set of national income estimates showed that real GDP was higher in 1983 than in the peak year of 1979 — by about 0.7%. What had happened was that productivity (GDP per person) had increased by some 8% in the four years since 1979, whilst demand had increased by less than 1% — hence there was a shortfall of 7% between actual and potential employment.

---

1 7% of an estimated GDP at factor cost of £270bn for 1984.

The main elements in the rise in GDP from 1979 were consumer spending and government consumption, both of which were up by about 5%. Consumption per employed person was up even more, so that the employed could be said to have been substantially better off in 1983 than they were in 1979. These increases were enough to offset the lower levels of fixed investment and stockbuilding, whilst exports were much the same as in 1979. Comparing 1983 with the trough year of 1981 there had been increases in all categories of expenditure, and particularly consumption.

VI.2   Economic Prospects to 1989

The economic outlook was for a continuation of low inflation and high unemployment. The official forecast was that the RPI would rise by about 4½% in the year to the 4th quarter of 1984. The GDP deflator for financial years was put as rising by 5½% in 1983-4, by 5% in 1984-5 and, looking further ahead, by 3% in 1988-9. These were the assumptions underlying the Public Expenditure White Paper (Cmnd. 9143).

The Treasury's forecast for GDP made in March 1984 was for a moderate increase during 1984 and a slightly slower increase into the first half of 1985. The rate of increase from 1983 to 1984 was put at 3.1%, and the increase between the first half-years at 1984 and 1985 at 2.6%. In section III we estimated that the growth rate of productive potential for 1971-9 was about 2.1% a year on a constant-vacancy basis. For constant unemployment and employment it might have to be a little higher than this—say 2¼%—although the calculation cannot be precise. The outlook for GDP, therefore, implied a slight reduction in unemployment in 1984 and early 1985. But with a gap of less than 1% between the forecast growth rate and the growth rate of potential it was clear that there would be no appreciable impact on the level of unemployment.

The outlook after 1985 will depend upon economic policy. But the government's assumptions in the Public Expenditure White Paper (Cmnd. 9134) and in its Green Paper *The Next Ten Years* (Cmnd. 9189) were not encouraging. These took the average rate of growth for the whole period from 1983/4 to 1988/9 (financial years) to be 2¼% per annum. As this was roughly equal to the growth rate of productive potential, it must be assumed that the government was contemplating an unemployment level of 3 million, or not much less, for the next five years.[1] If the assumptions are not overturned by a change of policy this will make the 1980s the most depressed decade in the whole of our recorded history.

VI.3   Economic Policies

The main macroeconomic objective was the reduction of inflation. The election of 1983 had showed that it was quite possible for a government to be returned to power—even with an increased majority— despite the presence of 3 million unemployed. Thus the 1984 Budget speech spoke not only of a continued fight against inflation, but even of an 'ultimate objective of stable prices'.

---

1   This was conceded by the Minister for Employment, Mr King, in a submission to NEDO— see the *Guardian*, 5 April 1984, p. 19.

The ostensible weapon for dealing with inflation continued to be the Medium Term Financial Strategy, which was renewed for the fourth time in March 1984. The new targets for monetary growth were as follows:

	% change during year				
	1984–5	*1985–6*	*1986–7*	*1987–8*	*1988–9*
Narrow money – M_0	4–8	3–7	2–6	1–5	0–4
Broad money – $£M_3$	6–10	5–9	4–8	3–7	2–6

The main rationale of the strategy still seemed to be that the reduction of monetary growth was a necessary condition (rather than a necessary consequence) of reducing inflation.[1] Yet the paradox remained that in analysing and forecasting inflation the Treasury pays no evident attention to the money supply, but emphasizes factors such as wage costs per unit of output, import prices and the exchange rate, using a model not dissimilar from that set out in section IV of this chapter. Some would argue that there is no paradox involved since it is monetary growth which determines inflation expectations. But there is no real evidence for the importance of expectations in moderate inflations or for their dependence on monetary factors.

The other contradiction, which was rife at the time of the 1983 general election, was the doctrine that the government was impotent to influence demand or employment by means of expansionary fiscal policy. This view was plainly inconsistent with the rationale behind the Treasury's forecasting methods, and difficult to reconcile with the view that private-sector expansion *could* create jobs. Since Mr Lawson became Chancellor these views have not been heard and they were certainly not reiterated in the Budget speech of 13 March 1984.

The main obstacles to fiscal expansion in 1984 were the fear of renewed inflation and the fact that the next general election was several years away.

VI.4 Alternative Strategies

Whilst the government's understanding of inflation may have been open to question there were, nonetheless, genuine inflationary risks in any attempt to restore employment to the level of 1979. The first factor to be reckoned with was the Phillips Curve effect of lower unemployment on the rate of wage increase. The original Phillips Curve was flat for unemployment levels in excess of 4%. But with the experience of the 1970s and early 1980s it was probably optimistic to expect no response of wages to a recovery of demand.

A second factor was the effect of higher GDP on imports, the exchange rate, and hence on import prices. Here the effect depends partly upon the elasticities of demand for exports and imports. If these are -1.5 and -0.5 respectively, the exchange-rate decline would have to be about 1–1.5% for each 1% rise in GDP.[2]

---

1 'In order to reduce inflation further, the Government intends to continue reducing rates of monetary growth' (*FSBR*, March 1984).

2 The reasoning is as follows: a 1% fall in the exchange rate leads to a 1% fall in UK export prices in terms of foreign currency and a 1.5% rise in their volume. The value of exports in terms of £s rises by 1.5%. At the same time, import prices (in £s) rise by 1%, whilst the import volume falls by 0.5%. The value of imports must rise, therefore, by 0.5%. Thus a 1% exchange-rate reduction improves the foreign balance by 1.5% on exports *less* 0.5% on imports, making a net improvement of approximately 1% of the value of imports.

Even a 10% addition to GDP would, on those assumptions, add only 10 or 15% to import prices, and, in the first instance, 2 or 3% to final prices. Subsequent rounds of the wage-price spiral would, of course, raise this amount, but the main point is that the pure adjustment effects are not too serious.

There was, however, the further danger that anything that looked like a 'retreat from sound finance' would affect the exchange rate more dramatically through its effects upon the prejudices of foreign-exchange dealers. It seems possible that these dealers are deeply influenced by monetarist ideas, and even if they are not they may believe that others are.[1] Thus it might be feared that an expansion of the economy with a step-up in the monetary growth rate would trigger off a run on sterling with serious effects on import costs. It seems that this is what happened during M. Mitterrand's brief excursion into Keynesianism in 1981–2, and the same thing could happen to Britain.

These effects through the exchange rate, however, might be neutralized if all industrial countries could be persuaded to expand together. A concerted recovery would, of course, drive up the prices of primary commodities—to the advantage of third world countries—but it would probably be less inflationary for the UK than going it alone.

Some rise in import prices, therefore, together with some pressure on wages are almost inevitable consequences of any attempt to expand domestic demand. These effects, however, could be offset or partly offset by a judicious choice of instruments for demand expansion. A cut in VAT from 15 to 5%, would, for example, reduce domestic prices by a bit less than 6% whilst at the same time adding 3% to GDP. A reduction in employers' contributions to national insurance would be another way of increasing demand and reducing costs simultaneously. Such policies, moreover, might pave the way for wage restraint, although with the experience of 1972–3 behind it the present government is unlikely to introduce a formal incomes policy.

The central dilemma of current economic policy is that 3 million are denied employment in order to protect society from the ill effects of inflation. Whilst the objective is wholly understandable, the costs are very serious. It must be asked, therefore, whether there are not better ways of stopping inflation—or curing its consequences—than the policies which have been pursued for the past five years. If, as seems probable, the most serious result of inflation is the impoverishment of retired people on fixed money incomes from private sources, then it would seem sensible for the government to consider some form of indexation for these incomes. The state pension scheme is already indexed to the cost of living. The extension of indexation to private pensions and retirement incomes would *not* be inflationary because it would simply maintain real demand at existing levels. It would, however, enable the government to help the unemployed without injuring a defenceless social group, and without having to wait until the danger of inflation had completely disappeared.

---

1 On this and the need for international co-operation, see Michael Stewart, *Controlling the Economic Future*, Wheatsheaf, 1983.

REFERENCES AND FURTHER READING

F.T. Blackaby (ed.), *British Economic Policy 1960-74*, NIESR and Cambridge University Press, 1979.

Sir Alec Cairncross, 'Is Employment Policy a Thing of the Past?', *Three Banks Review*, September 1983.

S.T. Cook and P.M. Jackson (eds.), *Current Issues in Fiscal Policy*, Martin Robertson, 1979.

Economic Policy Review, Department of Applied Economics, University of Cambridge.

Sir Bryan Hopkin, M. Miller and B. Reddaway, 'An Alternative Economic Strategy – A Message of Hope', *Cambridge Journal of Economics*, March 1982.

C.H. Feinstein, *National Income, Expenditure and Output of the United Kingdom 1855-1965*, Cambridge University Press, 1972.

A.P. Lerner, 'Functional Finance and the Federal Debt', *Social Research*, 1943, reprinted in M.G. Mueller (ed.), *Readings in Macroeconomics*, Holt, Rinehart and Winston, 1966.

R.C.O. Matthews, C.H. Feinstein and J.C. Odling-Smee, *British Economic Growth 1856-1973*, Stanford University Press, 1982.

Midland Bank Review.

National Institute Economic Review.

D. Savage, 'The Channels of Monetary Influence: A Survey of the Empirical Evidence', *NIER*, February 1978.

D. Savage, 'Fiscal Policy, 1974/5-1980/81: Description and Appraisal', *NIER*, February 1982.

M. Stewart, *Politics and Economic Policy in the UK Since 1964*, Pergamon, 1978.

M. Stewart, *Controlling the Economic Future – Policy Dilemmas in a Shrinking World*, Wheatsheaf, 1983.

Treasury, *Economic Progress Report*.

Treasury, *Financial Statement and Budget Report 1984-85*.

2

The monetary, financial and fiscal systems

N.J. Gibson

I   INTRODUCTION: THE POLICY DILEMMA

The previous chapter conveys an overall picture of the UK economy, paying particular attention to fluctuations in economic activity, demand management, inflation and economic growth. This chapter concentrates on a more restricted subject area. It describes the monetary, financial and fiscal systems and examines the monetary, credit and fiscal policies of the authorities, that is, the UK government and the Bank of England.

The term 'policy' implies the existence of goals or objectives, and a strategy or instruments to achieve them. For twenty years after the Second World War the most frequently cited policy goals in the UK were the maintenance of full employment, price stability and fixed exchange rates, the encouragement of economic growth and the achievement of a 'satisfactory' balance of payments.[1] However, since the late 1960s the emphasis on the maintenance of fixed exchange rates has all but disappeared and more flexible exchange rates have become the norm, though this does not mean that the balance of payments has become a matter of little concern. Furthermore, reducing the rate of inflation, rather than the maintenance of full employment, has come to dominate the policy goals of the authorities. The former is considered to be of crucial importance in laying foundations conducive to economic growth. But as will be seen this whole matter is highly controversial.

The standard policy instruments at the disposal of the authorities are monetary, credit and fiscal. The first includes measures which alter the money supply; the second, the cost and availability of credit; and the third, tax rates and government expenditure. By using these instruments the authorities hope to realize some or all of their policy goals. But in addition to the instruments mentioned, the authorities may alter exchange rates, restrict imports and impose controls on prices and incomes. They may even go beyond this, particularly in periods of extreme economic difficulty, and introduce rationing and other interventionist measures.

The policy problem is clearly a complex one. In dealing with it the authorities may attempt to use their policy instruments to influence what are called target variables, sometimes known as intermediate targets to distinguish them from the goals or ultimate targets described above. The belief or hope is that the instrument and target variables are causally related and that in turn there is a reasonably stable

1   See chapters 3 and 5 respectively for explanation and discussion of the balance of payments and incomes controls. A 'satisfactory' balance of payments is best seen as a constraint to be satisfied rather than a goal to be realized.

link between the target variable and the desired goal. For instance, the authorities may assume that by manipulating interest rates they can affect the amount of money in the system or its rate of growth and that there is, at least in the longer term, a link between the latter and the rate of inflation.

But the foregoing is evidently a somewhat idealized picture. Once a set of goals is chosen, a host of questions arise. Can they be defined precisely? Are they mutually compatible within the particular economic system, given the policy instruments at the disposal of the authorities? If they are not, which goals should be sacrificed or modified? Are there alternative policy instruments that might be used to achieve one or more of the policy goals? Have the authorities, or for that matter has anyone else, the necessary knowledge about the relationships between instruments and goals? Do they know exactly when and by how much to manipulate the policy instruments they need? More fundamentally, is this whole methodological approach too mechanistic, and does it make insufficient allowance for individuals and groups to adapt their behaviour to actual and anticipated policy measures? These questions, which are easier to pose than to answer, highlight what may be called the policy dilemma.

Implicit in this discussion of goals and instruments are questions concerning both value judgements and how an economic system works. Each of these questions is a recurring theme in this chapter. Section II looks briefly at the theoretical and empirical basis of monetary and fiscal policy. Section III discusses the structure of the banking and financial system, and examines some money and credit theories. The taxation system is considered in section IV, which also includes a brief discussion of taxation within the EEC. Finally, in section V, policy since the 1960s is briefly surveyed and also included is a short discussion of the prospects and possible implications of economic and monetary union within the EEC.

II   SOME THEORETICAL AND EMPIRICAL BACKGROUND
II.1   Certain Keynesian and Monetarist Positions

If the policy dilemma is as difficult as the foregoing discussion suggests, what has economics to say about it? To attempt to answer this question is to enter the highly controversial debate which has been over-simply and crudely described as Keynesianism versus Monetarism.

Keynesianism does, of course, trace its lineage from the writings of Keynes and especially *The General Theory of Employment, Interest and Money*.[1] In writing *The General Theory*, Keynes set himself the task of providing a general theory of the working of the aggregate economic system but one which allowed involuntary unemployment of labour to persist. The term 'involuntary' has the connotation that it is undesired and that unemployed workers would provide their services at the existing real wage (or even a lower one) if there were only a demand for them; the persistence of involuntary unemployment was taken to suggest that there were no automatically working market forces which would tend to eradicate the involuntary unemployment and that, in particular, a willingness of workers to accept a reduction in money wages would not solve the problem.[2] For Keynes and

---

1   Macmillan, 1936.

2   The concept of 'involuntary unemployment' is not a simple one. For further discussion, see Don Patinkin, *Money, Interest and Prices*, 2nd edition, Harper and Row, 1965, pp. 313-34.

his followers the answer lay in expanding aggregate demand for goods and services and so indirectly for labour.

The preferred policy instrument for influencing aggregate demand was fiscal policy, either through changing government expenditure or taxation or a combination of both. Monetary policy might also be used to influence interest rates and so aggregate demand, though for some Keynesians this approach was less reliable as they were sceptical about the impact of changes in interest rates on investment expenditure and felt that in some circumstances, such as that of a deep recession, the demand for money, if it could be relied on at all, might be so elastic that interest rates could not be made low enough to stimulate expenditure.

This approach to policy — variously called demand management or the 'neoclassical synthesis', as it stressed that, so long as aggregate demand was sustained, market processes could be relied upon to allocate resources more or less efficiently — dominated economic thinking in the period immediately following the Second World War. There was considerable confidence amongst economists and governments that by manipulating aggregate demand — sometimes known as fine-tuning — full employment could be maintained.

However, by the 1950s there was some concern about the ability to generate full employment and at the same time achieve price stability. This concern came eventually to be formulated in terms of the so-called 'Phillips Curve', which purported to have found an inverse relationship, over a lengthy historical time-period, between the rate of unemployment and the rate of change of wages.[1] That is, as unemployment became smaller, the rate of increase of wages got larger. The first may be taken as a proxy for growing aggregate demand and the second puts pressure on prices generally to rise. Policy-makers seemed to be posed with a fundamental dilemma; they could not have full employment and price stability at the same time. Nevertheless, many Keynesians welcomed the advent of the Phillips Curve as they had been unhappy with the traditional emphasis on the downward rigidity of nominal wages and prices.

There were, however, other Keynesians who never accepted the neoclassical synthesis and emphasized other and perhaps more radical aspects of *The General Theory*. For them wages and wage costs are basically exogenous, or at any rate largely the outcome of non-economic, social and political factors, and any attempt to restrain them by controlling aggregate demand through, for example, restrictions on public expenditure will result in falling output and rising unemployment with perhaps little or no effect on wages and prices; or indeed falling output and employment together with rising prices may occur; this latter combination of phenomena is commonly called stagflation. Economists who hold these views feel extremely strongly about the restrictive public expenditure policies followed by Mrs Thatcher's government. The protagonists of this approach also tend to emphasize the inherent uncertainty of economic life, stressing the importance of unpredictable expectations about the future and their impact on economic activity. If this approach is accepted, it rules out attempts to rely on the existence of reasonably stable investment and monetary relationships as a basis for economic policy. Incomes and prices policies and other forms of government intervention in the areas of finance, investment, foreign trade and exchange rates are generally suggested as the type of policy required to sustain the growth of output and employment, though even these policies require some reliance on

---

1   For a more extensive discussion of the Phillips Curve, see chapter 1, section IV.5.

market processes.

In addition to the foregoing there is a less extreme strand of the Keynesian tradition which also attacks the assumption of the automatic working of market processes and, in particular, the notion of general flexibility of prices and instead emphasizes that prices may be sticky and adjust at varying rates in different markets. This became known as disequilibrium analysis, and of necessity stresses the importance of quantity adjustments as well as price adjustments. They too would expect attempts to control inflation solely by restrictive fiscal and monetary policies to lead to unemployment and loss of output. However, they still consider such policies to be important but would buttress them by some form of incomes and prices policy and perhaps other types of intervention such as in the foreign-exchange market. In general, however, they still place considerable reliance on market processes and their ability to allocate resources comparatively efficiently.

A particularly noteworthy contribution in this context is due to Professor James Meade and his associates and which they have called 'New Keynesianism'.[1] A central conviction of the New Keynesianism is that to overcome stagflation it is necessary to attack it with two distinct weapons. The first requires the introduction of decentralized institutional arrangements, backed by statutory authority, to fix wages for the different sectors of the economy, paying careful attention to the demand and supply of labour with a view to achieving a satisfactory level of employment. The second, within which the first would operate, is demand-management arrangements in the form of monetary, fiscal and exchange-rate policies which maintain the total demand for goods and services on a steady, expansionary and low-inflationary path. These proposals are clearly an interesting and radical departure from orthodox Keynesianism and, as will be seen, are distinctively different from the monetarist tradition. If they stand the test of criticism and can be made to work, they would be of the greatest importance.

There were, of course, economists who never saw themselves as part of the Keynesian tradition, notably a group of University of Chicago economists under the intellectual leadership of Milton Friedman. In 1956 in his famous article, 'The Quantity Theory of Money—a Restatement',[2] Friedman powerfully challenged those versions of Keynesianism which had tended to play down or dismiss the relevance of money to the operation of the economic system. He did this by recasting the traditional quantity theory of money as a theory of the *demand* for money; a demand that was stable and could be specified in terms of a small number of key variables. He also contended that there were factors affecting the supply of money which did not affect its demand; hence on these arguments the way was open to trace out the effects of changes in the supply of money on such key variables as nominal income. Monetarism had been born, though it was more than a decade before the label was invented.

The term seems to owe its origin to Karl Brunner, another famous monetarist, who in 1968 attached the term to three major conclusions which he claimed had

---

1   J.E. Meade, *Stagflation*, vol. 1: *Wage-Fixing*, Allen and Unwin, 1982, and David Vines, Jan Maciejowski and J.E. Meade, *Stagflation*, vol. 2: *Demand Management*, Allen and Unwin, 1983.

2   In Milton Friedman (ed), *Studies in the Quantity Theory of Money*, University of Chicago Press, 1956.

emerged from intensive research work in the previous ten years or so: 'First, monetary impulses are a major factor accounting for variations in output, employment
and prices. Second, movements in the money stock are the most reliable measure
of the thrust of monetary impulses. Third, the behaviour of the monetary authorities dominates movements in the money stock over business cycles.'[1] These
statements constituted a strong challenge to the whole Keynesian tradition, with its
relative neglect and in some instances dismissal of the importance of money in the
operation of the economic system.

A further forceful attack on an element in the Keynesian tradition came from
Friedman in the late 1960s. He convincingly questioned the validity of a stable
trade-off between inflation and unemployment; the Phillips Curve thus came under
strong critical pressure. Friedman argued that the Phillips Curve as ordinarily understood assumed that the anticipated rate of inflation was given. His position was that
this could only be a short-run phenomenon and that the experience of rising prices
would lead to a revision of anticipated inflation and an upward shift in the Phillips
Curve. In the long term there was for him no trade-off between inflation and
unemployment; indeed the long-run Phillips Curve was vertical, defining what he
called the 'natural rate of unemployment', that is, the rate which in the long run
emerged from the interaction of real market forces, though it was not to be seen as
a constant.

Friedman felt that his criticisms of the original Phillips Curve and his argument
that the long-run Phillips Curve was vertical carried important implications for
monetary policy. In particular, any attempt to reduce unemployment below
its natural rate through monetary expansion, or indeed expansionary fiscal policies,
would not succeed in the long run but would lead to greater inflation and, if the
attempt was maintained, to accelerating inflation. This point of view would seem to
have had a great influence on the policies of Mrs Thatcher's government. Moreover,
any reduction in the rate of monetary expansion once the process is under way
could be expected, for a considerable period, to be accompanied by both rising
prices and rising unemployment; in other words, stagflation is again observed. And
more generally the effectiveness of demand-management policies is seriously open
to doubt.

Running through the immediately preceding account is the notion that people's
adjustments to rising prices take time. This notion became formalized in terms of
what is called the adaptive expectations hypothesis. Briefly this suggests that people
form their expectations about future prices by extrapolating their past experience
of actual prices, giving most weight to the recent past. On the face of it, if this type
of lagged response does exist it would seem to allow for some element of demand
management or fine-tuning. Friedman would, however, be inclined to reject this
inference on a number of grounds, in particular because of the variability of the
lagged adjustments and hence the extreme difficulty in following a policy which is
really stabilizing in its effects.

However, the adaptive expectations hypothesis has itself come under strong
criticism from what has come to be called the 'rational expectations' or 'new
classical' economics. The basis of the challenge to adaptive expectations is that if
people generally operate on that basis, then they are going to be systematically in

---

1   'The Role of Money and Monetary Policy', *Review,* Federal Reserve Bank of St Louis, July
1968, p. 9.

error and this is clearly not rational. More positively, rational expectations require that views about the future be formulated in the light of all the available information. The implication of this is far-reaching, as it implies, for instance, that people in making their decisions will take into consideration anticipated government policy. But this in turn carries the consequence that the objectives of government policy may then be frustrated. If, for example, government hopes to encourage a growth in output and employment through expansionary monetary policies and people generally anticipate that this will result in rising prices, then in this approach they will take the latter into account in their own decision-making and the objectives of government may in part be undermined. In other words, the rational expectations approach casts doubt on the effectiveness of government demand-management policies.

This approach, as indicated above, is also described as the 'new classical' economics. The reason for this term is that like the old classical economics (some would say neoclassical), the new relies heavily on market-clearing processes, discounting the importance of price rigidities and so-called persistent disequilibria, and postulates optimizing behaviour on the part of economic agents, with the optimization extending to expected future events; it is the latter that is 'new'. This whole approach has encountered strong criticism, frequently on the grounds of the lack of realism of its assumptions, especially the one relating to market clearing. If the latter is dropped then the way seems to be open for Keynesian-type macro policies which would generate adjustments in the growth of output and employment.

It should be evident from the foregoing discussion that a highly intensive and at times conflicting debate has been and still is in progress about the operation of the economic system and what may be appropriate policy measures for governments to employ in their attempts to stabilize it. Nevertheless, it is possible to discern some areas of broad agreement or at least of a coming closer together. The branch of Keynesianism which has come to stress the importance of quantity as well as price adjustments, that rates of adjustment in different markets may vary greatly, being particularly rapid for foreign-exchange rates but sluggish in many labour markets, are views which would be shared by some monetarists. In particular, the New Keynesianism has some features in common with aspects of monetarism, though they differ considerably about the operation of labour markets and the former stresses the significance of a steady growth of money incomes whilst the latter emphasizes the importance of the growth of the money supply. There is also a widespread recognition that expectations about the future are of importance to the effectiveness of policy measures. However, the areas of agreement should not be overstated and they do not necessarily imply agreement on the appropriate policy responses that should be followed at a particular point of time. Thus the task of the policy-makers remains extremely difficult. It is time to explore some of their views about these matters.

II.2　Views of the Authorities

The Bank of England has made it clear that, like many others, they were strongly influenced by Keynesian thinking for a considerable number of years after the Second World War. A Governor of the Bank has stated as regards the early part of this period that 'the doctrine of Keynes, at least as interpreted by his followers . . .

had led to a totally new emphasis on fiscal policy . . . monetary policy went into limbo. There was a general scepticism about its relevance.'[1]

The scepticism would seem to have persisted, except perhaps for a brief interlude in the mid-1950s, until the later 1960s. By the latter period the Bank had come to be influenced by the rise of monetarism and especially by empirical evidence 'suggesting that there might well be a stable relationship between the demand for money and the level of income and interest rates'. For the Bank, 'The identification of this function appeared to provide a sound intellectual basis for monetary policy'.[2] In particular, other things being equal, if the authorities could control the appropriate interest rates the quantity of money demanded would be given, though, of course, it was never believed that matters were as clear-cut as this statement suggests.

However, it was from around the late 1960s and partly because of pressure from the IMF, which provided the United Kingdom with standby facilities following the devaluation of sterling in 1967, that the authorities paid increasing attention to the growth of what have come to be called the monetary aggregates. There are a number of these, but the two most relevant to this discussion are M_1 and M_3. M_1 refers to notes and coin in circulation with the public, plus sterling sight deposits held by the private sector. M_3, which subsumes M_1, originally consisted of notes and coin in circulation with the public, together with all deposits whether in sterling or other currencies, held by UK residents in both the public and private sectors. However, the Chancellor of the Exchequer announced on 10 February 1984 that M_3 was to be redefined to exclude public-sector deposits. This matter is considered below in section III.8, where other monetary aggregates are also discussed, including M_0, M_2 and sterling M_3 ($£M_3$).

Despite the increasing attention which the Bank claims to have given to monetary aggregates from the late 1960s, M_3 grew extremely rapidly in the early 1970s and it was not until the end of 1973 that they adopted unpublished targets for the rate of growth of M_3.[3] Publication of targets did not take place until the autumn of 1976. The Bank saw the introduction of targets as providing 'the framework of stability within which other policy objectives [could] be more easily achieved'[4] and that there was a 'relationship between monetary growth and inflation over the longer term'.[5]

These statements might suggest that around the mid-1970s the Bank had become converted to monetarism. This would, however, overstate the case, though it should also be noted that the Bank would seem to have begun to share the scepticism of many economists about frequent fiscal-policy adjustments or 'fine-tuning' as a means of demand management. Nevertheless, the Bank cannot be simply labelled as monetarist since the mid-1970s in their approach to economic policy; they are rather more eclectic and pragmatic than this would imply. A Governor of the Bank has, however, referred with approval to the label 'practical monetarism', though even this term needs to be interpreted with caution, since another senior official of

---

1 'Monetary Management in the United Kingdom', *BEQB*, Vol. II, No. 1, March 1971, p. 41.

2 'An Account of Monetary Policy', *BEQB*, Vol. 18, No. 1, March 1978, p. 32.

3 For further discussion of this period, see below, p. 119.

4 'An Account of Monetary Policy', p. 34.

5 ibid., p. 35.

the Bank has referred to this period as representing 'monetarily constrained Keynesianism'. Furthermore, the Bank has subsequently become increasingly sceptical about relying on any single monetary aggregate as a basis for judging the appropriateness of policy in relation to ultimate policy objectives.

It is clear that the evolution of the views of the Bank away from a Keynesian perspective to one with a monetarist emphasis has been shared by the authorities generally. The Treasury has stated that 'There is a clear relationship between the growth of the money stock and the rate of inflation in the medium term. This is the foundation of the Government's strategy for reducing inflation by means of monetary control.'[1] It may, however, be doubted whether this statement would be made so categorically today.

The mention of the medium term is important because it allows that in the short term the effects of, say, a reduction in the rate of growth of the money supply may adversely affect output and employment. The Treasury took the view that the consequences for output and employment would depend crucially on price expectations, and that if these were revised downwards and reflected in money wages the impact on output and employment would be reduced. Central to this revision was the perception of the commitment by government to its money-supply targets. Although the Treasury was not optimistic that adverse effects on output and employment could be avoided in the short term, it saw no reason why the effects should permanently damage potential growth. However, the authorities have clearly been disappointed and perhaps surprised that the adjustment process has been so painful in terms of its output and employment effects, though it would be argued that these effects have occurred in part because of long-standing rigidities in the economic system.

The Treasury explained the differences between the short- and medium-term effects of a restrictive monetary policy in terms of the rapidity of the response of different markets. Financial markets, including foreign-exchange markets, were understood to respond much more quickly than labour markets. As regards the foreign-exchange markets, a restrictive policy would strengthen the exchange rate and tend to make domestic economic activity less competitive, putting pressure on output, prices and wages. In the long run it was considered that once prices and wages had adjusted, there would be no effect on the real exchange rate. Thus the Treasury like the Bank has taken up what perhaps may be called a qualified monetarist approach to economic policy.

II.3   Empirical Evidence

It might have been hoped that the conflict of views on how the economy works and the appropriate policies for the authorities to follow in order to achieve their goals could have been resolved by the building and testing of macro-econometric models. However, as the introduction to this chapter implies, this hope has not so far been realized. The Treasury and Civil Service Committee referred to in the footnote below expressed deep disappointment at the dearth of empirical evidence

---

1   'Memorandum by H.M. Treasury', Third Report from the Treasury and Civil Service Committee, Session 1980–81, *Monetary Policy*, Vol. II, Minutes of Evidence, HC, 163–II, 24 February 1981, p. 90. See also Vol. I, 163–I and Vol. III Appendices, 163–III.

presented to it in its enquiry into monetary policy.

One of the difficulties is, of course, that different models may suggest substantially different answers not only on how the economy works but what would be the consequences of following a carefully specified monetary or fiscal policy. Testing these matters with a model is known as simulation. However, there is a more fundamental difficulty in relying on simulation exercises as a means of providing definitive answers to policy questions. In so far as an econometric model incorporates optimal behaviour of economic units, then a change in policy may be expected to require an alteration in the structure of the model and to that extent reduce or undermine the predictive capacity of the original model. On the other hand, for the policy-makers to be able to anticipate and allow for the structural changes which their policies may give rise to, clearly poses formidable problems and might presumably require that the public be taken into their confidence.

Notwithstanding these difficulties, there is some measure of agreement between econometric model-builders in the UK and the US that both monetary and fiscal policies have in the short run important effects on output, employment and prices. with the price effect coming about more slowly than the other two effects. The actual impact of the policies will, of course, depend in part on the initial state of the economy as well as unpredictable events which may subsequently impinge upon its operation. In the longer term, there is a presumption, at least as regards the US, that 'the response of the economy to both monetary and fiscal policy is . . . consistent with the views advanced by Friedman and the monetarists'.[1] However, these conclusions are of little comfort to policy-makers acutely aware of both the costs of unemployment in the short and medium term, and the inefficiencies and inequities of continuing and variable inflation. What in some sense constitutes an optimum or best set of policies is clearly elusive.

III   THE MONETARY AND FINANCIAL SYSTEM
III.1   Introduction

The monetary and financial system is made up of a set of institutions which trade in or exchange financial instruments of various types and maturities. These include deposits of banks and building societies, notes and coin, loans (whose attributes may vary greatly), company and government stocks and securities, and many other kinds of instrument. The trade in instruments necessarily gives rise to a host of financial markets of varying degrees of interdependence, which are of fundamental importance to the efficient operation of the economic system and which extend outside national boundaries into the world at large. In this chapter, however, attention is concentrated on the major domestic financial institutions, beginning with a discussion of the monetary sector; other financial institutions are discussed later.

---

1 F. Modigliani, 'The Channels of Monetary Policy in the Federal Reserve–MIT–University of Pennsylvania Econometric Model of the United States', in G.A. Renton (ed.), *Modelling the Economy*, Heinemann, 1975, p. 241.

III.2   The Monetary Sector

The monetary sector is officially defined to include the following institutions:

(i)   all recognized banks and licensed deposit-takers (LDTs);

(ii)   the National Girobank;

(iii) those institutions in the Channel Islands and the Isle of Man which have opted to comply with the new monetary control arrangements introduced in August 1981;

(iv)   the trustee savings banks;

(v)   the Banking Department of the Bank of England.

The terms 'recognized banks' and 'LDTs' are new to the UK banking system and were introduced under the 1979 Banking Act. To acquire the status of a recognized bank, an institution or parent institution has to satisfy the Bank of England that it enjoys 'a high reputation and standing in the financial community' and provides or will provide, directly or through a subsidiary, 'a wide range of banking services or a highly specialized banking service' and can meet certain minimum capital and reserve requirements.[1] Under the Act, 'a wide range of banking services' is defined to include both domestic and foreign banking services, though the Bank has some discretion in what it requires to satisfy the conditions.

To become LDTs, institutions have also to meet requirements similar to those specified for recognized banks but without any conditions as regards the range of services they offer. In fact, a number of institutions which sought recognized-bank status were not granted it and had to be content with the status of a LDT: the grounds for refusal would seem often to have been the extent of the range of services offered.

There are some 600 recognized banks and LDTs, with the former making up about half of the total number. As might be expected, this large number of institutions covers banks—where the term is used to refer to both recognized banks and LDTs unless the text specifies otherwise—with enormous variation in size and range of activities. It includes the six large London clearing banks with some 11,000 branches between them, the three Scottish clearing banks, the four Northern Ireland banks, discount houses, accepting houses, and highly specialized investment banks and trust companies, finance houses, consortium banks and literally hundreds of overseas banks with offices in London.[2]

Putting aside the National Girobank which is discussed below, the monetary sector includes certain institutions in the Channel Islands and the Isle of Man which accepted an invitation to become part of the monetary sector, although the Banking Act does not apply to either area. In doing so they have, of course, to comply with the official monetary control provisions; the latter are examined below. There are over 60 Channel Islands and Isle of Man institutions which have opted to become part of the UK monetary sector; some of the institutions concerned are branches of mainland banks. The major reason for the large number of financial institutions in the Channel Islands and the Isle of Man is that they find distinct tax advantages in being outside the jurisdiction of the UK fiscal authorities.

The remaining institutions that are part of the monetary sector, the trustee

---

1   Quotations from the 1979 Banking Act (1979 c. 37), Schedule 2, Part 1.

2   For further discussion, see below, sections III.6 and III.7.

savings banks and the Banking Department of the Bank of England, are discussed later.

The Governor of the Bank of England recently described the UK as 'a relatively small country with a relatively very large financial centre exposed to international monetary forces acting in a turbulent world'.[1] Table 2.1 shows a highly aggregated picture of the monetary sector at the end of 1983; the figures are intended to exclude double counting and to show the position of the sector *vis-à-vis* third parties. Total deposits were just under £459,000 million, with approximately £115,000m in sterling and £343,000m in other currencies. In comparison with most other countries, these figures are relatively large in relation to GDP and clearly do expose the UK to the influence of 'international monetary forces', especially those reflected in eurocurrency markets. (See section III.5 *et seq.*)

TABLE 2.1
UK Monetary Sector, end-December 1983 (£m)

	Sterling	Other currencies	Total
(i) *Liabilities*			
Domestic deposits	92,212	16,601	108,813
Overseas-sector deposits	23,234	326,603	349,837
Non-deposit liabilities (net)	n.a.	n.a.	19,280
			477,930
(ii) *Assets*			
Lending:			
to public sector	18,357	1,443	19,800
to private sector	94,394	24,658	119,052
to overseas sector	18,752	320,326	339,078
	131,503	346,427	477,930

Source: *BEQB*

It should be noted that in aggregate there is a rough matching of sterling assets and liabilities and similarly for other currencies, though this does not necessarily imply a similar matching of maturity dates. Indeed, one of the fundamental functions of financial institutions is to operate in ways which allow a mismatch of maturity dates to persist without any threat to the stability of the particular institution and ultimately the whole system. This function used to be called borrowing short and lending long, but is now more aptly referred to as maturity transformation. The capacity to engage in this practice hinges crucially on the ability of the institutions to pool independent risks, in the sense of, say, deposit withdrawals being offset by new deposits and similarly for transactions on the assets side of balance sheets. There are, of course, in addition other important factors at work including economies from large-scale operation and the system of

---

1 'Recent Changes in the Monetary and Regulatory Framework', *BEQB*, Vol. 22, No. 1, March 1982, p. 102.

prudential and supervisory controls applied by the monetary authorities. The particular controls operated in the UK are discussed under the activities of the Bank of England.

III.3 The Bank of England

The Bank of England acts as the main banker to the government and plays a basic role in smoothing government cash transactions between the government and the banking system and in administering and managing the national debt—broadly speaking, the debt liabilities of the state to its nationals, to its own agencies and to overseas holders. As agent of the government, the Bank helps to regulate foreign-exchange transactions and manages the Exchange Equalization Account, which holds the official gold, foreign-exchange reserves and SDRs of the UK. The Bank is also banker to the banking system and has a major responsibility for the carrying out of monetary policy and for the prudential supervision of the monetary sector; in short, the Bank of England is a central bank.

The Bank is divided into two parts for accounting purposes; it produces two balance sheets, one for the Issue Department and one for the Banking Department. The origin of the double-balance-sheet system is to be found in monetary controversies during the first half of the nineteenth century and was introduced under the 1844 Bank Charter Act, separating the note-issue function from all other functions of the Bank. But the two balance sheets still retain a certain, if somewhat artificial, significance in that the Issue Department is classified in the national accounts as part of the public sector whereas the Banking Department is classified for banking purposes with the banking sector. The position of the Issue Department in December 1983 is shown in table 2.2.

TABLE 2.2

Issue Department (selected items), 14 December 1983 (£m)

Liabilities		*Assets*	
Notes:			
in circulation	12,152	Government securities	4,699
in Banking Dept.	8	Other securities	7,461
	12,160		12,160

Source: BEQB

The notes in circulation are necessarily held by persons, companies and financial institutions. Notes in the Banking Department would, of course, disappear from the accounts if the two balance sheets were amalgamated. The assets of the Issue Department are classified as government securities and other securities. The latter 'include commercial bills, local authority bills, and on occasion, local authority deposits and bonds . . . and company securities and other miscellaneous securities'.[1]

'Government securities include British government and government-guaranteed

---

1 'Notes and definitions to the tables,' *BEQB*, Vol. 24, No. 1, March 1984, p. 1.

securities, Treasury bills, ways and means advances to the National Loans Fund . . . and any special Treasury liability';[1] the latter arises when the total market value of assets is less than the note issue. Any increase in the note issue implies an equal addition to holdings of securities. In other words, when the Issue Department supplies additional notes, which it does via the Banking Department, it obtains interest-earning securities in exchange, which are then held within the public sector.

The Issue Department uses its assets to facilitate the issue and redemption of the national debt; it underwrites all new issues of government stock, taking up any stock that is not bought by the public on the day of issue and subsequently sells it as demand appears. Similarly, it purchases stock nearing redemption, avoiding large cash payments to the public when the actual redemption date arrives. The Issue Department may in fact be in the market as a buyer or seller of government securities, or both, almost continuously. That is, it engages extensively in open-market operations, largely by means of transfers between one form of debt and another. The latter are not, of course, confined to transactions involving government securities. In particular, in its money-market operations it deals extensively in commercial bills.

The balance sheet of the Banking Department is shown in table 2.3.

TABLE 2.3

Banking Department (selected items), 14 December 1983 (£m)

Liabilities		*Assets*	
Deposits:			
Public	44	Government securities	383
Bankers	650	Advances and other accounts	947
Reserves and other accounts	1,648	Premises, equipment and	
Special deposits	–	other securities	1,018
		Notes and coins	8
	2,342		2,356

Source: BEQB

Note: The balance sheet does not exactly balance because certain subsidiary items, such as capital, have been omitted.

Public deposits are all government balances. They include those of the Exchequer, the National Loans Fund, HM Paymaster General, the National Debt Commissioners, Dividend Accounts and certain other government accounts. The total amount involved is relatively small by comparison with bankers' deposits despite the enormous scale of government transactions. The main reason for this is that the government, with immediate access to the banking system, does not need to have large holdings of deposits to carry out its daily expenditure. Any so-called surplus balances are used to buy back government debt in an attempt to keep down costs. As may be seen from table 2.3, net payments from the government to the private sector will have an immediate effect on bankers' deposits, increasing the cash holdings of the banking system whilst reducing public deposits.

---

1 ibid.

The reverse is true for net payments from the private sector to the government, and so smoothing-out movements of funds between public and bankers' deposits is a major preoccupation of the Bank day by day; they use the resources of both the Banking Department and the Issue Department for these operations which generally take place in the money market (this matter is returned to below).

Bankers' deposits have taken on an enhanced significance since the introduction of the new monetary control arrangements from August 1981.[1] Previously, bankers' deposits were mostly current accounts of banks, predominantly those of the London clearing banks and discount houses. But since August 1981 they consist of what are called operational deposits and non-operational, non-interest-bearing cash-ratio deposits. As their name suggests, operational deposits are those held, mainly by the London clearing banks, for settling clearing transactions and the purchase of Bank notes. Non-operational, non-interest-bearing deposits refer to those deposits held to satisfy the new cash ratio imposed by the authorities on all recognized banks and licensed deposit-takers above a minimum size (see section III.4 *et seq*. below). The deposits are designed to provide the Bank with resources and to enable it to earn income from the corresponding assets.

Reserves and other accounts include balances of overseas central banks, certain dividend accounts, local authority and public corporation accounts, unallocated profits of the Banking Department and the accounts of the Bank's remaining private customers. These accounts are clearly not without importance but they are not central to the purpose of this chapter and so are not discussed further.

Special deposits were first introduced in April 1960. Under the initial scheme, the London clearing banks and Scottish clearing banks were from time to time obliged to transfer special deposits to the Bank in support of monetary and credit policy. This scheme came to an end in September 1971 when all outstanding special deposits were repaid and was replaced by a new scheme covering a much wider range of banks. The new monetary control arrangements introduced from August 1981 also involve a special-deposits scheme. Special deposits are further discussed below.

Government securities introduce the assets of the Banking Department and include Treasury bills and government and government-guaranteed securities and ways and means advances to the Exchequer.[2] These advances occur if the Exchequer finds itself short of funds at the end of the day and wishes to make up its balance: the advances are generally only overnight loans, being repaid the following day.

The Banking Department, through sales and purchases of Treasury bills and government securities, affects the volume of bankers' deposits and hence the cash holdings of the banking system. In general, government securities in the Banking

---

1   See 'Methods of Monetary Control', *BEQB*, Vol. 20, No. 4, December 1980, pp. 428-9; 'Monetary Control: Next Steps', ibid., March 1981, pp. 38-9; and 'Monetary Control – Provisions', ibid., September 1981, pp. 347-9.

2   A 'bill' in the sense used here is a piece of paper which is evidence of indebtedness on the part of the person or body on whom it is drawn. The bill is said to be 'discounted' when it is purchased at a price below its value on maturity. Hence Treasury bills are evidence of indebtedness of the Treasury. These bills initially have usually 91 days to run to maturity and might be acquired by the discount houses at, say, £98 per £100, which would represent a discount of approximately 8% per annum on the value at maturity and a yield to the holder of about 8.16%.

Department can be used in much the same way as those in the Issue Department to facilitate debt management and monetary policy. However, the assets at the disposal of the Banking Department are rather smaller than those available to the Issue Department.

Advances and other accounts are of three main types: market advances to the discount market, loans to the remaining private customers of the Bank, and what are called support loans to deposit-taking institutions. The first are discussed in the section below dealing with the discount market. The third refers to loans made by the Bank to a number of secondary banks which had got into liquidity difficulties in the early 1970s through lending to certain property companies.

Premises, equipment and other securities and notes and coins can be dealt with briefly. Other securities are non-government securities and include commercial bills purchased by the Bank in order to keep a watch on the quality of such bills circulating in the London market. The Bank will not purchase bills of which they disapprove and this acts as a deterrent to their circulation. Other securities also include local authority bills and bonds and some holdings of equity share capital of other companies. Notes are the counterpart of the items in the Issue Department and some coin is held for ordinary business purposes.

III.4   The Discount Market

The term discount market refers to the ten discount houses that are members of the London Discount Market Association (LDMA). The discount houses constitute a unique set of highly specialized banking institutions which are at the centre of the day-to-day money market operations of the Bank of England as it implements its monetary and credit policies. Indeed the term money market is frequently restricted to operations involving the discount houses, though it is also used to cover all markets, including interbank markets, which deal in wholesale (large) sums for same-day settlement. The Bank went to considerable lengths when introducing its new monetary control arrangements in 1981 to preserve and sustain the significance of the discount market in the operation of the monetary system. An examination of the balance sheet of the discount market makes this clear.

The borrowed funds from the Bank of England pinpoint one aspect of the special relationship between the discount houses and the Bank. Apart from some institutions in the gilt-edged market—the market for government and government-guaranteed securities—the discount houses are the only financial institutions which may, when they cannot obtain funds from other sources, approach the Bank for funds. The Bank is then prepared to lend to the discount houses against suitable collateral but only 'on terms designed to discourage their use'.[1] In other words, the Bank will impose stiff conditions as regards collateral, duration and interest rates for this type of assistance; it is intended to be a 'last resort' form of help and not part of the day-to-day operations of the Bank.

By far the greater amount of borrowed funds, which, of course, constitute the liabilities of the discount houses, are denominated in sterling and come from the rest of the UK monetary sector in the form of call money, that is, a deposit which is placed on a day-to-day basis and which can be withdrawn any day before noon.

---

1 'The Role of the Bank of England in the Money Market', *BEQB*, Vol. 22, No. 1, March 1982, p. 87.

TABLE 2.4

Discount Market (selected items) 14 December 1983 (£m)

	Sterling	Other currencies	Total
Liabilities: Borrowed funds			
Bank of England	55	–	55
Other UK monetary sector	5,838	49	5,887
Other UK	738	14	752
Overseas	36	8	44
TOTAL	6,667	71	6,738
(of which call and overnight)	(6,132)		
Assets			
Cash-ratio deposits with Bank of England	3	–	3
Treasury bills	31	–	31
Local authority and other public-sector bills	206	–	206
Other bills	3,371	13	3,384
Funds lent:			
UK monetary sector	96	–	96
UK monetary sector certificates of deposit (CDs)	2,044	–	2,044
Building society CDs and time deposits	280	–	280
UK local authorities	149	–	149
Other United Kingdom	79	–	79
Other CDs	–	70	70
Investments:			
British government stocks	364	–	364
Local authorities	154	–	154
Other	46	10	56
Other sterling assets	37	–	37
	6,860	93	6,953

Source: *BEQB*.

Under the new monetary control arrangements, what are called 'eligible banks', that is, recognized banks whose acceptances are eligible for rediscount at or sale to the Bank,[1] have undertaken to hold on any day not less than the equivalent of 2½% of their eligible liabilities (ELs) as secured funds with the members of the LDMA.[2] The 2½% holding is defined as an average which is to be maintained by each eligible bank over either a discrete six- or twelve-month period.

The reason given by the Bank for introducing this requirement for eligible banks – they must also similarly hold up to 2½% of their ELs (making 5% in total) as secured call money with money brokers and gilt-edged jobbers[3] – was to ensure

---

1 An 'acceptance' is a commercial bill on which a reputable bank has placed its name, thus undertaking to honour the bill when it matures. An acceptance is also known as a bank bill, in contrast with a trade bill which is a commercial bill that has not been accepted by a bank.

2 Eligible liabilities of the banks are defined in section III.5.

3 There are six recognized money brokers; the amount of secured call money they can take is limited by the Bank. See 'Monetary Control – Provisions', op. cit. p. 348, fn. 3.

that there existed 'a market in bills of the size necessary for the Bank's open market operations'.[1] The Bank feared that with the abolition of the bank's reserve assets ratio (RAR), there might not be a market of sufficient scale for its money market activities (the RAR is discussed in section III.8 below). Implicit in this new emphasis on the market in bills — Treasury bills, local authority bills and commercial bills — is a determination of the Bank to allow market forces greater freedom to influence the rates ruling in bill markets and to avoid as far as possible secured lending to the discount market. These developments are all part of the new approach to monetary control.

From the definition of call money and more generally the secured money discussed above, it is evident that it is a highly liquid asset from the point of view of the banks, subject, of course, to eligible banks maintaining their required percentages. If for some reason, perhaps because of large net payments to government, the banks find themselves running short of funds, they may decide not to renew some of their call money with the discount houses. The latter will then generally have to find funds by offering bills to the Bank. But under the new arrangements of 1981 the Bank no longer announces rates at which it will deal in bills and may refuse the offer in whole or in part if it is not satisfied with the rates involved. By this technique it is in a strong position to influence market rates in ways it considers consistent with its overall interest-rate policy. This policy at any point of time is defined in terms of maintaining short-term rates within unpublished maturity bands. Notwithstanding the wish of the Bank to operate as described, it still retains the right to lend to the discount houses at rates of its own choosing. Thus the banks need have no fear that funds will ultimately be forthcoming if they decline to renew some or all of their secured money with the discount houses.

Turning to the assets of the discount market, it will be noticed that they have a small holding of cash-ratio deposits with the Bank of England. These are, in fact, part of the non-operational, non-interest-bearing deposits already mentioned in the discussion of the balance sheet of the Banking Department of the Bank. The members of the LDMA, like other banks, are now required since August 1981 to hold one-half of one per cent (½%) of their ELs in such deposits.[2] The deposits play no part in day-to-day money market management and are fixed in amount twice a year for a period of six months. The ELs of the discount houses constitute their sterling deposits 'other than from institutions within the monetary sector and from money brokers and gilt-edged jobbers in the Stock Exchange'.[3] Since the bulk of the borrowed funds of the discount houses come from the rest of the monetary sector, it is not surprising that their cash deposits are relatively small in amount.

The discount houses occupy a very special position in the market for UK Treasury bills though these are in quantitative terms less important than formerly. One reason is that the authorities in the second half of the 1970s came increasingly to concentrate on controlling the rate of growth of the money stock and in so doing found it desirable and possible to press sales of government securities on the non-bank private sector; this enabled the authorities to reduce the volume of Treasury bills on offer. Nevertheless, the long-standing arrangement remains

---

1 'Monetary Control: Next Steps', op. cit., p. 39.

2 The ½% cash-ratio requirement applies only to monetary sector institutions whose ELs average £10m or more over the calculation period.

3 'Monetary Control — Provisions,' op. cit., p. 347.

whereby the discount houses tender week-by-week for the whole issue of Treasury bills.[1] Each discount house determines the rate or rates at which it will tender. In the past if the discount houses did not have adequate funds to take up the whole tender, the Bank stood ready to help by open-market purchases which provided the market with the necessary additional funds to acquire the new Treasury bills. This is tantamount to the Bank lending directly to the Treasury and is clearly open to abuse by an impecunious government. It must be presumed that with a commitment to let market forces have greater influence in determining interest rates this form of assistance by the Bank will disappear or be used infrequently.

It may be seen from table 2.4 that in terms of volume Treasury bills are greatly outweighed by other bills including local authority bills and commercial bills. The Bank in its market activities now operates on a large scale in both these latter categories of bills.

The remaining asset of the discount houses which is of particular importance to the monetary management of the authorities is British government stocks. These consist of short-term government securities with less than five years to run to maturity. Their ownership by the discount houses facilitates the debt-management policies of the authorities, as the latter can generally replace the stocks on or before maturity by sales of new stock and so avoid having to make large cash payments.

It is evident from this discussion that the discount market has a pivotal role in monetary management and that the authorities have gone to considerable lengths in their new monetary arrangements to see that it is sustained and even strengthened.

III.5 Retail Banks

The Bank of England in September 1983 introduced for statistical purposes a new way of classifying British banks. It was felt that a more functional grouping of these banks was desirable and three categories are now used: retail banks, accepting houses and a residual category — other British banks.

The retail banks group is intended to bring together those banks which provide an extensive current- and savings-account service to individuals.[2] The group includes the London clearing banks (LCBs), the Scottish clearing banks, the Northern Ireland banks, the trustee savings banks (including the Central Trustee Savings Bank), the National Girobank, the Co-operative Bank and the Yorkshire Bank. A central feature of these banks is that they either have extensive branch systems or are major participants in a UK clearing system. In fact, these banks play a dominant role in money transmission through cash distribution and by processing an enormous volume of transfers both by paper (or voucher) and increasingly by electronic methods.

---

1 The Bank also makes, from time to time, special issues of Treasury bills of less than 91 days to maturity to remove funds from the market. A recent example took place in September 1981, when large VAT refunds were expected; a dispute had delayed their earlier repayment.

2 Whilst the retail banks come under the general heading of British banks, they in fact include the branches of banks in the Channel Islands and the Isle of Man which the parent banks have opted to bring under the UK monetary control arrangements and, in addition, the heading includes the branches in Great Britain and Northern Ireland of Allied Irish Banks and the Bank of Ireland, both of which are incorporated in the Republic of Ireland.

The Banking Department of the Bank of England is also included—somewhat surprisingly—in this group. The reason given is that of the three groups this one seemed to be the most appropriate. This, of course, begs the question why it does not constitute a 'group' on its own.

The London and Scottish clearing banks, the Northern Ireland banks, the Co-operative Bank and the Yorkshire Bank clearly do engage in what can be legitimately described as retail banking activities, though they carry on many other banking activities besides.

The trustee savings banks require a special word of explanation. A trustee savings bank is an unincorporated society run by trustees and offering a range of banking services, mostly to individuals. For some 160 years until 1976 they had been obliged to invest most of their funds with the public sector. But the 1976 Trustee Savings Bank Act made provision for a gradual relaxation of government controls over their activities, and since then they have increased the banking services offered, including lending to the general public. The number of trustee savings banks has been gradually reduced from over 70 in the early 1970s to TSB England and Wales, TSB Scotland, TSB Northern Ireland and TSB Channel Islands. Between them they have some 1,600 branches. Proposals are under way to launch in 1985 a new public limited company, TSB Group plc, of which the four banks above will be subsidiaries. It is hoped that these and other developments will enable the TSBs to compete more effectively with other retail banks and especially the clearing banks.

The National Girobank (it was called the National Giro until 1978) aims to provide a simple, cheap, accessible money-transmission service. Accessibility is facilitated by offering its services through some 21,000 post offices throughout the UK. Following a review of its activities, the National Giro decided in 1975 to extend its range of banking services and now offers customers both current and interest-bearing deposit accounts and certain limited lending facilities to persons. The National Giro has not grown as expected when first established.

As may be seen in table 2.5, the retail banks have a small note issue. In fact, the notes are liabilities of the Scottish clearing banks and the Northern Ireland banks and are a survival from the banking legislation of the mid-nineteenth century.

A feature of the retail banks is that, of their total deposit liabilities, the greater proportion is denominated in sterling: on 14 December 1983 £88,900m, as compared with £30,400m in foreign currencies. This position, as may be seen below in section III.6 and III.7, contrasts strongly with that of many other banking institutions where foreign or eurocurrency business is the dominant activity (eurocurrency business being transactions denominated in currencies other than that of the country or jurisdiction in which the institution is located). The ownership of the deposits of the retail banks is heavily concentrated with the UK private sector, which also contrasts with the position of the accepting houses and other British banks and overseas banks; these groups are much more dependent on overseas deposits.

Putting aside the currency distinction, deposits are of two main types: sight deposits and time deposits. Sight deposits, which may or may not be interest-bearing, are transferable or withdrawable on demand without interest penalty; they include the well-known current or chequeing accounts on which no interest is paid but where an abatement in charges may be allowed, depending on the balances maintained and the scale of transmission activity. Time deposits refer to

TABLE 2.5

Retail Banks, 14 December 1983 (£m)

	Sterling	Other currencies[1]	Total
(i) Liabilities			
Notes issued	836	–	836
Deposits:[2]			
UK monetary sector	10,125	6,461	16,586
UK public sector	1,767	} 3,190	} 70,747
UK private sector	65,790		
Overseas	6,250	18,800	25,050
Certificates of deposit (CDs)	4,989	1,961	6,950
Capital and other funds and items in suspense, etc.			17,943
Total liabilities			138,112
(ii) Assets			
Notes and coin	1,915	–	1,915
Balances with Bank of England:			
Special and cash-ratio deposits	310	–	310
Other	141	–	141
Market loans:[3]			
Secured money with LDMA	3,975	–	3,975
Other UK monetary sector	10,215	11,796	22,011
UK monetary sector CDs	1,600	239	1,839
UK local authorities	1,840	–	1,840
Overseas	350	–	350
Bills:			
Treasury bills	246	–	246
Eligible local authority bills	338	–	338
Eligible bank bills	1,898	–	1,898
Other	81	56	137
Advances:[4]			
UK public sector	968	76	1,044
UK private sector	57,085	2,947	60,032
Overseas	4,859	15,466	20,325
Investments:			
British government stocks	5,334	–	5,334
Other	3,242	1,561	4,803
Banking Department lending to central government (net)	387	–	387
Sterling and other currencies miscellaneous assets	–	–	11,185
Total assets	–	–	138,110

Source: BEQB.

Note: This table and tables 2.6 and 2.7 present data for what are called monthly reporting institutions, which are those members of the monetary sector which report to the Bank of England on a monthly basis – the members of the LDMA have already been considered – and generally have a total balance sheet of £100m or over or ELs of £10m or over.

1   Other currency liabilities and assets are valued in sterling at the closing middle-market spot rate on reporting days.

2   Sterling sight deposits amounted to £32,954m and were 37% of total sterling deposits (including CDs) of £88,921m. ELs totalled £71,057m on 14 December 1983.

3   Market loans may include some advances in other currencies.

all other deposits, except certificates of deposit which are shown separately in table 2.5. Time deposits include the traditional interest-earning 7-day deposits, that is, deposits which require 7 days' notice of withdrawal, although it is common practice to waive this requirement and to adjust interest payments in lieu of notice. In addition, time deposits include wholesale deposits; these are large deposits, usually for amounts in excess of £50,000, which carry interest at rates reflecting conditions in the money markets both at home and abroad. The time-period of the deposits may vary from as little as 8 days up to 5 years and over.

The advent of wholesale deposits – they first appeared in the 1960s – has given rise to what is called liability management. The latter is said to occur when a bank is approached for a loan or loans for specific time-periods, known as term loans, and matches the loans by bidding for or seeking out in the money markets deposits of corresponding term; thus in these circumstances little in the way of maturity transformation may take place, though risk transformation may still occur. Liability management is particularly widespread amongst other British banks and overseas banks in what is known as the inter-bank market and is of considerable importance for the authorities in their attempts to control the rate of growth of bank deposits. The interest rate which emerges in the inter-bank market is known as the London Inter-Bank Offered Rate (LIBOR) and is a basis for determining corresponding term loan rates.

A certificate of deposit (CD) is a negotiable instrument, denominated in sterling or dollars, issued by a bank in receipt for deposits for a fixed period of time and at a fixed rate of interest. The minimum amount of a CD is usually £50,000 and with an original term to maturity of between three months and five years. CDs have advantages for both the issuers and the holders. Issuing banks have found them to be a useful means of raising large amounts for strictly fixed periods – unlike the so-called fixed-term deposit where payment may be requested before maturity and be hard to refuse. Holders of CDs, including banks, have found them highly convenient as they can sell them in the secondary market if they need immediate funds for liquidity or other purposes. The discount houses are major operators in the secondary market but there is also an extensive inter-bank market.

The remaining liabilities entry is items in suspense and transmission and capital and other funds. The former refers to credit balances received but not yet credited to customers' accounts, and to items such as standing orders and credit transfers already debited to customers' accounts but not yet paid to the receiving body. Capital and other funds include capital and reserves and internal accounts of the banks. Capital and reserves are of fundamental importance as a protection against insolvency through default on loans, investment losses and foreign-exchange losses. The Bank of England is paying increasing attention to the adequacy of bank capital reserves, and it will be recalled that to acquire the status of a recognized bank or a licensed deposit-taker, under the 1979 Banking Act an institution has to satisfy the Bank about the adequacy of its capital. This matter falls under the heading of prudential control of banking activities and is discussed further in section III.8 below.

Turning to the assets of the retail banks, notes and coin are required for their ordinary day-to-day business. Special and cash-ratio deposits with the Bank refer only to the latter category, as at the present time (April 1984) there are no special deposits. Cash-ratio deposits were defined earlier in the discussions of the Bank and the discount houses. At £310m in December 1983, they amounted to exactly 62% of all cash-ratio deposits with the Bank on that date and at current rates of interest should earn the latter some £27m in a year and so may be considered as a substantial charge on the retail banks.

Eligible liabilities (ELs) for the retail banks and other banks are not defined in quite the same way as for the discount houses. Broadly speaking, they comprise sterling deposit liabilities, excluding deposits with an initial maturity of over two years since these are considered as more akin to loan capital than deposits; in addition ELs include any sterling resources obtained by switching foreign currencies into sterling; finally offsets to the foregoing are allowed for inter-bank transactions, except for cash-ratio and any special deposits with the Bank, and adjustments are made for items in transit. The offsets mean that in the calculation of ELs those funds lent by one institution to another in the monetary sector are deductible as well as 'money at call placed with money brokers and gilt-edged jobbers in the Stock Exchange, and secured on gilt-edged stocks, Treasury bills, local authority bills and eligible bank bills'.[1]

The other balances of the retail banks with the Bank are their operational deposits and are voluntarily held for clearing and reserve purposes. It is noticeable that on 14 December 1983 at £141m they were actually smaller in total than the compulsory cash-ratio deposits, and even when the former are combined with the £1,915m of their notes and coin holdings their total 'cash' of £2,056m represents only 2.3% of their total sterling deposits, putting aside their foreign-currency deposit liabilities. Bearing in mind that the remaining banks in the UK monetary sector, as indicated in sections III.6 and III.7 below, hold relatively little cash resources, there is clearly an enormous pyramid of credit built on a slender cash base; this is the actual fulcrum of the monetary system on which the Bank operates through its open-market operations. The slenderness of the base is not necessarily a matter for alarm but neither is it a matter that should be ignored and it is certainly relevant to the whole issue of the prudential control of the monetary sector.

The next major category of assets is market loans. Market loans refer to loans made at rates determined in the various money markets and are often made through the agency of money brokers; the loans may take a number of forms and are mainly with other members of the monetary sector, but also include some loans lent through the local authority money market and some overseas funds and may be denominated in sterling or other currencies.

The secured money with the LDMA, that is, money backed by suitable collateral—which is considerably in excess of the minimum requirement of 2½% of ELs for eligible banks—together with most bills and other balances with the Bank, formerly constituted the major part of the reserve assets the banks were required to hold under the 1971 Competition and Credit Control (CCC) arrangements. The actual RAR was originally 12½% of ELs but, in preparation for the introduction of the new monetary control arrangements, was reduced to 10% in January 1981 and, following a temporary reduction to 8% for most of March and April 1981, was abolished in August 1981. The CCC arrangements and the reasons for the abolition of the RAR and the alternative supervision by the authorities of liquid asset holdings of the banks are discussed below in section III.8.

Bills were considered in section III.4. Advances include all direct lending to customers, with or without collateral, and may take the form of fixed-term loans

---

1   'Monetary Control—Provisions', op. cit., p. 347.

or overdrafts. With loans, the customer's account is credited in accordance with the agreed drawing arrangements, whereas the overdraft is literally an overdrawing of a current account which is correspondingly debited. In principle, the overdraft is repayable on demand and its size is subject to an agreed limit which may be revised from time to time. Loans may be for different periods; from 5 to 7 years is quite common and it is possible to negotiate longer-term loans.

The interest rates charged on loans and advances vary considerably, depending on the duration as regards loans, the creditworthiness of the borrower, the purposes for which funds are required and the security provided by the borrower. At any point of time the actual rates charged will be related directly or indirectly to those ruling in the wholesale deposit and other money markets. The link may be indirect. For example, each of the LCBs declares a base rate which is itself related to rates in the money markets and may then use its base rate to determine charges for advances; most rates are between 1% and 5% higher than base rate.

Sterling advances by the retail banks to the private sector totalled £57,000m on 14 December 1983 and are clearly very important to the operation of the economic system; they constituted some 65% of all advances of monthly reporting banks in the UK. Moreover, the sterling advances of the retail banks to the private sector have been growing extremely rapidly in the last few years.

Investments are of two kinds: British government stocks, which include all stocks issued by the government, and those stocks of the nationalized industries which carry a government guarantee. The amount of government stock held by the retail banks is less than 6% of their total assets and is relatively small by historical standards.

A further asset which should be mentioned is net lending by the Banking Department of the Bank of England to the central government. The net position is arrived at by subtracting from the Banking Department's holdings of all forms of central government debt, including bank notes, its deposit liabilities to the government under the headings of the National Loans Fund and the Paymaster General. It is felt that this is the best way to present the banking relationship between the central government and the Banking Department of the Bank; it is, in fact, sterling borrowing from the Bank as defined in the central government's borrowing requirement. It should be noted that the net figure can, of course, be negative as well as positive, that is, the central government can be a lender to the Banking Department, though this was not the case in December 1983.

Finally, there is a wide-ranging category called miscellaneous assets, which includes items in suspense and collection and covers things like debit balances awaiting transfer to customers' accounts and cheques drawn on, and in course of collection from, other members of the monetary sector. Premises and physical assets generally are included, as are leased assets; the latter are assets which are beneficially owned by the reporting bank but have been leased to customers. An additional interesting item which is included and which has just recently become available is CDs issued by building societies.

III.6   Accepting Houses and Other British Banks

Accepting houses and other British banks are classified separately in the statistical tables of the *BEQB* but they have sufficient monetary and financial activities in common to justify discussing them together. The term 'accepting houses' as used here refers to the members of the Accepting Houses Committee and certain of their banking subsidiaries in the Channel Islands and Isle of Man. But the term originally arose because of the important role the houses played and still play in accepting commercial bills on behalf of clients; for this service they receive a commission, which clients are willing to pay because accepted bills command a lower rate of discount in the market.

Accepting houses are also known as merchant banks since the banking activities of a number of them emerged as a consequence of their business as merchants, particularly in overseas trade. The accepting houses now provide a wide range of banking services, mainly for the corporate sector. Their activities encompass operations in the following areas: the wholesale deposit markets for both sterling and foreign currencies—the latter is now the larger of the two; large-scale term lending to corporate borrowers; the foreign-exchange market; the gold and silver bullion markets; in the making and underwriting of new issues both in sterling and other currencies—the main accepting houses are all members of the Issuing Houses Association; advising on mergers and takeovers; managing investments on behalf of clients, including investment trusts, unit trusts, insurance companies and pension funds; and acting as trustees.

The accepting houses and other British banks as deposit-takers are subject to the requirements of the 1979 Banking Act and to the new (1981) monetary control arrangements. These requirements are, in part, reflected in the aggregate balance sheet for the two sets of institutions. It may be seen in table 2.6 that on 14 December 1983 these institutions held £92m of cash-ratio deposits in fulfilment of the ½% of ELs requirement under the new monetary arrangements and £758m secured money with the LDMA. It should also be noted that for the two sets of institutions the distinguishable sterling and other currency assets at £40,891m and £59,955m (the totals are not shown in table 2.6) slightly exceeded the corresponding sterling and other currency deposits; in other words, there is an approximate matching of liabilities and assets as regards sterling and other currencies respectively. This suggests that there may be relatively little switching from, say, foreign currency assets into sterling assets, which is a matter of some significance for monetary and credit policy. Such switching could, for instance, permit an extension of domestic credit. This matter is returned to in section III.8.

Other British banks refers to all other UK registered institutions including certain institutions in the Channel Islands and the Isle of Man. Banks operating in the UK but controlled by overseas companies, including the subsidiaries of Allied Irish Banks and the Bank of Ireland, are classified as 'other overseas banks'.

The composition of the other British banks group is evidently highly varied, covering international banks which transact much of their business abroad; merchant and wholesale banking subsidiaries of the clearing banks, which operate in much the same way as the accepting houses; and former finance houses and leasing companies which as deposit-takers come under the provisions of the 1979 Banking Act.

On 14 December 1983 their total balance sheet at £80,900m represented some 13% of the corresponding balance sheet for all monthly reporting institutions. Of their total deposits of £72,500m, some 37% were denominated in sterling and 63% in other currencies. However, the ratio of sterling deposits to other currency deposits varies widely between institutions, ranging from zero to nearly 100%.

The finance houses included in the group, whilst carrying out many typical banking functions as regards both the type and management of their liabilities and

The monetary, financial and fiscal systems

TABLE 2.6

Accepting Houses and Other British Banks, 14 December 1983 (£m)

	Sterling	Other currencies[1]	Total
(i) Liabilities			
Deposits:[2]			
UK monetary sector	14,193	17,127	31,320
UK public sector	433	} 3,407	} 17,203
UK private sector	13,363		
Overseas	5,570	33,872	39,442
Certificates of deposit	1,490	4,106	5,596
Capital and other funds and items in suspense, etc.	–	–	10,857
Total Liabilities			104,418
(ii) Assets			
Notes and Coin	5	–	5
Balances with the Bank of England:			
Special and cash-ratio deposits	92	–	92
Other	2	–	2
Market loans:[3]			
Secured money with LDMA	758	–	758
Other UK monetary sector	11,303	10,808	22,111
UK monetary sector CDs	2,237	1,130	3,367
UK local authorities	1,741	–	1,741
Overseas	1,208	40,375	41,583
Bills:			
Treasury bills	32	–	32
Eligible local authority bills	6	–	6
Eligible bank bills	271	–	271
Other	61	98	159
Advances:[4]			
UK public sector	362	669	1,031
UK private sector	18,502	4,372	22,874
Overseas	1,842	–	1,842
Investments:			
British government stocks	725	–	725
Other	1,744	2,503	4,247
Sterling and other currencies miscellaneous assets	–	–	3,574
Total assets			104,420

Source: *BEQB*.

1 3 4   See corresponding footnotes to table 2.5.

2 Sterling sight deposits amounted to £7,960m and were 23% of total sterling deposits of £35,049m. ELs totalled £19,437m on 14 December 1983.

assets, employ considerable amounts of funds in instalment lending and leasing to industrial and other companies, as well as engaging in consumer instalment lending. Finance houses commonly operate through branch offices but they also offer their facilities through retailers or dealers at the point of sale. The customer of the product is generally able to arrange through the retailer or dealer an appropriate form of loan, hire-purchase or similar type of finance. The provisions of the 1974 Consumer Credit Act are central to the activities of finance houses and similar bodies. Broadly speaking, the Act regulates all lending to non-corporate borrowers for amounts up to £5,000 except that under the 1979 Banking Act bank lending by way of overdrafts is exempt. The Act also provides for a system of licences relating to the consumer credit and hire-purchase industry, and controls the form of credit advertisements.[1]

III.7   Overseas Banks and Consortium Banks

Overseas banks are classified into three categories: American, Japanese and other overseas banks. The number in each category at the end of 1983 were 63, 25, and 229 respectively. Branches as well as subsidiaries of foreign banks are included in the overseas category, as are certain branches and subsidiaries in the Channel Islands and the Isle of Man. By no means all of these banks are monthly reporting institutions, as defined earlier. Only those which are have their balance sheets included in table 2.7.

Consortium banks are UK registered institutions which are owned by banks or financial institutions but in which no one bank or financial institution has a direct shareholding of more than 50%, and in which at least one shareholder is located overseas. The activities of both overseas banks and consortium banks are heavily concentrated on foreign or eurocurrency business; such banks are frequently referred to as eurobanks and the markets in which they operate as euromarkets. These markets are truly international in that they involve banks outside the UK and link together the major banking centres of the world; indeed, much of the trading in the euromarkets is inter-bank and may give rise to a chain of transactions between banks before funds end up with non-bank customers. It is evident that the activities of eurobanks and the existence of eurocurrency markets raise important issues for domestic monetary control and for the prudential supervision of banking systems.[2]

The scale of eurocurrency business undertaken by the overseas banks and consortium banks may be appreciated from table 2.7. On 14 December 1983 the foreign-currency deposits of these banks totalled £350,000m (the total is not shown in the table), representing some 80% of all foreign-currency deposits of monthly reporting institutions; and of the total of £350,000m, about 64% were overseas deposits, mostly with overseas banks. Moreover, the foreign-currency deposits of the overseas banks and consortium banks were over ten times as large as their sterling deposits at some £33,000m. This is not intended to imply that the latter are insignificant; they constituted some 21% of sterling deposits of monthly reporting institutions and were equivalent to nearly 37% of the sterling deposits of the retail banks. However, the private-sector sterling deposits of the overseas banks and consortium banks were only 22% of their total sterling deposits, whereas the corresponding figure for the retail banks was 83%. But this relative dominance of the retail banks in the private sector may not last as other banks and even some building societies are making determined efforts to move into retail banking.

---

1   There are a great many small companies and other bodies involved in consumer credit activities besides the finance houses discussed in this section; but in financial terms their activities are small.

2   See 'Eurobanks and the Inter-Bank Market', *BEQB*, Vol. 21, No. 3, September 1981, pp. 351–64. See also section III.8 below.

TABLE 2.7

Overseas Banks and Consortium Banks, 14 December 1983 (£m)

	Sterling	*Other currencies*[1]	*Total*
(i) *Liabilities*			
Deposits:[2]			
UK monetary sector	11,639	63,854	75,493
UK public sector	162	} 8,834	} 16,218
UK private sector	7,222		
Overseas	10,448	213,300	223,748
Certificates of deposit	3,313	64,389	67,702
Capital and other funds and items			
in suspense, etc.	–	–	5,858
Total liabilities			389,019
(ii) *Assets*			
Notes and coin	18	–	18
Balances with Bank of England:			
Special and cash ratio deposits	96	–	96
Other	4	–	4
Market loans:[3]			
Secured money with LDMA	1,031	–	1,031
Other UK monetary sector	11,347	61,162	72,509
UK monetary sector CDS	1,142	9,244	10,386
UK local authorities	1,488	–	1,488
Overseas	3,076	250,464	253,540
Bills:			
Treasury bills	55	–	55
Eligible local authority bills	7	–	7
Eligible bank bills	118	–	118
Other	117	1,087	1,204
Advances:[4]			
UK public sector	1,283	629	1,912
UK private sector	11,888	16,815	28,703
Overseas	3,279	–	3,279
Investments:			
British government stocks	559	–	559
Other	661	9,578	10,239
Sterling and other currencies			
miscellaneous assets	–	–	3,873
Total assets			389,021

Source: *BEQB*.

1, 3 and 4   See corresponding footnotes to table 2.5.

2   Sterling sight deposits amounted to £5,073m and were 15% of total sterling deposits of £32,784. ELs totalled £20,858m on 14 December 1983.

On the assets side of the balance sheet of the overseas banks and the consortium banks, the predominant foreign-currency asset is overseas market loans at £250,000m; these funds are mostly on loan to overseas banks. Of their sterling assets, their cash-ratio deposits of £96m are less than one-third as large as the corresponding deposits of the retail banks, again reflecting the smaller involvement of the former in sterling banking. Nevertheless, the overseas banks and the consortium banks are of major importance to the UK monetary and financial system. How the authorities attempt to influence and control that system is the subject of the next section.

III.8   The Authorities and Monetary and Prudential Control

It was mentioned in section II.2 that the Bank in its approach to monetary policy had come to espouse 'practical monetarism' or perhaps more accurately, 'monetarily constrained Keynesianism'. One reason was the belief that the demand for money is stable in terms of its relationship to certain income concepts and interest rates. This belief seemed to hold out the possibility that if the authorities could control the relevant interest rates for any given level of income, the short-run demand for money would be determined, except for random components, and with it the stock of money in existence. However, the confidence of the authorities that they could determine the stock of money in this way may never have been great and, at least as regards the M_3 definition of money, was severely shaken in the two years following the introduction of their CCC measures in September 1971: these measures were designed to encourage greater competition throughout the monetary system and permit more reliance on market methods of control instead of restrictions.

The CCC measures also imposed a minimum RAR of 12.5% across the banking system and extended to all banks (except the NI banks) the special deposits scheme. The theory was that open-market operations and/or calls for special deposits would influence interest rates and the banks' holdings of liquid assets, with consequential effects on the money stock. However, the theory did not work as envisaged and contributed to distortions in the interest-rate structure and, in any event, the 1½% of their ELs that the LCBs had to hold as balances with the Bank became the effective fulcrum for the Bank in affecting interest rates in the money market. In the light of this the authorities eventually concluded that they no longer required the RAR and, as already indicated, abolished it in 1981. However, they saw the RAR as not just having relevance as an instrument of monetary control but also as a prudential liquidity requirement for the banks; this aspect of the matter is returned to below.

The initial experience of the working of the CCC measures was particularly unfortunate. Between the fourth quarters of 1971 and 1973 the minimum lending rate (MLR) at which the banks lent funds to the discount market was raised from 5% p.a. to 13%, a very large nominal increase by historical standards; and yet M_3 increased by the extraordinary figure of 64%.

Faced with this problem the authorities had to modify their immediate commitment to the objectives of CCC, and in late 1973 they introduced the supplementary special deposits (SSD) scheme, which came to be known as the 'corset'. In broad terms, the SSD scheme, which was a form of direct control, required banks (and certain finance houses) whose interest-bearing deposits grew at more than a prescribed rate, to place non-interest-bearing deposits with the Bank. The faster the banks' interest-bearing deposits grew in excess of the prescribed rate, the more deposits the banks had to place with the Bank. In short the scheme was designed to penalize severely the banks for any 'undue' expansion of their interest-bearing deposits.

The distortions brought about by the RAR and SSD scheme caused the authorities increasing concern about what is called 'disintermediation'; this arises where funds get diverted by the imposition of controls and restrictions away from the channels through which they would otherwise flow. This response defeats the purposes of the authorities in whole or in part, distorts competition and is generally economically inefficient, and may create additional problems in that once controls are introduced it may be difficult to find an opportune time for their removal, partly because of the 'reintermediation' which is then likely to take place. The SSD scheme was, however, abolished from June 1980.

Mention was made above of the authorities' interest in the short-run demand for money. But from about the middle of the 1970s the authorities gave more attention to the longer-run demand for money. The justification for this would seem to be that, notwithstanding the experience of 1972 and 1973, there was evidence suggesting that the longer-run demand for money was reasonably stable. It is a plausible step from this position to suggest that there should be target rates of growth of the money stock over a period of years and that it is unnecessary to be too concerned about temporary departures from the growth path; which is not to say it is easy to recognize what is a temporary departure.

But the question arises which monetary aggregate or aggregates should be employed for target or control purposes? The initially preferred concept of the authorities was M_3 and later $£M_3$; the latter excluded from M_3 foreign-currency deposits of the private and public sectors. However, as stated previously, the authorities introduced from February 1984 new definitions of both M_3 and $£M_3$. The difference between the old and new definitions is straightforward. The old definitions included public-sector bank deposits and these are excluded from the new definitions. Two main reasons are given for making the change. First, public-sector deposits and changes in them, which can be substantial from month to month, have little or no bearing on the expenditure of the public sector and hence on economic activity. Secondly, the new definition is more in keeping with practice in other countries and is in line with a revised definition of the public-sector borrowing requirement (PSBR); the latter is discussed below.

A major reason why the authorities concentrated their attention on $£M_3$ is that it can be related, at least in an arithmetic sense, to changes in some key credit counterparts which in turn link it to the fiscal, credit and exchange-rate policies of the authorities. The term 'credit counterparts' refers in the first instance to the assets side of the balance sheet of the monetary sector; and overall monetary policy can be formulated in terms of influencing the rate of growth of these assets and is sometimes referred to as a 'supply side' approach to monetary control. In other words, the thrust of monetary control is not towards a direct effect on the demand for money but to influence the 'supply' of those assets which are the counterparts of the money stock and, by this means, attempt to control its rate of growth.

It is helpful in following this argument to make use of a stylized and simplified balance sheet of the monetary sector. The balance sheet on the liabilities side include private-sector sterling deposits which are the main component of $£M_3$. The other component is notes and coin in circulation with the public. The latter do not appear in the balance sheet since they are liabilities of the Issue Department of the Bank of England and the Royal Mint respectively.

Monetary Sector Balance Sheet

Liabilities	Assets
Sterling deposits:	Sterling lending to:
UK private sector	UK public sector
Overseas sector	UK private sector
Foreign-currency deposits	Overseas sector
Non-deposit liabilities (net)	Foreign-currency assets
Total liabilities	Total assets

It follows from the definition of $£M_3$ that:

the change in $£M_3$ = the change in notes and coin in circulation with
the public *plus* the change in sterling deposits of
the UK private sector.

It also follows from re-arranging the monetary sector balance sheet that:

the change in sterling
  deposits of UK private sector   =   the change in sterling lending to:

    UK public sector
    UK private sector
    overseas sector

    less the increase in:
    overseas-sector sterling deposits
    foreign-currency deposits net of foreign-
        currency assets
    non-deposit liabilities (net)

The next step is to consider the financing of the public sector, and in particular, the PSBR, broadly the difference between public-sector expenditure and receipts. Now the PSBR can be financed by borrowing from the private sector and the monetary sector, and through transactions with the overseas sector. Alternatively, whatever part of the PSBR is not financed by the private and overseas sectors is financed by the monetary sector under the heading of the change in sterling lending to the public sector. Hence it follows that:

the change in sterling lending
  to the UK public sector
  (by the monetary sector)   =   the PSBR (surplus = –)
                       less
                       net purchases of public-sector debt by the
                          UK private sector
                       less
                       external and foreign-currency finance of
                          the public sector.

Thus the items on the right-hand side of the equality sign may be substituted into the re-arranged balance sheet of the monetary sector for the change in sterling lending to the public sector. This is in fact presented in a simplified form below, making use at the same time of the definition of the change in $£M_3$ mentioned above. It may be noted that the main debt instruments involved in purchases of public-sector debt by the UK private sector are national savings, certificates of tax deposit and government securities. The outcome is as follows:

the change in £M_3 =
Domestic counterparts {
the PSBR
less net purchases of public-sector debt by the UK private sector
plus the change in sterling lending to the UK private sector (including Issue Department purchases of commercial bills)
}
less external and foreign-currency counterparts
less the change in non-deposit liabilities (net).

Thus putting aside the non-deposit liabilities of the banks, the credit counterparts to the increase in £M_3 may be related to what the authorities call 'domestic counterparts' and 'external and foreign-currency counterparts'. Hence the supply-of-assets approach to monetary control may be formulated in terms of policies to influence the behaviour of the domestic and external and foreign-currency counterparts to £M_3.[1] The actual counterparts in recent years are shown in table 2.8.

TABLE 2.8

Counterparts to and Changes in the Money Stock, 1978/9 to 1982/3 (£m)

	1978/9	*1979/80*	*1980/81*	*1981/2*	*1982/3*
1. PSBR	9,222	9,919	13,187	8,785	9,164
2. Net acquisition of public-sector debt by private sector	8,512	9,188	10,872	11,270	8,290
3. Sterling lending to private sector	6,296	9,330	9,248	14,928	14,360
4. External and foreign counterparts	760	2,422	−601	893	2,746
5. Non-deposit liabilities (net)	982	1,199	1,470	1,742	2,380
6. Change in £M_3 (old definition)	5,262	6,443	10,693	9,808	10,108

Source: *FS*, Table 11.3, March 1984.
Note: Relationship between rows: 6 = 1 − 2 + 3 − 4 − 5; and 1 − 2 + 3 = domestic counterparts.

Broadly speaking, the PSBR may be seen as related to fiscal policy, the sale of public-sector debt to debt-management policy, sterling lending to credit policy, and currency flows to exchange-rate policy. This is not to say that the policies are or can be independent; a change in fiscal policy, for example, is likely to have repercussions on not only the PSBR but also public-sector-debt sales, interest rates and credit conditions generally, and exchange rates.

Approaching the problem of monetary control from the supply-of-assets side is

1 A variation of this approach to monetary control emphasizes domestic credit expansion (DCE). DCE has two main components, the domestic counterparts referred to in the text and monetary sector lending in sterling to overseas residents. Since the abolition of exchange controls in 1979, the growth in gross movements of funds involving banks abroad has somewhat obscured the concept of DCE.

necessarily hazardous. The different credit counterparts can and do vary greatly in ways that are clearly not amenable to fine-tuning by the authorities. Furthermore, it is unlikely that there is any simple causal relationship between the major credit counterparts and $£M_3$; a change in one may be offset in whole or in part by changes in the others. In particular, there may be no systematic causal link between the PSBR and changes in $£M_3$.

Notwithstanding this, and the authorities are perfectly aware of it, they remain convinced that over the longer term it is essential to reduce the PSBR as part of the medium-term financial strategy (MTFS) for bringing down the rate of growth of the money stock, reducing the rate of inflation and encouraging economic growth. In taking up this position, which is a controversial one, they are, of course, espousing a view about the operation of the economy over time, rather than relying on balance-sheet arithmetic as outlined above. However, it is possible to sympathize with the medium-term goals of the authorities without endorsing their supply-side approach to monetary control (see section V.1 below).

As regards debt-management and credit policies, or more generally interest-rate policies, the authorities have on the one hand emphasized their need to be able to vary interest rates as a means of influencing some of the credit counterparts in order to control $£M_3$, and on the other stressed their wish to give market forces greater play in the determination of interest rates. On the face of it there is some contradiction between these positions. The former is wedded to the assets-supply-side approach to monetary control, whereas the latter would seem to lean towards a monetary base control system (see below). But perhaps it would be fairer to interpret the difference in emphasis between the two positions as indicating an evolution in their thinking and policy.

Indeed the authorities have in the last few years moved away from concentrating on a single monetary aggregate as the basis of their monetary policy. Experience quickly showed that $£M_3$ was subject to many influences outside the immediate control of the authorities with the consequences for the economy being far from clear. These developments called for the most careful interpretation in trying to assess the stance of monetary policy.[1] Greater emphasis came to be placed on a range of monetary and liquidity aggregates. In the 1982 Budget M_1 and PSL_2 (private-sector liquidity) were included along with $£M_3$ in the target ranges for monetary growth. Meanwhile for a number of years before this the authorities had engaged in and encouraged an intensive debate on 'monetary base control'.

A monetary base system generally means one in which the banks hold, either because it is mandatory or for prudential reasons, base money which may be defined to include bankers' deposits with the central bank and may also include their holdings of central-bank notes and official coin as well as those held by the public. Thus in the widest sense, base money constitutes deposit and note liabilities of the central bank plus official coinage. In principle, this base money is under the control of the authorities, and by regulating its supply they can, on certain conditions, control or at any rate influence the volume of deposits of the banking system and more generally the supply of money.

The most widely understood monetary base system is probably the textbook mandatory one where the banks are required to hold base money in a fixed proportion to deposits. The simplest is where the proportion relates to deposits and

1 See 'Setting Monetary Objectives', *BEQB*, Vol. 23, No. 2, June 1983, pp. 200–8.

base money on the same date—known as current accounting—but it is possible to envisage a lagged accounting system where 'current base requirements are fixed by reference to deposits in a previous period. . . [or] lead accounting where the holding of base assets would put a limit on deposits for some future date'.[1] Alternatively, a monetary base system might be non-mandatory or voluntary, where the banking system finds it desirable to maintain a fairly systematic relationship through time between its deposit liabilities and base money.

It is apparent, however, that the authorities in their Green Paper on *Monetary Control* were not thinking in terms of a monetary base system as outlined above. For them a monetary base system 'is intended to provide a means for the markets to generate the interest rates necessary to bring the rate of growth of the money supply back towards the desired path'.[2] Thus the authorities would seem to be thinking in terms of influencing the credit counterparts to the money stock rather than in terms of a monetary base system as indicated above, which, if implemented, would impinge directly on the operations of the banks. The latter would, of course, bring about changes in interest rates, but these would be consequential instead of being an intermediate target and the question of how they affected the so-called credit counterparts would not be of direct concern. Friedman and other economists would argue that this approach is the more efficient way to tackle monetary control.[3] The authorities have still to be convinced and the debate is far from settled.

It is perhaps significant, however, that in the 1984 Budget base money, defined to include the banks' till money, their operational balances with the Bank plus notes and coin in circulation with the public and called M_0—the wide monetary base—was given a target range for its growth, together with £M_3. M_1 and PSL_2 have for the moment not been given target ranges for their growth. M_1 had become particularly difficult to interpret and had ceased to be a good measure of transaction balances because of the increasing proportion of interest-bearing deposits included in the total. It is hoped that in due course a new monetary aggregate M_2 may be an improvement on M_1. The whole series of monetary and liquidity aggregates and the relationships between them are summarized in a simplified form in the attached table reproduced from the *Bank of England Quarterly Bulletin*.

It would be a mistake to assume that the difficulties encountered in finding a single suitable monetary aggregate or 'money supply concept' as a basis for monetary policy represents a weakening of monetary control. In the words of the article mentioned in note 1, page 91, 'the difficulties that. . . seem inherent in short-term monetary targetry are by no means fatal to the associated counter-inflationary strategy . . . . what matters is the refusal of the authorities to stimulate demand in "Keynesian" fashion, or to "reflate", as conditions develop that would in the past have justified and provoked such a response. The fact that the monetary targets have not concurrently been met, or that the meaning of particular developments in this or that aggregate has become very ambiguous, is of much less importance.'[4]

---

1 *Monetary Control*, Cmnd. 7858, HMSO, March 1980, p.10.

2 ibid., p. 8.

3 Milton Friedman, 'Memorandum on Monetary Policy', Treasury and Civil Service Committee, Session 1979–80, *Memoranda on Monetary Policy*, HC, (1979–80) 720, HMSO, pp. 55–61.

4 op. cit., p. 207.

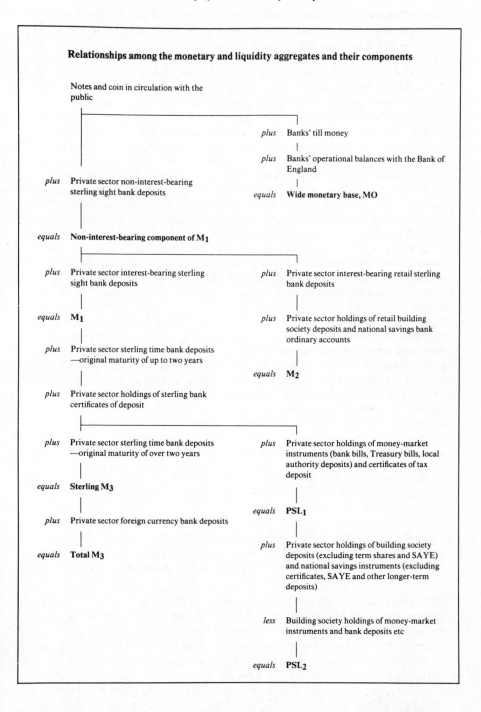

Relationships among the monetary and liquidity aggregates and their components

Notes and coin in circulation with the public

plus Banks' till money

plus Banks' operational balances with the Bank of England

plus Private sector non-interest-bearing sterling sight bank deposits

equals **Wide monetary base, M0**

equals **Non-interest-bearing component of M1**

plus Private sector interest-bearing sterling sight bank deposits

plus Private sector interest-bearing retail sterling bank deposits

equals **M1**

plus Private sector holdings of retail building society deposits and national savings bank ordinary accounts

plus Private sector sterling time bank deposits —original maturity of up to two years

equals **M2**

plus Private sector holdings of sterling bank certificates of deposit

plus Private sector sterling time bank deposits —original maturity of over two years

plus Private sector holdings of money-market instruments (bank bills, Treasury bills, local authority deposits) and certificates of tax deposit

equals **Sterling M3**

equals **PSL1**

plus Private sector foreign currency bank deposits

plus Private sector holdings of building society deposits (excluding term shares and SAYE) and national savings instruments (excluding certificates, SAYE and other longer-term deposits)

equals **Total M3**

less Building society holdings of money-market instruments and bank deposits etc

equals **PSL2**

Source: *BEQB*, Vol. 24, No. 1, March 1984, p. 79 (reproduced with permission of the Bank of England).

What the article goes on to say does matter is 'the exercise of judgement' in the situation; indeed, the tradition of British pragmatism is strongly praised, albeit one purged 'of earlier permissiveness'.

Closely related to the issue of monetary control is the prudential control of the monetary system. By prudential control is meant the oversight by the authorities of the banks and other financial institutions to ensure that their capital and reserve assets and their liquid assets are sufficient to enable them to meet their domestic and foreign-currency liabilities. The matter of prudential control has become of increasing importance in the last ten years. During 1973-4 there occurred a so-called 'fringe' or secondary banking crisis, when to avoid their likely default a number of financial institutions had to be extensively supported by the Bank and the London and Scottish clearing banks; the support scheme became known as the 'lifeboat' operation. This experience has prompted a more active interest in bank supervision. In addition the Directive of the European Community on Credit Institutions requires the UK to authorize institutions taking deposits from the public; indeed, this was one reason for the introduction of the 1979 Banking Act.

The Bank, in approaching the task of more formal prudential control of the banks, has issued a number of papers dealing with different but related aspects of the problem: 'The Measurement of Capital', 'The Liquidity of Banks', 'Foreign Currency Exposure', 'Prudential Arrangements for the Discount Market' and 'The Measurement of Liquidity'; published respectively in the *Bank of England Quarterly Bulletin* of September 1980, March 1981, June 1981, June 1982 and September 1982. Prudential controls, like all administered controls, impose costs on institutions and to that extent may give rise to some disintermediation. This possibility has become particularly important as banking has developed into an international industry, able to offer highly competitive services outside the jurisdiction of any single country. The authorities are undoubtedly aware of these matters and decide their policies accordingly.

III.9   Other Financial Institutions

The United Kingdom is particularly rich in the variety and number of its financial institutions. The term 'rich' is used advisedly for financial institutions able to engage in maturity and risk transformation of securities or otherwise mediate freely between borrowers and lenders, facilitate the achievement by both parties of a preferred distribution of their assets and liabilities, and help to make the allocation of scarce resources more efficient; limitations on space prevent more than a brief mention of certain activities of some major financial institutions.

Building societies: Building societies are known as mutual bodies in that they are owned by their customers and do not distribute profits; they do, of course, earn surpluses and accumulate reserves. They specialize in raising and providing finance for the purchase of both new and secondhand houses. There are some 200 building societies, about 9% of the number at the beginning of the century. Between them, they had some 6,700 branches at the end of 1983. The individual societies vary greatly in size, from some very large ones with a national network of branches to those with only one office. The five largest societies account for over half of all building society assets.

Some 90% of the liabilities of the building societies are shares and deposits.

Both are essentially deposits, so that the term 'share' is something of a misnomer. However, the shareholder is a member of the society whereas the depositor is not, and the latter has a prior right of liquidation over the shareholder. The variety of the terms and conditions governing the payment of interest on, and the withdrawal of, shares and deposits has increased greatly in recent years as the societies have found it necessary to compete for funds, particularly with the national savings movement and with the banks. Ordinary shares and deposits are subject to notice of withdrawal, though in practice both are paid on demand or on very short notice. Term shares and other similar accounts are subject to specific withdrawal conditions.

Some of the larger building societies are also now raising funds in the wholesale markets through syndicated bank loans, the issue of negotiable bonds and certificates of deposit. With this development, building societies are, of course, offering a new form of competition to the monetary sector and, indeed, some have gone further by introducing interest-bearing chequeing accounts and entered into certain arrangements with a bank or credit-card company for the issue of credit cards. These latter developments are, however, hindered by the legislative restrictions under which building societies operate since they cannot offer loans or overdrafts other than on the security of a mortgage. The government has, however, undertaken to introduce legislation during the current Parliament which may be expected to reduce the restrictions now inhibiting the building societies from offering a wider range of financial services.

The interest rates on the bulk of shares and deposits are quoted net of income tax, which is paid by the societies at an average or composite rate and is less than the basic rate of tax. In early 1984 the interest rate suggested by the Building Societies Association for ordinary shares was 6.25%. This rate is net of tax and is equivalent to 8.93% before deduction of basic-rate tax. The composite tax rate procedure is to be applied to banks from April 1985.

The rate of growth of the balance sheets of the building societies has been very rapid. In 1970 total shares and deposits were about £10,000m and by 1983 they were approaching £80,000m; this latter figure compares with the £89,000m sterling deposits at the end of 1983 of the retail banks.

Mortgages generally account for about 80% of the assets of building societies and are predominantly for private house purchase. Most mortgages are for between twenty and thirty years, with continuous repayment by instalments. The average life is generally about seven years, making the assets of building societies much shorter-lived than they might appear. The recommended interest rate on new mortgages to owner-occupiers was 10.25% in early 1984. But this is the gross rate, as interest payments on a housing loan — up to £30,000 for a principal residence — are allowable against income-tax assessments: if allowance is made for income-tax relief at the basic rate, the interest rate is reduced to 7.175% net.

All the other assets, except such things as office premises, are classified as liquid assets by the societies. Liquid assets must be at least 7.5% of total assets, and both the type of asset and the maturity distribution are regulated by the Chief Registrar of Building Societies. At the end of 1983 the actual liquid-assets ratio was over 19% of total assets. Cash holdings and balances with banks are relatively small and vary a lot seasonally. The societies cannot for long expand the supply of finance to borrowers unless there is a corresponding net inflow of funds from new shares and deposits; otherwise they would deplete their liquid assets and in time risk upsetting public confidence in their management. The interest rates the societies pay and the relationship they bear to the competing rates would appear to be a major determinant of the net inflow of funds to the societies.

The building societies have for many years dominated the market for the raising and provision of finance for home purchase. However, in the last few years they have experienced strong competition in house-mortgage lending from the banks. The societies have in turn responded with much more flexible methods of fund-raising, as briefly outlined above. At the same time the authorities have indicated a willingness to examine the legislative framework within which the societies operate. There can be little doubt that the range of financial services offered by the building societies will be extended in the next few years, that the distinctions between their activities and those of the banks will be further eroded, and that as a consequence they are likely to be brought under the monetary and, perhaps in due course, the prudential control arrangements of the Bank of England.

Insurance companies: There are some 850 insurance companies, which vary greatly in size, engaged in business in the UK, though the principal business of a considerable number is overseas. By far the greater part of UK business is carried on by the members of the British Insurance Association, which has less than 300 members. The fundamental purpose of insurance is to facilitate the spread of risk between persons and bodies and through time.

Insurance falls into two main categories: life assurance, and a catch-all, general insurance, which includes fire, marine, motor and other accident insurance. The insurance companies also operate the pension schemes of many industrial and commercial companies. Life assurance for the most part gives rise to long-term liabilities which the companies must be in a position to meet. This gives them an interest in long-term investments and in assets that may be expected to increase in capital value over the years. General insurance, on the other hand, is carried on much more on a year-to-year basis, ideally with premiums for the year being sufficient to cover the risks underwritten and to allow for expenses and the accumulation of limited reserves. So the disposition of funds arising from general insurance is largely governed by short-term considerations; assets must be quickly realizable without undue fear of capital loss. The insurance companies as a whole, with total investments at the end of 1982 of some £96,000m, are of great importance in the UK's capital markets. They are large holders of both government and company securities. Their growth has been encouraged by tax privileges, though tax relief on life-assurance premiums was abolished in the 1984 Budget.

The Department of Trade under the 1974 Insurance Companies Act has extensive powers of supervision over the activities of insurance companies. These powers are mainly designed to give protection to policyholders and have been influenced by membership requirements of the European Community. Insurance companies must demonstrate annually that their assets exceed their liabilities to policyholders. If the Department of Trade suspects that a company might be unable to meet its liabilities, it may take certain measures including the strong sanction of prohibiting the company from undertaking new business. Policyholders have also the protection of the 1975 Policyholders Protection Act, which broadly speaking provides that where an insurance company goes into liquidation its liabilities to policyholders will be met up to 90%—and in certain cases 100%—by a levy on other insurance companies.

Superannuation funds: Superannuation or pension funds are financial institutions which, on the basis of contributions, often by both employees and employers, undertake to provide future incomes to their members. Their size and form of organization facilitates risk-sharing and the exploiting of economies of scale. Pension funds have grown very rapidly during the past twenty-five years; their growth has been stimulated by tax incentives. Pension funds approved by the Inland Revenue (including those managed by insurance companies) are known as gross funds; such funds do not have to pay tax on their investment earnings nor tax on their capital gains. Pension funds are also of major significance to the UK capital market.

Investment trusts: Investment trusts are limited companies which specialize in the investment of funds provided by their shareholders or borrowed from debenture holders or other lenders, thus enabling investment risks to be shared and economies of management to be gained. Despite the term 'trust', investment trusts do not operate, as do the unit trusts, under trust deeds which specify the terms and conditions governing the management of investment funds, but are, in fact, limited companies whose assets consist mainly of company securities and who are not allowed by their articles of association to distribute capital gains as dividends. In addition to investment trusts, there are private investment companies and investment-holding companies which often perform similar functions. But these are not discussed in this chapter. There are about 200 investment trusts that are recognized as such for tax purposes by the Inland Revenue, but the statistics below are based on returns from about 150 of the larger companies.

Investment trusts expand by raising funds from new capital issues, borrowing in the form of loan capital and by retaining some of the income and capital profits from previous investments. But it is the assets side of the balance sheets that is of chief interest. At the end of 1982 the total market value of investments of reporting investment trusts was about £10,000m. Most of this was invested in company securities, practically all ordinary shares; some £4,600m was invested in securities of overseas companies.

The size of the investment trusts makes them important operators in the ordinary share market. They also fulfil a useful function in helping to finance small companies by holding unlisted securities.

Unit trusts: Unit trusts perform a similar function to investment trusts. But unlike the latter they do operate under trust deeds and have trustees, often a bank or insurance company. The unit trusts are authorized by the Department of Trade and are run by managers who are quite distinct from the trustees. Returns are collected from some 540 unit trusts; in 1960 the figure was fifty-one.

Unit trusts do not issue share capital and are not limited companies, but they issue units which give the owners the right to participate in the beneficial ownership of the trusts' assets. The units are highly marketable, as they can always be bought from or sold to the managers at prices which reflect the market value of the underlying assets. As more units are demanded, the managers provide more; for this reason they are sometimes called 'open-end' trusts, as opposed to 'closed-end' trusts such as the investment trusts which do not expand in this way.

Like the investment trusts, the assets of the unit trusts are almost entirely company securities, made up of ordinary shares. At the end of 1982 the total holdings of UK government and company securities of the unit trusts were £5,000m; they also held £2,300m of securities of overseas companies. Their rate of growth has been rapid; in 1960 their total assets were only £190m.

The Stock Exchange: The Stock Exchange is not strictly a financial institution but an association of stockjobbers and stockbrokers which provides a market for variable-price securities, both government and company securities. Without this market where securities may readily be bought and sold, the whole business of raising funds through outside sources would tend to be more expensive and less efficient. Since March 1973 the Stock Exchange comprises the Stock Exchange of the UK and the Republic of Ireland. Before that date, though with close links, they were distinct organizations.

A traditional feature of the Stock Exchange has been the distinction between jobbers and brokers. Jobbers are traders in securities; they act as principals, buying and selling on their own account and making their profits on the difference between their buying and selling prices, which they generally stand ready to quote for the securities in which they specialize. This function can be extremely important in giving stability to the market which might otherwise be much more volatile and possibly mislead investors. Brokers generally act as agents for customers, buying and selling on their behalf, usually but not always through jobbers.

However, the forces of competition, innovation and change which are powerfully affecting the monetary and financial system generally are increasingly impinging on the Stock Exchange. A major departure is the start of the abolition of a fixed scale of commissions on transactions. Many observers believe that this change will lead to the breakdown of the distinction between jobbers, who are principals, and brokers, who are agents, and that much greater capital will be called for in carrying out these functions. A number of banks have already indicated their wish to establish closer links with both firms of jobbers and brokers. The Bank of England is monitoring these developments with interest and is concerned that the Stock Exchange as a central market for securities should be preserved and that investors should be adequately protected.

An idea of the scale of Stock Exchange activities can be obtained from the figures on turnover; that is, sales and purchases. The total turnover during 1983 was almost £290,000m. Turnover of UK government securities was some £210,000m. The latter compares with a total of government stocks outstanding of some £80,000m. The Stock Exchange is of major importance to the financial activities of both the public and private sectors of the economy.

IV   TAXATION
IV.1   Introduction

Taxation and the economic role of government in society are necessarily closely linked and discussion of the one involves some consideration of the other. It is often said that taxation in a market economy has three main functions:

(1)   to provide or encourage the provision of goods and services that are not easily or adequately supplied by the market if left to itself, and also to discourage the provision of those goods and services that are considered to have harmful effects on society—and perhaps the reverse for those goods and

services which are considered beneficial to society;

(2)   to redistribute income and wealth; and

(3)   to facilitate the exercise of fiscal policy as a means of economic stabilization. (The latter has been encountered earlier in this chapter and in the preceding one, and is not discussed further.)

The first may be approached by making a distinction between so-called private and public goods, and noting a possible discrepancy between private and public costs and benefits—what has come to be called the externalities problem. Private goods refer to those goods where the utility a person gets from their consumption depends on how much of them he has, and at the same time the more he has the less anyone else gets. Public goods, on the other hand, are such that, once the goods are produced, their consumption by one person does not diminish the amount available to others. Any kind of food is an example of a private good and some forms of national defence are an example of public goods. The market system can by and large handle the problem of producing and pricing private goods but not public goods, since the price system cannot operate effectively to determine an appropriate amount to produce, nor determine its distribution. It needs to be stressed immediately that pure private goods and pure public goods are extreme cases and that, in general, elements of both may be combined in the same good.

Externalities are said to arise when the costs and benefits are not internalized to the individual producer or consumer. A typical example is what has been called the 'smoke nuisance', when a producer engages in a productive activity that gives off smoke and spreads grime and dirt in the immediate neighbourhood and possibly causes chemical erosion of buildings in the surrounding area. The costs of these nuisances are generally not voluntarily paid for by the producer or reflected in the quantity produced or price of his product. This kind of example could be greatly extended as could similar examples on the benefits side. Indeed, in so far as a so-called public good was provided privately, it would be an example of external benefits being conferred widely throughout a community. Clearly, externalities pose a fundamental problem for society, and in particular suggest that where they are present in a market-based economy, the market if left to itself will produce too much of a good which imposes external costs on the society and too little of a good which confers external benefits. In such circumstances there seems to be no simple answer to the question, on the one hand, of the appropriate domain of market processes and, on the other, of the role of government. These are difficult and far-reaching issues in political economy.

The second function of taxation—the redistribution of income and wealth—is closely related to the matters just discussed. Because there is no self-evident reason why a competitive market economy should lead to an optimum distribution of income and wealth—however difficult that may be to define—so governments have come to use taxation and the revenue raised thereby to bring about some redistribution. It should perhaps be said that there is also no obvious reason why government redistribution policies will be optimal, since the distribution and ability to exercise political power may itself be far from optimal; clearly these issues beg some fundamental and intractable questions.

A further feature of taxation that should be mentioned is its so-called 'supply-side' effects. Broadly speaking, the argument is that taxation distorts the choice at the margin between work and leisure, investment and saving, risky versus less risky investments, one type of good or service and another, and is also a stimulus to the 'black economy', that is, the illegal carrying on of economic activity outside the tax net. The conclusion of those who stress the importance of supply-side effects is that, in general, taxation adversely affects output and economic growth and that on these grounds tax rates should be lower rather than higher and the role of the government in the economy smaller rather than larger. The subject is, of course, a highly controversial one, but it certainly cannot be lightly dismissed by anyone who has some confidence in traditional microeconomic analysis.

IV.2   The Size of Government

It is well known that in this century governments have become, in terms of their own activities, far more important in relation to the economic life of the community. Nevertheless, it is by no means straightforward to measure the size of government economic activity relatively to the rest of the economic system. Perhaps the best that can be done is to take a number of different measures.[1]

One of these is the direct claims the general government makes through its own economic activity on the volume of goods and services available to the community. In this context, 'general government' includes central and local government, but excludes such things as the nationalized industries or, more generally, public corporations. Table 2.9 shows that government expenditure on goods and services claimed about 22% of the Gross National Product in 1972, gradually increased to over 26% by 1975, fell to almost 22% by 1979 but was over 23% in 1982. Clearly, notwithstanding the aim of Mrs Thatcher's government to bring down public expenditure it has remained persistently high.

TABLE 2.9

General Government: Total Expenditure on Goods and Services as a Percentage of GNP at Market Prices, 1972–82

Year	1972	1973	1974	1975	1976	1977	1978	1979
%	22.5	22.8	24.7	26.3	25.3	23.6	22.6	22.3
Year	1980	1981	1982					
%	23.8	23.5	23.4					

Source: *NIE*, 1983 edition.

It is arguable that the data in table 2.9 understate the 'size' of government. They take no account of subsidies, grants and debt interest paid by the government, and ignore its net lending. The reason for this is that these transactions are mainly classified as transfer payments. That is, the government raises the necessary funds by taxation and borrowing, and transfers them back to the community and overseas. Thus the government does not buy goods and services directly as far as this type of expenditure is concerned. But there is no doubt that these transfers are extremely important in relation to taxation and government borrowing, and

---

1 See A.R. Prest and N.A. Barr, *Public Finance in Theory and Practice*, 6th edition, Weidenfeld and Nicolson, 1979, chapter 8, for a discussion of the issues involved.

greatly influence the economic system. When they are included in government
expenditure, the previous percentages are markedly increased. Table 2.10 shows
that for 1972 the percentage was just over 38% of Gross National Product and that
a jump occurred in the mid-1970s to a peak of 45% in 1975; the percentage then
fell to 42% in 1979 but increased to over 45% in 1982, despite the efforts to curb
public expenditure. It is arguable that the figures are not completely comparable
over time and, in particular, that net lending should be excluded; the correction
would make little difference to the overall picture. Clearly, grants, subsidies, debt
interest and net lending have been of major importance in recent years as a component of government expenditure and, as will be seen, the financing of total
government expenditure has posed formidable problems for government and the
monetary authorities.

TABLE 2.10

**General Government: Total Government Expenditure as a Percentage of GNP at
Market Prices, 1972–82**

Year	1972	1973	1974	1975	1976	1977	1978	1979
%	38.5	38.8	43.5	45.0	44.2	42.5	42.0	41.9
Year	1980	1981	1982					
%	44.3	45.2	45.4					

Source: *NIE*, 1983 edition.

IV.3   The Budget and Borrowing Requirements

The Budget is traditionally the annual financial statement which the Chancellor of
the Exchequer makes in the House of Commons either in March or early April,
around the end of each financial year. The statement includes an account of the
revenue and expenditure for the previous financial year and forecasts for the year
ahead. In the ordinary way there is only one Budget but the Chancellor has power
to alter taxation and expenditure at other times of the year. In particular, since
1982 the Chancellor makes each autumn a statement both written and oral to the
House of Commons and known as the Autumn Statement, which expounds government economic policy and may include decisions and recommendations about
public expenditure and revenue. Tables 2.11, 2.12 and 2.13 bring together in an
aggregated form the main features of the 1984–5 Budget accounts.

The gross tax revenue of government, less repayments, plus all other public
monies payable to the Exchequer are paid into the Exchequer's Account at the
Bank of England; the amount standing to the credit of this account at any point of
time is known as the Consolidated Fund. Virtually all expenditure by the government, with the major exceptions of government loans and national insurance
benefits, is paid out of issues from this fund.[1] In table 2.11 is shown the Consolidated Fund Revenue as it appears in the *Financial Statement and Budget
Report*. The receipts fall under four main headings: inland revenue, customs and

---

1   *Financial Statistics: Explanatory Handbook*, HMSO, April 1984, p. 38.

excise (including EEC own resources), other duties and charges, and miscellaneous receipts. The first two refer to the great revenue-collecting departments of state, and major taxes and duties collected by these are discussed below.[1] Vehicle excise duties are collected by the Department of the Environment. Miscellaneous receipts include interest and dividends, broadcast-receiving licences and certain other receipts, of which one of the most important is oil royalties.

TABLE 2.11

Consolidated Fund Revenue, 1984–5 (Forecast) (£m)

Inland Revenue		
Income tax	33,800	
Corporation tax	8,400	
Petroleum revenue tax	6,000	
Capital gains tax	710	
Development land tax	75	
Capital transfer tax	680	
Stamp duties	860	
Total Inland Revenue		50,525
Customs and Excise		
Value added tax	18,000	
Oil	6,100	
Tobacco	4,100	
Spirits, beer, wine, cider and perry	4,000	
Betting and gaming	650	
Car tax	700	
Other excise duties	20	
EEC own resources		
Customs duties, etc.	1,230	
Agricultural levies	200	
Total Customs and Excise		35,000
Vehicle excise duties		2,140
National insurance surcharge		900
Total Taxation		88,565
Miscellaneous receipts		9,480
Grand Total		98,000

Source: *Financial Statement and Budget Report 1984–5* (Grand Total rounded).

The two main categories of expenditure shown in table 2.12 are supply services and consolidated fund standing services.The first, which covers the expenditure of all the major departments of government, including Defence, Health and Personal

---

1 EEC own resources include revenue from the Common External Tariff, agricultural levies and sugar levies that, under the EEC Treaty and subsidiary legislation, are considered as belonging to the European Community and available for its budgetary purposes. See *Official Journal of the European Communities*, 94, of 28 April 1970.

Social Services and Social Security, is voted annually by Parliament, and the second is a standing charge against revenue and includes the cost of servicing the national debt.[1]

The National Loans Fund is a cash account at the Bank of England and was set up in 1968. Most of the domestic lending of the government and all transactions relating to the National Debt, including its creation, the repayment of loans from the Fund and interest payments thereon, now appear in the National Loans Fund. Table 2.13 shows that the central government is an important source of loans for the local authorities. The government must raise these funds either through taxation or other receipts or by borrowing. In these accounts there is a deficit of £5,400m forecast for the Consolidated Fund and a net borrowing of £10,300m by the National Loans Fund.

The net borrowing by the National Loans Fund, the 'central government borrowing requirement' (CGBR) and the PSBR are closely inter-related, as illustrated below with the forecast figures for 1984-5:

	£m
Net borrowing by National Loans Fund	10,300
Other funds and accounts (net)	800
CGBR	11,100

The other funds and accounts refer to the national insurance fund, certain departmental balances and Northern Ireland central government debt. The central government is, however, only one part of the public sector, the others being the local authorities and public corporations, and their borrowing has to be taken into consideration to arrive at the PSBR. This is indicated below for 1984-5:

	£m
CGBR *less* on-lending to local authorities and public corporations	5,300
Local authorities borrowing requirement	1,300
Public corporations borrowing requirement	600
PSBR	7,200

The foregoing shows that the central government has an 'own' borrowing requirement of £5,300m and thus anticipates on-lending of £5,800m to the local authorities and public corporations. As already stated, the authorities finance the PSBR by borrowing from the non-bank private sector, the monetary sector and the overseas sector. The financing takes a number of forms including notes and coin, national savings, Treasury bills, government securities, specialized forms of debt, and changes in the official foreign-exchange reserves. A number of these require special mention.

National savings refer to a variety of savings media provided by the state and originally designed mainly to attract the smaller saver. Two main forms of national savings are national savings certificates, including some issues which are index-linked, that is, their repayment value is linked to the retail prices index and is tax-

---

1 The detailed estimates for supply services are published in a *Memorandum by the Chief Secretary to the Treasury*, Cmnd. 9161, HMSO, March 1984.

free, and savings through National Savings Bank (NSB) accounts. The NSB has two types of account, the ordinary and the investment account. The ordinary account offers limited facilities for withdrawal of funds on demand, and carries interest at 3% on amounts up to £500 and 6% if a minimum balance of £500 is held for the 12 months ending 31 December 1984; the first £70 of interest is tax-free. The investment account requires one month's notice for the making of withdrawals and paid 9¼% before deduction of tax from 2 April 1984. All forms of national savings raised over £3,000m towards the financing of the PSBR 1983-4.

TABLE 2.12
Supply and Consolidated Fund Standing Services, 1984-5 (Forecast) (£m)

Supply Issues		91,700
Consolidated Fund Standing Services		
Payment to the National Loans Fund for service		
of the National Debt	6,800	
Northern Ireland — share of taxes, etc.	1,700	
Payments to the European Community, etc.	3,200	
Other services	60	
Total Consolidated Fund Standing Services		11,760
Total		103,400
Consolidated Fund Deficit		−5,400
Grand Total		98,000

Source:. Financial Statement and Budget Report 1984-5 (Total rounded).

As regards government securities, the 1982 Budget included a notable innovation with the first issue of an index-linked government stock which may be bought by the general public; previous index-linked issues could only be held by pension funds and similar bodies. Both the principal and the interest on such stocks are index-linked and, hence, if held to maturity are a complete protection against inflation. This development should have the effect as inflation falls of reducing the ongoing cost of servicing the government stocks' component of the national debt.

The annual Budget as an instrument of fiscal policy has frequently been criticized because of its inflexibility. In the ordinary way the major taxes such as income tax and corporation tax cannot be varied between Finance Acts.[1] Thus though it might be thought desirable by those who favour activist fiscal policies to alter these taxes more frequently, this cannot be done without all the inconvenience of a supplementary Budget. However, the authorities have more leeway over some other sources of revenue. From the point of view of flexibility one of the most important has been the power, first granted in the 1961 Finance Act, to vary by not more than 10% the rates of nearly all customs and excise duties and,

---

1 The Finance Act puts into law the Budget proposals, subject to the Provisional Collection of Taxes Act which allows certain tax changes to take effect immediately and in advance of the enactment of the Finance Bill; the latter is subject to any amendments made to it by the House of Commons.

since the introduction of value added tax in 1973, to vary it by not more than 25%.[1] Thus there are now substantial powers to vary taxes between Budgets. This, of course, leaves other crucially important problems, such as the timing and scale of tax changes and their anticipation by the public; more generally it raises the issue of the ability of the authorities to 'fine-tune' the operation of the economy.

TABLE 2.13

National Loans Fund, 1984–5 (Forecast) (£m)

(i) *Receipts*		
Interest on loans, profits of the Issue Department of the Bank of England, etc.	5,800	
Service of the National Debt – balance met from Consolidated Fund	6,800	
Total		12,600
Net borrowing by the National Loans Fund		10,300
Grand Total		22,900
(ii) *Payments*		
Service of the National Debt:		
Interest		12,500
Management and expenses		140
Consolidated Fund Deficit		5,400
Loans (net)		
To nationalized industries	130	
Other public corporations	400	
Local authorities	4,400	
Other loans	−10	
Total		4,920
Grand Total		22,900

Source: *Financial Statement and Budget Report 1984–5* (Grand Total rounded).

Alterations in government expenditure are also, in principle, a possible way of making fiscal policy more flexible. But government expenditure may be planned years in advance of its formal inclusion in the Budget estimates, and periodic modifications of the plans may give rise to problems, since much of the expenditure is on a continuing basis and cannot be easily varied. Furthermore, it may be extremely costly to slow down or postpone some kinds of expenditure, particularly investment expenditure. Hence frequent variation of government expenditure is not an ideal instrument of fiscal policy.

The Budget accounts, as already indicated, are incomplete in a number of ways. They deal, for example, only peripherally with local government finances and the national insurance funds.

The latter are known as extra-budgetary funds and include national insurance, national health, redundancy fund and maternity pay fund contributions, both

---

1 Thus if the customs or excise rate of duty was 10%, it might be varied between 9% and 11%, and, as regards a VAT rate of 15%, between 11¼% and 18¾%.

those of employers and employees. The estimated receipts for 1984-5 are £23,000m, which compares with £33,800m for income tax and £18,000m for value added tax. In short, national insurance contributions are an important source of revenue to government. From an employer's point of view, his contribution is a tax on employment and one which was particularly resented was in the form of the national insurance surcharge, which is treated in the government accounts as a tax on expenditure and not as contribution to the national insurance funds. The surcharge was abolished in the 1984 Budget with effect from October 1984.[1]

IV.4   Income Taxation

Up to April 1973, individuals were subject to income tax and surtax, with the latter chargeable in addition to income tax on incomes in excess of a certain level. From that date, the former income tax and surtax were replaced by a single graduated personal tax, known as unified tax. The main aims of unified tax were to simplify the tax structure, permit a smoother graduation in tax rates as income rises and simplify the administration of the whole system. The unified tax is constructed on the concept of earned income and so manages to dispense with the calculation of earned-income relief, which was required under the previous system since it was constructed in terms of unearned or investment income. As well as earned income and investment income, a further concept requires to be mentioned, that is chargeable income. Chargeable income is the income which remains from all sources after deduction of personal, family and certain other allowances.

The main personal allowances since an amendment to the 1977 Finance Act have, with the exception of the year 1981-2, been linked to the retail price index – an example of indexation. For 1984-5 the single and married personal allowances have been raised by 12½%, some 7% more than required to take account of inflation over the past year, and are as follows: for single persons £2,005 and for married couples £3,155. The age allowances for the elderly are £2,490 for a single person and £3,955 for a married couple, and were increased broadly in line with inflation.

Once taxable income has been determined, the various tax rates come into operation. For 1984-5 the tax bands, or ranges of income in relation to each tax rate, are as follows:

£	%
0–15,400	30
15,401–18,200	40
18,201–23,100	45
23,101–30,600	50
30,601–38,100	55
Over 38,100	60

The unified tax retains the former distinction between earned and investment income, but the previously existing surcharge of 15% on investment income above £7,100 was abolished for individuals in the 1984 Budget.

---

1   National Insurance is discussed further in Chapter 5, section III.5.

It is evident that one of the main features of income taxation is its progressive-ness. This is, of course, by design; it can be traced to notions of ability to pay. It is assumed that those with larger incomes are or should be able to pay propor-tionately more of them in taxation. In addition, progressive taxation lends itself to income redistribution, to the extent that government expenditure benefits the less well-off in the community. But progressive taxation also diminishes the direct reward for extra work as income increases, and may act as a disincentive to more effort.

It is also possible that steeply progressive taxation is a disincentive to move-ment from one job to another; it may be difficult to get a sufficiently large income after tax to compensate for the costs of upheaval and change. If this is correct, then the tax system may misallocate resources and be a drag on economic efficiency and growth. There is also no doubt that highly progressive taxation stimulates tax avoidance—the search for loopholes in the law permitting a reduced tax bill—and indeed tax evasion which is, of course, illegal. If it is possible to spend less than a pound on advice to save a pound in tax, then clearly this is a powerful incentive. The energies and resources of lawyers, accountants and tax experts generally may thus be diverted into socially costly tasks.

To the extent that some or all of these problems arise, the community may have to make difficult choices between more redistribution and a smaller total income, or somewhat less redistribution and a larger total income, with each choice being associated with varying degrees of social and political conflict. Once more, there would seem to be no escape from the difficult problems which arise in sustaining the ongoing life of a complex and diverse society.

It has long been a goal of taxation policy that the system of taxation should be easy to understand, equitable and cheap to administer. How far this continues to be true of the system in the UK is open to question. Concern has been expressed about the distortions and inefficiencies generated by the complex interdependencies of the whole system of taxation and the social-security system.[1] In particular, there is concern about what has come to be called the 'poverty-trap', where people who are in low-paid jobs or unemployed may find that the effective marginal tax on their additional earnings may be extremely high—in excess of 100% in some circumstances—when both taxation and loss of social-security benefits are taken into consideration. The introduction of tax-free child benefit helped to alleviate this problem.

There are, however, various proposals for dealing more radically with these and related problems by, in effect, integrating to some degree the direct-taxation and social-security systems. One proposal is known as 'the negative income tax', which ideally is designed to permit a single assessment of income and provide either for calculating the tax due, if income is above a certain level, or for a transfer to be paid, if it is below that level. The particular scheme that has received most official attention in the UK is known as a 'tax credit system'.[2] There seems to be little doubt that a tax-credit scheme such as that proposed could achieve some

---

1   See *The Structure and Reform of Direct Taxation*, Report of a Committee chaired by Professor J.E. Meade, Institute for Fiscal Studies, Allen and Unwin, 1978; and also below, chapter 5, section III.5.

2   See *Proposals for a Tax-Credit System*, Cmnd. 5116, HMSO, 1972.

simplification and economies in present arrangements for taxation and in the administration of at least some social-security benefits. However, it would be a mistake to assume that it offers a simple panacea to the problem of all those with low incomes.

IV.5   Capital Gains Taxation and Development Land Tax

Under the capital gains tax, gains are taxable on the disposal of most assets. Important exemptions are principal private residences, private motorcars, National Savings securities, most life-assurance policies and betting winnings, gifts to charities and, if sold more than one year after purchase, British government and government-guaranteed securities and most corporate fixed-interest securities. In addition, the first £5,600 of net annual gains of individuals are exempt, which is an increase of £300 over 1983-4 to allow for inflation. The rate of capital gains tax is 30%. All gains at death are exempt; and there are various special provisions for taxing gains on gifts. There are also provisions generally allowing losses to be offset against gains on those assets that are subject to tax. Gains realized by companies are ordinarily chargeable to corporation tax, which for the year 1984-5 is to be 45%. However, for many years the effective rate of tax on company gains has been only 30%—achieved by the expedient of leaving out of account a fraction of the gain. Authorized unit trusts and approved investment trusts are exempt from capital gains tax.

The major justification put forward for the introduction of capital gains taxation is on grounds of equity. The argument, ignoring dividends, is roughly as follows. An individual may purchase £100 worth of securities in 1983 and—if he is lucky—find that in 1984 they are worth £200. If he sold the securities and if there were no capital gains tax, he could maintain his capital intact and still have £100 to spend, therefore his £100 is essentially income and should be taxed as such. But is this really equitable with progressive income-tax rates? It might be that in some years he would have no gain and that if the £100 were spread over a number of years a lower tax charge would arise. Does this mean that gains should be averaged over a number of years, or would a compromise solution be to charge rates somewhat less than income-tax rates? The UK capital gains tax seems to favour the latter.

In discussing the £100 gain above, nothing was said about prices. But if prices have risen by 10% over the period, then £110 would be required to maintain his capital intact in real terms, leaving £90 in current prices as the income he might spend without eroding the former; in effect, inflation is a form of tax and indeed may be said to be levied without Parliamentary approval. The question arises—is it legitimate to tax gains which are only nominal? The usual answer is 'No' and the government now not only provides for changing the exemption limit in line with inflation but in 1982 also introduced complex provisions for deducting some of the elements of nominal from total gains.

Capital gains taxation is, of course, important for other reasons besides equity. It may affect investment and saving and the functioning of the capital markets, and pose difficult problems of administration. To the extent that the return on investment takes the form of capital gains—especially the return on risky investment—taxing them may discourage such investment. This discouragement may, however, be mitigated to some extent, since the tax is postponable and payable only on realized capital gains and there are special provisions for retirement relief for those who sell a business or shares in a trading company. The allowance of losses against gains also works in the same direction. Nevertheless, the overall effect may well be to depress investment.

The effects on savings are perhaps even more problematical but may also be adverse, as may the effects on the operation of the capital markets. Since the tax is on realized gains, this encourages the retention of the same securities as, of course, the holder has the income on the tax that would otherwise have to be paid if the securities are realized. There is therefore a discouragement to switching between securities, which reduces the flexibility of the market and perhaps makes the raising of capital more costly. A possible offset to these effects is the realization of capital losses since these are allowable for tax purposes against corresponding capital gains.

The administrative problems with the tax are particularly great where difficulties of valuation arise. This is especially true of changes in the value of assets which do not ordinarily have a market value; an example is unquoted securities. The problem of valuation may become less acute as time proceeds and the community gets accustomed to the tax.[1]

The Development Land Tax makes development value arising from land subject to a special development tax, but there is no liability to income tax, corporation tax or capital gains tax on gains subject to development land tax. The term 'development value' refers to the difference between the base value of the land and its value for development purposes. The base value 'is the highest of:

(1)   cost of acquisition plus the cost of "relevant improvements", plus any increase in current use value since the date of acquisition; or
(2)   current use value at the date of disposal, plus 15%; or
(3)   acquisition cost of the land, including all improvements, plus 15%.'[2]

The first £75,000 of realized development value in any financial year after 1 April 1984 is exempt from tax. The standard rate thereafter is 60% of development value.

Various people and bodies are exempt from development land tax, including the main residence of owner-occupiers for land up to one acre, and certain co-operative housing associations provided that if they dispose of dwellings or land they do so to 'a housing association registered with the Housing Corporation or to the Housing Corporation itself'.[3]

No doubt the development land tax is an attempt by the state to appropriate what it considers to be inequitable capital gains from certain forms of land development. However, it is difficult to see how it can fail to raise the costs of new housing and in so doing confer actual or potential capital gains on owners of existing houses.

---

1   For further discussion of all of these issues, see Prest and Barr, *Public Finance in Theory and Practice*, op. cit., pp. 333–44.

2   *The British System of Taxation*, HMSO, 1977, p. 24.

3   Ibid. For a fuller discussion of the whole subject see A.R. Prest, *The Taxation of Urban Land*, Manchester University Press, 1981.

IV.6   Corporation Tax, Depreciation and Other Allowances, and Oil Taxation

Corporation tax draws a strong distinction between the company and the share-holder, taxing each as separate entities. A basic argument used in favour of corporation tax is the opportunity it gives the authorities to distinguish between the personal and company sectors for policy purposes. They may wish, for instance, to curtail consumption expenditure with as little adverse effect as possible on investment expenditure. An increase in income tax, leaving corporation tax unchanged, may tend to have the desired effect and may even encourage smaller dividend distributions, leaving more funds available to companies for investment purposes.

The foregoing analysis begs, however, a number of important questions. Among these are the following. Should future consumption be preferred to present consumption, in so far as larger current investment makes possible a larger future income and so consumption? Are the companies with retained profits the ones which should grow? This is not at all self-evident. It means that companies avoid the discipline of having to raise funds in the market and probably favours the larger established company at the expense of the smaller or newer company. Furthermore, greater encouragement of profit retention tends to reduce the flow of funds through the capital market to the detriment of companies dependent on it. Corporation tax may also tend to distort the operation of the capital market by encouraging firms to rely more on loan or debenture capital at the expense of ordinary or other forms of share capital, since the interest on the former is allowed as a cost in the calculation of profits and hence liability for tax, whereas this is only partly true of the latter. It may indeed be argued that the gains from introducing corporation tax outweigh all the disadvantages. However, once a tax has been in operation for a period of years, to remove it may give rise to inequities.

Corporation tax is based on what is known as the imputation system. Under it, all profits, whether distributed or not, are subject to the same corporation-tax rate, but part of the tax is imputed to shareholders, and collected from the company at the time of payment of dividends. If, for instance, the corporation-tax rate is 45% and the basic income-tax rate is 30%, then a company whose activities are entirely within the UK and which had profits of 100 would have a corporation-tax liability of 45. If during a year it paid a dividend of 21 to its shareholders, it would be treated as a gross dividend of 30 from which income tax of 30% had been deducted. The company would pay the 9 to the Inland Revenue and this, which is called advance payment of corporation tax (ACT), would be credited against the company's corporation-tax liability of 45. Shareholders subject to basic-rate income tax would be deemed to have discharged their tax liabilities; only in the case of those exempt or subject to higher rates would a refund or additional charge be necessary.

The 1984 Budget substantially reduced corporation-tax rates. The rate, which for many years was 52%, was reduced as follows:

Rate (%)	Year ending 31 March
50	1984
45	1985
40	1986
35	1987

Small companies whose annual profits do not exceed £100,000 are subject to a reduced rate of corporation tax and had their rate lowered from 38% to 30%. Special marginal rates exist for companies with profits between £100,000 and £500,000.

The imputation form of corporation tax has certain advantages over the two-rate system when it comes to negotiating double-taxation agreements with other countries; it also facilitates the movement towards tax harmonization within the European Community, as it puts Britain broadly in line with French and German company taxation and with EEC policy.

In assessing liability to corporation tax, allowance is made, broadly speaking, for all the costs incurred by the company, including the wear and tear of physical capital and, as mentioned above, interest on loans and debentures. However, depreciation is not allowed on all physical assets; there are generally no allowances on such things as retail shops, showrooms and offices, except in Enterprise Zones where there are 100% capital allowances for commercial and industrial buildings.

In addition to depreciation allowances for wear and tear, successive governments have attempted to influence investment by various kinds of incentive. The basis of the system was to permit accelerated depreciation of physical assets, that is, their writing-off more quickly than warranted in terms of actual economic costs incurred through wear and tear. However, the Chancellor of the Exchequer in his 1984 Budget introduced measures which have radically altered previous practice.

For some time what is called the first-year allowance for plant and machinery had been 100%, permitting the complete writing-off of the asset in the first year, irrespective of depreciation through wear and tear. But in the 1984 Budget the Chancellor announced the phasing-out of first-year allowances over a two-year period. The 100% allowance was reduced to 75% for the year up to 31 March 1985, 50% for the year ending 31 March 1986 and nil subsequently. Thereafter expenditure on plant and machinery will only qualify for annual depreciation allowances on a 25% reducing-balance basis.

The comparable system for expenditure on industrial buildings formerly gave an initial allowance of 75%. But this too is to be abolished in two steps by 31 March 1986; there was an immediate reduction to 50% for the year to 31 March 1985 and to 25% for the following year. After 31 March 1986, expenditure is to be written off on an annual 4% straight-line method.

The foregoing discussion refers to the general position; special depreciation arrangements exist, as well as the provision of cash grants, in relation to investment in both plant and equipment and industrial buildings for the development areas and for Northern Ireland.

With the rapid rise in prices in the 1970s many companies found themselves subject to heavy taxation on the increase in the nominal value of their stocks, and special provisions were made to allow a measure of tax relief. This too was abolished in the 1984 Budget on the grounds that it was no longer necessary because of the fall in inflation.

The whole system of allowances and grants gives rise to many complicated issues, some of which are accentuated by rapid inflation. A few of the issues are touched on here. First, should depreciation allowances be on an original or a replacement-cost basis? This question would be of little or no significance if prices were generally stable. But in periods of rising prices it would seem that, if the community is to preserve intact its physical stock of capital it is preferable to have allowances based on a replacement-cost basis. However, if the problem is approached in a different way the argument may not be so clear-cut. Suppose a firm purchases a piece of equipment and thereafter prices rise, including the price of the equipment, then the capital value of the old equipment also rises, giving a capital gain to the firm. If allowances are permitted on a replacement-cost basis the firm is, in fact, receiving untaxed capital gains. Is this equitable in relation to other sections of the community or is it a useful compromise to allow only original costs in calculating depreciation, so that the apparent capital gains are subject to corporation and income tax, as was the practice in the UK until the modification in the seventies relating to the increase in the value of stocks? The answer is far from obvious, but clearly the issues become more acute in periods of rapid inflation.[1]

Initial and first-year allowances and cash grants should on the face of it act as a stimulus to investment and encourage economic growth—the first may be regarded as reducing the amount of tax payable on a profitable investment, and the second is, of course, a direct subsidy which does not depend upon the availability of profits. The Chancellor, however, in his 1984 Budget speech stated that 'there is little evidence that these incentives have strengthened the economy or improved the quality of investment. . . . Too much . . . investment has been made because the tax allowances make it look profitable, rather than because it would be truly productive.'[2] His 1984 Budget measures are consistent with this outlook.

A major feature of cash grants and regional development grants is the extent to which they are discriminatory. They make investments in certain places more profitable than in others and some types of investment more profitable than other types. This, of course, is by design and is intended to stimulate investment in the places and in the forms the government desires. The basis for this intervention is the conviction that the market, reflecting the interacting decisions of consumers, savers and investors, if left to itself will lead to misallocation of investment and to under-investment, and to regional imbalance in the levels of employment and economic activity. However, as far as the latter is concerned, it is not at all obvious that this form of capital subsidization, which cheapens capital relatively to labour with the latter generally in excess supply, is the best way to proceed either regionally or nationally. But the problem of regional development is extremely complex. Some of the issues, such as the distribution of income and wealth in society, were referred to in the introduction to this section but cannot be explored further here. On the whole, however, it is difficult not to feel a sense of disappointment about the effectiveness of capital subsidization as an instrument of regional development.

Oil taxation has become increasingly important as a consequence of exploitable North Sea oil and gas discoveries. The tax system has three main components, though there are differences depending on the location of the oil fields. The first is royalties based on the well-head value, though these can be relieved in whole or in part to encourage a licensee to develop or continue production from a commercially marginal field. The second is petroleum revenue tax (PRT), which is chargeable on each field separately on net income, defined as receipts from oil sales less royalties and operating costs (excluding interest payments) and less certain

---

1   See Prest and Barr, *Public Finance in Theory and Practice*, Chapter 16.

2   HC, *Official Report*, Weekly Hansard, Vol. 56, No. 117, cols. 295–6.

important reliefs. The third component is corporation tax, which is levied on net income after deducting royalties and PRT. Total revenues from North Sea oil and gas production for 1984-5 are estimated at £10,200m which, as may be seen from table 2.11, constitutes a major contribution to government revenue. The contribution is expected to decline in the future.

IV.7 Value Added Tax

Value added tax (VAT), as its name implies, taxes value added at each stage of the productive process, with the final selling price to the consumer being made up of the cost of production plus the rate of tax. An example may help to make the matter clearer. Suppose the value added tax rate is 10%—the standard rate for 1984-5 is 15%—and that a manufacturer buys all his raw materials at a cost of 110 including tax. The 10 is known as input tax. The manufacturer processes the raw materials and sells the final product to a retailer for 220 including tax. The 20 is known as output tax, and the manufacturer pays the difference between the output tax and the input tax to Customs and Excise, namely 10. The retailer may be supposed to sell the product to the consumer for 330 including tax. Thus the output tax of the retailer is 30 and the input tax is 20, so he also pays 10 to Customs and Excise.

Thus the tax, as it were, comes to rest with the consumer, and this is why VAT is frequently described as an indirect tax on consumer expenditure. It should be stressed, however, that the foregoing is intended only as a simple arithmetical explanation of the VAT method and should not be interpreted as implying that tax is necessarily wholly passed on to the final consumer or does not affect his behaviour. The problems of tax incidence are extremely complex.

VAT is a broadly based indirect tax covering a wide range of products and is intended to cause as little as possible distortion of consumer choice. This, however, is difficult to achieve, partly because it is not easy to tax certain services. VAT is also widely used throughout the EEC and has been encouraged as a step towards tax harmonization.

A problem with VAT, however, is that a general tax on consumer expenditure is regressive and discriminates against those on lower incomes. Successive governments have attempted, and it would seem with some success at least as far as short-run consequences are concerned, to get round this criticism by what is called zero-rating most food, coal, gas, electricity, public transport fares, and drugs and medicines supplied on prescription. Zero-rating means that the trader does not have to charge tax on his sales, and, in addition, he can claim a refund of any tax he may have paid to his suppliers because of tax paid on inputs entering into the final product.

Certain other features of value added tax deserve to be mentioned. As well as a zero-rated category of goods, there is also an exempted category. For exempted goods the trader does not have to charge tax on his sales but he cannot claim a refund for any tax included in the price of his purchases. Exempted goods and services include land, insurance, postal services provided by the Post Office, betting and gaming (which already carry excise duty), finance, education and health services. Small traders with a business turnover of less than £18,700 a year or £6,200 a quarter in taxable goods and services are exempt from the tax. In 1984-5 VAT is expected to raise £18,000m in revenue, well over 50% of the income-tax total.

IV.8   Excise Duties and Protective Duties

Until recently the practice in the UK has been to distinguish between customs duties, which were imposed on imports, and excise duties, which were levied on home-produced goods and services. External duties had two functions: one, to raise revenue in a similar way to excise duties, and two, to give protection to British-produced goods or preference to goods from specified countries. However, membership of the EEC has obliged the UK to bring its practices into line with the rest of the Community. Thus duties for revenue purposes are now known as excise duties and are levied on both home-produced and similar imported goods. Protective duties refer to what was formerly the protective part of customs duties, and these have been generally brought into line with the Common External Tariff of the EEC. This means that the UK, like other members of the Community, now operates a common tariff on imports from non-members, whilst trade between the member countries is free of customs duty. As may be seen from table 2.11, the products which are large revenue-yielders are oil, tobacco and alcohol with a total estimated yield of £14,200m in 1984-5, or 16% of total revenue from taxation. Moreover, this does not take account of VAT on these products.

An outstanding feature of the duties and taxes on oil, tobacco and alcohol is the large proportion that they represent of the purchase price. Ordinarily it might be expected that something which has the effect of substantially increasing the price of a product would lead to less of it, perhaps much less of it, being bought. By and large this does not seem to have happened with these three products – their demands are inelastic with respect to price. However, some doubts are beginning to be expressed about the buoyancy of the revenue from tobacco, though this may be due to other causes besides the scale of taxation. The inelasticity of demand with respect to price implies that these duties and taxes may have little direct effect on the allocation of resources. But there will be an indirect effect because the funds withdrawn by taxes from consumers will scarcely be spent by the state in the same way as if they had been in the hands of the former.

It is often argued that indirect taxes are to be preferred because they are less of a disincentive to the supply of labour than direct taxes. This is an extremely difficult issue and depends on many factors, such as the scale of duties and taxes to be substituted, say, for a reduction in direct taxes or for forgoing an increase, the type and range of the goods involved and, in particular, whether they are considered as substitutes or complements for leisure. For an individual, in choosing between additional work or leisure, may well consider not only the direct tax on extra earnings but also the type of goods and services that can be bought with additional income either now or in the future and either by himself or those who may inherit from him.[1]

It is also arguable that, on equity grounds, indirect taxes are regressive in that they fall more heavily on relatively low-income groups. There would seem to be some truth in this as far as tobacco and beer are concerned, but possibly to a lesser extent for petrol. On the other hand the relatively less well-off obtain benefits from government welfare and other services. If the community wants extensive government expenditure on welfare services and education, it seems unavoidable that one way or another a large proportion of the tax revenue must be raised from the mass

---

1   See *The Structure and Reform of Direct Taxation*, op. cit.

of taxpayers. If at the same time the latter are important beneficiaries from government expenditure then they are indirectly paying for perhaps all of or a major part of these benefits. This is in no way to deny, however, the power of taxation, or at least certain forms of it, to redistribute income and wealth.

IV.9   Capital Transfer Tax and Wealth Tax

Capital transfer tax (CTT), often called a gifts tax, applies, subject to certain exemptions, to gifts made during life and to transfers on death. Transfers of what is called settled property or property held in trust are also subject to the tax. The tax is chargeable as the gifts or transfers occur and is cumulative over a maximum period of ten years. That is, in calculating the tax due on successive gifts or transfers, the ones made over the previous nine years are taken into account and progressively higher rates of tax apply. The rates of tax on what are known as lifetime transfers are lower than for transfers on death. The tax is in general payable by the donor but may be recovered from the beneficiary.

The main exemptions are transfers between husband and wife both in life and on death; transfers in any one year of up to £3,000 plus any unused part of the previous year's exemption; outright gifts to any one person during the tax year up to a value of £250; and transfers made out of income after tax as part of normal expenditure which leave the donor sufficient income to maintain his usual standard of living. Marriage gifts are given special treatment; transfers by a parent up to £5,000 are exempt and up to £2,500 by any other ancestor and £1,000 by anyone else. Business owners and working farmers also get special relief; for purposes of the tax, value transferred is reduced by 50%. All outright gifts and bequests to charities are completely exempt. There are also special provisions relating to the exemption of gifts of works of art and historic buildings made during the individual's lifetime.

The first £64,000 of transfers, after taking into consideration all exemptions, is tax-free whether made during lifetime or on death. The rates for lifetime transfers then rise from 15% on the next £21,000 by gradual steps to 30% on lifetime transfers over £285,000. For transfers on death the rate is twice that for lifetime transfers. Rate bands are indexed for inflation. Transfers made within three years of death are subject to the rates applicable on death.

The intention behind the introduction of the CTT was to reduce the inequality of wealth distribution. However, it is arguable that an accessions tax, that is a tax on recipients rather than on donors, would have been more effective as a means of achieving greater wealth equality. For an accessions tax would encourage a spreading of gifts between recipients in a way that would reduce tax liability; this is not true of the CTT.

The precise form of the CTT and the exemptions it incorporates make it extremely important for individuals with even quite modest capital assets to plan their affairs carefully if they wish to minimize their tax liability. This too could be a source of inequity, depending on the foresight and luck of donors. Finally, like all such taxes it may encourage increased consumption expenditure and perhaps expenditure on education, travel and the like.

From time to time, official consideration has been given to the introduction of an annual wealth tax. A Green Paper was published in 1974 outlining proposals the government had in mind. In a foreword the then Chancellor stated that 'income by itself is not an adequate measure of taxable capacity. The ownership of wealth, whether it produces income or not, adds to the economic resources of a taxpayer so that the person who has wealth as well as income of a given size necessarily has a greater taxable capacity than one who has only income of that size.'[1] It is not clear what precise form the wealth tax might ultimately take; it encountered much criticism both in and outside Parliament. A Select Committee of the House of Commons established to examine a wealth tax did not find it possible to present an agreed report, and for the present, especially since the change of government in 1979, the matter would seem to be in abeyance.

IV.10   Taxation and the European Community[2]

It is evident from the preceding discussion that some of the recent tax reforms of the UK were designed to bring its taxes, or at any rate some of them, more closely into line with those of the EEC. Members are obliged under the Treaty of Rome and subsequent directives to harmonize their tax legislation as regards turnover taxes, excise duties and other forms of indirect taxation. In particular, the Community has adopted value added taxation as its main general indirect tax and this is binding on all members, though there remains considerable variety in the number and scale of rates levied. Contributions to the Community budget are in part calculated on the basis of value added tax.

The Community intends to harmonize the main excise duties on tobacco, oil and alcohol. As far as the UK is concerned, this may eventually mean a reduction in the duties on tobacco and alcohol (wine duty was reduced in 1984) since these are much higher than in most of the countries of the present Community. Corporation-tax harmonization remains under consideration within the Community but it is likely that the credit or imputation system will be adopted. The Community does not require harmonization of direct personal taxation.

The fundamental justification for tax harmonization within the Community stems from the very concept of the Community as, amongst other things, a common, unified competitive market. This requires, it is argued, the disappearance of all artificial barriers to trade and capital flows between the member countries, including those that might be created by different tax systems. On the basis of this approach, the impetus towards uniformity or harmonization of taxation is immense. This is especially clear in the case of value added tax and excise duties and is becoming more so, as far as corporation tax is concerned, with the increasing importance of international companies and the mobility of capital, which the Community is determined to foster among its members. The need to harmonize personal direct taxation is not felt to arise as it is believed that mobility of labour is not greatly affected by differences between member countries in this type of tax.[3]

---

1   *Wealth Tax*, Cmnd. 5704, 1974.

2   See chapter 4, section II, on the Common Agricultural Policy; and also chapter 3, section III.7.

3   However, the Community intends to harmonize such matters relating to direct taxation as tax-deduction of dividends at source.

The whole process of tax harmonization carries important consequences for both the Community and its member countries. By implication it places great stress on the efficient allocation of resources as indicated by the static competitive model. By the same token it neglects, or at least puts on one side, the fundamental questions of externalities and of income and wealth distribution, except to the extent that these will or can be dealt with by harmonization of social-security arrangements and with the help of the Community budget, and by regional policy measures. Up to the present, none of these areas is well developed, though some progress has been made in each of them. Finally, harmonization is relevant to the whole issue of stabilization policy. It remains to be seen to what extent it will be possible for individual members to vary indirect taxes such as value added tax as an instrument of fiscal policy. This could obviously pose serious problems for member countries and, not least, the relative fiscal power of the Community vis-à-vis its individual members. These matters have, as yet, had little public discussion in the UK.

V　POLICY IN RETROSPECT AND PROSPECT
V.1　The 1960s and After

In the brief review of policy below, attention is concentrated on the record of the authorities in the pursuit of their major policy goals. For most of the 1960s the authorities were preoccupied with the achievement of high levels of employment, price stability, economic growth, fixed exchange rates and a 'satisfactory' balance of payments. But in the late 1960s the commitment to fixed exchange rates became less strong and was abandoned in the early 1970s; and in the last few years a reduction in the rate of inflation has dominated the other policy goals including full employment and economic growth. Indeed, the authorities now see the curtailment of inflation as a necessary means to achieving more employment and faster economic growth.

During the 1960s unemployment in Great Britain averaged less than 2%, though from 1967 onwards it was in excess of this figure. But for the 1970s it averaged 4.0% with the trend rising ominously; and for 1980 the average was 6.4% and for 1983 12.4%. Thus the policy goal of high levels of employment is far from being currently achieved.

Retail prices rose over the 1960s at a compound rate of some 3.8% a year, with the rate of increase accelerating in the later years to around 5%. However, even this latter rate seems low in comparison with the rates experienced since. Over the 1970s the annual rate was over 13%, which implies that during the period prices rose by more than 300%. But even 13% is relatively mild in comparison with a rate of 24% between 1974 and 1975 and the rate of 18% in 1980. The decline since then has been marked with a fall to 11.9% for 1981 and to 5.3% for 1983. Thus whilst there was a complete failure to achieve price stability during the 1970s there has been a distinct improvement in the early 1980s.

If economic growth is measured in terms of gross domestic product (GDP), then this grew at a compound rate of around 2.8% a year during the 1960s, though by no means regularly, and just about 1.5% a year in the 1970s. Between 1972 and 1973 GDP increased by about 7% but fell by almost 3% between 1973 and 1975. GDP also fell in 1980 and 1981, and has only recently recovered to its 1979 level. Thus whilst some economic growth has taken place, it has been far from regular and has been low by international standards for developed countries.[1]

For the first half or more of the 1960s, fixed exchange rates were a major goal of economic policy.[2] But in the year or two leading up to the devaluation of sterling in November 1967 this policy came increasingly under question and by 1972 the Chancellor of the Exchequer was prepared to say in his Budget speech that 'it is neither necessary nor desirable to distort domestic economies. . . in order to maintain unrealistic exchange rates, whether they were too high or too low'. In the light of the exchange-rate fluctuations in recent years it seems doubtful that such a statement would be made now, as there is a renewed concern about the behaviour of the exchange rate, though this is not to say that fixed exchange rates have once more become a widely accepted policy goal in the UK. Whatever may be true of the official attitude to exchange rates, and whether it be regarded as a goal or policy target, there is no doubt about the authorities' concern over the balance of payments. For most of the 1960s and in the 1970s the balance of payments has been a preoccupation of the authorities and from time to time they have felt constrained to take drastic action to improve the position.

Since June 1972 the exchange rate of sterling has been allowed to float, though by no means free from official intervention. During 1973 it averaged about $2.45 to the pound, falling to $1.75 in 1977. However, since the US dollar has itself experienced variations in its exchange rate during this time, a better indicator for sterling is what is called the 'sterling effective exchange rate' which is a weighted index of movements against a basket of other currencies; the base year is 1975 with the index set equal to 100. From 1973 to 1977 the rate declined from 112 to 81, a depreciation of 28%; between 1977 and 1980 the index increased from 81 to 96, a rise of over 18%, and by 1983 had fallen to 83.

Thus during the 1970s and into the early 1980s the UK, like much of the rest of the world, has experienced relatively variable exchange rates. This outcome must be expected when exchange rates are allowed to float, with or without official intervention (in the foreign-exchange market) by monetary authorities and especially if different countries are pursuing divergent monetary policies; in November 1979 the MLR of the Bank of England was raised to 17%, an historically high level for the UK and also high relative to rates in other countries. Variability of exchange rates has important consequences for the domestic economy. In particular, a sharp appreciation in the effective exchange rate, such as occurred between 1979 and 1980, seriously affects the competitiveness of exports and puts great pressure on the profits of those companies heavily involved in export markets. This, in turn, will tend to depress domestic economic activity and increase unemployment, especially when real wages are inflexible downwards. This is essentially the pattern of events that took place in the UK in 1980 and into 1981. Since then, there has been an improvement in both competitiveness and company profitability.

If the economic record of the 1960s and especially the 1970s is disappointing, what were the roles of monetary policy and fiscal policy over these periods?

---

1   Taking the EEC (of the nine countries) as a norm and equal to 100, GDP per head in the UK in 1962 at current official exchange rates was 109.7 and at current purchasing-power parities was 108.3. By 1977 the corresponding figures were 71.7 and 91.8. Over these 15 years the UK has fallen far behind West Germany, France, Holland and other countries in terms of GDP per capita.

2   See chapter 3, section III, for detailed discussion of exchange-rate policy.

Throughout the 1960s little or no attention was given to the behaviour of the monetary aggregates. Monetary policy, or more accurately credit policy, was largely seen in terms of using quantitative restrictions to control particular credit magnitudes together with the manipulation of interest rates, with the latter geared to government financing requirements. Nevertheless, it is instructive to examine the growth of the monetary aggregates during part of the 1960s.

From 1963I to 1970I (where I refers to the first quarter and the data are seasonally adjusted), M_1 grew at an average rate of 3% a year and £M_3 at 5.4%. The contrast with the next 3 years to 1973I is striking when M_1 and £M_3 grew respectively at average rates of 13% and 18.4%. It will be recalled that this period overlapped with the introduction of the CCC measures. It should also be noted that it predates the first oil crisis; the latter is important to bear in mind in assessing the 'causes' of inflation in the UK since the mid-1970s. More specifically, and notwithstanding certain problems of interpretation because of the removal of restrictions on the activities of the banks, the rapid growth in these monetary aggregates is suggestive of a boost to inflation quite distinct from the oil crisis.

From 1973I to 1979I, just before Mrs Thatcher's government took office, the respective annual rates of growth of M_1 and £M_3 were some 14% and 12%, again relatively high rates of growth by historical standards, though attempts were being made to slow these growth rates down from 1976 onwards.

As regards fiscal policy, difficulties arise in trying to determine whether or not a so-called 'fiscal stance' is, in some sense, expansionary, contractionary or neutral in its effects on the economy. For some years discussions of fiscal policy at the macroeconomic level have concentrated on the PSBR as an indicator of fiscal stance. Four measures of PSBR may be distinguished: (1) the nominal or actual; (2) the demand-weighted; (3) the cyclically adjusted; and (4) the inflation-adjusted or 'real'.[1]

The first is the familiar one and requires no further discussion. The second is based on the proposition that changes in different kinds of government expenditure and revenue may have different multiplier effects on output, and it attempts to weight these in relation to any actual PSBR. It is recognized that the attempt to measure such multipliers is highly precarious, thus casting doubt on the usefulness of the demand-weighted PSBR.

The cyclically adjusted PSBR is intended to compensate for the fact that even with fixed expenditure programmes, rates of tax and social-security benefits, 'fluctuations in economic activity would lead to movements in the PSBR'. For example, the heavier than expected unemployment during 1981 increased the PSBR. The cyclically adjusted PSBR tries to correct for these cyclical effects and estimate what the PSBR would be if they were removed and the economy was growing at its trend rate. In periods of recession this results in the cyclically adjusted PSBR being less than the actual PSBR. Some would wish to infer from this that the actual PSBR should be increased to keep the cyclically adjusted PSBR stable. But this suggestion raises all sorts of questions about the overall policy of government and would not necessarily be appropriate.

The fourth measure, the inflation-adjusted or real PSBR, refers to the nominal or actual PSBR corrected for the erosion through inflation of the real value of the

---

1 The discussion that follows relies heavily on the Treasury *Economic Progress Report*, 'The Budget Balance: Measurement and Policy', No. 144, April 1982.

outstanding public-sector debt. The argument is that inflation is, in effect, a form of tax on the holders of the public debt, reducing the real value of their assets, which, of course, reduces the real value of government liabilities. This latter reduction should, in principle, be offset against the nominal interest payments on the public debt, thereby reducing the nominal PSBR to arrive at the inflation-adjusted or real PSBR.

The calculation of the real PSBR raises both conceptual and practical difficulties. As regards the former, for instance, the question arises: what is the appropriate offset for inflation? There is no unique answer to this question and this needs to be kept in mind in interpreting the discussion which follows.[1]

Despite the difficulties with the notion of a real PSBR, it has significant implications for the operation of the economy and the assessment of the fiscal stance of government. In particular, there is reason to believe that if inflation erodes the real value of the private-sector's monetary assets – and it is the assets of the private sector that have been seriously eroded – it will respond, at least in part, by attempting to restore them through an increase in the savings ratio with consequential effects on consumption expenditure and economic activity.

With the nominal net amount of public-sector debt outstanding over the last ten years averaging some 40% of GDP at market prices, corrections for inflation, especially if it is in double figures, are likely to be relatively large and hence substantially reduce the nominal PSBR. The scale of the corrections may be seen in table 2.14. An average nominal PSBR of £1.1bn for the early 1970s becomes real net lending by the public sector of £1.9bn, suggesting a restrictive fiscal stance.

TABLE 2.14

Nominal and 'Real' PSBR: 1970–83 (£bn) (borrowing = −; lending = +)

	Annual Averages				Years	
	1970–72	1973–5	1976–8	1979–81	1982	1983[1]
Nominal	−1.1	−7.0	−7.8	−11.8	−5.4	−11.7
'Real'	+1.9	+1.4	0.0	+1.6	+1.8	−5.8

Sources: BEQB, vol. 24, no. 2, June 1984, p. 233.

1   Provisional.

During the following three years, though the real PSBR remains positive, some relaxation is apparent, accompanied by a rising nominal PSBR. For the three years 1976–8, the nominal PSBR is slightly larger than in the previous three years but the real PSBR became zero, indicating a more expansionary fiscal emphasis.

With the advent of Mrs Thatcher's government in 1979 a new importance was placed on reducing the nominal PSBR absolutely and as a percentage of GDP at market prices. This was understandably not achieved in 1979 and it was only in 1982 that the nominal PSBR showed a marked decline. However, the real PSBR,

---

1   See 'Real National Saving and Its Sectoral Composition', *BEQB*, June 1980, Vol. 20, No. 2. pp. 196–202; also Marcus Miller, 'Inflation-Adjusting the Public Sector Financial Deficit', in J. Kay (ed.), *The 1982 Budget*, Basil Blackwell, 1982.

which averaged zero for the three years 1976-8, increased to £1.6bn for the period 1979-81 and to £1.8bn for 1982. These figures indicate a distinct tightening of fiscal policy from about 1979. But, insofar as one year can be relied upon, the year 1983 brought a considerable change in emphasis. The real PSBR became negative, namely −£5.8bn, reflecting in part the smaller adjustment of the nominal PSBR as inflation declined. Whilst caution needs to be exercised in assessing the monetary and economic significance of the PSBR, both in its nominal and real forms, the switch from a positive to a negative PSBR suggests an expansionary fiscal stance.

In 1980 the government launched its Medium-Term Financial Strategy (MTFS) to reduce inflation and create conditions for a sustainable growth of output and employment. Central to that strategy is the announcement of declining target rates of growth for one or more monetary aggregates for a period of years ahead and the structuring of fiscal policy consistently with those targets. It is argued that if these are to be achieved and if interest rates are to decline, which is particularly important for the private sector, the nominal PSBR must be reduced as a percentage of GDP at market prices.

To begin with, as stated earlier, the target ranges for monetary growth were expressed in terms of $£M_3$ but subsequently M_1, PSL_2 and, most recently in 1984, M_0 were also included. The target rates of growth of M_0 and $£M_3$ and the projected path for the PSBR, which is not seen as a target, are shown in table 2.15 for the period 1982-4, together with the actual outcomes.

TABLE 2.15
Growth of Monetary Aggregates and the PSBR/GDP Ratio, 1982-9 (%)

	1982-3	1983-4	1984-5	1985-6	1986-7	1987-8	1988-9
Target for Narrow Money: M_0	–	–	4.8	3.7	2.6	1.5	0.4
Actual growth of M_0	3½	6	–	–	–	–	–
Target for Broad Money: $£M_3$	8-12	7-11	6-10	5-9	4-8	3-7	2-6
Actual growth of $£M_3$	10	9	–	–	–	–	–
Projected PSBR as % of GDP at market prices	3.3	3	2	2	2	1	1
Actual PSBR as % of GDP at market prices	3.2	3	–	–	–	–	–

Source: *Financial Statement and Budget Report (FSBR)*, 1983-4 and 1984-5.

Note: The projected PSBR/GDP ratios are as revised in the 1984-5 *FSBR*.

The relative uncontrollability of the growth of $£M_3$ and the inability or reluctance of the authorities in the first years of the MTFS to keep it within the target ranges has clearly been a source of some concern. For 1980-81 and 1981-2 the actual rates of growth were 18% and 14½%, whilst the target ranges were 7-11% and 6-10% respectively. It must, however, be conceded that there were major factors at work 'distorting' the growth of $£M_3$, including the ending of the SSD scheme in June 1980, which led to some reintermediation for the banks. But this, of course, implies that $£M_3$ is not an ideal monetary target and experience since then supports this view, though for 1982-3 and 1983-4 the actual growth of $£M_3$ fell within the target ranges (see table 2.15), albeit ones which had been increased in absolute terms and re-based on the actual growth which had occurred.

Notwithstanding the problems encountered in meeting the $£M_3$ target and if allowance is made for special factors and for inflation, as measured by the retail price index, then it is reasonable to conclude that on the whole monetary policy has been quite tight over most of this period and particularly in the first couple of years. This view is also supported by the relatively high nominal interest rates which have operated during this time, which in turn have generated high real interest rates. Thus, despite difficulties with its implementation, the MTFS has brought about broadly restrictive monetary and fiscal conditions, though considerable relaxation of fiscal policy would seem to have occurred in 1983.

There can be little doubt that these policies have contributed to the marked fall in inflation over the past four years. This is not to say that the monetary and fiscal policies of the authorities are perhaps as soundly based as they might be. They have shied away from a proper monetary base approach to monetary control which really would leave the market to determine interest rates and instead emphasize the so-called supply-side approach; they remain apprehensive about the effects of interest-rate fluctuations in the money markets and the consequences for the foreign-exchange market. This approach in turn has encouraged them to put great stress on the nominal PSBR which, as has been seen, is open to question.

That the price of restrictive monetary and fiscal policies may have been high is evident in so far as it has contributed to the loss of output and the massive and disturbing growth of unemployment. But it is also clear that the costs of inflation may be high and that a society which is determined to reduce inflation may have little alternative but to accept for a time unemployment and some loss of putput, hopefully as a means to more soundly based economic recovery, aided perhaps by more strongly competitive markets. But the question remains—might different policies have made the cost of adjustment lower.

V.2   Policy and the European Community[1]

Whatever may be the merits or demerits of past monetary and fiscal policy, there is no doubt that the UK is, and has been, affected by the moves to establish economic and monetary union amongst the members of the EEC. Some twelve years ago this was envisaged as involving absolutely fixed exchange-rate margins, or, alternatively and preferably, a single Community currency and the establishment of a Community system for the central banks of the member countries, possibly along the lines of the Federal Reserve System of the United States and with analogous powers. The harmonized management of national budgets was also envisaged as taking place under the auspices of a Community decision-making body which would have authority to influence member countries' levels of revenue and expenditure, as well as the methods employed to finance deficits and the disposal of surpluses.[2]

However, these far-reaching proposals received a cool response from member countries and little progress was made towards implementing them. But more recently the matter was again taken up by the Community and eventually led to the establishment of the European Monetary System (EMS).

---

1   See also chapter 3, section III.7.

2   *Report to the Council and the Commission on the Realization by Stages of Economic and Monetary Union in the Community*, Werner Report, Supplement to *Bulletin* 11/1970 of the European Communities.

The EMS came into operation in March 1979 and is designed, in the words of the European Council, 'to establish a greater measure of monetary stability in the Community'.[1] One of the basic features of the EMS is the agreement between the fully participating members to maintain their exchange rates, except for Italy, within ±2¼% of agreed central rates. Italy was allowed a margin of ±6% because its currency was floating at the time. The UK decided not to participate in the exchange-rate arrangements but is a party to other aspects of the scheme.

The participating members have found it necessary to realign their exchange rates on a number of occasions since the inauguration of the scheme, but despite these it is fairly claimed that the new arrangements have helped to stabilize exchange rates between the members. Whether or not they will be able to sustain this relative stability of exchange rates depends considerably on their ability to avoid substantially divergent inflation rates.

One of the implications of a strictly fixed exchange-rate relationship between currencies, according to the monetary approach to exchange-rate behaviour, is the need to ensure that monetary policies are consistent with its maintenance. This requires, in particular, that the money supply of the subordinate or satellite currencies should be geared to this end and in effect become endogenous, and that other policies, including fiscal policies, be similarly directed. Ideally these arrangements would be carried out by careful co-ordination of policies between the members, and this would certainly seem to be what the Community has in mind. For the European Council has stated that 'The European Monetary System will facilitate the convergence of economic development and give fresh impetus to the process of European Union.'[2] It still remains to be seen if the Community will be able to achieve the kind of co-ordination required and if the UK will become a full participant of the EMS.

V.3   Conclusions

The monetary and financial sectors of the UK economy have developed enormously over the last twenty years in terms of the number and range of the institutions involved. The processes of development and change can be expected to continue under the twin spurs of growing competition, both domestic and international, and technological innovation. The authorities will continue to be faced with the erosion of what formerly seemed to be clear-cut distinctions between one type of institution and another—such as used to be broadly true of the banks and the building societies—posing searching questions about the effective implementation of both monetary and prudential controls.

The policy record of the UK for the period since the 1960s has been disappointing. The simultaneous achievement of the various goals over a sustained period has continuously eluded the authorities. This failure or relative failure raises far-reaching questions about the choice of policy goals, the nature and adequacy of the policy instruments at the disposal of the authorities, and the limitations on our knowledge of the detailed and interdependent relationships between goals,

---

1 *European Economy*, Commission of the European Communities, No. 2, March 1979, p. 7. See also chapter 3, section III.7, on this whole subject.

2 *European Economy*, ibid.

instruments and targets. Moreover, these questions ultimately go far beyond the realm of economic considerations.

The discussion in section V.1 suggests that policy errors and misjudgements have contributed significantly to the economic problems of the UK. Both monetary and fiscal policy have from time to time been used in ways which could only be expected to give rise to future economic problems; the monetary and budgetary policies of the early to mid-1970s come particularly to mind, and, to a lesser extent, the policies pursued in 1977 and 1978. However, there seems to be a greater acceptance across a range of political opinion that rapid and variable inflation imposes serious costs on the community, putting at risk both employment and living standards; and that both monetary and fiscal policy can be managed in ways that contribute to its curtailment. The reduction in inflation since 1980 is encouraging, as is the recovery of output since 1981, though the problem of persistent unemployment remains. The fundamental policy dilemma is to try to quicken economic growth and reduce unemployment whilst continuing to curtail inflation. Sound monetary and fiscal policies can help this process but more is required; greater economic efficiency and more competitive markets, including labour markets, are also essential. But the latter relate to the supply side of the economy which is the primary concern of other chapters.

REFERENCES AND FURTHER READING

M.J. Artis and M.K. Lewis, *Monetary Control in the United Kingdom*, Phillip Allan, 1981.
A.D. Bain, *The Economics of the Financial System*, Martin Robertson, 1981.
Bank of England Quarterly Bulletin.
Committee to Review the Functioning of Financial Institutions (Wilson Committee), *Report*: Appendices, Cmnd. 7937, HMSO, June 1980.
Corporation Tax (Green Paper), Cmnd. 8456, HMSO, January 1982.
C.A.E. Goodhart, *Monetary Theory and Practice: The UK Experience*, Macmillan, 1983.
David Gowland, *Controlling the Money Supply*, Croom Helm, 1982.
M.A. King and J.A. Kay, *The British Tax System*, 3rd edition, Oxford University Press, 1983.
D.T. Llewellyn, G.E.J. Dennis, M.J. Hall, and J.G. Nellis, *The Framework of UK Monetary Policy*, Heinemann Educational Books, 1982.
Monetary Control (Green Paper), Cmnd. 7858, HMSO, March 1980.
A.R. Prest and N.A. Barr, *Public Finance in Theory and Practice*, 6th edition, Weidenfeld and Nicolson, 1979.
The Structure and Reform of Direct Taxation, Report of a Committee chaired by Professor J.E. Meade, Allen and Unwin, 1978.
Treasury and Civil Service Committee, *Memoranda on Monetary Policy*, House of Commons, Session 1979-80, 720, July 1980; 720-II, November 1980, HMSO 1980.
Treasury and Civil Service Committee, *Monetary Policy*, Vol. I: *Report*; Vol. II: *Minutes of Evidence*; Vol. III: *Appendices*, House of Commons, Session 1980-81, 163-I, III, HMSO, 1981.
D. Swann, *The Common Market*, 4th edition, Penguin Books, 1978.

3

Foreign trade and the balance of payments

J.S. Metcalfe

I THE UK BALANCE OF PAYMENTS
I.I Introduction

The importance to the UK of foreign trade, foreign investment and the balance of international payments will be obvious to anyone who has followed the course of events since 1960. The growth of the UK economy, the level of employment, real wages and the standard of living have been, and will continue to be, greatly influenced by external economic events. It is the purpose of this chapter to outline the main features of the external relationships of the UK and to discuss economic policies adopted to manipulate these external relationships, with the primary focus of attention being on the years since 1960.[1]

To begin with, it is often said that the UK is a highly 'open' economy, and some indication of the meaning of this is given by the fact that, in 1983, exports of goods and services were 30.9% of GDP and imports of goods and services were 29.5% of GDP, both figures being greater than the corresponding figures for the mid-1960s and substantially greater than those for 1938.[2] A high degree of openness implies that the structure of production and employment is greatly influenced by international specialization. For the UK it also means that about 36% of the foodstuffs and the bulk of raw materials necessary to maintain inputs for industry have to be imported. In the sense defined, the UK is a more open economy than some industrial nations, e.g. West Germany and France, but less open than others such as Belgium.

I.2 The Concept of the Balance of Payments

The concept of the balance of payments is central to a study of the external monetary relationships of a country but, as with any unifying concept, it is not free from ambiguities of definition and of interpretation. Such ambiguities stem from at least two sources, *viz.* the different uses to which the concept may be put − either as a tool for economic analysis or as a guide to the need for and effectiveness of external policy changes; and the different ways in which we may approach the concept − either as a system of accounts or as a measure of transactions in the foreign-exchange market.

---

1 Earlier editions of this volume contain a discussion of external developments between 1945 and 1960. See, e.g., the 5th edition (1974).

2 In 1938 the export:GNP ratio stood at 14%, and the import:GNP ratio at 18.9%.

From an accounting viewpoint, we may define the balance of payments as a systematic record, over a given period of time, of all transactions between domestic residents and residents of foreign nations. In this context, residents are defined as those individuals living in the UK for one year or more, together with corporate bodies located in the UK, and UK government agencies and military forces located abroad. Ideally, the transactions involved should be recorded at the time of the change of ownership of commodities and assets, or at the time specific services are performed. In practice, trade flows are recorded on a shipments basis, at the time when the export documents are lodged with the Customs and Excise, and at the time when imports are cleared through Customs. The problem with this method is that the time of shipment need bear no close or stable relationship to the time of payment for the goods concerned, and it is this latter which is relevant to the state of the foreign-exchange market, although over a year the discrepancies between the two methods are likely to be small. All transactions are recorded as sterling money flows, and when transactions are invoiced in foreign currencies their values are converted into sterling at the appropriate exchange rate. Because sterling is a 'key' or 'vehicle' currency, and is used as an international medium of exchange, it transpires that 76% of UK exports and roughly 38% of UK imports were invoiced directly in sterling.[1]

Like all systems of income and expenditure accounts, the balance-of-payments accounts are an *ex-post* record, constructed on the principle of double-entry bookkeeping. Thus, each external transaction is effectively entered twice, once to indicate the original transaction, say the import of a given commodity, and again to indicate the manner in which that transaction was financed. The convention is that credit items, which increase net money claims on foreign residents, e.g. exports of goods and services and foreign investment in the UK, are entered with a positive sign, and that debit items, which increase net money liabilities of domestic residents, e.g. imports of goods and services and profits earned by foreign owned firms operating in the UK, are entered with a minus sign. It follows that, in sum, the balance-of-payments accounts always balance and that the interpretation to be read into the accounts depends on the prior selection of a particular sub-set of transactions. It will be clear, therefore, that there can be no unique picture of a country's external relationships which may be drawn from the accounts.

When analysing the balance of payments, it can be useful to make a distinction between autonomous external transactions, transactions undertaken for private gain or international political obligation, and accommodating external transactions, transactions undertaken or induced specifically to finance a gap between autonomous credits and autonomous debits. This distinction is by no means watertight, as we shall see subsequently, but it provides a useful starting point when structuring the accounts and when trying to formulate notions of balance of payments equilibrium.

The structure of the external accounts of the UK: It is current practice to divide the external accounts of the UK into three sets of items: (i) current-account items; (ii) capital-account items; (iii) official financing items. Current-account items and all, or part (depending on taste), of capital-account items can as a first

---

1 Cf. the article by S.A. Page, 'The Choice of Invoicing Currency in Merchandise Trade', *NIER*, No. 98, 1981.

approximation be treated as if they correspond to autonomous external trans-actions. The structure of the external accounts and figures for the period 1979–83 are shown in table 3.1.[1]

Current-account items consist of exports and imports of commodities (visibles) and services (invisibles, e.g. insurance, shipping, tourist and banking transactions), profit and interest payments received from abroad less similar payments made abroad, certain government transactions, e.g. maintenance of armed forces over-seas, and specified transfer payments, e.g. immigrants' remittances, payments to and from the EEC budget and foreign aid granted by the UK government. The rationale for collecting these items together is that the majority of them are directly related to flows of national income and expenditure, whether public or private. In particular, visible and invisible trade flows are closely related to move-ments in foreign and domestic incomes, the division of these incomes between expenditure and saving, and the division of expenditure between outlays on foreign goods and services and outlays on domestic goods and services. It should be remembered, however, that trade flows may change not because of changes in incomes, but because of spending out of past savings (dishoarding) or because of the need to build up inventories of means of production, changes which correspond to variations in holdings of assets. Profit and interest flows are classified in the current account because they correspond directly to international flows of income.

Capital-account items can be arranged in several ways. One may distinguish official capital flows (line 3) from private capital flows (e.g. lines 4, 5 and 6). Alternatively, one may classify by the maturity date of the assets involved and distinguish long-term capital flows (e.g. lines 3–6 inclusive) from short-term capital flows (e.g. lines 7–14 inclusive). Equally one could, in principle, distinguish capital flows according to the implicit time-horizon of the investor undertaking the appropriate decisions. The inevitable limitations of alternative classificatory schemes should not be allowed to hide one basic point, that all capital flows corres-pond to changes in the stocks of foreign assets and liabilities of the UK, although not necessarily to changes in the net external wealth of the UK. As such, these capital flows are motivated primarily by the relative rates of return on domestic and foreign assets after due allowance is made for the effects of risk and taxation. Flows of direct and portfolio investment in productive capital assets (lines 5 and 6) thus depend on prospective rates of profit in the UK compared to those abroad, and changes in holdings of financial assets depend on relative domestic and foreign interest-rate structures. A relative increase in UK profit and interest rates will normally stimulate a larger net capital inflow or a smaller net capital outflow, and vice versa for a relative fall in UK profit and interest rates. One important factor which should not be overlooked here, is the influence of anticipated exchange-rate changes upon the capital gains and losses accruing to holdings of assets denominated in different currencies. If a sterling depreciation is anticipated, for example, this will provide a powerful incentive for wealth-holders to switch any sterling-denominated assets they hold into foreign-currency-denominated assets, in order to avoid the expected capital losses on holdings of sterling assets.[2] The

---

1 For further details the reader may consult the *UK Balance of Payments 1983*, HMSO 1984. This annual publication is known as the *Pink Book*.

2 Subject to the possibility that forward exchange cover may have been taken.

TABLE 3.1

UK Summary Balance of Payments 1979-1983 (£m)

		1979	1980	1981	1982	1983
Current account (credit +/debit −)						
Exports (fob) (+)		40,687	47,422	50,977	55,565	60,658
Imports (cif) (−)		44,136	45,909	47,325	53,181	61,158
Visible-trade balance		−3,449	+1,513	+3,652	+2,384	−500
Government services and transfers (net)		−2,800	−2,456	−2,215	−2,642	−2,901
Other invisibles and transfers (net)		+5,696	+4,773	+5,835	+6,259	+5,450
Invisible-trade balance		+2,896	+2,137	+3,620	+3,617	+2,549
Current balance	1	−553	+3,650	+7,272	+5,551	+2,049
Capital transfers	2	−	−	−	−	−
Investment and other capital flows:						
Official long-term capital	3	−401	−91	−336	−337	−562
Overseas investment in UK public sector[1]	4	+902	+589	+188	+320	+693
Overseas investment in UK private sector	5	+3,381	+4,619	+3,270	+3,289	+5,712
UK private investment overseas	6	−6,802	−8,033	−10,670	−10,872	−10,895
Overseas currency borrowing (net) by UK banks	7	+1,623	+2,054	+1,462	+4,271	+1,104
Exchange reserves in sterling:						
British Government stocks	8	+247	+945	+267	−52	+284
Banking and money market liabilities	9	+509	+317	−118	+438	+726
Other external banking and money market liabilities in sterling	10	+2,580	+2,558	+2,607	+4,134	+3,203
External sterling lending by UK banks	11	+205	−2,500	−2,954	−3,299	−1,440
Import credit	12	+64	−254	+122	−224	−63
Export credit	13	−856	−902	−969	−1,165	−1,461
Other short-term flows[2]	14	+383	−757	−221	+239	+655
Total investment and other capital flows	15	+1,835	−1,455	−7,352	−3,258	−2,044
Balancing item	16	+428	−1,003	−765	−3,577	−821
Balance for Official Financing	17	+1,710	+1,192	−845	−1,284	−816
Allocation of SDRs and gold subscriptions to IMF	18	+195	+180	+158	−	−
Total lines 17-18	19	+1,905	+1,372	−687	−1,284	−816
Official financing						
Net transactions with IMF	20	−596	−140	−145	−163	−36
Net transactions with overseas monetary authorities plus foreign borrowing by HM government[3]	21	−250	−312	−353	+26	+249
Drawing on (+)/additions to (−) official reserves	22	−1,059	−291	+2,419	+1,421	+603
Total Official Financing	23	−1,905	−1,372	+687	+1,284	+816

Source: *ET*, March 1984.

Notes: 1 Excludes foreign-currency borrowing by the public sector under the exchange cover scheme.
2 Includes other external borrowing and lending.
3 Includes foreign-currency borrowing by the public sector under the exchange cover scheme.

'capital value' effect is particularly important in inducing changes in the flow of short-term capital.

It is worth commenting at this stage upon lines 8, 9 and 10, which correspond to changes in sterling balances. Sterling balances arose out of the key currency role of sterling which led to private traders and foreign banks holding working balances in sterling, and which also led governments to hold part of their official exchange reserves in sterling. This latter aspect was particularly important for the overseas sterling area (OSA) countries who traditionally maintained their domestic currencies rigidly tied to sterling, maintained the bulk of their foreign-exchange reserves in sterling, and pooled any earnings of gold and non-sterling currencies in London in exchange for sterling balances. Furthermore, between 1940 and 1958, OSA countries were linked to the UK through a tightly knit system of exchange controls which discriminated against transactions with non-sterling area (NSA) countries, and especially those in the dollar area. The sterling area was effectively a currency union which allowed members to economize on their total holdings of gold and non-sterling currency reserves. One important consequence of this was that the sterling-area system created substantial holdings of UK liabilities to foreigners which had no maturity date and which could be liquidated at a moment's notice, so forming a permanent fund of contingent claims on the UK gold and foreign-currency reserves. OSA countries could acquire sterling balances in the following three ways: by having a current-account surplus with the UK; as the result of a net inflow of foreign investment from the UK; and from pooling in the UK any gold and foreign currency earned from transactions with NSA countries.

At the beginning of World War II, the total of sterling balances stood at approximately £500m; by the end of the war they had risen to £3.7bn, around which figure they fluctuated between 1945 and 1966. In contrast to the stability in the total quantity of sterling balances, there were marked changes in the country composition; some countries, e.g. India and Pakistan, ran down their wartime accumulation of balances, while other countries, e.g. some Middle East countries, acquired new holdings of sterling balances.[1] The continued existence of the sterling-area financial arrangements depended upon two conditions being satisfied. Firstly, the OSA countries required to have a high proportion of their transactions with each other and with the UK. Secondly, there had to be a continued confidence in the ability of the UK, in its role of banker to the OSA, to match short-term sterling liabilities with an equivalent volume of official reserves or other short-term assets. From 1958 onwards, neither of these conditions was satisfied. The OSA countries began to transact more intensively with NSA countries, and the UK moved into a position of seemingly permanent deficit on her basic balance, thus increasing short-term liabilities relative to official reserves and other short-term assets and creating the conditions for the sterling crises which became frequent in the 1960s.[2] It was not unexpected, therefore, when the sterling area

---

1 Detailed information on this may be found in Susan Strange, *Sterling and British Policy*, Oxford, 1971, Chapters 2 and 3.

2 If official short-term and medium-term foreign borrowing by the UK government is subtracted from the official exchange reserves, this gives a measure of 'cover' for the sterling liabilities. In 1962 the ratio of 'cover' to total sterling liabilities was 51%. By end 1967, the 'cover' had disappeared entirely and outstanding official borrowing exceeded the official reserves by £3.8bn.

effectively ceased to exist in June 1972.[1]

We come next to the balancing item (line 16), which is a statistical item to compensate for the total of measurement errors and omissions in the accounts, arising from, for example, the under-recording of exports and the reliance upon survey data for certain items such as foreign investment and tourist expenditure. A positive balancing item can reflect an unrecorded net export, an unrecorded net capital inflow, or some combination of the two. The major source of changes in the balancing item is likely to be unrecorded changes in net trade credit, reflecting discrepancies between the time goods are shipped and the time when the associated payments are made across the exchanges. As can be seen from table 3.1, the balancing item is very volatile and can on occasions, e.g. in 1982 or 1983, be of a magnitude far greater than the surplus or deficit on visible trade. The total of investment and other capital transactions together with the balancing item is known as the balance for official financing (BOF, line 17), which can, in principle, be treated as the net balance of autonomous transactions.[2] Before we come to accommodating transactions, two adjustments to the BOF have to be made in line 18, both of which relate to the UK's membership of the IMF. First, we have the allocation of special drawing rights which is treated as a credit item since it effectively adds to the official reserves of the UK (line 22). Secondly, we have the UK's reserve tranche subscription to the IMF. When the UK's IMF general quota is increased, the UK is obliged to subscribe 25% of the increase to the IMF in the form of SDRs or other convertible foreign exchange (up to April 1978 this subscription was paid in gold and the reserve tranche was known as the gold tranche) and the official reserves fall by the corresponding amount. The corresponding item in line 18 is the requisite double entry to balance the accounts and may be treated as the acquisition of assets at the IMF.

The total of lines 17-18, the *adjusted balance for official financing* (line 19), has to be matched by an equal amount of official financing. If, for any one year, line 19 has a negative sign, then the authorities must reduce the official external assets or increase the official external liabilities of the UK, undertaking the reverse operations if line 19 is positive in sign. There are three ways in which the necessary adjustments can be made. First, the UK may draw upon or add to the official gold and currency reserves (line 22). Over the period 1970-76, the average annual value of the UK's gross reserves was $5.41bn, but since then they have increased fourfold with an average value for 1979-83 of $21.6bn. During the period since 1970, the composition of the reserves has also altered considerably, through policy decisions and changes in the market values of the various assets. At end-1970 the reserves consisted of 48% gold, 43% convertible currencies and 9% SDRs. However, by December 1983, the gold portion had fallen to 33% and the convertible currency portion had risen to 51%. During 1979, the basis on which the gold and SDR portions of the reserves are to be valued was changed to a market-price-related basis. Since then, the gold reserves have been revalued annually

---

1 Prior to 1972, the OSA consisted of the Commonwealth, except Canada, and South Africa, Iceland, Ireland, Kuwait, Jordan and some others. Before June 1972, these countries were known as the scheduled territories but after June 1972 only Ireland and Gibraltar remained in this category. The demise of exchange control in October 1979 has formally ended the OSA, NSA distinction.

2 Prior to 1976, this measure of external transactions was known as the total currency flow.

according to a formula based on the average London fixing price in the three months prior to March. Similarly, SDRs are now valued at their average dollar exchange rate in the three months to end-March. Both these valuation rules are subject to annual revision. At end-1983, SDRs accounted for only 4% of UK reserves. Over the period 1979–83, the UK reserves averaged 18% of total imports, the ratio of reserves to total imports reaching a peak of 22% in 1977. As a second line of defence, the UK can borrow foreign currencies from the IMF. An amount equal to 25% of the UK's quota may be borrowed automatically, the so-called reserve tranche position which is classed as part of the official reserves.[1] The UK has further access to four credit tranches, each of which corresponds to 25% of quota, but access is dependent upon the UK government adopting economic policies which meet with the approval of the IMF, this being particularly so for drawings beyond the first credit tranche. The maximum amount the UK could borrow at year-end 1983, including the reserve tranche position, stood at SDR 8.8bn. The points to remember about IMF finance are that it is temporary (borrowings have to be repaid within 3–5 years), conditional, and cheap, relative to current commercial rates of interest. Finally, the UK has access to a considerable network of borrowing facilities built up with foreign central banks in the 1960s, primarily as a short-term defence against speculative capital flows. These have proved to be of considerable value to the UK, and have been supplemented since 1973 by direct government borrowing, mostly from the Eurodollar market.

It may already be apparent that the distinction between autonomous and accommodating transactions, upon which this discussion is based, is not entirely satisfactory. For example, by manipulating UK interest rates, the government can create an inflow of short-term capital to accommodate a given current-account deficit, even though from the point of view of individuals or banks buying and selling the assets, the transactions are autonomous. Similarly, autonomous government items such as foreign aid may be deliberately adjusted to accommodate a deficit elsewhere in the accounts. At a more general level, whenever the government adopts policies to change the balance of payments, the effects of these policies will influence the totals of autonomous transactions so that they cease to be independent of the underlying state of the balance of payments. Despite these difficulties, the autonomous-accommodating distinction provides a useful starting point for any arrangement of the external accounts.

So far we have examined the external accounts in isolation, but they may equally be examined as an integral part of the national income and expenditure accounts.

From this viewpoint, the balance-of-payments deficit (surplus) on current account is identically equal to the excess (shortfall) of national expenditure over national income and hence to the reduction (increase) in the net external assets owned by UK residents. It follows that the UK can only add to its external net assets to the extent that it has an equivalent current-account surplus.

Finally, we should note that, although the accounts separate current-account items from capital-account items, there are several important links between the two sub-sets of transactions. We have already pointed out that a non-zero current

---

1 Automatic borrowing can exceed the reserve tranche position to the extent that the total IMF holding of sterling falls below 75% of the UK quota.

account results in changes in the net external assets of the UK. As these assets and liabilities have profit and interest flows attached to them, any change in the total of external net assets will feed back into changes in the interest, profit and dividend flows which appear in the current account. Furthermore, because they also result in equivalent changes in national income, they will affect the current account indirectly through any effects on national expenditure and the demand for imports. Similarly, within the context of a given current-account position, capital flows which change the composition of external net assets will change the average rate of return on these assets and so react back on the current account. These are perhaps the more straightforward links, but others exist, for example between trade flows and the balance of export and import credit and between trade and investment flows and changes in total sterling balances. As has often been said, the balance of payments is a seamless web and it can be grossly misleading to treat individual items in isolation from the rest of the accounts.

I.3   Equilibrium and Disequilibrium in the Balance of Payments

It is obviously important, both for purposes of economic policy and historical analysis, to have clear notions of balance-of-payments equilibrium and disequilibrium. However, the formulation of such concepts is not easy and depends upon the exchange-rate regime which is in operation. It is tempting to begin by defining balance-of-payments equilibrium as a situation in which, at the existing exchange rate, autonomous credits are equal to autonomous debits and no official financing transactions are required. Unfortunately, this definition raises more questions than it answers. The time-span over which equilibrium is defined is obviously important. A daily or even monthly span of time would be of little value and it is generally accepted that a sufficient span of years should be allowed so that the effects of cyclical fluctuations in income will have no appreciable net impact on external transactions. However, if the exchange rate is allowed to fluctuate freely to equate the demand with the supply of foreign exchange, then equilibrium is always attained automatically, and any notion of payments disequilibrium based on a discrepancy between demand and supply of foreign exchange becomes redundant. By contrast, if the exchange rate is managed in some way to make it partially or completely independent of market forces, we must then accept that policies can be adopted to manipulate autonomous transactions in such a way as to make them balance over any given period of time. The problem which this raises is that the attainment of external equilibrium, at a given exchange rate, may involve unacceptable levels of employment or inflation, an interest-rate structure which is counter to economic-growth objectives and a trade policy inconsistent with international obligations.

Since 1972, successive UK governments have allowed sterling to float but subject to a variable degree of exchange-market intervention. The problems of balance-of-payments disequilibrium which troubled governments in the 1960s have been avoided, and, as we shall see in section III, the general movement of the exchange rate has been in line with the principle of purchasing-power parity. Nonetheless, it is still of some interest to focus attention on particular groups of transactions within the accounts which provide particularly important economic information. Of central interest is the balance on current account, since the UK is adding to its net external wealth whenever this is positive. Within the current account, the balances of trade in goods and in services provide an important indication of trends in the UK's position in international competition. If attention is directed to other items in the accounts, we find additional clues on the changes in the external capital structure of the UK.

The basic balance, defined as the sum of the current account and the net flow of long-term capital, attracts attention on several grounds, not least as one indicator of secular trends in external transactions. If the basic balance is zero, any net outflow (inflow) of long-term capital corresponds to an equivalent increase in the stock of external assets (liabilities) of the UK. Furthermore, all net flows of short-term capital must be matched by equivalent offsetting changes in official financing. Thus, the basic balance puts below the line all capital flows essentially related to the role of the UK as an international banking and financing centre; capital flows which may be particularly sensitive to accommodating monetary manipulation and speculation on short-run movements in the exchange rate.

Although sterling has floated against all currencies since June 1972, this does not mean that at each moment in time the net balance of autonomous transactions has been zero, as table 3.1 illustrates. In these circumstances, the BOF is an appropriate indicator of the balance of autonomous pressures on the exchange rate. In contrast to the basic balance, this places all short-term capital flows above the line, so that a zero BOF corresponds to a situation of constancy in the total of officially held external net assets. There are several arguments in favour of the BOF, *viz.* (i) many short-term capital flows are linked to items in the trade balance, e.g. trade credit, or to the financing of long-term investment, and cannot sensibly be separated from items in the basic balance; (ii) short-term private capital flows are inherently volatile and, therefore, they provide poor accommodation; and (iii) the BOF avoids the problem of separating the balancing item from the basic balance, with the attendant danger of a misleading treatment of any errors and omissions. In the short term, of course, the BOF is more volatile than the basic balance, but over the longer run, the two measures should coincide, provided that short-term flows net out to zero. A further advantage of the BOF is that it shows the potential increase (decrease) in the UK money supply as a result of a surplus (deficit) in the aggregate of autonomous balance-of-payments transactions.

I.4   The Balance of Payments 1961–83

We now turn to assess the balance-of-payments performance of the UK since 1961. To assist in this, table 3.2 contains average annual figures for selected items in the balance of payments in the periods 1961-4, 1965-7, 1968-71, 1972-8 and 1979-82, with 1983 entered separately for comparative purposes. The first sub-period covers a complete short cycle ending in a boom year, while the remaining four are somewhat arbitrary and may be separated in the reader's mind by the 1967 devaluation, the floating of sterling in June 1972, and the second oil price increase in 1979. The averages, of course, hide substantial annual variations but they will suffice for present purposes.

In the *Brookings Report*, R. Cooper suggested that the UK balance-of-payments position, at least up to 1966, could be summarized in terms of four propositions: (i) the UK is normally a net exporter of long-term capital, with a surplus on the current account; (ii) the visible trade balance is normally in deficit, but the invisible balance shows a surplus more than sufficient to offset this; (iii) the role of the UK

TABLE 3.2

Trends in the UK Balance of Payments, Annual Average for Selected Periods (£m) and Average Growth Rates for UK Real GDP amd World Exports of Manufacturers

	1961-4	1965-7	1968-71	1972-8	1979-82	1983
1 Visible balance	−226	−322	−191	−2,825	+728	−500
Balance on NS oil	−	−	−	−2,676	+1,825	+7,002
2 Govt. services and transfers net	−377	−459	−485	−1,251	−2,528	−4,018
Net transfers to EEC	−	−	−	−282	−772	−827
3 Private invisibles, transfers, IPD	+595	+725	+1,228	+3,337	+5,427	+6,567
4 Invisible balance	+218	+266	+743	+2,086	+2,899	+2,549
5 Current balance	−8	−56	+552	−739	+3,627	+2,049
6 Balancing item	−35	+35	+25	+654	−902	−821
7 Balance of long-term capital	−139	−161	−223	−345	−5,224	−5,052
8 Balance of total capital flows	−183	−506	+350	+412	−3,185	−2,044
9 Basic balance (5+7)	−147	−217	+329	−1,084	−1,597	−3,003
10 Basic balance + balancing item (9+6)	−182	−182	+354	−430	−2,499	−3,824
11 Balance for official financing (5+6+8)	−226	−527	+927	+327	−460	−816
12 Gold subs to IMF and SDRs	−	−15	+65	+18	+133	−
13 Total (11+12)	−226	−538	+992	+345	−327	−816
Official Financing						
14 Net foreign-currency borrowing by HMG	+144	+420	−594	+425	−296	+213
15 Transfer from $ portfolio	−	+173	−	−	−	−
16 Drawing on(+) or additions to(−) official resources	+82	−55	−398	−770	+623	+603
17 Total (14−16)	+226	+538	−992	−345	+327	+816
18 Average annual growth, UK real GDP, %	3.30	1.86	2.56	2.10	−0.08	3.01
19 Av. annual growth, volume world exports of manufactures, %	7.95	6.77	11.45	5.64	2.10	1.98

Sources: ET, March 1984, and *AAS*, various.

as a banker to the OSA and to the world financial community in general gives volatile short-term capital flows an important position in the balance of payments; and finally, (iv) the trading, investing and international financial activities of the UK are carried out with a very inadequate underpinning of foreign-exchange reserves.[1]

Certainly, the years 1956-60 discussed by Professor Cooper fit into this pattern, with an average annual long-term capital outflow of £189m offset by a current-account surplus of £149m per annum and a net short-term capital inflow of £53m p.a. After taking account of the balancing item and other factors, the UK was able to add to its reserves at an annual rate of £79m. Some of these characteristics have

---

1   R. Caves (ed.), *Britain's Economic Prospects*, Allen and Unwin, 1968, chapter 3.

also extended into the period to 1982, as table 3.2 indicates. The visible balance is generally in deficit and the total invisible balance in surplus, despite a growing deficit on government services and transfers to which a substantial contribution is made by EEC transfers. The chief source of the strength of the invisible balance has been the growing surplus on trade in services, rather than a surplus on interest, profits and dividends, though this does make a positive but declining contribution to the invisible balance. From line 7 we see that the UK has maintained its position as a long-term capital exporter, while line 8 and its differences from line 7 indicates the volatility and magnitude of short-term capital flows. The surplus on the visible balance between 1979 and 1982 is clearly a reflection of North Sea oil exploitation, and to this extent it is a temporary phenomenon, as the figure for 1983 perhaps illustrates.

In other dimensions the traditional picture has ceased to be applicable. The first two columns of table 3.2 indicate an unmistakeable slide into fundamental disequilibrium at the prevailing exchange rate, in terms of the current-account deficit and the basic balance. The chief proximate source of this deterioration was the worsening balance of visible trade which occurred despite the rapid growth in the volume of world trade in manufactures. A reduction in the net long-term capital outflow, relative to that of the late 1950s, helped cushion the basic balance but the improvement here was more than offset by the short-term capital outflows during the sterling crises of 1961, 1964 and each of the three subsequent years. The deficit in the BOF is reflected in reserve losses, the incurring of substantial foreign debts and the liquidation (in 1967) of the government's portfolio of dollar securities.

The inevitable devaluation, which took place in November 1967, was followed by a remarkable turn-around in the external payments position, although it is not completely clear to what extent this is attributable to the devaluation alone, to the contemporaneous acceleration in the growth of world trade or, indeed, to measures to restrict demand growth and money-supply growth after 1968 (between 1969 and 1971 the average rate of growth of real GDP fell to 1.70%). During this period of severe domestic restraint, the visible deficit was almost halved which, when combined with the continuing increase in the invisible surplus, resulted in the current account moving back into substantial surplus. Though the net outflow of long-term capital also increased during this period, this was not sufficient to prevent a very strong position emerging in the basic balance, especially when account is taken of the balancing item. Furthermore, confidence in sterling returned after 1968, no doubt helped by the Basle Arrangements of that year, and short-term capital flowed back into the UK at an identified annual average rate of £573m. So strong was the improvement in the payments position, that the UK was able to repay a substantial part of the debts raised in defence of sterling in the previous two periods and, at the same time, add to the official reserves. It cannot be claimed that this period saw a return to equilibrium in the external accounts, simply because of the severe restraint on domestic growth which took place. However, it can at least be argued that the foundations were laid for a return to equilibrium once the foreign debts had been repaid.

With the benefit of hindsight, it is clear that the years 1968-71 marked a watershed in the balance-of-payments performance of the UK. The subsequent decade is played out within an entirely different international economic environment from that which formed the postwar framework. With the adoption of a floating exchange rate in 1972, the rules of balance-of-payments management changed drastically, while the increases in the real price of oil in 1973 and 1979 resulted in major disruption to the postwar system of international trade and investment. Indeed, the world recession which followed the 1979 oil price increase was associated with a decline in world trade volume of 2.8% between 1981 and 1983. The resulting sharp deterioration which occurred in the UK visible balance during the years 1972-8 is clearly illustrated in table 3.2, with average deficits of quite unprecedented magnitude. Even the record invisible surpluses of this period could not prevent the average current-account deficit reaching £0.74bn. Capital outflows added to the basic-balance deficit despite the growth in private imports of long-term capital (primarily to exploit North Sea oil and gas resources). To accommodate the negative balance of official financing, the governments of the period quite sensibly drew on the reserves and engaged in substantial foreign borrowing, effectively mortgaging a portion of anticipated future North Sea oil revenues. The current-account and basic-balance deficits were thus absorbed without an immediate cutback in output levels and the standard of living in the UK. This policy was not without its moments of difficulty as the events of 1976 and 1977 demonstrated. With overseas confidence weakened by the basic-balance position and the rapid rate of UK inflation, short-term capital flowed out of the UK on an unprecedented scale in 1976, placing substantial downward pressure on the exchange rate and resulting in heavy reserve losses. The official UK reserves fell from $7.20bn in February 1976 to $4.13bn at the end of that year, only to be replenished even more rapidly in 1977 following the successful negotiation of support from the IMF. By the end of 1977, the reserves had increased to a total of $20.5bn. The policy of official borrowing to finance the oil-related deficits resulted in total official foreign debts of $14.2bn at the end of 1976, of which $11.2bn was due for repayment by the end of 1984.[1]

By comparison, the period after the second oil price shock indicates a remarkable turnround in the external situation. The chief element here is, of course, the growth of production from the North Sea oil and gas fields and the effect on the visible trade balance. When combined with the ever-strengthening invisible balance – despite, we may note, the growth of net government transfers to the EEC amounting to £282m p.a. in 1972-8 and £772m p.a. in 1979-82 – we find a surplus on the current account of quite unprecedented magnitude. A second, but important, element from 1979 onwards was the rapid decline in UK industrial output and the associated reduction in inventory holdings, a factor which will be rapidly reversed if recovery continues after 1984. With respect to capital flows, the relaxation of exchange controls in 1979 clearly contributed to the tremendous outflow of long-term capital, while the petrocurrency status of sterling encouraged short-term inflows which offset some 40% of the longer-term outflows. Taking account of the balancing item, we can see that the basic balance has moved into a position of substantial deficit despite the surplus on current account. The negative balance of official financing in this period is reflected in a decline in the level of official reserves from a peak of $27.5bn at end-1980 to $17.8bn at end-1983. Part of the reserve loss reflects a reduction in official external debt of $5.5bn over the same period.

---

1 Cf. *BEQB*, March 1982, Appendix Table 17, and the article 'UK Official Short Term and Medium Term Borrowing from Abroad', *BEQB*, March 1976, pp. 76-81. Approximately $10.4bn represented public-sector borrowing under the exchange cover scheme introduced in 1973. The IMF standby arrangements and oil facility borrowings of early 1977 added a further $4.2bn to official debts.

The period since 1971 is clearly *sui-generis* as far as the balance of payments is concerned. Even though the exchange rate has been nominally free to float, it is clear that it has been actively managed since 1972 and that the fixed-rate system could not have coped with the strains of this period. Looking forward from 1983, the picture does not appear promising. The continuing competitive weakness of UK industry (discussed in section II) is reflected in the fact that the balance of trade in manufactures became negative for the first time ever in 1982 and, with the prospect of economic recovery, this situation is unlikely to improve, at least in the short term. Moreover, the marginal costs of oil extraction are rising sharply as less productive strata are exploited and this raises the prospect that the flow of production from the North Sea oilfields will decline from 1985 onwards. Once the underpinning of North Sea oil disappears, one may reasonably conjecture that the familiar questions of trade performance and an excessive propensity to export long-term capital will emerge again to dominate discussion of balance-of-payments policy, as they did in the 1960s.

I.5   North Sea Oil and Gas

Much recent economic policy discussion in the UK has been concerned with the economic effects of the exploitation of oil and gas resources in the North Sea. Although exploration began around 1960, the production of North Sea oil first became substantial in 1975 and self-sufficiency was reached during 1981. It is generally argued that the net effect on GDP will be relatively small, effectively offsetting the loss of real income imposed on the UK by the increase in the relative price of oil since 1973, and the direct effects on employment negligible.[1] However, the effects on the balance of payments and public-sector revenue are substantial. The major effect will, therefore, be to alter the environment in which economic policy is formulated and to underpin prospects of substantial real growth, unimpeded by trade-balance constraints, over the next decade. Section III.5 discusses some of the policy options opened up by North Sea oil. In this section, we briefly outline some calculations of the likely effects of North Sea oil upon the balance of payments and the difficulties surrounding such calculations.

The major difficulties relate to important areas of uncertainty, e.g. with respect to oil yields, trends in exploitation and development costs, the share of extractive equipment provided by UK firms and most importantly in the sterling price of oil. This latter element will depend jointly on the ability of the OPEC cartel to determine the future real increase in the dollar price of oil, a decision over which the UK as a minor world producer accounting for 5% of world production will have no influence, and upon the policies which the UK government adopts with respect to the exchange rate. The more sterling appreciates relative to the dollar, the smaller will be government tax revenue from the North Sea. Other aspects of government policy, as yet uncertain, will be of equal importance – in particular, the production and depletion policy adopted, whether it matches production to domestic demand or allows net exports of crude oil, and the levels of royalty and petroleum revenue tax charged, which will determine the proportion of profits left to the oil

---

1   At 1978 prices, North Sea oil and gas contributed gross some 7.3% extra to GDP in 1980, perhaps rising to 9.6% in 1985. *TER*, No. 112, August 1979.

producers for potential remission overseas. One further obvious difficulty is that the total benefits from North Sea oil to the balance of payments will not be independent of how the government feels able to exploit these benefits for domestic purposes.[1]

When calculating the direct impact of North Sea oil and gas on the UK balance of payments, account has to be taken of the following items. First, the net effect on the balance of trade in oil and gas as home output is exported or substituted for imports. Second, the net trade in equipment and technical services to discover and extract the oil and gas. Third, the inflows of foreign capital to finance extraction and development, and finally, the net flows of interest, profits and dividends, remitted overseas by the foreign-owned firms operating in the North Sea. It is worth remembering that the balance-of-payments effects of these operations began well before the flow of North Sea oil commenced. Thus, in the years 1973-6, total net imports of equipment and services to exploit North Sea resources amounted to £2.49bn, an amount which was almost covered by a cumulative net capital inflow of £2.38bn. During 1983, the contribution to the balance of official financing was made up as follows: balance-of-trade effects +£7.0bn, net IPD due overseas −£3.0bn, and capital inflow net of imports of goods and services to exploit North Sea resources +£0.18bn, to give a total effect on the BOF of +£4.18bn. The most recent calculations of the effect on the BOF in 1985 suggest a net oil- and gas-related contribution in the range £10.5bn to £15bn, though this figure is subject to all the previously noted uncertainties.[2]

To calculate the net contribution to the balance of payments is, of course, more difficult. With the exchange rate floating freely, an oil-wealth-induced appreciation will 'crowd out' exports of non-oil manufactures and services and stimulate competing imports to an extent which depends on the magnitude of the appreciation. This, in turn, depends upon the capital-movement effects of North Sea oil and gas and the extent to which the authorities wish to turn North Sea surpluses into foreign-exchange reserves. Tentative calculations would indicate that North Sea oil and gas activity had pushed the effective rate for sterling roughly ten to fifteen percentage points higher than the value it would otherwise have taken during the period.[3]

II   FOREIGN TRADE OF THE UK
II.1   Structure and Trends 1955-83

In this section, we shall examine the major structural features and trends in the

---

1   In particular, the exchange-rate policy adopted to accommodate North Sea oil is an important determinant of the total economic effect on government revenue and the balance of payments. For a useful account of the effect of different exchange-rate assumptions, see S.A.B. Page, 'The Value and Distribution of the Benefits of North Sea Oil and Gas, 1970-1985', *NIER*, No. 82, 1977, pp. 41-58.

2   Cf. 'NS Oil and Gas − Costs and Benefits', *BEQB*, March 1982. The figures quoted in this paragraph are at constant 1980 prices and are not directly comparable with estimates produced in Page, op. cit.

3   Cf. F.J. Atkinson *et al.*, 'The Economic Effects of North Sea Oil', *NIER*, No. 104, 1983, pp. 38-44.

foreign trade of the UK between 1955 and 1983.[1] In focusing attention upon certain longer-term trends, we will find evidence of a marked decline in the international competitive performance of UK manufacturing industry; a decline which, it may reasonably be claimed, is the proximate source of the unsatisfactory behaviour of the balance of payments noted in the previous section.

Geographical and commodity trade structure: The traditional picture of UK foreign trade was one in which manufactures were exchanged for imports of foodstuffs and raw materials, with the bulk of the trade being carried out with the Commonwealth and overseas sterling area countries. That this picture is now completely out of date is shown in tables 3.3, 3.4 and 3.5, which illustrate the radical changes in trading structure which have occurred in the quarter century since 1955. To some small extent, these changes reflect the relaxation of wartime import restrictions and the general postwar movement toward trade liberalization associated with the several rounds of GATT tariff reductions. But, in general, they are the outcome of more deep-seated changes in competitive forces.

The major changes in the geographic composition of UK trade are shown in table 3.3. Several general trends are immediately apparent. Compared to 1955, the following years show a decreased dependence on trade with developing countries, a trend which has been primarily at the expense of trade with the less developed members of the OSA,[2] and the four major Commonwealth nations, Canada, Australia, New Zealand and South Africa. An interesting development since 1970 is the increased importance, for obvious reasons, of the oil-exporting countries as a market for UK exports. The decline in their importance as a source of UK imports between 1980 and 1983 reflects the exploitation of the UK's North Sea oil resources. As far as trade with the developed nations is concerned, the most striking trend is the increasing importance of trade with the EEC. In 1972, the year prior to entry, the current nine EEC members accounted for approximately 30% of UK exports and imports, but by 1983 the export share had risen to 43.8% and the import share to 45.6%. The growing importance of Japan as a source of UK imports may also be noted. In broad terms, the EEC now occupies the same position in the UK trade structure that the Commonwealth countries occupied in 1955.

The switch towards a greater trade dependence on the industrialized, urbanized, high *per capita* income countries of Western Europe, Japan and North America has been matched, not unexpectedly, by significant changes in the commodity structure of UK trade, particularly in respect of imports. The changing structure of UK import trade is shown in table 3.4. Most important here is the increase in the proportion of imports of finished manufactures, the share of which increased eightfold between 1955 and 1983, and the decline in the proportion accounted for by

---

1 Since, over the period, some 65%-70% of total exports and imports reflected commodity transactions, we here concentrate solely on commodity trade. For a treatment of invisible items in the current account, see P. Phillips, 'A Forecasting Model for the United Kingdom Invisible Account', *NIER*, No. 69, 1974. Interest, profit and dividend flows are discussed in section III.7 below. For further details on invisibles, consult the COI pamphlet, *Britain's Invisible Exports*, HMSO, 1970.

2 In 1955, these countries provided 22.8% of UK imports and absorbed 21.6% of UK exports; the corresponding figures for 1977 were 6.3% and 9.4%.

TABLE 3.3

Area Composition of UK Merchandise Trade, Selected Years 1955–83 (percentages)

	Imports, c.i.f.				Exports, f.o.b.			
	1955	1970	1980	1983	1955	1970	1980	1983
Western Europe	25.7	41.5	55.9	61.4	28.9	46.2	57.6	56.2
EEC[1]	12.6	27.1	41.3	45.6	15.0	29.4	43.4	43.8
North America	19.5	20.5	15.0	13.7	12.0	15.2	11.2	15.4
USA	10.9	12.9	12.1	11.3	7.1	11.6	9.6	13.8
Other developed[2]	14.2	9.4	6.8	7.8	21.1	11.8	5.6	5.2
Japan	0.6	1.5	3.4	5.1	0.6	1.8	1.3	1.3
Total developed countries	59.4	71.4	77.7	82.9	62.0	73.2	74.5	76.8
Centrally planned economies	2.7	4.2	2.1	2.3	1.7	3.8	2.8	1.8
Oil-exporting countries	9.2	9.1	8.6	4.3	5.1	5.8	10.1	10.1
Other developing countries[3]	28.7	15.3	11.3	11.5	31.2	17.2	12.4	11.3
Total	100.0	100.0	100.0	100.0	100.0	100.0	100.0	100.0

Sources: AAS, MDS, various; TI, 16 March 1972.

Notes: 1 Excluding Greece.
2 Japan, plus Australia, New Zealand and South Africa.
3 Subject to minor changes in classification over time.

TABLE 3.4

Commodity Composition of UK Imports, Selected Years 1955-83 (percentages)

SITC Group	Description	1955	1970	1980	1983
0, 1	Food, Beverages, Tobacco	36.2	22.6	12.4	11.9
3	Fuel	10.4	10.4	13.8	10.7
2, 4, 5, 6	Industrial Materials and Semi-Manufactures	47.9	42.7	35.2	32.8
7, 8	Finished Manufactures	5.2	22.9	35.6	42.4
9	Unclassified	0.3	1.4	3.0	2.2
	Total	100.0	100.0	100.0	100.0

Source: AAS, MDS, various.
Imports are measured on an overseas trade statistics basis and are valued c.i.f.

foodstuffs, beverages and tobacco. Imports of finished and semi-manufactures now account for some 60% of total UK imports. This same trend has also been experienced by other EEC countries although it remains the case that the UK is more dependent upon imports of non-manufactures than are, for example, France or West Germany.[1] On the export side, table 3.5 shows that changes in structure

1   M. Panic, 'Why the UK's Propensity to Import is High', LBR, No. 115, 1975.

TABLE 3.5

Commodity Composition of UK Exports, Selected Years 1955-83 (percentages)

SITC	Description	1955	1970	1980	1983
7, 87	*Engineering Products*	36.9	43.6	37.5	32.7
	Machinery	21.1	27.4	25.3	21.3
	Road Motor Vehicles	8.9	10.7	6.7	5.1
	Other Transport Equipment	5.7	3.7	3.5	3.9
	Scientific Instruments	1.2	1.8	2.0	2.4
5, 65, 67-9	*Semi-Manufactures*	29.7	26.4	22.7	20.6
	Chemicals	7.8	9.5	11.2	11.4
	Textiles	10.1	5.1	2.9	2.1
	Metals	11.8	11.8	8.6	7.1
Remainder 6 and 8	*Other Semi-Manufactures and Manufactures*	12.6	14.7	13.4	12.7
0, 1, 2, 3, 4 and 9	*Non-Manufactures*	21.2	15.3	26.4	34.0
	Food, Beverages and Tobacco	6.5	6.3	6.9	7.0
	Basic Materials	5.6	3.0	3.1	2.5
	Fuels	4.6	2.6	13.6	21.7
	Others	4.5	3.4	2.8	2.8
Total		100.0	100.0	100.0	100.0

Source: AAS, MDS, various.

Exports are measured on an overseas trade statistics basis and valued f.o.b.

are less noticeable.

The most obvious trends are the declining shares of textiles and metals and less obviously of road motor vehicles and other transport equipment. Clearly, though, it is the increased share of fuel exports, predominantly North Sea oil related, which commands most attention, and this has largely been at the expense of the sectors noted above. It should also be pointed out that the share of machinery in total exports reached a peak of 30.4% in 1975 from which it had fallen substantially by 1983. The general weakness of the UK engineering sector is a matter of some concern given its dominant position in the UK export structure.

It will be apparent from this that UK trade is increasingly dominated by an exchange of manufactures for manufactures with the advanced industrialized nations. These structural changes would imply that UK manufacturing industry has experienced and will continue to experience greater foreign competition in home and export markets. They also help to explain the disintegration in the sterling-area system which occurred after 1964.

II.2   The Decline in Competitive Performance

The trend toward increasing visible-trade deficits, which became evident in the early 1960s, has rightly been taken as an indication of a widespread lack of competitive edge in UK industry relative to foreign industry. Evidence to support this view is provided by the progressive decline of the UK's share of world exports of manufactures[1] and by evidence of the increased import penetration of the UK market by foreign competitors. The net effect of these trends is to substantially limit the scope for the UK to grow without coming up against a balance-of-trade constraint. Thus, for example, a well-known study by Houthakker and Magee found a UK income elasticity of demand for imports of 1.66, double the corresponding world income elasticity of demand for UK exports of 0.86. Starting from balanced trade, these figures would suggest that the UK can only grow at half the world average rate if balanced trade is to be maintained.[2] Some further indication of the problem may be gained by the fact that between 1971 and 1980, when UK manufacturing production grew at an average annual rate of *0.7%*, the volume of exports of finished manufactures increased by an average of *3.36%* per annum, while the volume of imports of finished manufactures increased at an average annual rate of *13.4%*. A growth of imports of this magnitude, in the industries in which the UK's traditional comparative advantage is thought to lie, is obviously a serious matter. Indeed, it has prompted widespread fears of the imminent de-industrialization of the UK, with the manufacturing base so eroded by foreign competition that full employment and payments equilibrium cannot be achieved without a substantial reduction in real income.[3]

The statistics of the decline in the UK share of world exports of manufactures are dramatic and indicate that the share fell from 20.4% in 1954, to 17.7% in 1959, 11.9% in 1967 and a low of 8.8% in 1974. Rough calculations for this period would suggest that a 10% increase in world exports of manufactures was associated with a 5-6% increase in UK exports of manufactures.[4] Since 1974, however, the position has changed substantially. Indeed, despite a 36% increase in world exports of manufactures between 1975 and 1983, the UK share of world trade appears to have stabilized at an average figure of 9.0%.[5]

---

1   'World', in this context, means W. Germany, France, Italy, Netherlands, Belgium, Luxemburg, Canada, Japan, Sweden, Switzerland, USA and UK. In 1977, they accounted for 75% of manufactured exports from all industrial nations. See *TI*, 7 June 1978, p. 22.

2   H.S. Houthakker and S.P. Magee, 'Income and Price Elasticities in World Trade', *REST*, Vol. 51, pp. 111-25. This study covered the period 1951-66. For a critique, see A.D. Morgan, 'Income and Price Elasticities in World Trade: A Comment', *Manchester School*, Vol. 38, 1970, pp. 303-14. A more recent study for the period 1968-78 of the income elasticity of demand for non-oil imports finds a figure of 2.7 for the UK, with comparable figures for Japan and Germany of 1.9 and 1.6 respectively; cf. M.A. Akhtar, 'Income and Price Elasticities of Non-Oil Imports for Six Industrialised Countries', *MS*, Vol. 49, 1981, pp. 334-47. For a critical assessment of such estimates, on the grounds that they overstate the true elasticity values, see M. Beenstock and P. Warburton, 'UK Imports and the International Trading Order', *Weltwirtschaftliches Archiv*, Vol. 118, 1982, pp. 707-25.

3   Cf. the various contributions to F. Blackaby (ed.), *Deindustrialization*, Heinemann, 1979.

4   *NIER*, No. 73, 1975, p. 12.

5   The decline in the UK manufactured exports share has also been matched by a similar fall in her share of world invisible exports, from 20.9% in 1960 to 12.5% in 1976. Unlike manufactures, however, the UK share of world invisible imports has fallen along with the share in invisible exports. Cf. J.R. Sargent, 'UK Performance in Services', in F. Blackaby (ed.), op. cit.

Of itself, the decline in export share need not give rise to concern, since it may simply reflect a decline in the UK share of world manufacturing production, the natural result of her early industrial start. (In 1899, the UK accounted for 32.5% of world exports of manufactures and 20% of world manufacturing production.) However, this is far too complacent a view. Once it is recognized that between 1959 and 1975 the volume of world trade in manufactures grew at historically unprecedented annual rates of between 7% and 13% per annum, and that the UK was alone among the major industrial countries in experiencing a substantial drop in export share, there are grounds for disquiet. Furthermore, the decline in the UK's share in world manufacturing production may itself reflect the same factors which hinder UK trade performance. In this respect, it is worth noting that during the long industrial boom of the 1960s and early 1970s, the UK share of OECD manufacturing output fell from 9.6% in 1960 to 5.8% in 1973.

On the import side, the evidence for a loss of competitive edge is equally disturbing. Even though all the major industrialised nations, with the exception of Japan, have experienced a rising import share since 1955, the UK seems to be relatively more import prone than her competitors and to have a relatively high income elasticity of demand for imports.[1] Recent calculations show that over the period 1968-83, the ratio of imports of manufactures to the value of domestic consumption of manufactures increased from 17% to 30%. This trend appears widespread across manufacturing industry and is particularly significant in certain sectors, e.g. motor vehicles, office equipment, construction equipment and miscellaneous metal goods.[2] Some care, however, is required in interpreting these figures since, in part, they reflect the increasing division of labour in the international economy which has occurred since 1958. Similar calculations on the export side indeed show a corresponding trend increase in the proportion of UK output which is exported, with the average ratio of UK manufacturing exports to manufacturing production rising from 17.6% in 1968 to 27.0% at end-1983.[3]

To explain these developments in any precise sense is not easy; several interrelated factors are involved and the relative weight to be attached to each is difficult to establish and may vary over time. At the most general level, and since

---

1   A.D. Morgan, 'Imports of Manufactures into the UK and other Industrial Countries 1955-69', *NIER*, No. 56, 1971; M. Panic, op. cit.; L.F. Campell-Boross and A.D. Morgan, 'Net Trade: A Note on Measuring Changes in the Competitiveness of British Industry in Foreign Trade', *NIER*, No. 68, 1974, suggest that from 1963, UK manufacturing industry had never been sufficiently competitive to restore the country's trade situation to the position held in that year.

2   J.J. Hughes and A.P. Thirlwall, 'Trends in Cycles in Import Penetration in the UK', *Oxford Bulletin of Economics and Statistics*, Vol. 39, 1977, pp. 301-17. See also *BB*, 19 June 1981, p. 348.

3   It may be noted that the sectors experiencing the greatest improvement in export performance, e.g. chemicals, electrical engineering, mechanical engineering and scientific instruments, are also the sectors which perform two-thirds of the non-aerospace research and development carried out in UK manufacturing industry. See 'Manufacturing Industry in the Seventies: An Assessment of Import Penetration and Export Performance', *ET*, 1980. Import-penetration ratios and export-sales ratios are now published on a monthly basis in *MDS*. A useful account of some of the pitfalls of interpreting movements in these ratios, pitfalls which arise out of the foreign trade multiplier links between exports, imports and home output, is contained in C. Kennedy and A.P. Thirlwall, 'Import Penetration, Export Performance and Harrod's Trade Multiplier', *OEP*, July 1979, pp. 303-23.

it is trade in manufactures which is crucial, there would seem to be two potential sources of the poor UK trade performance: an increasing lack of price competitiveness; and a failure to produce and market commodities of the right quality, in the face of rapidly changing technologies and world demand structures. Certainly in the period up to 1967, the movement of UK export prices relative to the export prices of her major trade competitors can explain some of the loss of export share. Averaged over the period 1959-67, UK dollar export prices rose at an annual rate of 2%, compared to 1.3% for the other major industrial nations.[1] It follows that the relative price of UK manufactures rose by some 6.4% over this period and, assuming an export share elasticity of -2, this could account for 39% of the decline in UK export share between the two dates.[2]

The problem with this line of argument is applying it to developments since 1967. Between then and 1974, UK relative export prices fell by 13% and yet the UK export share still declined by 26%. If we maintain an assumed export share elasticity of -2, this suggests that other factors, in the absence of any change in competitiveness, would have resulted in a decline in the UK share of world trade to 4.2% in 1974. With an elasticity of -1, the corresponding hypothetical share of the UK in world trade in 1974 is 5.4%. It would appear from this that other factors, as yet unspecified, have come to play a dominant part in determining UK export performance in the 1970s. The case for a structural break in the UK export environment is reinforced by considering the period 1974-80, prior to the world recession which followed the second oil price increase. During this period, the volume of world exports of manufactures increased at an annual percentage rate of 6.5%, and UK price competitiveness declined by an average of 5% points per annum. On past performance, both factors should have reduced the UK share of world exports but, as we have seen, the share appears to have stabilized. This combination of circumstances lends weight to the view that non-price factors have come to play the dominant role in UK export performance.[3] On the import

---

1 Figures calculated from *NIER*, Appendix tables, which also provide a valuable summary of international trends in labour productivity, unit costs and industrial output.

2 A share elasticity of -1 would account for 21% of the loss in export share. Batchelor and Bowe, 'Forecasting UK International Trade: A General Equilibrium Approach', *Applied Economics*, Vol. 6, 1974, estimate price elasticities for UK export volume of between -1.13 and -2.80. One difficulty with any elasticity estimates is in evaluating the length of time it takes for the effects of price changes to be fully reflected in volume changes. Some estimates suggest up to five years as being the appropriate time-lag. See, e.g., H. Junz and R. Rhomberg, 'Price Competitiveness in Export Trade Among Industrial Countries', *AER*, May 1973, pp. 413-18. The export share elasticity can be taken as one plus the export volume price elasticity.

3 Other econometric research suggests that relative price movements can only account for one-half at most of the UK's loss of export share between 1956 and 1976, and one-fifth of the loss between 1970 and 1976. See M. Fetherstone, B. Moore and J. Rhodes, 'Manufacturing, Export Shares and Cost Competitiveness of Advanced Industrial Countries', *Economic Policy Review*, No. 3, Department of Applied Economics, Cambridge, 1977. More recent research suggests a representative price elasticity for UK manufactured exports, for the period 1967-75 of -1.4, while for the period 1967-77 (2nd quarter) the representative elasticity is reduced to -1. Cf. C.A. Enoch, 'Measures of Competitiveness in International Trade', *BEQB*, June 1978. This article also contains a useful review of alternative measures of price competitiveness. A summary of recent estimates suggests a price elasticity for both exports and imports of UK finished manufactures of -1.25. Cf. J.R. Artus and A.K. McGuirk, 'A Revised Version of the Multilateral Exchange Rate Model', *IMF Staff Papers*, Vol. 28, 1981, p. 294.

side there is strong evidence that the ratio of imports of manufactures to domestic demand has increased due to the decline in the competitiveness of UK manufactures. Independently of this, however, there is also a well-defined trend increase in the degree of import penetration of about 2% per annum,[1] which again suggests an important role for non-price factors. We have already noted the progressive shift in the pattern of UK trade toward exchanges of manufactures with the advanced industrial nations. It is plausible to argue that the oligopolistic conditions found in such markets are bound to increase the importance on non-price factors in competitive performance and to reduce the relative influence of prices on the demand for traded goods.[2] The type and quality of manufactures produced, delivery lags and after-sales service, and the general quality of marketing effort, it is frequently claimed, play a significant part in explaining the relatively poor UK trade performance.[3]

Unfortunately, the precise role of these factors has proved impossible, as yet, to determine, although it is interesting to note that similar explanations of poor British competitive performance were employed at the end of the nineteenth century.[4]

Explaining trade performance: Some guidance on these matters may be provided by a brief consideration of theories of comparative advantage. Traditional trade theory explains patterns of international trade by reference to national differences in endowments of productive factors, a country exporting those commodities which use relatively intensively its abundant factors. While this may have some relevance to the explanation of exchanges of manufactures for raw materials between industrialized and developing countries, it is of less obvious relevance to the explanation of the dominant component of world trade, exchange of manufactures between industrialized nations. Indeed, the assumptions of traditional theory immediately invite a cautious interpretation of its content, for they specify homogeneous outputs of each industry, equal access to technical knowledge in all countries, and factors of production of equal quality. Prima facie, they do not reflect the reality of modern industrial competition, i.e. conditions of imperfect competition. A powerful indication of the weakness of traditional theory is provided by the phenomenon of intra-industry trade — the simultaneous importing and exporting of products of the same industry — which is estimated to comprise some 60% of trade between developed countries.[5] In part, of course, this

---

1 C.A. Enoch, op. cit., who finds an import-penetration price elasticity of -0.4 for 1967-77 (2nd quarter).

2 Recent evidence suggests that in 1981, 84% of UK exports were accounted for by 1,858 enterprises and that 30% of UK exports came from foreign-owned UK firms. See, Business Statistics Office, *Business Monitor MA4: Overseas Transactions 1981*, HMSO, 1983.

3 *NEDO*, 'Imported Manufactures', HMSO, 1965 and *NEDO*, 'International Price Competitiveness, Non-Price Factors and Export Performance', HMSO, 1977. See also Report of the Committee of Enquiry into the Engineering Profession, *Engineering Our Future*, Cmnd. 7794, January 1980, chapter 1, and *Facing International Competition*, HMSO, July 1982.

4 R. Hoffman, *Great Britain and the German Trade Rivalry 1875-1914*, Pennsylvania University Press, 1933, pp. 21-80.

5 D. Greenaway and C. Milner, 'On the Measurement of Intra-Industry Trade', *EJ*, 1983, Vol. 93, pp. 900-8.

phenomenon is a statistical aberration, reflecting the lack of detail within even the finest classification of industrial statistics. For example, within the steel industry, there are many qualities of steel each of which is a poor substitute for the other in many applications but which are treated statistically as if they were perfect substitutes. More fundamentally, it reflects the role of intra-industry product differentiation as a key element in the competitive process.[1] It is no puzzle that the UK should simultaneously import and export whisky of different brands or equally automobiles, given the many grades of product which exist within this commodity group, each model type defined by a unique set of characteristics. Design, technical sophistication, after-sales service, durability and reliability are easily recognized as elements which successfully differentiate products in the mind of the consumer, whether a household or a firm.

The major determinants of intra-industry trade thus relate to product differences rather than cost differences, and may be outlined as follows. First, the existence of diversity of preferences for commodities of many different kinds within industrial countries, with the degree of overlap of preference distributions being determined by the similarity of per capita income levels.[2] Secondly, the importance of a domestic market to the initial development of a new commodity, which implies that the types of commodities produced in an economy reflect the pattern of domestic preferences. The same industry within different countries will then produce different product designs. Thirdly, the importance of economies of scale, including in this category the spreading of overheads, marketing and R and D expenses, leading firms to specialize within particular product niches. In general, specialization will be directed to those products in which home demand is greatest. Economies of scale and diversity of preferences then create the basis for intra-industry trade between industries organized in an imperfectly competitive fashion. The conditions which generate intra-industry trade also make technological innovation an important element in trade performance. Economists have long recognized the connection between technical innovation, technology transfer and changes in the structural pattern of foreign trade. Three factors are recognized as being of proven importance here: time-lags in the inter-country transfer of technology; differences in the national rate of consumer acceptance of innovations; and differences in the rates of growth of national production capacity to exploit innovations.[3] From this perspective, a country's trade performance is determined by the rate at which it acquires and exploits new technologies relative to its major competitors. Moreover, as technologies mature, the inputs which are required for effective exploitation change significantly. A new technology, in a fluid state, requires major scientific and technical manpower inputs to compete effectively but, as it matures, production processes become standardized and the emphasis shifts to exploitation of economies of scale and access to cheap labour.[4]

---

1 Cf. H. Grubel and P. Lloyd, *Inter-Industry Trade*, Macmillan, 1975, for an exhaustive discussion of this phenomenon. Also P. Krugman, 'New Theories of Trade Among Industrial Countries', *AER*, 1983 (May), Vol. 73, pp. 343-7.

2 Cf. S.B. Linder, *An Essay on Trade and Transformation*, Almqvist and Wicksell, 1961.

3 The classic reference is M.V. Posner, 'International Trade and Technological Change', *OEP*, 1961, Vol. 13, pp. 323-41.

4 R. Vernon, 'International Trade and Investment in the Product Cycle', *QJE*, Vol. 80, 1966, pp. 190-207.

Although one can recognize the historical force of these arguments in the study of individual industries,[1] it has proved difficult to identify the role of innovation-related factors in UK trade performance as a whole. Some pieces of evidence may, however, be relevant. First, if one divides UK trade according to the R and D intensity of the underlying industries, one finds that throughout the 1970s, R and D-intensive industries consistently experience a trade surplus while other industries are in deficit.[2] Secondly, a variable which reflects the employment of professional and technically qualified manpower is statistically important in explaining UK trade performance.[3] These findings fit naturally with any explanation of trade in terms of human capital inputs. More generally, there is also evidence to show that export success in the advanced industrialized nations is positively related to the resources devoted to R and D and to measures of inventive activity, e.g. patenting.[4] Here, it is important to remember that 44% of UK exports in 1983 were in the R and D-intensive and high-patenting areas of engineering and chemicals.

It will be clear that these dynamic considerations do not fit well with the factor endowments theory of trade. The important endowments of skills available to innovate and exploit new technology quite naturally differ in quality between countries and, moreover, change over time as new knowledge is discovered and transmitted into the workforce via formal education and practical experience. At root, it is the vague cultural attitudes towards change and innovation, summarized as industrial dynamism, which are impossible for the economist to measure but yet underpin the long historical trends of trade performance.

Much of what we have said stresses the role of non-price factors in trade performance. It must not be read as implying that price factors are unimportant. The econometric evidence suggests that price elasticities are important in deter-mining traded quantities, even if they are not the overwhelming determining factor in trade performance. However, an important aspect of pricing is missing from this conventional view. Namely that the relation of prices to costs determines the financial base from which firms may engage in R and D and competitive marketing expense. Prices are a key determinant of the resources available for innovation and thus of the relative dynamic performance of different national industries. Price elasticity evidence is important but it is only part of the picture. Nonetheless, indices of relative unit labour costs, adjusted for exchange-rate change, do provide evidence of trends in competitive strength, depending as they do on the

---

1 Cotton textiles and the computer industry are excellent examples. On micro-electronic innovations and trade, see E. Braun and S. McDonald, *Revolution in Miniature*, Cambridge, 1978; E. Tilton, 'International Diffusion of Technology: The Case of Semi Conductors', *Brookings Institution*, 1971, and B.A. Majumdar, *Innovations, Product Developments and Technology Transfers*, University Press of America, 1982.

2 *Business Monitor*, MA4. High-technology industries are those with a ratio of R and D expenditures to value added greater than 3%.

3 S.R. Smith *et al.*, 'UK Trade in Manufacturing: The Pattern of Specialization During the 1970s', *GES Working Paper, No. 56*, June 1982.

4 For a review, see the valuable paper by C. Freeman, 'Technical Innovation and British Trade Performance ', in F. Blackaby (ed.), op. cit. See also the study by K. Pavitt and L. Soete, chapter 3 of K. Pavitt (ed.), *Technological Innovation and British Export Performance*, Macmillan, 1980.

relationships between money wages and labour productivity in different countries. It is disturbing, therefore, to find that between 1975 and 1982, UK relative competitiveness declined by 40% on this measure, largely because of the North Sea oil-induced appreciation of sterling.

It is not difficult to link together the relative contributions of price and non-price factors, at least in theory if not in practice. The central point is that we have a sequence of interacting and mutually reinforcing proximate sources of the trend deterioration in UK trade performance. A convenient place to begin is with the well-documented fact that since 1950 the rate of growth of labour productivity in the UK has been inferior in comparison with the other major industrial nations.[1] A relatively slow growth rate of productivity implies a trend reduction in the relative level of UK industrial efficiency, which contributes to an increasing lack of price competitiveness for UK manufactures and to a relative shortage of resources for investment directed toward capacity expansion, marketing and innovative activities. A low rate of export growth combines with rising import penetration and a low rate of industrial investment feedback to reinforce the relatively slow growth of output. In turn, a low rate of output growth reduces the scope for the UK to exploit static and dynamic economies of scale, and scarcely provides a climate conducive to risk-taking and successful innovative activity. Consequently, the growth of productivity and quality change is held back and we come full circle again to the initial source of the poor UK trade performance. A country such as the UK has no option but to maintain its technological level close to 'world best practice', if it is to maintain its historically high standards of living. As technologies mature, the centre of comparative advantage inevitably moves to low-real-wage countries, so an advanced country can only maintain its living standards by shifting its resources into new areas opened up by technological advance. Like the Red Queen, the UK has to run to stand still, and if it fails, it will enter the ranks of the underdeveloped nations from the wrong direction.

Other factors: While it is the inadequate industrial growth performance which is chiefly responsible for the poor UK trade performance, several additional factors should not be ignored. On the export side, it is possible that an undue concentration on the supply of relatively slow-growing markets and on the production of commodities for which world demand was growing relatively slowly could explain the decline in export share. Appealing though this hypothesis is, evidence does not support the view that the structure of UK trade is responsible for poor export performance. A NEDO study finds no evidence in support of the view that the UK export structure is biased adversely toward the slower-growing commodities in world trade.[2] Furthermore, a study by R.L. Major has shown that only 9% of the total loss in UK manufacturing exports between 1954 and 1966 can be attributed to exporting to relatively slow-growing markets.[3]

---

1 See, e.g., E.H. Phelps Brown, 'Labour Policies', in A. Cairncross (ed.), *Britain's Economic Prospects Reconsidered*, Allen and Unwin, 1971 and A.D. Smith *et al.*, 'International Industrial Productivity: A Comparison of Britain, America and Germany', *NIER*, No. 101, 1982.

2 M. Panic and A.H. Rajan, *Product Changes in Industrial Countries' Trade 1955-68*, NEDO, monograph, No. 2, 1971.

3 R.L. Major, 'Note on Britain's Share in World Trade in Manufactures 1954-66', *NIER*, No. 44, 1968.

It may also have been the case that preferential trading arrangements have changed to the disadvantage of UK exporters. Isolated examples of this can be found, for example in the relaxation by certain Commonwealth countries of import-quota restrictions, which led to substantial export gains for Japan and the USA at the expense of UK producers. Of much greater importance has been the formation of the EEC. Although UK exports to the EEC have clearly benefited, it also seems likely that the effects of selling to a large and rapidly expanding market have been more than offset by reductions in UK exports to non-EEC countries, possibly due to the adverse effects of discrimination against the UK. Equally, EEC entry has clearly contributed to the recent growth of imports.[1]

One final factor which may be important in explaining the rising share of imports into the UK is the substantial reduction in tariff and other import restrictions which occurred after 1945. Between 1947 and 1959, the war-time restrictions on imports were virtually eliminated,[2] and from 1955 onwards the UK tariff was progressively reduced in line with agreements concluded through GATT. The UK tariff, introduced in 1932, had developed as a two-part structure with many imports from Commonwealth producers entering the UK duty-free, and imports from the rest of the world being subject to duties which, in the case of manufactures, ranged from 10% to 33%.[3] Between 1959 and 1975, the average UK tariff on semi-manufactures fell from 16.2% to 10.5% and that on finished manufactures from 21.4% to 12%. Despite the magnitude of these changes, a recent study suggests that their overall effect has proved to be relatively small, increasing imports for semi-manufactures by 13% and that of finished manufactures by 9% relative to the values they would otherwise have had in 1971.[4]

1   UK membership of the EEC is treated in section III.8 below. See also M. Fetherstone, B. Moore and J. Rhodes, 'EEC Membership and UK Trade in Manufactures', *Cambridge Journal of Economics*, December 1979, where it is suggested that the net (trade-creation minus trade-diversion) effect of EEC membership between 1973 and 1977 was to reduce average UK exports by £152m and to increase average UK imports by £994m p.a. at 1970 prices.

2   For details, see M.F.W. Hemming, C.M. Miles and G.F. Ray, 'A Statistical Summary of the Extent of Import Control in the UK Since the War', *RES*, Vol. 26, pp. 75-109.

3   In 1957, the average margin of preference on dutiable Commonwealth imports was 9%. See PEP, *Commonwealth Preference in the UK*, 1960. The swing in UK trade toward manufactures and the advanced industrialized nations progressively made this degree of preference less important.

4   A.D. Morgan and A. Martin, 'Tariff Reductions and UK Imports of Manufactures 1955-71', *NIER*, No. 72, May 1975. It is possible that this study understates the true reduction in protection afforded to UK manufacturing industry because it deals only with nominal tariff rates and not effective tariff rates – the effective rate taking into account the impact of tariff changes on the cost of imported means of production. Recent calculations for the period 1968-72 show that while the nominal rate on manufactures fell by 36%, the effective rate fell by 46%. N. Oulton, 'Tariffs, Taxes and Trade in the UK: The Effective Protection Approach', *Government Economic Service Occasional Papers*, No. 6, 1973, p. 9.

III   ECONOMIC POLICY AND THE BALANCE OF PAYMENTS
III.1   Introduction

The coverage of this section is limited in two ways. First, pressure of space precludes more than a passing reference to events and policies prior to the floating of sterling in June 1972. Second, the concept of economic policy is limited to government intervention where the prime concern is to produce alterations in flows immediately affecting the balance of payments.

It may be argued that *all* economic policy affects the balance of payments, since any non-trivial intervention in the economy is likely to produce at least minor alterations in the balance of forces affecting trade and payments flows and the exchange rate. Some policies may well have major implications for trade but, for present purposes, are not regarded as balance-of-payments policies. Thus, attempts to control inflation or to stimulate innovation, efficiency and growth are likely if successful to have substantial impacts on trade flows, but these problems are discussed elsewhere in this book and, in any case, may be judged desirable for reasons other than those concerned with the balance of payments. Equally, policies which are directed explicitly at trade flows may involve related adjustments in 'domestic' policy, as we shall see below in the discussion of exchange-rate management. Manipulation of tariff and other barriers to trade is a legitimate branch of balance-of-payments policy, but, in practice, government action of this nature is circumscribed by international agreements and membership of the EEC, so again pressure of space precludes more than a cursory discussion of what might be done within these constraints. Entry to the EEC was obviously a policy decision of incalculable magnitude affecting all aspects of economic behaviour, but this section will confine itself to some balance-of-payments implications of that decision. The external debt problems facing less developed countries and the influence of the international monetary system upon UK policy is so important that we conclude the section by looking at recent developments in these fields.

When interpreting the following discussion, it is important to remember that the conduct of balance-of-payments policy, or for that matter of economic policy in general, is not a matter of 'fine-tuning'. In part this reflects the fact that UK balance-of-payments performance is as much determined by the economic policies adopted in other countries as it is by policies adopted in the UK. On top of this, familiar problems of forecasting the direction and rate of change of economic variables, political and other limitations on the values of policy variables, and conflict between different policy objectives, taken together, mean that practical policy-making is more an art than a science.

III.2   The Exchange Market Framework

It is a familiar proposition that modern industrial economies have evolved by means of a progressive division of labour and that one important pre-condition for this is the adoption of a single internal currency, to act as an intermediary in all economic transactions. The international division of labour has so far proceeded without this advantage. Since nations continue to maintain separate currencies for internal use, it follows that international transactions must proceed with the simultaneous exchange of national currencies, apart, that is, from those transactions conducted in key currencies. This exchange of currencies takes place in the foreign-exchange market and it is there that the relative prices of different national currencies — exchange rates — are established.

An important policy issue which faces the government of any country is, therefore, that of the degree of restraint which it wishes to place on the exchange of its own currency with the currencies of other nations. Not only will the chosen restraints limit the type and geographical direction of transactions which domestic residents may make with foreigners, but they will also have an important bearing upon the conduct of policy to achieve internal objectives such as full employment and price stability. Successive UK governments have exercised their options in two ways: by adopting particular forms of exchange-rate policy, and by placing restrictions upon the currencies against which sterling may be exchanged for the pursuit of specified transactions, i.e. by exchange control.

Between 1945 and June 1972, the UK operated the foreign-exchange market for sterling in accordance with the rules of the par-value system.[1] This required the official adoption of a par value to be expressed in terms of gold or the US dollar of 1944 fineness, which determined the central value of the spot-market rate for sterling,[2] together with the acceptance of a band of fluctuation of the spot rate around the par value.[3]

Provided the spot rate for sterling, as determined by market forces, lay within the permitted band, the UK exchange authorities did not need to take any action. Should the exchange rate be under pressure to stray outside this permitted band, then the exchange authorities were obliged to intervene in the foreign-exchange market, selling foreign exchange from the reserves when sterling was at its lower limit and purchasing foreign exchange to add to the reserves when sterling was at its upper limit. Thus, the par-value system allowed some degree of variability in the foreign-exchange rate but it also required that the UK keep a buffer stock of foreign-exchange reserves which it could use to keep the exchange rate within the specified bounds.

It must be noted that the par value of a currency was not fixed for all time once a country decided to abide by this system. On the contrary, a country could, when its balance of payments was in 'fundamental disequilibrium' and after consultation with the IMF, change its par value. This UK governments did twice, devaluing sterling in 1949 and again in 1967.

In contrast to what is required in the market for spot exchange, IMF rules placed no formal restrictions on the movements of forward exchange rates for a currency. Nor were any necessary. In normal circumstances, the forward exchange

---

1 This is the name given to the exchange-rate system adopted by the majority of Western nations after the Second World War. The central body of the system is the International Monetary Fund (IMF).

2 A distinction must be made between the spot market and the forward market exchange rates for a currency. The spot exchange rate is the price of foreign currency for immediate delivery, that is, at the time the rate for the transaction is agreed. A forward exchange rate is the price of foreign currency for delivery at a specified date in the future.

3 Until December 1971 the permitted band of fluctuation was 1% either side of par. Under the Smithsonian reforms of that time, the band was widened to 2.25% either side of par.

rate will stand in a simple relationship[1] to the spot-exchange rate, reflecting the role of the forward market in providing cover for the exchange risks inherent in spot-market transactions.

A major change in UK policy occurred in June 1972, when the par-value system was 'temporarily' abandoned and sterling allowed to take whatever values the balance of demand and supply for foreign exchange might dictate. However, a policy of allowing sterling to float has not meant that the exchange market ceases to be an object of policy concern. The government still has to decide to what extent sterling will float freely, without official constraint, and thus to what extent it is going to manage the exchange rate. Recent UK experience suggests a considerable degree of exchange management to iron out potentially violent fluctuations in the spot rate without, if possible, influencing its longer-term trend.

The second important aspect of UK exchange policy is that of exchange control, and here 1979 saw some important changes when, in October, the exchange-control restrictions which had been built up since 1945 were abolished. Exchange control is a complex issue with a detailed history of evolution, so that space precludes more than the most general remarks.[2] The legal basis of exchange control is contained in the Exchange Control Act of 1947, which assigns to the Treasury the authority to formulate exchange-control policy. The day-to-day responsibility for implementing the exchange-control provisions is delegated to the Bank of England, while, in turn, the daily volume of foreign-currency transactions is handled by authorized exchange dealers, e.g. the commercial banks. The Exchange Equalization Account acts only as a residual purchaser or seller of foreign exchange in order to support a given exchange rate. As far as UK residents were concerned, practice after 1960 was to allow complete freedom for current transactions[3] but to restrict transactions on capital account in various ways. Exchange control in the UK was greatly complicated by the international-reserve and medium-of-exchange functions of sterling, which result in foreigners holding sterling balances. After 1958, a distinction was maintained between two such categories of sterling: external-account sterling and resident sterling. External-account sterling consisted of sterling balances held by non-sterling area residents. This was freely convertible into any currency for current and capital transactions. Resident sterling consisted of sterling balances held by residents of the UK and of the overseas sterling areas, who were treated in the same fashion as UK residents, i.e. allowed full convertibility on current account but restricted convertibility for capital transactions to non-sterling area countries.

---

1   This is the interest parity relationship. Provided interest arbitrage funds are in perfectly elastic supply, then the percentage difference between spot and forward exchange rates for any pair of currencies will equal the interest differential on assets of the appropriate maturities denominated in those currencies. However, with arbitrage funds not in infinitely elastic supply, the forward rate will deviate from the interest parity value. In the limit, when the supply of speculative funds to the forward market is infinitely elastic, the forward rate will equal the value of the spot rate expected to hold at the time forward contracts mature.

2   A useful historical account of UK exchange control will be found in B. Tew, *International Monetary Co-operation 1945-1970*, Hutchinson, 1971. The interested reader may also consult the IMF *Annual Reports on Exchange Restrictions*.

3   Apart from certain restrictions on the availability of exchange for foreign travel and for the making of gifts and other transfers to non-sterling area residents.

From 1960, UK exchange-control regulations stayed broadly unchanged. However, with the float of sterling in 1972, several modifications were required, which essentially involved giving the former sterling area countries external-account status. By October 1979, the sterling area, for exchange-control purposes, consisted only of a handful of countries.[1] The major implications of the abandonment of exchange controls relate to capital-account transactions and these are discussed in more detail in section III.6.

III.3 External Economic Policy with a Floating Exchange Rate

In June 1972, the UK abandoned its commitment to the par-value system and sterling began to float relative to other currencies. By the middle of 1973, sterling had been joined in this respect by all other major currencies so that, for the advanced industrial nations as a whole, the par-value system had been abandoned. With sterling only one of the many currencies engaged in a simultaneous float, there is no simple index of movements in the international value of sterling. Sterling may appreciate in terms of some currencies while, at the same time, it depreciates in terms of others. Current practice is to rely upon the so-called 'effective exchange rate', which is a suitably weighted average of the movements of sterling compared to the currencies of those countries which are most important in UK trade.[2]

The movement in the effective exchange rate since June 1972 can be divided conveniently into three phases. The first, to November 1976, was one of almost continual depreciation with the movement being particularly rapid after February 1976. In the last quarter of that year, the effective rate (with 1975 = 100) averaged 78.1 compared to an average of 94.0 in the first quarter and an average of 105.0 in 1972. Between the end of 1976 and the end of 1978, the effective rate was remarkably stable, rarely deviating more than 2% points either side of an average quarterly value of 81.3, but it then appreciated rapidly from January 1979 to reach a value of 100.6 in the last quarter of 1980. In the final stage, since 1980, the effective rate has drifted gradually downwards, averaging 95.3 during 1981, 83.3 during 1983 and 82.0 during the first two months of 1984. The movement of sterling relative to individual currencies, in particular the dollar, has been much more volatile although the broad trends have mirrored that of the effective exchange rate. Before we analyse the causes of this sustained depreciation, it will prove useful to outline some of the more important economic implications of floating exchange rates.

Floating rates and economic policy: The case for floating exchange rates rests, in large part, upon the alleged simplicity and automaticity of the free-market mechanism in reallocating resources in response to changing circumstances. In a dynamic world in which comparative advantages change rapidly and national inflation rates differ, changes in exchange rates are necessary if widespread under-utilization or misallocation of productive resources is to be avoided. The

---

1 See footnote 1 on page 130.

2 For details see *ET*, June 1974; *BEQB*, March 1977; *TER*, March 1977; and *BEQB*, March 1981.

advantage of floating rates, it is argued, is that the necessary changes can occur progressively at a pace dictated by the costs and profitability of resource allocation, and not, as with the par-value system, by sudden, discrete jumps dictated by speculative pressure and political expediency. The resource-allocation advantages are only one aspect of the benefits derivable from the adoption of a floating exchange rate. More important for present purposes are the implications for the conduct of macroeconomic policy. For it seems clear that, with a more flexible exchange-rate policy, the UK could have avoided most of the policy dilemmas of the period 1960-71 and that the period since 1971 would have generated impossible policy contradictions had the UK adhered to the par-value system.

There is, first, the minor point that the government no longer has to decide what constitutes an equilibrium exchange rate; to a large extent, this will be decided automatically within the foreign-exchange market. One cannot go from this, however, to suggest that the conduct of domestic economic policy can proceed independently of developments in the foreign-exchange market. The correct management of domestic demand is just as important with a floating exchange rate as it is with a fixed exchange rate. Balance-of-payments problems do not disappear with the adoption of a floating exchange rate, they simply appear in different forms. Developments that would lead to a loss of reserves with a fixed exchange rate, lead to a depreciation in the foreign-exchange value of the currency if the exchange rate is allowed to float. In the first case, the loss of reserves will result, unless it is a once-and-for-all loss, in a policy-induced contraction in domestic income; while with a floating rate, the loss in real domestic purchasing power occurs automatically as the prices of tradeable commodities rise with the currency depreciation.

The main advantage of a floating rate is that it allows a greater independence of domestic economic policy-making. In particular, full-employment objectives may be more consistently pursued; there being some value of the exchange rate which will give exactly a zero currency flow at any, non-inflationary, level of employment. Furthermore, since a floating rate provides the minimum of linkage between the circular income of different trading nations, it follows that a floating exchange rate will isolate the level of demand for UK goods from changes in foreign incomes and preferences for UK goods. An increase in foreign demand which, under a fixed rate, would generate a multiple expansion in UK incomes, now generates an appreciation of the sterling rate of exchange, such that the final increase in the value of UK exports is exactly matched by an appreciation-induced increase in the value of UK imports, i.e. in the domestic expenditure on foreign goods. The total demand for UK goods and, therefore, UK incomes will remain unchanged.[1] The isolation of domestic incomes from external changes in demand has, of course, as counterpart the proposition that the level of domestic income is more sensitive to changes in the level of *domestic* money expenditure. In this respect, an economy with a floating exchange rate will behave in the same manner as a closed economy; the effects of changes in foreign trade upon the circular flow of income are completely negated. The policy consequence of this is that the multiplier repercussions of monetary and fiscal policy will be greater in an economy with a floating

---

1   A more detailed discussion would have to modify this argument in respect of any change in the aggregate savings ratio which followed the exchange appreciation and the possible effects on demand of any changes in international interest-rate levels.

exchange rate than in the same economy with a fixed exchange rate.[1] Correspondingly, the cost of mistakes in demand management will be increased with a floating rate and so policy must be conducted with greater attention to underlying circumstances.

Other implications of floating rates: The relative merits of fixed and floating exchange rates are matters of considerable controversy among economists. Some of the alleged advantages of flexible exchange rates have already been mentioned. The object of the present section is to deal with two less clear-cut aspects of the controversy. In particular, the view that private speculation will convert floating exchange rates into wildly fluctuating rates, and the view that a floating rate increases the uncertainty faced by international traders and investors to the detriment of the international division of labour.

The case for and against floating rates depends essentially on the view taken of the effects of speculators in the operation of free markets. If these markets are to be cleared continuously without undue fluctuations in the exchange rate, it is essential that speculators take over the role of the monetary authorities and operate in a stabilizing manner, selling sterling when the rate is temporarily 'too high' and buying sterling when the rate is temporarily 'too low'. Temporary fluctuations in the exchange rate follow, in part, because daily imbalances in the demand and supply for foreign exchange will result from random and seasonal factors, even if the balance of payments is basically in equilibrium over a longer time-span, and because short-period trading adjustments to relative price changes are likely to be inelastic. The proponents of floating exchange rates argue that speculative activity will be stabilizing and that the speculators will be able to predict the trend value of the exchange rate so as to ensure minimal variations in the actual exchange rate around the trend value. Opponents fear that this will not be the case, and the exchange market will be dominated by too much uncertainty for speculators to recognize the appropriate trend. Successive waves of optimism and pessimism will follow the frequent revision of expectations and generate substantial movements in exchange rates, out of all proportion to the volume of trading.

The difficulty with the above arguments is that we have little factual evidence to decide either way. Certainly the period with floating rates has witnessed some sudden, sharp movements in exchange rates, out of step with underlying economic circumstances. Thus, for example, between 11 November and 16 December 1983, sterling depreciated by 4.6% against the dollar, and then appreciated to reverse this movement completely by the beginning of March 1984. On the other hand, the average quarterly movement of the sterling-effective rate over the same period comes to 0.54 percentage points, which is not excessive and is well within the limits permissible under the par-value system. However, should private speculation prove to be less stabilizing than is thought desirable, there is no reason why the authorities should not engage in 'official' speculation, if necessary at the

---

1   Again this is subject to qualifications, depending upon the sensitivity of international capital movements to policy-induced changes in interest rates and the time-span considered for analysis. With floating exchange rates, a greater degree of interest sensitivity of capital flows enhances the potency of monetary policy and limits the potency of fiscal policy for the management of aggregate demand.

expense of private operators. Indeed, this is precisely what the authorities have undertaken when supporting the sterling par value against speculative pressure and when actually managing the exchange rate over various periods since June 1972. The implication is, of course, that even with a floating exchange rate, the authorities must maintain a stock of exchange reserves. Widespread adoption of exchange-management practices would also require the institution of international co-ordination and surveillance of exchange-rate practices; this appears neither impossible nor undesirable within the framework of an existing body such as the IMF (see section III.8 below). Finally, it must not be overlooked that destabilizing speculation can disrupt any exchange-rate framework and clearly did so with the par-value system. One of the major drawbacks of the par-value system was that it gave a one-way option to currency speculators. A currency under pressure would be pushed to one of the official intervention limits. This immediately signalled the possibility of a change in par value in a direction in which no one could have any doubt. Naturally, a large and cumulative movement of funds across the exchanges was thereby encouraged. A likely advantage of floating exchange rates is that the problem of a one-way speculative option will be much reduced.

The view taken of the effects of speculation determines the importance of the arguments on uncertainty and the inhibition of trade and investment. Provided that floating rates do not fluctuate wildly, there is no reason why the bulk of trade and investment should be seriously affected. After all, exchange risks can always be covered with simultaneous deals in spot and forward markets. For sterling transactions involving the major currencies, the foreign-exchange market currently provides active dealings for contracts up to one year in duration. Since some 92% of UK exports are financed on credit terms of less than six months' duration,[1] with, no doubt, a similar proportion for imports, there should be no difficulty in traders covering their exchange risks. Longer-term trade contracts and international investment projects will face problems, but then in an uncertain world they always will. In addition, it is argued that, should the forward premium on sterling exceed the appropriate interest differential, then traders will have to face extra costs of finance. There are two counter-arguments to this. First, the difference between forward premia and interest differentials will be smaller, the greater is the response of international capital flows to arbitrage possibilities. Particularly now that UK exchange controls have been relaxed, there is no reason to expect the costs of forward cover to be prohibitive. Secondly, suppose it could be demonstrated convincingly that additional exchange-rate uncertainty had reduced trade and investment. This could still not constitute an argument against floating rates, until the claimed costs could be shown to be greater than the employment and resource-misallocation costs imposed under a par-value system

III.4· The Exchange Rate and the Balance of Payments 1972-83

In section I.4 we outlined the considerable changes in the UK's external position in the period since 1972, showing that from an initial surplus the current account moved into deficit during 1972-8 and then recovered, with substantial surpluses

---

1   See Business Statistics Office, *Business Monitor MA4: Overseas Transactions 1977*, HMSO, 1979.

from 1979 onward. On the domestic front, as other chapters show, this period was also one of very rapid and variable inflation rates, high and variable interest rates, steadily increasing unemployment and slow growth, terminating in a 2.5% decline in GDP between 1979 and 1982. The purpose of this section is to outline some of the major factors leading to the changes in the current account and the exchange rate during the period, and their relation to domestic and international events.

The first point to be reminded of when interpreting the events of the period is that the exchange rate for sterling has not been allowed to float freely, rather it has been managed quite actively, and this policy has produced economic effects which are a mixture of those occurring under the extremes of fixed and freely floating rates. We return to this point subsequently. It will also be clear from an examination of table 3.2 that a wide variety of transactions involve payments across the exchanges but that it is the net balance of payments which is the crucial factor. Since the equilibrium exchange rate at any point in time reflects the balance of demand and supply of foreign exchange, it is useful to begin with an outline of the major forces affecting the volume of autonomous external transactions. Here we make an important distinction between those determining factors related to changes in national price levels, and those related to the real forces of production, consumer preferences, productivity and thrift. It is to the former that we turn first.

Purchasing-power parity: A convenient place to begin is the theory which relates the values taken by a currency's exchange rate to its purchasing-power parity. Broadly speaking, this means that the equilibrium exchange rate between the currencies of two countries is proportional to the ratio of the price levels in the respective countries. Moreover, providing this factor of proportionality remains constant, the proportionate rate of change of the exchange rate will be approximately equal to the difference between the inflation rates in the two countries.[1] With the exchange rate at par, the current account would then balance in the absence of net capital flows. The proximate source of the rapid depreciation of sterling between 1972 and 1976 can then be found in the excess of the UK rate of inflation over a suitably weighted average of the inflation rates in our major trading partners; it being a matter of indifference what the source of this inflation differential may be, whether it be related to excessive monetary expansion in the UK or to excessive wage-push by UK trade unions. Similarly, the rise in sterling after 1978 would be related to a lower UK inflation rate in comparison to that of our major trade partners. To investigate this further, we may compare the movement in the UK's effective exchange rate, in the computation of which the OECD countries have a weight of 89%, with the movements in the consumer price indices in the UK and the combined OECD countries. The consumer price index is not perfect for this purpose but it will suffice. Between 1972 and 1978, the ratio of the OECD to the UK price levels fell by 24.4%, while the effective rate of sterling fell by 33.9%. Clearly, sterling depreciated more quickly than purchasing-power

---

1 Probably the clearest statement of the purchasing-power parity theory is still contained in J.M. Keynes, *A Tract on Monetary Reform*, Macmillan, 1923, pp. 70-93. For a recent survey, see L.H. Officer, 'The Purchasing Power Parity Theory of Exchange Rates: A Review Article', *IMF Staff Papers*, Vol. 23, 1976. The exact formula for the percentage change in purchasing-power parity between two dates is $(P'-P)/(1+P)$, where P and P' are the proportionate changes in the domestic and foreign price levels.

parity would suggest, particularly during 1976 when the exchange rate was on average 13.6% points below purchasing-power parity. The effective rate remained roughly constant to the end of 1978 but it then appreciated rapidly during 1979 and 1980 despite a further 7.4% decline in its purchasing-power value. As a consequence, sterling stood 10% points on average above purchasing-power parity during 1980, a very sharp reversal from the position in 1976. Since 1980 the UK inflation rate has matched the average for the OECD countries so that the purchasing-power-parity value of sterling has remained constant. In contrast, the effective rate for sterling has depreciated continually, so that by 1983 its value stood 2% points on average below purchasing-power parity. Thus, from 1979 to 1982, the effective rate for sterling was generally above the purchasing-power parity and it is not surprising to find that this period was one of deep recession in UK manufacturing, nor to read of the vociferous concern of UK industrialists that an overvalued exchange rate was adversely affecting UK exports and encouraging import penetration. Of course, these calculations are rather rough and ready and depend crucially upon an assumption that sterling was at purchasing-power parity in 1972. Nevertheless, they are sufficiently robust to serve as a basis for discussion, and indicate that purchasing-power parity is not an exact guide to movements in the effective exchange rate even though it captures the longer-term trend.[1]

How are we to explain these substantial short-run deviations from purchasing-power parity? A vital point to remember here is that purchasing-power parity is only relevant if three stringent conditions hold true during the relevant period: the national inflation rates must be correctly anticipated by economic agents; there must be no net capital movements across the exchanges, including in this category government intervention in the foreign-exchange market; and there must be no relevant changes in economic structure affecting the current account of the balance of payments. Not one of these conditions can be said to have applied over the period since 1972, and it is convenient to seek the proximate sources of deviations from purchasing-power parity in terms of capital movements and structural change, particularly in relation to the exploitation of North Sea oil. As far as capital movements are concerned, a full treatment is given in section III.6, and for the present it is sufficient to note that changes in international interest differentials and in expected international inflation differentials are a potent source of deviations from purchasing-power parity. The period of sterling over-valuation since 1979 has certainly been one in which short-term interest rates in the UK have been almost always greater than in the United States, with the gap virtually vanishing in 1983. Given the tenuous nature of expectations and market sentiment, one must recognize that the short-run relation between the exchange rate and purchasing-power parity will be difficult to predict. Short-run exchange-rate movements will tend to be volatile and to pre-date measured changes in purchasing-power parity by a time-period of indeterminable length.

On the question of economic structure, several factors are relevant. The first is the effect of UK membership of the EEC and the associated longer-term trends in UK trade patterns, referred to in sections II and III.7. *A priori*, it is impossible to say how these factors have affected the purchasing-power parity value of sterling.

---

1   A recent study of the movements of seven other major currencies besides sterling also finds substantial short-run deviations from purchasing-power parity. Cf. G. Hacche and J. Townsend, 'A Broad Look at Exchange Rate Movements for Eight Currencies, 1972-80', *BEQB*, December 1981.

Certainly they are slow-moving, persistent forces which could reasonably be relegated to a minor role in this account. Of much greater importance have been sharp changes in the terms of trade and the progression of the UK toward self-sufficiency in oil production.

These important changes in economic structure were bound to make our simple purchasing-power-parity calculation a poor guide to short-run and even long-run movements in the exchange rate. Without question, the most significant price change was the quadrupling of the posted price of oil by the OPEC nations at the end of 1973 from $3.45 to $11.58 per barrel.[1] The implications of this development were considerable and worldwide, affecting not only individual economies but also the stability of the international monetary system. (Some of the wider issues are treated in sections III.8 and III.9 below.) Between 1975 and 1978, the price of oil remained within the range $12 to $14 per barrel but rose sharply again from June 1979, with a price at the beginning of 1981 of $36 per barrel. However, the deepening world recession and the declining demand for energy gradually created a world oil glut so that, in the first quarter of 1982, the price of oil fell by between $4-$5 per barrel and averaged $30 per barrel in 1983. Relative to the average price of world manufactured exports, however, the real fall in the price of oil between 1980 and 1983 amounts to 4.1%.

As the short-run elasticity of demand for oil and commodity imports does not differ appreciably from zero, the impact effect of the oil price increases was simultaneously to worsen the trade balance and to generate deflationary pressures in the UK economy. It is as if the UK government had raised indirect taxes, so cutting the demand for UK output and had then transferred the tax proceeds to the oil-producing and primary-commodity-producing nations. In addition, the similar effects on other industrial economies produced cuts in the demand for UK exports and so provided a further deflationary stimulus; while very little help could be expected in the short run from the spending of OPEC funds on UK-produced goods.

Several options were open to the government to deal with the first oil shock. First, it could have attempted to eliminate the current-account deficits either by a severe policy-induced cut in aggregate demand, or by allowing the exchange rate to depreciate sufficiently to improve the non-oil trade balance of the UK at the expense of the other industrialized countries. Neither option proved to be feasible or otherwise desirable. The only effective policy was one of substantial foreign borrowing, combined with a broadly neutral stance toward domestic aggregate demand.[2]

Foreign borrowing took place under three separate headings. Prior to 1972, the OPEC oil-producers traditionally received about 25% of their oil revenues in

---

1 The posted price should not be confused with the market price of oil. The posted price is the administrative price from which the OPEC countries assess the royalty payments and tax payments from the oil-extracting companies.

2 Although the March 1975 budget was intended to produce substantial cuts in the government borrowing requirement, it can be argued that their net effect on the aggregate demand was negligible. See *NIER*, May 1975, p. 11. A more deflationary stance was adopted in 1976 and 1977 announcing further reductions in future public expenditure. Calculations suggest, however, that over the period 1975-7, the net stance of fiscal policy had a small stimulating effect on the economy. See the article 'Why is Britain in Recession?', *BEQB*, March 1978.

sterling and normally deposited this as sterling balances in London. With the increase in oil revenues following the Tehran agreement, the immediate response was to place much of the surplus in London. In 1974, some 37% of surplus oil funds, a total of $21bn, was placed in London. In the subsequent years, the total amount of short-term finance made available in this way declined considerably, as a result of falling surplus oil revenues and an increasing unwillingness to deposit funds in a depreciating currency. In fact, between 1975 and 1977 only $4-4.5bn flowed into the UK, on an annual basis, representing 12-14% of surplus oil funds. The second important source of finance was nationalized industry and local authority borrowing under the Treasury exchange cover scheme. Much of this was in the form of OPEC funds taken from the Eurodollar market in the form of medium-term (3-7 year) loans. Some $3.4bn was raised in this way in the two years to the end of 1975, and a further $3.6bn to the end of 1977. Finally, the UK government itself engaged in substantial borrowing. Most important here was the $2.5bn and $1.5bn loans raised from the Eurodollar market in 1974 and 1977, the $2bn borrowed from the IMF at the end of 1975 – 60% of which represented a drawing on the specially created oil facility – and the stand-by agreement with the IMF agreed at the end of 1976 under which the UK could draw $3.9bn from its remaining credit tranches – $1.2bn being taken in January 1977.

While the policy of foreign borrowing allowed the UK to accommodate its payments deficit in anticipation of the benefits of North Sea oil, it also clearly prevented the exchange rate from dropping even further below purchasing-power parity than it did. As pointed out in section I.4, this increased external debt created an interest and amortization burden which implies the need for a substantial UK current-account surplus in the 1980s to service the interest and amortization payments.

Turning now to the period after 1978, the most important fact to be explained is the rapid appreciation of sterling during 1979 and 1980. The major structural factor of relevance here is the growth in production from the North Sea oil fields, which have made by far the largest contribution to the growing current-account surpluses after 1977, as well as effectively insulating the terms of trade from the second major increase in the relative price of oil in 1979. The direct effect on the current account has been reinforced by the indirect effects on confidence and capital flows. With the UK payments position now unaffected by oil price changes, sterling is a safe haven for OPEC and other capital funds – free from the exchange risks attached to the currencies of net oil-importers such as the USA, Japan and Germany. This renewed confidence in sterling, its petrocurrency status, is adequately reflected in the average annual rate of recorded overseas investment in the UK, which amounts to £7.7bn annually during the years 1979-82. The comparable figure for the period 1972 to 1976 is a mere £1.7bn. A further structural factor which has to be taken into account is the relatively greater depth of the UK recession. While the appreciation of sterling has helped to reduce aggregate demand for UK goods, there is little doubt that a further major depressing factor has been the stance of UK fiscal and monetary policy. Between 1978 and 1981, UK industrial output fell by 6.8% while, in the whole OECD area, industrial output *expanded* by 6%. Naturally, this relative decline, together with the associated reductions in inventory levels in the UK, has been an important factor contributing to the large current-account surpluses and thus the buoyancy of sterling. It remains an open question as to what value of sterling would currently correspond to full employment and external equilibrium in the UK.

So far we have looked at deviations from purchasing-power parity in terms of shifts in several autonomous real factors impinging upon the exchange rate. Equal weight must also be given to government intervention in the foreign-exchange market. The next section deals with the theoretical pros and cons of intervention, so here we simply record that the float of sterling has been heavily managed since 1972. For example, between 1974 and 1976, annual reserve losses of $1.3bn were incurred to prevent an even more rapid slide of the exchange rate, while during 1977, by contrast, the reserves were allowed to increase by the historically unprecedented sum of $16.4bn when the effective rate was stabilized. Further reserve gains of approximately $9bn (after allowance for valuation changes) during 1979 and 1980 also prevented even greater appreciation above purchasing-power parity, while the decline in sterling since 1981 has been ameliorated by some reductions in reserves.

To sum up. Over the longer term, a simple, indeed crude, measure of purchasing-power parity adequately captures the trend in the effective sterling rate. However, in any short period, it is clear that the market-clearing value for sterling deviated significantly from this purchasing-power-parity figure, largely as a response to structural factors and net capital flows. Moreover, it is clear that government intervention in the foreign-exchange market prevented even greater deviations from purchasing-power parity than would otherwise have been imposed by a free market for sterling.

III.5   Management of the Exchange Rate

In the previous section we have indicated how the sterling exchange rate has been heavily managed during the period since 1972, the primary weapons in this management being foreign-currency borrowing and changes in the stock of UK foreign-exchange reserves.

There are several important reasons why a government may wish to manage the exchange rate. In the first instance, it may view changes in the demand and supply of foreign exchange as temporary and so act as a speculator to prevent such transitory changes in the balance of autonomous transactions from influencing the exchange rate. This policy could be justified as one way to minimize the disruptive effects of transitory exchange-rate variations on trade and investment. As a second example, the government may take a view that the balance of autonomous transactions has shifted permanently but at the same time consider that an immediate full adjustment of the exchange rate would be too disruptive to patterns of employment and resource allocation. The exchange rate could then be actively managed toward its new long-run level at a pace which allows the pattern of resource allocation to change smoothly. The problem with this line of argument is, of course, the familiar one — how does the government know the exchange rate appropriate to different sets of internal and external circumstances? Too easily a policy of 'leaning into the wind' may become a policy of manipulation of the exchange rate to satisfy other objectives.

One very important objective in the UK context could be that of engineering a depreciation of sterling to maintain or increase the competitiveness of UK manufacturing exports and import substitutes. This policy could be justified in terms of offsetting the medium-term effects on the sterling exchange rate of North Sea oil which, if left unchecked, could undermine the competitiveness of UK industry and leave the country with greatly diminished foreign-exchange earning power when the North Sea oil resources are exhausted. The appreciation of sterling during 1979 and 1980 brought this problem to the forefront of discussion with the increasing concern about de-industrialization of the non-oil sector of UK industry. The mechanism of a managed depreciation would be as follows. The impact effect would be to change relative prices. The relative prices of tradeable commodities, exports, imports and their close substitutes will increase and, depending on the pricing policies of domestic and foreign firms,[1] the terms of trade will typically deteriorate as sterling import prices rise relative to sterling export prices. The changes in relative price then induce substitutions in patterns of production and consumption, which, though they may at first be negligible, grow in magnitude as contracts are renegotiated and as new plant and equipment is installed to take advantage of changed profit opportunities. Available evidence would suggest that the magnitudes of these quantitative responses do produce a long-run improvement in the trade balance.[2] There may, however, be an initial deterioration as a result of the adverse terms-of-trade effect, the so-called 'J' curve response to depreciation, as the immediate effects on relative prices precede the longer-term quantitative responses of trade flows.

Even if the elasticities of foreign and domestic demand and supply are of the right magnitude, the effects do not stop there. To the extent that the trade balance improves in terms of home currency, the aggregate demand for UK goods will be increased and this, via the multiplier effects on income, will create subsequent and partially offsetting increases in the demand for imports. Furthermore, if the economy is at or near to full employment, the devaluation-induced expansion of aggregate demand will have inflationary implications which can only be prevented if domestic expenditure is reduced to make room for the improvement of the trade balance. Finally, account must be taken of the import content of domestic production, and the effect of the devaluation in raising domestic costs of production and of its effects in creating pressure for higher money wages.[3] This latter qualification is of prime importance. For unless the depreciation is associated with a reduction in real wages, then the only effect of a real depreciation of sterling will be to lower the long-run profitability of UK manufacturing industry. If, however, domestic firms follow pricing policies to maintain rates of return, then the real depreciation will be prevented, the ultimate effects of the depreciation will be purely nominal and there will not be any long-run effect on flows of exports and imports.

---

1 On the pricing policies of UK firms following the 1967 devaluation, see P.B. Rosendale, 'The Short-Run Pricing Policies of Some British Engineering Exporters', *NIER*, No. 65, 1973, and the valuable study by D.C. Hague, E. Oakeshott and A. Strain, *Devaluation and Pricing Decisions*, Allen and Unwin, 1974. Professor Cooper has suggested that foreign suppliers cut down their foreign-currency prices on average by 4%. See A.K. Cairncross (ed.), *Britain's Economic Prospects Reconsidered*, Allen and Unwin, 1971, p. 181.

2 In the special case in which there is initial balanced trade and supply elasticities of traded goods are infinite, then the depreciation improves the trade balance provided that the sum of the foreign and domestic elasticities of demand for imported goods exceeds unity. For a more general statement, see Kindleberger and Lindert, *International Economics*, Irwin, 1978, chapter 15 and Appendix H. Evidence suggests that this so-called 'Marshall–Lerner' condition would be satisfied for the UK.

3 The average import content of UK manufacturing output is currently 21%.

The conclusion to be drawn from this is that powerful forces are at work to offset the initial effects of a managed depreciation on the balance of trade. Indeed, recent calculations show that the effects of a hypothetical depreciation in sterling are largely transitory with respect to the level of output and the current balance of payments and that, after six years, a devaluation of 5% would produce a 4% increase in the UK's retail price index. These calculations also make clear that the effects of a devaluation depend on the fiscal policies and other policies to control money income which accompany the depreciation.[1] Certainly, the depreciation of sterling in 1976 only produced a temporary increase in the international competitiveness of UK goods which had been entirely eroded by the beginning of 1979.

Discussion of the inflationary effects of an exchange depreciation raises another reason why a government may wish to manage the exchange rate actively. Some of the arguments here were stimulated by the sharp depreciation of sterling in 1976, which occurred after a period in which domestic incomes restraint had reduced the annual rate of increase of unit labour costs in UK manufacturing from 30% between 1974-5 to 11.2% between 1975-6. It has been suggested, therefore, that a managed appreciation of sterling would help to combat domestic inflation. The argument surfaced again in 1981 when the decline in sterling was alleged to threaten the then current anti-inflation policy. The main proposition here is that the rate of inflation is influenced by the pressure of demand in the labour market and by expectations of inflation, so that a currency appreciation reduces inflation on three fronts: it directly lowers domestic production costs via the cost of imported means of production, it reduces the pressure of demand for labour by its adverse effects on the demand for UK output, and, by reducing inflation in this direct fashion, it has the indirect effect of lowering the anticipated rate of inflation thus moderating money wage demands and possibly increasing the viability of attempts to directly influence money wages. The effectiveness of such a policy must, however, be questioned, not least because of the ambiguity over whether any persistent change in the exchange rate is a cause of, or only an implication of, domestically generated inflation. Indeed, to take one extreme, if it were the case that inflation expectations were formed, as some economists suggest, from a knowledge of rates of growth of UK monetary aggregates, then the exchange rate will also reflect this information and its movements should not have any independent influence on the UK inflation rate. It will be clear that the competing claims of 'industrial competitiveness' and 'anti-inflation policy' upon exchange-rate policy are inconsistent, and for the present it would appear that the anti-inflation motives governing exchange-rate policy have the upper hand.

So far we have taken for granted the view that the exchange rate can be managed to achieve either balance-of-payments or inflation-rate effects. Such a view may prove excessively optimistic outside the short period. First, one has to recognize that in a world where all the major currencies are floating, governments may follow mutually inconsistent exchange-rate targets and find themselves in a situation of

---

1 Cf. *TER*, March 1978, No. 96. It is particularly important that the money supply is not allowed to expand and negate the effects of depreciation in reducing real money balances and absorption. A more recent study suggests that, holding money wages constant, a 10% effective depreciation of sterling would be followed after three years by a 4% increase in wholesale prices and a 2.5% increase in consumer prices. See the article, 'Sterling and Inflation', *BEQB*, September 1981.

competitive exchange-rate management in which one country's policies are nullified by the action of others. Secondly, experience gained with sterling and other currencies during the 1960s and the 1970s showed that it becomes increasingly difficult for the authorities to maintain an exchange rate substantially different from its equilibrium value without inducing disruptive flows of speculative short-term capital which ultimately force a change in policy. Thirdly, and more funda-mentally, there are strong arguments to suggest that any attempt to maintain an exchange rate other than that dictated by purchasing-power parity must be a failure in the long run. This argument simply takes account of the fact that any artificial, disequilibrium exchange rate will, in general, be associated with a non-zero BOF and thus with changes in the stock of foreign-exchange reserves and the domestic money supply.[1] One version of this proposition is as follows. If the exchange rate is notionally depreciated, the effect on the domestic price level will reduce the real value of monetary assets in general and induce a temporary trade surplus as agents attempt to restore real asset holdings to their equilibrium levels. This surplus will expand the reserves and the money supply until balance sheets are returned to equilibrium and the pre-devaluation structure of relative prices regained. The only permanent effect of the devaluation will be an equal proportionate increase in the price level and an increase in the stock of foreign-exchange reserves. It must be stressed that this is a long-run argument, and that the links between changes in the reserves and the domestic money supply can be offset by domestic monetary policy. However, despite these qualifications, it throws into perspective the point that management of the exchange rate is only likely to prove successful in the short run.

Unresolved issues: We have already described the direct effects on the balance of payments of the growing production of North Sea oil and gas since 1973, and argued that this was a key factor behind the appreciation of sterling between 1979 and 1980. In 1983, the price of oil relative to world exports of manufactures was four and a half times greater than in 1973 (this calculation leaves aside the quality premium on UK crude), and the UK has indeed been fortunate to capitalize on this change in world relative prices. Yet many doubt that the benefits are real, and even industrialists are sometimes prone to suggest that the UK would have been better off without the exploitation of North Sea resources. The key issue here is the effect of the oil revenues on the exchange rate and whether any oil-induced appreciation of sterling above purchasing-power parity is inevitable. Two facts are crucial to this issue and must be borne in mind in what follows: that as much as 80% of North Sea revenues will accrue in taxes to the Exchequer; and that all UK production represents an equivalent gross gain to the balance of visible trade.[2] The impact effect of increased UK production is necessarily one of improving the current account and putting upward pressure on the exchange rate — an effect enhanced by the petrocurrency issues discussed in the next section. The high

---

1 For useful accounts of the links between external transactions and the domestic money supply, see 'Of DCE, M_3 and Similar Mysteries', *MBR*, February 1977, and 'External and Foreign Currency Flows and the Money Supply', *BEQB*, December 1978.

2 The tax revenue figure comes from P.J. Forsyth and J.A. Kay, 'The Economic Implications of North Sea Oil Revenues', *Fiscal Studies*, 1980, pp. 1-28.

exchange rate crowds out the production of non-oil tradeables in the UK and, since these are labour-intensive relative to oil, has the effect of reducing the aggregate demand for labour at current levels of real wages. What is the appropriate policy response to this so-called 'Dutch disease' phenomenon?[1] Whatever policy is adopted, the objective must be to generate a countervailing increase in the supply of sterling in the foreign-exchange market and thus prevent any oil-induced appreciation of the spot-exchange rate.

A first priority will be to expand the economy and reduce current levels of unemployment and spare capacity using tax cuts or public expenditure increases financed directly from North Sea tax receipts. Via the familiar multiplier mechanisms, these policies will increase the demand for net imports of goods and securities, and thus help to hold down the exchange rate. Alternatively, a reduced PSBR would allow some reduction in interest rates, with additional beneficial effects on capital flows and the exchange rate. Now suppose, as seems plausible, that full employment is reached before the North Sea resources effect on the exchange rate is eliminated. Further tax cuts will have a relatively small effect on imports of consumption goods and the best policy option would be for the government to make those socially profitable investments in infrastructure which have either a high import content, or a substantial capacity for generating employment in order to absorb resources displaced from the non-oil traded goods sector, e.g. investment in health, education, research and training. In this way, the North Sea oil benefit could be translated into physical and human capital assets with positive effects on UK industrial competitiveness in the medium and long term when North Sea production begins to decline.[2]

An alternative line of policy would be for the government to invest the additional tax revenues in foreign assets, either directly by exchange-market intervention and the repayment of foreign debts sensibly accumulated during the period 1974-7, or indirectly by running a lower PSBR, so potentially leaving a large fraction of domestic savings free for private overseas investment. While the short-term effects of this strategy will certainly limit any appreciation of sterling, it is easy to see that, in the longer term, it would of itself only delay the oil-induced exchange-rate appreciation as the return flow of interest and profits swells current-account receipts.[3]

It is difficult to avoid the practical conclusion, once full employment is restored, that the exploitation of the North Sea will leave the UK with a higher exchange rate than would otherwise prevail. Some structural change is certain to follow from this, with adverse consequences for employment in the production of manufactured tradeable goods. The pattern of comparative advantage has changed and in a way which allows a higher *average* level of UK income than would otherwise prevail. The proper response is surely not how change can be prevented but

---

1 On this, see the interesting article by M. Ellman, *Cambridge Journal of Economics*, 1977.

2 Cf. *The Challenge of NS Oil*, Cmnd. 7143, HMSO, 1978.

3 If X is the annual capital outflow 'financed' out of North Sea revenues and r the interest return on these investments, then after T years, the return flow of interest will be rXT. The net annual gain in the supply of sterling is thus $X(1-rT)$, which is smaller the longer the policy is maintained. Thus if r is 6%, the policy will become self-defeating after 16.5 years. Investment in barren assets would avoid this problem and, of course, dissipate entirely the benefits of North Sea oil!

how the consequences of North Sea resources can be accommodated with a minimum of transitional cost and a maximum of longer-term benefit.[1]

The second related issue is that of persistent unemployment in the UK, currently well above the average levels of the 1960s, and the view that in order to eliminate this and at the same time revive UK industry, some substantial protection in the form of import restrictions will be required. The argument here is complex and hotly debated, but the broad issues are clear enough. To the extent that unemployment in the UK is a reflection of the general world recession, induced by the past and recent oil price increases, there is little to commend import restrictions. To adopt such a policy would be in the worst tradition of beggar-thy-neighbour diplomacy. However, to the extent that the UK's employment and lack of competitive edge in world markets reflect structural problems unique to UK industry, then general import restrictions, provided they are linked to a policy of investment and industrial reconstruction, merit at least a hearing if only because the alternative policy of a sterling depreciation may not prove viable for the reasons outlined above.[2] In response to the argument that foreign retaliation will be provoked, it should be remembered that any policy which improves the UK's trade balance and competitive strength, whether it be import restriction, export subsidy or devaluation, must 'harm the foreigner', so that the precise way this is achieved should be a relatively minor matter dictated by the net advantages of each policy for the UK. It should also be remembered that the purpose of such a policy is primarily to stimulate the demand for UK output so that its final effect on UK imports would be smaller than its impact effect, the difference reflecting the induced increase in imports as domestic incomes and employment increase. Indeed, as the economy grows, the permitted volume of imports can also be allowed to grow in step. Practical objections to such a policy are essentially twofold. First, there are the immediate political difficulties of obtaining EEC and IMF approval, especially as any sensible policy of import restrictions would have to last for fifteen years or so, and would have to be implemented when the favourable balance-of-payments effects of North Sea oil are at their height. Second, and more fundamentally, there is no guarantee that higher levels of output and employment will lead to more productive investment, more flexible working practices and a willingness to take innovative risks. If they do not, the import restrictions could prove a recipe for stagnation rather than industrial regeneration.[3] The diagnosis, then, is quite simple. Without a significant increase in the competitive ability of UK industry, the long-term prospects for employment and living standards in the UK are quite grim. It is the nature of the medicine which is unknown, and while import controls may possibly be a part of any cure, they will certainly not be sufficient of themselves to regenerate the UK's industrial structure.

---

1   On the inevitability of structural change, see Forsyth and Kay, op. cit. We leave aside any discussion of a further policy option, i.e. managing the production flow from the North Sea to minimize the effect on the exchange rate. This involves complicated questions of intertemporal choice beyond the bounds of realistic policy formation

2   The most persistent advocates of this view have been the Cambridge Economic Policy Group. See, e.g., their *Economic Policy Review*, No. 4, March 1978, and the contribution by R. Neild to the book by R.D. Major cited at the end of this chapter.

3   The 7th edition of this volume contains a brief account of the temporary import restrictions employed by the UK in the 1960s.

III.6 Capital Flows and Balance-of-Payments Policy

In this section we shall investigate the relationship between capital movements, the balance of payments and the exchange rate. As we have pointed out in section I.2, the distinction between short-term and long-term capital flows is to a considerable extent arbitrary, and the distinctions drawn here reflect matters of convenience alone. By short-term capital movements, we shall mean transactions between UK and overseas residents, in currency, bank deposits and securities, transactions which are typically related to the finance of foreign trade or the optimal allocation of stocks of wealth between assets denominated in different currencies. In the case of long-term capital flows, we shall primarily be concerned with the international direct investment operations of companies and public-sector bodies.

Short-term capital movements have traditionally played an important role in the overall UK balance-of-payments situation. Their importance is the joint result of the position of London as an international financial centre, and of the historical role of sterling as an international reserve asset and medium of exchange. Thus, some short-term capital movements reflect changes in the sterling balances which foreign governments and individuals have acquired as matters of commercial and financial convenience. The remainder reflect the role of London as the major centre for the Eurocurrency, Euroloan and other international financial markets, with banks in the UK lending and borrowing extensively in dollars and other currencies. The development of the Eurocurrency and related markets since 1958 has meant the increasing integration of European and American capital and money markets.[1] The degree of integration increased particularly quickly in the 1970s with the rapid growth of the Eurocurrency market, with net deposits of $85bn in 1971 increasing to $932bn in 1982. The volume of deposits and the ease with which they may be switched between currencies have important implications for the stability of exchange rates and the conduct of national monetary policies.

The significance of short-term capital flows for the conduct of UK policy arises from their magnitude relative to the official reserves and from their volatility. It is convenient to divide the capital flows which influence the UK balance of payments into two broad classes: speculative and non-speculative. The motive behind speculative capital flows is one of making a capital gain from anticipated movements in spot exchange rates or interest rates. A currency speculator would be indifferent between holding sterling- or dollar-denominated assets, for example, if the interest rate on sterling assets equalled the interest rate on dollar assets plus the anticipated depreciation of sterling relative to the dollar – risk premium here being ignored. If the anticipated sterling devaluation exceeds the sterling interest advantage, holders of sterling assets will switch their assets into dollars while UK importers will accelerate (lead) dollar payments for imports and UK exporters will try to delay (lag) dollar payments due from foreigners. Non-speculative activities undertaken to avoid capital gains or losses associated with exchange-rate movements, involve simultaneous transactions in both spot and forward currency markets so that the risks associated with currency transactions may be shifted

---

1 Eurocurrency deposits are bank deposits in currencies other than that of the country in which the banks in question are located. For the working and development of the Eurocurrency markets, consult G.W. McKenzie, *The Economics of the Eurocurrency System*, Macmillan, 1976. See also, 'Eurobanks and the Inter-Bank Market', *BEQB*, September 1981.

onto speculators.[1] In sum, short-term capital movements depend on a complex set of interactions between national interest rates, spot and forward exchange rates and expectations of future changes in spot rates. Not surprisingly, short-term capital flows are highly volatile and are capable of creating substantial deviations of an exchange rate from its purchasing-power value. The fact that the exchange market is an efficient, competitive market means that mere changes in the news may result in sudden exchange-rate movements as expectations are revised. Indeed, it is quite plausible to argue that short-term exchange-rate movements will exceed those required to restore long-run exchange-market equilibrium in the face of exogenous disturbances.[2] The precarious nature of expectations in general, also implies that short-term capital movements are not necessarily amenable to official attempts at their control. During periods of rapidly diverging national rates of inflation, expectations of exchange-rate changes will be greatly influenced by expectations of differences in national inflation rates. In a world of high capital mobility, the short-term capital flows induced by the expectation of divergent national inflation rates can exert a dominant influence on the actual movements of the exchange rate.

The implications of short-term capital flows for external and internal policy depend upon the exchange market framework in operation. Under the par-value system, the first impact of a short-term capital outflow fell upon the exchange reserves and thus on the monetary base of the banking system, this being true of both speculative and non-speculative flows. Given the poor reserve/short-term liability situation of the UK, any such loss of reserves, if heavy, almost invariably provoked a change in demand-management policy. A 'run on sterling' was normally followed by a policy to contract domestic demand and restore 'confidence', frequently in conjunction with foreign borrowing by the government. With a freely floating exchange rate, however, the impact effect of a net capital flow falls not upon the reserves but upon the spot exchange rate and, in general, will not affect the money supply.[3] A capital outflow will now work to depreciate sterling, and an inflow to appreciate sterling. However, any such change in the exchange rate acts upon the current account in the same way as a policy-induced parity change. Hence, a capital inflow has effects akin to those of an appreciation; discouraging exports, encouraging imports, as well as influencing the price level.

It will be clear that large and sudden capital flows can provide difficult policy problems for economies operating with floating exchange rates and, in the light of this, it is relevant to enquire if the UK authorities can exert any substantial influence over short-term capital flows. In the first instance, some restraint on UK residents can be obtained via exchange-control provisions which, until 1979, were a major element in UK policy. Under these provisions, UK residents were denied the opportunity to purchase foreign currency except for authorized purposes, and direct limits were placed on the net foreign-exchange positions which banks and

---

1   See the 6th edition of this volume for a discussion of forward market transactions. More detailed treatments will be found in Grubel, *International Economics*; Irwin, 1977, chapter 12, and Kindleberger and Lindert, op. cit., chapter 13 and Appendix G.

2   An introduction to this technical phenomena known as 'exchange-rate overshooting' may be found in R. Dornbusch, *Open Economy Macroeconomics*, Basic Books, 1980, chapter 11.

3   For a statement of the exceptions to the general rule, see the article, 'External and Foreign Currency Flows and the Money Supply', *BEQB*, December 1978.

other exchange dealers could undertake in the course of their business.[1] A particularly important dimension of exchange control was that limiting purchases of overseas securities by UK residents. From 1947 onwards, purchases of securities issued in non-sterling area countries could not be financed with official foreign exchange, nor could the proceeds of the liquidation of such investments be converted back into sterling at the official exchange rate. Instead, all such transactions had to pass through the investment currency market at a separate exchange rate which balanced the desire to purchase foreign currency securities with the desire to liquidate existing holdings of NSA assets. Typically, the investment currency rate stood at a premium relative to the official exchange rate, the magnitude of the premium providing some indication of the degree of the restriction on potential capital outflows.

Numerous changes in the degree of restriction took place in the period from 1960 onwards, the most significant being the 25% surrender rule introduced in 1965 under which 25% of the foreign-currency proceeds of security transactions had to be converted into sterling at the official, spot exchange rate. Entry into the EEC, however, meant that the UK had to abide by the Community directives freeing capital movements within the Community from exchange restriction. To comply with EEC regulations, the surrender rule was abolished in January 1978 though the remaining network of controls was maintained under the escape clause, Article 108 of the Treaty of Rome, for balance-of-payments protection. The strength of sterling during 1979, and the prospective benefits of North Sea oil, rendered the balance-of-payments argument for controls nugatory and they were partially relaxed in June 1979 and finally abolished in October 1979. From this date, the capital and money markets of the UK become fully integrated with those of the rest of the world. The effects of this should not be exaggerated, since the exchange regulations applied only to UK residents and left untouched the activities of non-resident holders of sterling, who since 1958 have been free to switch between sterling and other currencies. Indeed, the major impact is likely to be felt through greater competition in capital and money markets rather than in any substantial long-term change in the net flows of capital across the exchanges. To be sure, the relaxation of exchange controls has allowed a once-for-all adjustment of the asset portfolios of UK individuals and financial institutions. Recent calculations do, indeed, indicate an effect of this nature, with the portfolio capital outflow in the years 1980 to 1983 roughly seven times greater than in the years 1977 to 1979.[2] To the extent that these figures accurately reflect the abolition of exchange controls, then it is clear that this policy could be justified as one means of limiting the oil-wealth effect on the sterling exchange rate.

Exchange controls apart, two alternative means of inducing capital flows may be employed. Manipulation of domestic interest rates is a powerful weapon in current circumstances, given the increasing integration of financial markets. Its use is subject to two limiting provisos: international retaliation, and conflict with the level of interest rates needed to attain internal objectives. The remaining policy option is official manipulation of the forward exchange rate, which would allow

---

1 For details, see the article 'Limits on UK Banks' Foreign Exchange Positions', *BEQB*, December 1975.

2 See also the article, 'The Effects of Exchange Control Abolition on Capital Flows', *BEQB*, September 1981.

the authorities to create for the UK a risk-free interest-rate advantage on short-term investments, as circumstances dictate. Between 1962 and 1967, the UK achieved some success with this policy, effectively counteracting pressure on the reserves on several occasions. Although such a policy may be run at a modest profit for the UK authorities, technical losses arise if the spot rate is changed while official forward contracts are outstanding. This occurred with the 1967 deval-uation, when the sum of £366m had to be paid out to foreigners who at the time held forward contracts to sell sterling. Since that episode, there has been little indication of official forward activity.

By far the most significant element influencing capital movements since 1973 has been the increase in the price of oil, which created a massive capacity to lend by the OPEC nations while simultaneously enhancing the desirability of depositing surplus funds in sterling. Indeed, the combination of London's financial infra-structure with the exploitation of North Sea oil wealth has been a major factor in keeping the value of sterling above the level which is indicated by purchasing-power-parity considerations. For example, in the period 1979-81, oil-exporting countries deposited $44bn in the UK, roughly 18% of the current-account surplus which followed the second oil price increase. With the evaporation of these surpluses from 1982 onwards, the inflow of funds was turned into an outflow of roughly $10bn per annum in 1982 and 1983. At the end of 1983, oil-exporting countries accounted for 22% of total sterling balances, which may be compared with the 20% held within the European Community.[1]

We turn now to consider long-term capital flows, and direct investment over-seas in particular. Foreign direct investment is one mechanism by which modern corporations seek to gain competitive advantages relative to their rivals, and the rate and direction of investment is determined by anticipated profit opportunities. Avoiding tariff barriers and taking advantage of cheap foreign labour are two underlying motives, although, increasingly, foreign direct investment must be considered in relation to exporting and foreign licencing of technology, as ways in which the firm may extract maximum advantage from its knowledge and human capital base.[2] Throughout the postwar period to 1979, investment overseas by UK firms was strictly controlled with the object not of preventing such investment but of ensuring that it was financed either from the retained profits of foreign operations or from currency borrowing.[3] Indeed, over the period from 1965 to 1978, roughly half of UK direct investment overseas was financed out of retained profits and the remainder largely from foreign borrowing. Quite how the relaxation of exchange controls will affect this financing pattern it is too early to say, but the initial indications are that finance from UK retained profits is being substituted for foreign borrowing.

Entry into the EEC as yet seems to have had a negligible effect on the pattern of the UK's overseas investment. During the period 1972-83, 43.5% of the total

1 The 9th edition of this volume contains an extended discussion of the evolution of sterling balances in the 1960s and 1970s and of the official measures taken to support the maintenance of the sterling holdings.

2 Cf. R. Caves, 'International Corporations: The Industrial Economics of Foreign Investment', *Economica*, Vol. 38, 1971, pp. 1-27.

3 The 9th edition of this volume contains details of the capital controls on overseas direct investment.

outflow was directed to North America, with the EEC accounting for 17.6%. Of the total stock of UK direct investment assets in the mid-1970s, 28% was located in Western Europe and 23% in North America, compared to figures of 13% and 23% in 1962.[1] This change in the share located in Western Europe is, of course, closely related to the change in the UK trade structure noted in section II.1. At the same time, it is interesting to note that 90% of the UK's foreign direct investment liabilities are owned by firms originating from Western Europe and North America.

The movements of capital funds across the exchanges cumulate over time to determine the net asset position of the UK vis-à-vis other countries. The balance of payments on current account is the chief element in this process, but valuation effects due to exchange-rate and national interest-rate changes are also an important factor. At end-1982, identified net assets amounted to £37.5bn or 19% of GNP. Largely as a consequence of North Sea oil exploitation, the ratio of gross external assets to GNP has risen from 0.9 in 1970 to 1.9 in 1982.[2]

Associated with the stocks of foreign assets and liabilities are return flows of interest, profits and dividends (IPD) which appear in the current account. For the UK, roughly 53% of the IPD credits are related to past direct investments by UK manufacturing firms, and 7% are derived from portfolio investments. It is worth noting that, throughout the period since 1960, the outflow of foreign investment from the UK has been smaller than the return flow of IPD credits on the existing stock of assets. While the net flow of IPD into the current account is positive, from year to year, the net receipts of foreign income are now less than 1% of GDP.

III.7   The UK and the European Economic Community

The question of UK membership of the EEC has always been controversial and the controversy has shown little tendency to abate since the UK became a full member in January 1973. The Labour government of 1974 declared its firm intention to renegotiate the original terms of entry,[3] completed the renegotiations in March 1975[4] and then settled the question in favour of membership with a referendum in July 1975. However, the case for EEC membership is still the subject of active political debate in the UK and there remains a possibility that the UK could terminate its full EEC links in the future. In this section we shall only comment upon the balance-of-payments implications of membership; other implications are treated in chapters 2 and 4 of this volume.

It was apparent at the time of the pre-entry negotiations that the full effects of entry into the EEC would imply a deterioration in the current account and possibly a deterioration in the long-term capital account of the balance of

---

1   For further details, see J.H. Dunning, 'The UK's International Direct Investment Position in the Mid-1970s', *LBR*, April 1978.

2   Cf. 'The External Balance Sheet of the United Kingdom: Developments to End-1982', *BEQB*, June 1983, pp. 240-8.

3   *Renegotiation of the Terms of Entry into the European Economic Community*, Cmnd. 5593, April 1974.

4   *Membership of the European Community: Report on Renegotiation*, Cmnd. 6003, March 1975.

payments. To offset this, the UK would have to depreciate the exchange rate or employ direct policies of expenditure reduction in order to achieve the cut in real income and expenditure necessary to eliminate the adverse balance-of-payments effects of entry. Against this 'real resource cost' could be set the dynamic, long-run benefit of selling in a greatly enlarged market; a benefit which, it was argued, would result from greater economies of scale in production and which would be reflected in an increase in the UK growth rate.[1] Improved growth performance, it was thought, would possibly yield some offsetting dynamic gains to the basic balance, provided productivity in the UK grew faster than the Community average. Unfortunately, while it proved possible to provide plausible estimates of the balance-of-payments costs, measurement of the potential dynamic gains has so far eluded any precise assessment. Certainly, membership of the EEC has not reversed the relative economic decline of the UK. Indeed, between 1972 and 1979 per capita GNP in the UK fell from 85% to 78% of the EEC average. Optimists may argue that there has been some convergence of the UK growth rate toward the EEC average[2] but to what extent this can be attributed to UK membership is not clear. At the time of writing, any belief in the dynamic effects of entry remains a matter of faith.

The effects on the UK current account can, in principle, be discussed under three headings: changes in the pattern of trade in manufactures, adoption of the common agricultural policy, and contributions to the Community budget.

The main implications for trade in manufactures follow from the customs union aspects of the Community, all tariffs on trade between the UK and other members having been reduced to zero in 1977 when the UK adopted the final stages of the common external tariff (CET) on trade with non-Community countries.[3]

It is impossible as yet to say what the final effects on the UK's pattern of trade will be. Adjustment to the tariff changes will not be immediate, and we must also take into account the discrimination which is now imposed against former Commonwealth countries (excluding signatories of the Lomé Convention) and the associated loss of UK export preferences in the same countries. We have already shown, in section II.1, that the direction of UK trade in the 1950s and 1960s swung progressively toward Western Europe and away from the traditional markets in North America and the OSA. It is clear that entry into the EEC has accelerated this trend. Over the years 1963 to 1973, UK exports of manufactures to the EEC increased at an average annual rate of 10.7%, while imports from the EEC increased by 16.6%. Between 1973 and 1983, these average annual growth rates of trade in manufactures increased dramatically, with exports to the EEC increasing by 21.1% and imports from the EEC increasing by 19.1%.[4] However, it remains the

---

1 *Britain and the European Communities: An Economic Assessment*, Cmnd. 4289, February 1970.

2 *European Economy*, November 1981.

3 The necessary tariff changes were to be achieved in stages. For details, see *The United Kingdom and the European Communities*, Cmnd 4715, July 1971. Following the completion of the Tokyo Round of multilateral tariff reductions in 1979, the average CET on industrial products will fall from 9.8% to 7.5% over an eight-year period.

4 For a more detailed analysis of the increasing intensity of UK–EEC trade, see A.E. Daly, 'UK Visible Trade and the Common Market', *NIER*, No. 86, November 1978. In this period to 1979, the value of Intra-EEC trade increased by approximately 16% per annum.

case that the UK trades with the EEC less intensively than do her fellow members of the Community. Thus, in 1983, roughly 45% of UK exports and imports were exchanged with EEC countries, compared to an average intra-trade of the whole Community of 52%. This divergence of trading patterns, which applies to agriculture as well as manufacturing, is an important factor behind the adverse net budgetary position of the UK which emerged after 1979.

Assessments of the balance-of-payments cost of entry for the UK have tended to concentrate upon the effects of adopting the CAP system of agricultural support in place of the deficiency-payments method formerly used by the UK. Under the deficiency-payments method, the UK imported foodstuffs at world prices, free of any import duty, and farm incomes were supported out of general taxation. Under the CAP, the UK is obliged to import all EEC foodstuffs at the common EEC prices, and to impose variable import levies and export subsidies on trade with non-EEC countries, so that the cost of support falls directly upon the consumer. At the time of the negotiation for entry, it was estimated that EEC prices were between 18% and 26% higher than world market prices and that, given an inelastic demand for imports of foodstuffs, the UK import bill would be increased accordingly.

Finally, the UK is obliged to contribute to the budget of the Community and this involves a transfer of funds across the foreign exchanges, the gross contribution of the UK being assessed by a complex formula (set out on page 175 below). The net contribution is smaller than the gross contribution to the extent that the UK receives reverse transfers from the EEC, for example in the form of regional aid, industrial development aid and agricultural support.[1]

Estimates of the static balance-of-payments cost of entry produced widely varying results, although most suggested a substantial balance-of-payments burden[2] and thus an implicit real resource cost of UK entry to be imposed by a devaluation or other means. It was in the light of the assumed adverse balance-of-payments implications that the UK government renegotiated the original terms of entry. The most concrete results of the renegotiation were the creation of a mechanism for reducing the gross budgetary contribution of the UK in line with the UK's share in the total GNP of the Community, and the guarantee of continued access to the Community for Commonwealth sugar and dairy products from New Zealand.[3]

It is remarkable how inaccurate the initial estimates of the balance-of-payments cost have proved to be. Three factors are relevant here. First, and most important, the food-related balance-of-payments cost depends on the gap between EEC prices and world market prices for foodstuffs and this gap varies over time, narrowing at times of world economic expansion and widening during periods of world

---

1 Cf. Cmnd. 4715, paras. 91-6 and Annex A.

2 The 1970 White Paper, Cmnd. 4289, suggested a balance-of-payments cost ranging between £100m and £1.1bn per annum. For a comparison with other, less extreme estimates, see J. Pinder (ed.), *The Economics of Europe*, Charles Knight, 1971, chapter 6 by M. Miller. For a more optimistic assessment, see R.L. Major and S. Hays, 'Another Look at the Common Market', *NIER*, November 1970.

3 Cmnd. 6003. For additional details of the convention which grants tariff preferences on exports to the EEC of industrial products, and some agricultural products from signatory developing countries, see P.L. Coffey, 'The Lomé Agreement and the EEC: Implications and Problems', *TBR*, No. 108, December 1975.

economic contraction. Thus, the increases in world food prices between 1971 and 1974 and between 1979 and 1980 substantially reduced the import cost of the CAP system. In the intervening periods, world prices fell below EEC levels, and the prospects of world food prices continuing to fall (they fell by 28% in dollar terms between 1980 and 1983) must raise once again a potentially formidable burden of UK entry, as well as swelling the proportion of Community expenditure devoted to the CAP.[1]

The second difficulty arises from the complexities of the CAP pricing system. The most important issue here is that the intervention prices are not only set above world market levels, but they are also set at levels which have encouraged substantial production surpluses for many commodities. Handling these surpluses either involves expenditure on storage, or subsidies to farmers to enable the surplus output to be exported to world markets. This policy is wasteful and absurd, providing no link between consumer preferences and food production. Clearly, it is in the UK's interest to press continually for more realistic food-pricing policies and limits on intervention buying, and to try and ensure that EEC prices fall in line with productivity gains in the more advanced farming units.[2] Formidable difficulties have also arisen because EEC food prices are set in terms of units of account and then translated into the respective member currencies at representative exchange rates, the so-called 'green currencies', fixed by administrative decision. Now as long as the ratio between any two green-currency rates is equal to the spot-market exchange rate between the corresponding national currencies, the system works as intended, in that any agricultural commodity will sell at a common price throughout the EEC. Unfortunately, following the collapse of the Bretton Woods exchange-rate system in 1971, spot-market rates for several EEC currencies have diverged substantially from the green-currency rates. In particular, the steady depreciation of sterling between 1972 and 1976 drove the spot rate for sterling below the green-pound rate, the percentage gap on some occasions reaching as much as 45%, despite frequent devaluations of the green pound.[3] The subsequent appreciation of sterling had by February 1981 taken the exchange rate between sterling and the European currency unit 18% above the green rate. The consequences of divergences between green and market exchange rates are extremely disruptive to agricultural trade and production in the EEC, since they undermine the principle of common prices for foodstuffs and create profitable opportunities for arbitrage between commodities and EEC currencies. To prevent this, border taxes and subsidies have to be levied on agricultural trade between EEC countries, the total amounts of subsidy involved being known as monetary

---

1   Recent calculations by the Institute of Fiscal Studies put the overall resource cost of entry for 1983 at 1.3% of GDP.

2   An indication of Community thinking on reform of the CAP may be found in *Bulletin of European Communities*, No. 6, 1981, pp. 12-13. Some 40% of CAP expenditure is on export subsidies and 20% on storage.

3   For further discussion, consult R.W. Irving and H.A. Fern, *Green Money and the Common Agricultural Policy*, Wye College, Occasional Paper No. 2, 1975, and C. Mackel, 'Green Money and the Common Agricultural Policy', *NWBR*, February 1978. The values for the green currencies are published monthly in *Bulletin of the European Communities*, Secretariat General, Brussels. An excellent account of the CAP and the green-currency system is given in A.E. Buckwell *et al.*, *The Costs of the Common Agricultural Policy*, Croom Helm, 1982.

compensation amounts (MCAs). As a substantial net importer of foodstuffs, the UK has been a major beneficiary from the MCA system, and, even though MCAs are now paid to the exporting country, the amounts can still be viewed as a corresponding subsidy to UK consumers and treated as a notional net UK budgetary receipt. Unfortunately for the UK, the appreciation of sterling after 1979 eliminated the need to pay MCA subsidies on UK food imports and thus any potential contribution to the net budgetary position. There can be little doubt that the MCA system is in need of reform. While it began as a temporary measure to maintain a common market in foodstuffs following the currency disruptions of 1972-3, it has subsequently developed into a permanent feature of the CAP. However, reform will require that green currencies are linked to currency exchange rates, and unless market rates are stabilized, this will raise formidable administrative difficulties for the CAP. It is easy to see how the establishment of a stable European currency area would provide a convenient means for shoring up the CAP and dismantling the MCA system.

The third area of difficulty, when estimating the balance-of-payments cost of entry, relates to calculation of the net budgetary contribution. This question has received a great deal of attention since 1979, because it was in 1980 that the UK shouldered for the first time the full budgetary cost of entry. The EEC budget is financed from the 'own resources' of the Community, which consist of all import duties and agricultural levies from non-EEC sources[1] plus a VAT contribution which does not exceed 1% of proceeds of a VAT levied on a uniform basis in the Community. On this basis, the gross UK contribution in 1984 is expected to be of the order of 20% of total own resources, even though the UK accounts for only 18% of Community GNP. The real problem for the UK, however, lies with the net contribution. After allowing for grants and loans, the UK can expect to receive only 10% of the Community's expenditure, leaving a net UK budgetary contribution, prior to any rebate, variously estimated to lie between £0.9bn and £1.2bn during 1984. This net contribution for one year may be compared with the cumulative gross contribution of £3.19bn over the calendar years 1973 to 1978 and a cumulative net contribution over the same period of £1.34bn.[2] The estimated net contribution represents a substantial transfer across the exchanges and, not surprisingly, the UK government has sought ways of reducing this burden.

In 1980, a special system of rebates for the UK was negotiated which, pending a more fundamental reform, reduced the net contribution to £800m in 1981/2 and £457m in 1983/4. Longer-term reform is more difficult and depends upon the adoption of a revised budgetary mechanism. The fundamental problem here is not so much the low level of GDP relative to other Community members but long-standing structural features of UK agriculture. The fact that the UK is more heavily dependent on imports from non-EEC sources enhances her gross contribution, whilst the small size and the greater efficiency of her agricultural sector mean that receipts from the agricultural funds are small.[3] At the root of this

---

1 Less 10% to cover costs of collection and administration.

2 At current prices. See *The Government's Expenditure Plans 1979-80 to 1982-83*, Cmnd. 7439, January 1979.

3 During 1984 the UK is expected to benefit from only 6% of farm price support expenditure but to contribute 27% of customs duty revenue and 19% of agricultural levy revenue in the EEC.

problem lies the continued growth in the amount of EEC expenditure devoted to the CAP, approaching 70% of the Community budget in 1984, which leaves relatively small amounts for the regional, social and other programmes from which the UK would be a major beneficiary.

The issue has been made particularly acute in 1984 by the fact that CAP expenditure is expected to exceed the own resources of the Community by as much as 18%, so creating a situation of technical bankruptcy. As is normally the case in human affairs, a crisis sharpens the mind, and considerable effort has been devoted to reforming the budgetary mechanism and the CAP. On the budgetary front, a proposal, at the 1984 Brussels meeting of heads of state, to raise the level of own resources by an increase in the VAT contribution limit to 1.6%, taking effect from 1986, fell foul of the conflict over the revised long-term formula for the UK's budget contribution.[1] More fundamentally though, the immediate problem is to control CAP expenditure, particularly with the prospect of accession by Spain and Portugal, both major producers of Mediterranean produce. As long as the basic principles of the CAP are adhered to, the two major avenues for economy are to link EEC prices more closely with world prices, and to place limits on the amount of farm production which will receive support. The 1984 price review certainly made limited progress in this direction with an average 0.5% cut in prices paid to farmers and, most significant of all, a 7% cut in milk-production quotas. Even so, the cost of support of the dairy sector is still expected to account for 21% of the total agricultural budget. The MCA system is also to be abolished by 1987, although Commission proposals to make food producers co-responsible for the cost of excess production were not acceptable. The fundamental problems remain, and advocates of reform must be concerned at the general willingness to increase the level of own resources and ease the pressures on this wasteful and inefficient system of farm support.

Although the CAP and budgetary contribution questions have tended to dominate practical discussion on EEC membership, it is important to recognize that the issue of monetary unification is potentially of greater significance to the UK. In 1971, the European Commission, following guidelines laid down in the Werner Report of 1970, adopted the goal of full monetary union to be achieved by 1980. In its fullest form, this would involve the irrevocable fixing of the parities of EEC countries one to another, full currency convertibility for current- and capital-account transactions and the creation of a Community central bank with full powers to determine monetary policy in each region of the EEC. In many respects, the case for monetary union is an integral part of the case for a common market in commodities. Creation of a single currency (*de facto* by fixing exchange rates, or by the adoption of a new currency unit) reduces transactions costs and promotes exchange and the division of labour which, it could be argued, is necessary if the dynamic gains from membership are to be maximised. Furthermore, it can be argued that once the members of the EEC develop intensive trade and investment links with one another, then adoption of a fixed pattern of exchange rates is the only foreign-exchange-market policy consistent with price stability. Stable EEC parities are, of course, a very necessary part of the operation of CAP and other Community-wide policies. Whatever the merits of these arguments, it should be

---

1 A side-effect of which was the freezing of the 1983 budget rebate.

realized that the costs of monetary unification are considerable.[1] As part of a monetary union, the UK would abandon the right to change its parity unilaterally against other currencies, having already surrendered the ability to impose import restrictions and export subsidies for balance-of-payments purposes by adopting the CET. Expenditure-switching instruments are, therefore, eliminated from the armoury of feasible economic policies. Adjustment to payments deficits must, then, be by domestic deflation and the creation of unemployment, with the harmful and ultimately self-defeating implications noted in section II.2 above. At best, a high degree of labour mobility to the other EEC countries may mitigate the effects on unemployment, while it is possible that sustained financial support from other Community members may ease, but not eliminate, the burden of adjustment. Equally, the commitment to capital-market integration would rule out restrictions on capital transactions in order to improve the basic balance.

An important step toward the objectives of monetary integration was taken in March 1979 with the formal adoption of the European Monetary System (EMS), the objective of which is the creation of a zone of monetary stability in Europe, and the return of the Community to the exchange-rate certainties of its first ten years of existence. The EMS consists of two principal components, an exchange-rate structure and intervention mechanism, and a system of credits for financing payments imbalances between members. It was planned that by 1981 the credit system would have evolved into a European Monetary Fund on the lines of the IMF, but little progress has been made towards this objective.[2] The exchange-rate mechanism is a logical development of the European snake. Following the collapse of the IMF adjustable-peg mechanism in 1971, the first concrete steps toward the creation of a European Monetary System were taken in April 1972 with the agreement to limit the margins of fluctuation between EEC currencies to one-half of the permitted 'Smithsonian' limits.[3] The system proved to be ill-fated. Sterling defected in June 1972, the Lira in February 1973 and the French Franc was forced out of the snake twice, the last of those departures being in March 1976. Despite these setbacks, the pressures toward currency stability have proved powerful and the EMS exchange-rate system is founded on a revitalized snake or currency grid.

Within this grid, each European currency is assigned a central rate against the other EEC currencies, together with a permitted band of fluctuation of 2.25%

---

1 The interested reader may consult Y. Ishiyama, 'The Theory of Optimum Currency Areas: A Survey', *IMF Staff Papers*, Vol. 22, 1975, pp. 344-83. For a discussion of the monetary union between the UK and Eire, see Whitaker, 'Monetary Integration: Reflections on Irish Experience', *Moorgate and Wall Street*, Autumn 1973.

2 Full details of the EMS mechanisms are given in Commission of the European Communities, *European Economy*, July 1979. A brief but useful summary is given in the article, 'Britain and the European Monetary System', *MBR*, Winter 1979. The arguments for monetary integration are set out by the then President of the European Commission, R. Jenkins, in 'European Monetary Union', *LBR*, No. 127, January 1978. See also, 'Intervention Arrangements in the European Monetary System', *BEQB*, June 1979.

3 This scheme was known as the 'snake in the tunnel', the 'snake' representing the closely linked EEC currencies which, under the pressure of market forces, was free to move up and down relative to the dollar in the 'tunnel' defined by the exchange-rate limits (see section III.8). The 'tunnel' disappeared in March 1973 when the EEC currencies engaged in a joint float against the dollar.

either side of this central rate. An exception is made for countries when they join
the system, who may initially adopt margins of 6% around central rates. Central
banks are obliged to keep their currencies within the margins of fluctuation but,
as became clear with the snake, this creates an asymmetric burden of obligation.
The weak currency country loses reserves and is always under pressure to adjust
its internal policies to a greater extent than is the strong-currency country. In the
EMS, an ingenious mechanism has been introduced to try and eliminate the asymmetries of adjustment and to enhance the convergence of exchange-rate and
economic policies. The key to this is the European Currency Unit (ECU), which is
a basket of the nine currencies, initially, but not irrevocably, of the same composition as the European unit of account. The ECU acts as numeraire for the
exchange-rate mechanism and, using the currency-grid exchange rates, each
currency is assigned its central value in terms of ECU together with a maximum
range of divergence around this central value.[1] From this basis, a divergence
threshold is defined whereby a currency may not diverge from its central ECU
rate by more than three-quarters of its divergence rate. The point of these restrictions is that, in general, a currency will reach its divergence threshold before it
reaches any of the bilateral intervention limits defined by the currency grid, and,
once this occurs, there is a presumption that consultation will be initiated with
all Community members to decide upon intervention policy, possible changes in
central parities and any necessary internal policy measures. In this way it is hoped
that burdens of adjustment will be more equally shared within the Community and
the asymmetries of bilateral intervention avoided. Certainly, the major realignment
of EMS parities which took place in October 1981 was achieved with the full
participation of member states, and in total seven such realignments had been
achieved up to March 1984.

Besides acting as numeraire in the EMS, the ECU has an important role as an
instrument of settlement between Community central banks and ultimately as the
planned reserve asset of the Community. Member countries deposit 20% of their
gold and gross dollar reserves with the European Monetary Co-operation Fund on
a three-month renegotiable basis, and in return have access to a variety of credit
facilities, to the total value of 25bn ECU, to finance payments imbalances within
the Community and to support the currency grid.[2] Of this total, 14bn ECU has
been allocated to short-term monetary support and the remainder to medium-
term credit facilities. Although the UK participated fully in the setting up of the
EMS, and contributes to the ECU credit arrangements, it has firmly declined to
join the exchange-rate system, on the grounds that the disparities of economic
performance within the Community make it unwise to fix parities within the
narrow limits set by the currency grid and divergence indicators.[3]

---

1   The maximum range of divergence for each currency is less than ±2.25% and is determined
by the formula ±2.25$(1-w_i)$%, where w_i is the weight of that currency in the value of the
ECU basket. The notional weight for sterling at end-September 1979 was 13.6%, giving a
notional divergence range of ±1.94% for sterling against ECU. The divergence threshold for
sterling is 75% of this, i.e. ±1.45%.

2   The gold contribution is valued at the average London fixing price during the six months
prior to valuation, and the dollar portion is valued at the market rate of the two working days
prior to valuation. At end-1982, ECUs contributed 13% to world foreign-exchange reserves.

3   Cf. *The European Monetary System*, Cmnd. 7405, November 1978.

The position is surely sound. The EEC countries have experienced widely different inflation rates and rates of monetary expansion, the budgetary mechanisms of the Community affect their current payments accounts in different ways, and they differ considerably with respect to the effect of oil price changes upon their respective basic balances. The gyrations of the European currencies against the dollar since 1979 have amply illustrated the difficulties of attempting to fix currency values when underlying circumstances differ between countries. To fix parities is surely folly, unless a common monetary and fiscal policy can be worked out and applied for the whole Community. But such far-reaching changes are a long way off; indeed any fiscal and monetary unification proposals are likely to run foul of strong pressures to maintain national sovereignty in the formulation and implementation of economic policy. The UK government in its pronouncements clearly appreciates the force of these arguments and it is unlikely that the UK will join the EMS in the medium term or even possibly the long term.

III.8   The Reform of the International Monetary System

If the quarter century from 1945 had one dominant characteristic in the international economic arena, it was the integration of national commodity and capital markets into a unified and rapidly growing system of world trade and investment. A key role in this process was played by the international financial rules established at the Bretton Woods conference of 1944, the supervisory institution of which is the International Monetary Fund (IMF).[1] The principal features of the Bretton Woods system were, in brief, its emphasis on mutual international co-operation and its creation of a system of fixed but, in principle, adjustable exchange rates – the par-value system – together with the provision of temporary and conditional balance-of-payments finance by the IMF to supplement reserve media in the form of gold and foreign exchange.

Throughout the 1960s, it became clear that the Bretton Woods system suffered from potentially lethal inconsistencies and that, in particular, it placed the United States in an economic position which the European industrial nations became increasingly unable to accept. The first weakness was the general unwillingness of the main industrial countries to adjust par values in the face of obvious fundamental disequilibria until the force of events, aided by currency speculation, drove governments into belated action. The case of sterling in the mid-1960s and of Germany and Japan in the late 1960s are obvious examples of this failure to use the par-value-adjustment mechanism in the way originally intended by the architects of Bretton Woods. Related to this was the asymmetry between deficit and surplus countries, in that the pressure of reserve losses bore far more heavily on the deficit countries than did the converse phenomenon of reserve gains in the surplus countries. In practice, the 'scarce currency' provisions of Article 7 of the IMF Agreement, which were meant to act as a sanction against persistent surplus countries, were never invoked.

The second weakness involved the supply of global reserve media, which under the IMF system consisted mainly of gold and foreign-exchange holdings, and in particular, of US dollars. The problem was that the supply of monetary gold depended on the vagaries of mining and speculative activity, and the supply of foreign

---

1   Cf. R.N. Cooper, *The Economics of Interdependence*, McGraw Hill, 1968.

exchange depended upon the balance-of-payments deficits of the US, which could prove to be temporary and, more important, unrelated to global reserve needs. In the light of this, there was considerable discussion in the 1960s of the alleged inadequacy of world reserves which took as its basis the observed decline in the ratio of world reserves to world imports, from a value of 68% in 1951 to one of 30% in 1969; the latter being less than the equivalent ratio for the depressed years of the 1930s. A difficulty with this type of discussion was that it failed to make clear that the demand for foreign-exchange reserves is a demand to finance balances-of-payments *disequilibria*, not a demand to finance the volume of trade. It failed, therefore, to recognize that the demand for reserve media will be smaller the more frequently exchange rates are adjusted in line with economic pressure, the more co-ordinated are national policies of demand management, and the greater the willingness of national governments and private capital markets to engage in mutual international borrowing and lending to finance payments imbalances. In the limit, for example, with a perfectly freely floating system of exchange rates, the demand for official reserves would be zero.

Finally, there was the so-called 'confidence' problem, which followed from the increasing degree of dependence of world reserve growth on foreign exchange in the form of the dollar and to a lesser extent sterling. The problem was simply that, by 1964, the total of outstanding dollar liabilities exceeded the gold reserves of the United States and from then on, this disparity between dollar liabilities and gold 'cover' increased. By December 1971, the US gold stock amounted to only 16% of the total of US short-term dollar liabilities held by overseas monetary authorities. *De facto* this meant that the dollar was no longer convertible into primary reserve assets, and so the willingness to hold dollars in official reserves decreased and the danger of a dollar crisis increased. As R. Triffin pointed out in 1960, the gold-exchange standard contained an automatic self-destruct mechanism,[1] with the potential risk of a severe liquidity crisis in which dollar and sterling reserves were liquidated and destroyed, while a given total of gold reserves was redistributed between countries.

Throughout the 1960s, the strains inherent to the system were manifested in a variety of ways. Most significant, perhaps, were the *ad hoc* measures taken by the industrial countries to supplement the existing sources of balance-of-payments finance. At one level were the General Arrangements to Borrow, organized in October 1962, in which the Group of Ten countries (UK, France, Germany, Belgium, Netherlands, Italy, US, Canada, Sweden and Japan) agreed to lend their currencies to the IMF should the latter run short of one of their respective currencies. These arrangements have been renegotiated on several occasions, most recently in February 1983, and the amount of support now totals about SDR 17bn, with the Swiss National Bank added to the list of participants. Recent years have seen increasing use of the GAB, indeed 76% of the finance for the standby arrangements negotiated by the UK in 1976 come from eight of the GAB countries. A second important manifestation of strain related to the official price of gold and the clear possibility that its price might have to be increased to boost world reserves and improve the asset:liability ratio of the US. Attempts to stabilize the free-market price of gold by the major central banks which had begun in 1961

---

1 R. Triffin, *Gold and the Dollar Crisis*, Yale, 1960, and R. Triffin, 'Gold and the Dollar Crisis: Yesterday and Tomorrow', *Essays in International Finance*, No. 132, Princeton, December 1978.

had to be abandoned in March 1968 following the loss of $3bn in monetary gold stocks, sold in an attempt to hold down the free-market price during the previous five months. The Washington Agreement of that time created a two-tier market for gold and effectively prevented national monetary authorities from using monetary gold stocks to finance payments disequilibria in the face of an ever-widening differential between the free-market and the official price of gold. This two-tier system was abandoned in November 1973.

The final, and some would say most significant, manifestation of strain was the increasing volume of speculative capital flows which from 1967 onwards repeatedly disrupted the working of foreign-exchange markets and threatened the parities of sterling, the deutschmark, the yen and the dollar. It became increasingly clear that the par-value system could not survive unless more effective methods for adjusting exchange rates in line with changing economic circumstances could be devised, and unless some means could be found for absorbing the increasing volume of short-term capital flows made possible by the growth of the Eurodollar market. Not surprisingly, in the face of such obvious strains, many proposals for reforming the system were put forward during the 1960s. On the fundamental question of the adjustment mechanism, proposals ranged from the adoption of freely floating exchange rates to mechanisms for ensuring the gradual and automatic adjustment of par values to payments disturbances, the crawling-peg proposal. However, the response of the IMF to such proposals was lukewarm; a study by the executive directors concluded by reaffirming faith in the viability of the par-value system, with the only concessions to flexibility being the suggestion of wider margins of fluctuation around par values and the temporary abrogation of par-value obligations.[1]

By far the most important development of the 1960s was international agreement on the creation of a new reserve asset, the Special Drawing Right. The outcome of several years of discussion, this scheme came into operation in 1970.

Special Drawing Rights: SDRs are book entries in the Special Drawing Account of the IMF, by means of which countries can give and receive credit on a multilateral basis to finance balance-of-payments deficits. At the outset, SDRs were to be held only by those national monetary authorities which participated in the IMF arrangements and which agreed to accept the provisions of the SDR scheme. The total of SDRs is agreed collectively by the members of the IMF, so that the supply of this new reserve asset is agreed by international decision; the basis for their creation being the provision of an adequate, but not inflationary, long-term rate of growth of world reserves. SDRs are thus superior to gold and foreign exchange in that their supply is not arbitrary but is, in principle, the outcome of rational discussion. The total of SDRs is revised on a five-year basis, the last revision in January 1981 taking the cumulative allocation to SDR 21.5bn.[2] Each country is assigned a net cumulative allocation of SDRs, in proportion to its quota

---

1   *The Role of Exchange Rates in the Adjustment of International Payment: A Report by the Executive Directors*, IMF, 1970.

2   The revised Articles of Agreement to incorporate SDRs may be found in the *IMF Annual Report* for 1968, or in the book by F. Machlup listed at the end of this chapter.

in the general account of the IMF, and can treat this allocation as 'owned reserves' to finance payments imbalances. A country in deficit, for example, may use its SDR quota to purchase needed foreign exchange from other countries. One of the most ingenious features of the scheme is that utilization of a country's SDR quota is subject to the supervision of the IMF, the object being to ensure a balanced and widespread activation of the SDR facility. Use of SDRs was initially subject to several provisions, of which the most important was the reconstitution requirement, that a country's average holding over a period of five years must not fall below 30% of its net cumulative allocation, a measure designed to prevent the persistent, as distinct from temporary, financing of a deficit with SDRs.

The fundamental question surrounding the SDR has always been that of whether SDRs simply co-exist with other reserve assets or whether they are destined to replace gold and foreign exchange, or both, as the reserve base of the system. In the initial arrangements, SDRs were effectively a gold substitute, they had a gold guarantee and carried a low rate of interest on net holdings of 1.5%. On the understanding that the dollar was not devalued relative to gold, then SDRs were inferior to the dollar as a reserve asset because of their lower interest yield and lesser convenience of use. However, the dollar devaluations of 1971 and 1973 upset this situation, as did the resort to a general floating of the important currencies relative to gold during 1973. In response to these changing circumstances, a series of steps have been taken since 1974 to enhance the use of the SDR as a store of wealth and as a standard of value. The first step in July 1974 was to value SDRs in terms of a basket of sixteen currencies, rather than in terms of the US dollar alone, and to set the interest rate on net SDR holdings at 60% of an average of short-term interest rates in the financial centres of the five countries with the largest SDR holdings. These rules have been progressively revised since 1974 and the latest developments in 1981 set the SDR interest rate at 100% of the market rate and based the valuation basket on the currencies of the same five countries.[1] Steady progress has also been made to promote the SDR as the logical principal reserve asset of the international monetary system. The most important changes came into effect with the adoption of the second amendment to the IMF Articles of Agreement in April 1978 (see below). These developments greatly extended the range of transactions for which SDRs may be employed by mutual agreement between countries without Fund authority, and reduced from 30% to 15% a country's minimum permitted holding of its SDR allocation over a five-year period. From 1 May 1981, this reconstitution requirement was eliminated.[2]

With effect from the Seventh General Increase in Quotas in 1980, members now contribute 25% of their additional quotas in SDRs. Finally, a multitude of developments have taken place, extending the right to hold SDRs to non-member organizations and legalizing the use of SDRs for currency swaps and forward

---

1 For details, see the article, 'The New Method of Valuing Special Drawing Rights', *BEQB*, September 1974, and *IMF Annual Report*, 1981. For further analysis of the issues discussed below, see F. Hirsch, 'An SDR Standard: Impetus, Elements and Impediments', *Essays in International Finance*, No. 99, Princeton, 1975, and K.A. Chrystal, 'International Money and the Future of the SDR', ibid., No. 128, December 1978.

2 *IMF Annual Reports*, 1978 and 1981, chapter 3, give relevant details.

transactions.[1]

Despite these developments aimed at enhancing the status of SDRs, the simple fact remains that SDRs only accounted for 5% of total world reserves at end-1983 and only 2.5% when gold reserves are valued at their market price. At best, all the IMF can press for is a continued enhancement of SDRs relative to currencies. In this respect, the proposed Substitution Account at the IMF, in which members would deposit currency reserves in return for SDRs, could be an important means of increasing the weight of SDRs in world reserves. Whether the proposals will come to anything during 1984 is doubtful, unless there is a sustained collapse in the dollar relative to other currencies.[2]

The future of the SDR is thus, for the moment, uncertain, not least because the tremendous growth in world reserves and rapid inflation over the 1970s has created fears of an excess of world liquidity rather than a shortage. Even valuing gold at the old official price of $35 per ounce, world reserves increased by 143% between end-1973 and end-1983. Of course, after allowing for inflation, these nominal reserve gains look less impressive, as can be seen by comparing the value of world reserves relative to the value of world imports. In particular, if gold is valued at its market price rather than the old official price, this ratio fluctuates narrowly around an average of 36% between 1973 and 1983. Indeed, on reflection, it is plausible to argue that the downfall of the Bretton Woods system proved to be its propensity to generate world liquidity, and from this stemmed the inflation tendencies of the 1970s and the collapse of the par-value system in 1973.

To the Second Amendment and beyond: Any illusion that the creation of the SDR had inaugurated a new period of stability for the par-value system was rudely shattered in August 1971, when the US government announced that the US dollar was no longer convertible into gold. The negotiations which followed this announcement set in train a review of the international monetary system under the direction of the so-called Committee of Twenty, but by the time of its final report in June 1974 its central concern with the maintenance of stable, but adjustable, par values had been overtaken by events.[3] Indeed, by April 1973, a succession of speculative crises meant that the exchange rates of all the major industrial countries were floating independently of their par values, while in December 1973 the increase in the price of oil dealt the final blow to the Bretton Woods consensus on exchange rates. The fact that the oil-producers could not rapidly convert export revenue into imports left them with little alternative but to invest in the industrialized countries, so returning on capital account the revenues extracted on current account.

The oil surplus raised three problems for the stability of the international monetary system. First, there is the potential havoc that can be wrought in foreign-exchange markets if surplus oil funds are invested in liquid assets and switched between currencies in search of interest return and the expected capital gain from

---

1 *IMF Annual Report*, 1981. The total number of prescribed 'other-holders' is currently fourteen.

2 Cf. 'The Proposed Substitution Account in the IMF', *MBR*, Winter 1979, and P.B. Kenen, 'The Analytics of a Substitution Account', *Banca Nazionale del Lavoro*, Quarterly Review, December 1981.

3 Cf. *IMF Survey*, June 1974 and J. Williamson, *The Failure of World Monetary Reform 1971-74*, Nelson, 1977.

exchange-rate alterations. Secondly, and more important, is the fact that the attractiveness of different oil-importing nations as havens for OPEC investment need bear no relation to the way in which their respective current-account balances have been affected by oil price increases. The possibility is, therefore, reinforced that individual countries will try to eliminate their deficits by deflation, trade restrictions or currency depreciation, the only outcome of which would be to depress world trade and output. Finally, there are the problems faced by the developing nations which have seen the real values of aid inflows virtually eliminated by the increase in oil prices, of which more will be said in section III.9 below.[1]

One response to these pressures has been to augment the resources at the disposal of the IMF, in fulfilment of its traditional function as provider of temporary balance-of-payments assistance. A number of temporary Financial Facilities were created from 1974 onwards, the latest example of which was the Supplementary Financing Facility. This came into effect in February 1979, with resources of SDR 7.8bn which members could borrow for longer than the normally allowed periods. Of more importance have been the greatly increased levels of general quotas in the Fund, which stood at SDR 39bn in 1976 and have been raised to SDR 90bn in the Eighth General Review due to come into effect in 1984.

The second major response has been a thorough reappraisal of the exchange-rate mechanism of the international monetary system, culminating in the Second Amendment to the Articles of Agreement of the IMF in April 1978. Without doubt, the most fundamental element is the amendment to Article 4 of the IMF Agreement. The main points of the new Article are as follows:[2] (i) a general return to stable but adjustable par values can take place with the support of an 85% majority in the IMF; (ii) such par values may not be expressed in terms of gold or other currencies but can be expressed in terms of SDRs, the margins of fluctuation around par values remaining at ±2.25%; (iii) with the concurrence of the IMF, any country may abandon its par value and adopt a floating exchange rate; (iv) the exchange-rate management of a floating currency must be subject to IMF surveillance and must not be conducted so as to disadvantage other countries; (v) the agreed practices with respect to floating rates will operate until such time as a general return to par values is attained. In effect, these changes legitimize floating exchange rates within the framework of the IMF system and without any diminution of the powers of the IMF.

A second aspect of the Second Amendment dealt with the relative positions of SDRs and gold. We have commented above on the attempts to enhance the reserve status of the SDR; the associated measures to demonetize gold were equally significant. In particular, the official price of gold was abolished and members were no longer allowed to use gold to make their general quota contributions.

---

1   For discussion of the adverse effects on developing countries and possible means of easing their problems, consult C. Michalopoulos, 'Financing Needs of Developing Countries: Proposals for International Action', *Essays in International Finance*, No. 110, Princeton, 1975.

2   The text of the proposed new Article 4 is contained in *IMF Survey*, 19 January 1976, pp. 20-1. Full details of the revised articles of agreement may be found in *The Second Amendment to the Articles of Agreement of the International Monetary Fund*, Cmnd. 6705, HMSO, 1977.

Furthermore, members were again allowed to trade in gold at free-market prices.[1]

The reforms embodied in the Second Amendment are undoubtedly important and reflect well on the IMF as an effective forum for international co-operation. However, they fall short of the ideals outlined by the C-20 and their long-run effects may be in doubt.[2] Of particular concern have been the large swings in nominal exchange rates that have occurred since 1978, swings well in excess of those which might be predicted by reference to purchasing-power parity, imperfect indicator though that may be. The volatility of capital flows at a time when capital restrictions in the UK and Japan were relaxed, the differing success of governments in controlling inflation, the structural problems induced by the OPEC cartel, and nominal interest-rate structures which have not reflected inflationary expectations, no doubt have each played a role in the appreciation of the dollar and the decline of the yen since 1980. These swings have been viewed with sufficient concern to result in a statement of objectives following the 1982 Versailles summit of world leaders which emphasized, *inter alia*, the need to avoid competitive exchange-rate policies and the legitimacy of exchange-market intervention to avoid disorderly market conditions.[3] The IMF response to exchange-rate volatility has been to emphasize the role of surveillance of member country practices, although it is doubtful whether this procedure can ensure greater harmonization of domestic economic policies – divergences between which are a powerful source of exchange-rate movements. Clearly, there is little prospect at present of a return to stable par values, whatever mechanisms may be invoked to ensure their adjustment to underlying circumstances. For the foreseeable future, the world will have to cope with managed flexibility. Relative to the problems associated with the world debt situation, however, those of exchange-rate management seem relatively innocuous.

III.9 World Debt and Bank Lending

A considerable degree of concern has been expressed in recent years over a further consequence of the oil price shocks, namely the implications for the international debt structure of non-oil exporting, less developed countries (non-oil LDCs) and the associated risks of an international banking crisis. This is an important issue but one which should be kept in its proper perspective.

It should be remembered, at the outset, that the efficient allocation of resources on a world scale will generally require international lending and borrowing.

---

1 At a meeting in Jamaica in 1974, it was agreed that the Fund divest itself of one-third of its stock of gold, with the profits on the free-market sale of one-half of this amount allocated to a special Trust Fund to provide balance-of-payments assistance on concessionary terms to very poor countries.

2 For somewhat jaundiced views of the Jamaica Agreement, see Bernstein *et al.*, 'Reflections on Jamaica', *Essays in International Finance*, No. 115, Princeton, 1976, and A. Kafka, 'The IMF: Reform Without Reconstruction?', *Essays in International Finance*, No. 118, Princeton, 1976. The Committee of Twenty (C-20) was the body established in June 1972 to advise on the evolutionary development of the international monetary system.

3 Cf. P.B. Kenen (ed.), 'From Rambouillet to Versailles: A Symposium', *Essays in International Finance*, No. 149, Princeton, 1982, and R.M. Dunn Jr., 'The Many Disappointments of Flexible Exchange Rates', *Essays in International Finance*, No. 154, 1983.

Countries with a surplus of savings will find it advantageous to lend to countries with a savings deficiency, through the medium of international capital flows. In the postwar world, the major savings-deficient nations have, of course, been the LDCs. The conditions for the international flow of capital to be sustainable are essentially twofold: the borrowing must be used to build up productive capacity in the debtor nation, with a gross rate of return on investment at least equal to the gross cost of borrowing; and the debtor country must be in a position to earn the foreign exchange required to service and repay the debt. This transfer requirement does not imply that the growth of debt-financed capacity be restricted to the direct production of traded goods but simply that the traded-goods sector expand at a rate consistent with the rate of foreign borrowing.

In fact, it is possible to identify for any country a set of circumstances which determines its capacity to accumulate external debt in a sustainable fashion. The simplest index of this capacity is measured by a ratio of foreign debt to gross domestic product. It may be shown that this sustainable ratio will be higher the greater the ratio of the trade surplus to national product, the greater the rate of growth of national product, and the lower the gross interest and amortization cost of borrowing. A country which is developing rapidly will enjoy a higher equilibrium debt:income ratio, and its total debt can increase over time at the rate of growth of income without any fear of insolvency.[1] The picture is complicated slightly by capital-market imperfections which mean that the interest rate at which any country can borrow is likely to rise with the debt:income ratio, so that a country enjoying a higher elasticity of supply of finance will, *ceteris paribus*, enjoy a higher equilibrium debt:income ratio. It is important to remember that sustainable debt:income ratios will be as varied as the circumstances which determine the respective country's international credit rating, capacity to generate a net export surplus and rate of economic growth.

One final point concerning the foreign debt mechanism is worth noting before we turn to the events of the 1970s, and this concerns the potential volatility of actual debt:income ratios. The problem is that when the actual debt:income ratio of a country diverges from the sustainable value, a process of cumulative divergence is set in train, so driving the debt:income ratio further from the equilibrium level unless corrective action is taken. For example, a reduction in net exports below the level required to service the current debt:income ratio requires recourse to further foreign borrowing to meet the foreign-exchange shortfall.[2] The increase in borrowing adds to the servicing burden and creates the need for even greater borrowing, and so the process of cumulative divergence is reinforced. Conversely, the effects of an improvement in the net export position will permit a

---

1   Thus, for example, a country exporting (net) 20% of its output, growing at 3% per annum and paying 10% gross on its foreign debt, would have a sustainable debt:income ratio of 2.85. Throughout the 1970s, the actual debt:income ratio of non-oil LDCs fluctuated between the values of one and five. The original statement of this condition is contained in E. Domar, *Essays on the Theory of Economic Growth*, Oxford, 1957, chapter 6.

2   We exclude here any temporary respite gained by drawing upon foreign-exchange reserves. For most LDCs, this option is of negligible importance. Instability depends upon the gross interest rate exceeding the growth rate of income in the LDCs. The average interest rate on total LDC debt averaged 6% in 1976/79 but rose to 10.25% in 1981. The median growth rates in non-oil LDCs are 5% and 3% for the same two periods. Cf. IMF, *World Economic Outlook*, 1983, Appendix B, Table 2.

cumulative contraction of debt. Of course, in practice, such movements are likely to be halted by remedial policy changes but, nevertheless, debt:income ratios are likely to show significant short-term instability.

We turn now to the practical implications of this analysis. Throughout the postwar period to 1970, the LDCs had been net importers of foreign capital, obtained primarily through direct foreign investment, official aid and official credits transferred through institutions such as the World Bank. The total foreign debt of LDCs increased against the backcloth of steadily expanding world trade and production, without servicing problems apart from those associated with export earnings instability in selected countries. The oil price shocks of 1974 and 1979 changed this situation rather drastically, creating a rapid growth in LDC debt and simultaneously reducing their capacity to borrow in a sustainable fashion. For non-oil LDCs as a whole, the ratio of outstanding debt to exports rose from 1.15 in 1973 to 1.40 in 1982, with a particularly sharp rise occurring after 1979. However, the aggregate figures conceal the extent to which external debt is concentrated in a small number of large and relatively developed countries of Europe, the Far East and Latin America, each enjoying good links with the international capital market. Taking the twenty largest borrowers (accounting for 85% of total debt to private creditors in 1982, but only 50% of non-oil LDC exports), we find the ratio of debt to exports rising from 1.50 in 1973 to 2.00 in 1982.[1] The connection with the oil price increase has both demand and supply aspects. On the demand side, the oil price shock had two adverse effects on the LDCs: it directly increased oil import bills, and indirectly reduced export revenues as the effect of the oil-price-induced recession in the industrialized countries worked its way through to lower export volumes and a worsening of the terms of trade.[2] In these circumstances, rapid structural adjustment was not to be expected, and between 1979 and 1982 the non-oil LDCs accumulated trade deficits of $257bn and current-account deficits of $344bn. By contrast, the corresponding figures for the industrial countries were $136bn and $50bn respectively. The associated increase in demand to borrow was readily satisfied due to supply-side changes in international credit markets which involved an increasing role for commercial banks in the industrial countries. BIS figures show that the gross foreign liabilities of commercial banks within its reporting area increased sixty-fold between 1973 and 1979, and that an increasing proportion of the lending was in the form of short-term 'roll-over' credits often with a floating interest rate. In 1982, some 30% of non-oil LDC borrowing was of this nature. The pressures for commercial-bank lending to LDCs are not difficult to identify. The recession reduced the demand for credit within the industrial countries, at the same time as their banking systems were receiving large flows of funds from the OPEC producers. Profit-seeking commercial banks were more than willing to lend to creditworthy LDCs on competitive terms which appeared to minimize risks, for each bank taken by itself.

The dénouement came in 1982, as the full effects of the decline in sustainable debt:income ratios became clear. The combination of world recession (world

---

1 IMF, *Annual Report*, 1983, p. 32.

2 For example, the real export value of primary commodities fell by 24% between January 1980 and January 1982.

trade fell by 2% in 1982) and high interest rates on commercial loans put an increasing number of LDCs in a position in which they could not meet the repayment schedules on a debt burden which was increasingly sensitive to short-term changes in interest rates. In quick succession, a small number of major borrowers, such as Mexico, Brazil, and for different reasons, Poland, announced their inability to meet immediate obligations. This naturally raised questions that bankers, in general, would prefer not to be asked. Was default a possibility? If so, would any commercial bank find that bad debts exhausted its capital resources? Would the appropriate national central bank act as lenders of the last resort in order to prevent a cumulative collapse in the credit structure, and what role might the IMF play in supporting this delicate situation?

At this stage, it seems reasonable to report that the serious danger of a collapse of the international capital market has passed. In the short term, LDCs have drawn on reserves where possible but otherwise turned to the IMF which financed 20% of LDC current-account deficits during 1983. However, IMF resources were limited, pending the Eighth General Review on quotas and additional GAB arrangements which have been discussed in the previous section. Moreover, financing the problem does not deal with the structural changes necessary to raise sustainable debt:income ratios. In general terms, a resolution requires that the net export-earning capacity of debtor nations be increased while, at the same time, their debt is rescheduled onto a longer time-scale, cutting the amortization·burden and reducing sensitivity to short-term interest-rate changes. The IMF has made significant efforts to impose import-reducing policies on countries in difficulty, while at the same time making its financial support conditional on continued lending by commercial banks in the industrialized countries.[1] It is vitally important that the flow of credit should continue, for fear of precipitating a default at a time when IMF resources are severely stretched. In the longer term, relief will come from more rapid world growth and a decline in nominal interest rates, although it may take several years for this to work to the benefit of the debtor nations.

In the background, as ever, is the prospect that world expansion will increase the demand for oil and precipitate a further increase in the price. It is sincerely to be hoped that the experience of the past two years will lead to a reappraisal of commercial lending practices, and the emergence of lending structures which permit LDCs to borrow in ways consistent with their long-term earning capacity.

---

1 Cf. T. Killick (ed.), *Adjustment Financing in the Developing World*, IMF/ODA, 1982.

REFERENCES AND FURTHER READING

Sir Alec Cairncross (ed.), *Britain's Economic Prospects Reconsidered*, George Allen and Unwin, 1971.

Sir Alec Cairncross, *Control of Long-Term Capital Movements*, Brookings Institution, 1973.

R.E. Caves and Associates, *Britain's Economic Prospects*, Brookings Institution and George Allen and Unwin, 1968.

R.E. Caves and L.B. Krause (eds.), *Britain's Economic Performance*, Brookings Institution, 1980.

H.G. Grubel, *International Economics*, Irwin, 1977.

H.G. Johnson and J.E. Nash, *UK and Floating Exchanges*, Hobart Paper, 46,

Institute of Economic Affairs, 1969.
C.P. Kindleberger and P.H. Lindert, *International Economics*, Irwin, 1978.
F. Machlup, *Remaking the International Monetary System*, Committee for Economic Development and Johns Hopkins, 1968.
R.L. Major, *Britain's Trade and Exchange Rate Policy*, Heinemann, 1979.
C. McMahon, *Sterling in the Sixties*, Oxford University Press, 1964.
J.E. Meade, *UK, Commonwealth and Common Market: A Reappraisal*, Hobart Paper, 17, Institute of Economic Affairs, 1970.
R.L. Miller and J.B. Wood, *Exchange Control for Ever*, Institute of Economic Affairs, London, 1979.
W.B. Reddaway, *Effects of UK Direct Investment Overseas: An Interim Report*, Cambridge University Press, 1967; *Final Report*, Cambridge University Press, 1968.
B. Tew, *International Monetary Cooperation, 1945–70*, Hutchinson, 1970.
B. Tew, *The Evolution of the International Monetary System, 1945–77*, Hutchinson, 1977.
S.J. Wells, *British Export Performance*, Cambridge University Press, 1964.
J. Williamson, *The Failure of World Monetary Reform, 1971–74*, Nelson, 1977.

Official Publications

Bank of England Quarterly Bulletin.
Commission of the European Communities, *European Economy*, Brussels (quarterly).
Economic Trends (regular analyses of balance of payments in March, June, September and December issues).
IMF *Annual Report* and IMF *Survey* (twice monthly).
Report of Committee on the Working of the Monetary System, Radcliffe Report, Cmnd. 827, 1959.
British Business (weekly) (previously *Trade and Industry*). Department of Trade and Industry, *UK Balance of Payments* (*Pink Book*, annual), CSO.

4

Industry

John Cable

I   UK INDUSTRIAL PERFORMANCE 1960-82

For much of the postwar period, industrial production in the UK has grown in line with the long-term trend over the previous century, yet has failed to match the much faster growth achieved in other countries. Between 1960 and 1982, UK industry expanded at a rate of only 1.7% a year on average, only half the rate of growth in America and West Germany, and less than half that in France (table 4.1). Consequently, while industrial production more than doubled over the period in these countries, in the UK it rose by less than half. Japan, however, was the international growth superstar, her industry expanding at more than 8% a year, and by more than fivefold overall.

TABLE 4.1

Growth of Industrial Production, UK and Selected Countries, 1960-82

	Annual average increase in industrial production (%)				
	1960-73	*1973-5*	*1975-9*	*1979-82*	*1960-82*
UK	2.9	−3.8	3.6	−2.7	1.7
USA	4.9	−4.7	5.7	−2.9	3.2
Japan	12.6	−7.1	9.2	1.5	8.2
France	5.9	−2.4	4.2	−0.8	3.9
W. Germany	5.5	−3.8	4.0	−1.2	3.4

Source: Derived from *NIER*.

All countries achieved much faster growth before the oil crisis of 1973, when world oil prices quadrupled, than in the subsequent period to 1982. After a very severe recession in the mid-1970s, strong expansion took place from 1975 to 1979, temporarily at more than the pre-1973 rate in the case of both the US and Britain. However these two countries were the most severely affected by the onset of further recession thereafter. Moreover, in the case of Britain it is not clear how much recovery there would have been after 1975 had it not been for North Sea oil.[1] Production rose from 1.6 million tonnes in that year to 103.1m tonnes in 1982, causing the output of the energy sector as a whole to double over the period

---

[1] For a discussion of the general impact of North Sea oil on the economy, see *NIER*, February 1978, and P.J. Forsyth and J.A. Kay, 'Oil Revenues and Manufacturing Output', *Fiscal Studies*, 2, 2 July 1981, pp. 9-17.

TABLE 4.2

Production in Industry 1973–82 (index numbers, 1980 = 100)

	1973	1974	1975	1976	1977	1978	1979	1980	1981	1982
Energy	55.8	52.1	54.5	60.8	74.8	85.0	100.5	100.0	103.8	110.2
Manufacturing										
Food, drink, tobacco	96.0	95.4	92.8	95.6	97.0	99.4	100.9	100.0	97.8	98.9
Chemicals	98.7	103.1	92.3	104.2	107.1	108.5	111.2	100.0	99.8	99.9
Metals	155.1	142.3	123.0	131.4	129.4	126.8	132.1	100.0	107.0	105.3
Engineering & Allied Inds.	114.2	116.1	110.0	107.8	110.0	109.6	107.2	100.0	91.1	92.2
Building materials	128.6	122.3	112.7	112.8	111.9	114.2	111.8	100.0	89.5	94.9
Textiles, clothing	128.7	121.6	116.7	117.1	120.6	119.4	117.9	100.0	91.5	88.4
Other manufacturing	114.6	109.7	98.5	103.4	106.5	109.2	111.7	100.0	93.2	89.5
Total manufacturing	114.1	112.7	104.9	106.9	108.9	109.6	109.4	100.0	93.6	93.7
Production Industries	99.4	97.4	92.2	95.2	100.1	103.1	107.0	100.0	96.3	98.0
Construction	122.4	109.7	103.9	102.5	102.1	105.0	105.6	100.0	90.4	91.8
Production and Construction	102.5	98.8	93.5	95.8	99.8	103.4	106.8	100.0	95.4	97.1

Source: NIER, MDS. The headings are those of the 1980 Standard Industrial Classification (SIC). This groups activities into broad 'Orders', with subdivisions into 'Minimum List Headings'. The industries shown are Orders or groups of Orders.

(table 4.2), even though coal production, the other main activity in this sector, only fluctuated around 125m tonnes p.a. Meanwhile, output fell by 17.9% in the manufacturing industries, and by 25% in construction.

The stagnation or decline of particular industrial sectors other than energy after 1973 is shown in table 4.2. During this period, industry was affected not only by the radical change in relative fuel prices following the oil crisis, but also by our entry into the EEC. Whereas all sectors had been expanding prior to 1973, the mid-1970s recession brought a fall in output in every case. Thereafter, the food, chemicals, metals and 'other manufacturing' industries all achieved relatively high growth up to 1979, while other sectors tended to stagnate. Severe recession then affected all sectors up to 1982, with especially dramatic declines in textiles, metals and 'other manufacturing'.

This pattern of UK industrial growth has brought changes in both the industrial structure of UK output, and in Britain's ranking among the world's richer nations. Once again the energy sector provides the most striking change, after which comes the decline of manufacturing's share from nearly a third of GDP in 1973 to under a quarter in 1982, while agriculture and construction have also declined relatively to other sectors (table 4.3).

TABLE 4.3

GDP by Industrial Origin, 1960, 1973 and 1982[1]

	1960		1973		1982	
	£m	(%)	£m	(%)	£m	(%)
Agriculture, forestry and fishing	912	(4.0)	2,010	(3.1)	5,752	(2.5)
Energy and water	1,304	(5.7)	3,013	(4.6)	26,037	(11.2)
Manufacturing	8,239	(36.5)	20,760	(32.0)	56,492	(24.3)
Construction	1,363	(6.0)	4,906	(7.6)	13,480	(5.8)
Transport and communications	1,953	(8.6)	4,898	(7.6)	17,164	(7.4)
Distributive trades	2,756	(12.2)	8,895	(13.7)	29,971	(12.9)
GDP[2] at factor cost	22,586	(100.0)	64,812	(100.0)	232,553	(100.0)

Source: NIE.

Notes: 1 Contribution of each industry to GDP before depreciation but after stock appreciation. 1960 figures are not strictly comparable because of revised SIC definitions.

2 Includes services, public administration and defence, and ownership of dwellings.

Statistics of income per head in different countries do not provide a very reliable indication of relative living standards, since official exchange rates may not accurately reflect international purchasing power.[1] Nevertheless, and subject to this caveat, table 4.4 shows a dramatic decline in Britain's position relative to the world's richer nations. In fact, France and Germany overtook Britain as long ago as 1961 and the EEC average passed us in 1967.

---

1 See I.B. Kravis *et al.*, 'Real GDP Per Capita for More than One Hundred Countries', *EJ*, June 1978, pp. 215–42.

TABLE 4.4

National Income per Head, UK and Selected Countries, 1960, 1973 and 1982 (£s per head at prices and exchange rates relevant each year)

	1960	*1973*	*1982*
USA	818	2,304	7,243
Canada	578	2,027	5,992
Japan	135	1,331	4,315[1]
France	368	1,745	4,639[1]
W. Germany	364	2,031	5,909
Italy	203	955	3,391
UK	398	1.409	4,276

Source: *IFS*.

Note: 1 1981.

Underlying Britain's relative industrial decline have been much lower productivity growth than in our competitors (except the USA), much higher growth of unit wage costs, and a much reduced share of world manufacturing exports (table 4.5).

TABLE 4.5

Productivity, Wage Costs and Share of Exports, UK and Selected Countries, 1965–82

	Annual average growth of:					
	Output per person-hour in mfg.	*Wage cost per unit of output*	*Share in total value of exports of manufactures [1] (%)*			
	(%) *1965–82*	*(%)* *1965–82*	*1960–65*	*65–70*	*70–75*	*75–82*
UK	3.0	10.4	15.3	12.2	9.9	9.2
USA	2.8	5.0	21.2	19.8	17.1	16.9
Japan	7.5	5.4	7.7	10.4	13.1	15.4
France	5.1	7.1	9.1	8.5	9.3	9.8
W. Germany	4.1	3.2	19.5	19.4	20.7	20.1

Source: *NIER*.

Note: 1 Total includes Italy, Belgium, Luxembourg, Canada, Netherlands, Sweden and Switzerland.

Many questions have been asked in the search for explanations of Britain's economic decline.[1] Have we fallen behind because of a lack of technical progressiveness and R and D spending? Is production carried on at too small a scale to compete in world markets? Is the blame due to militant unions or inefficient managers?

---

1 See also R. Bacon and W. Eltis, *Britain's Economic Problem: Too Few Producers*, Macmillan, 1976; M. Panic (ed.), *The UK and German Manufacturing Industries*, NEDC, 1976; J.C. Carrington and G.T. Edwards, *Financing Industrial Investment*, Macmillan, 1979; and S.J. Prais, *Productivity and Industrial Structure*, Cambridge University Press, 1982.

Has the financial system failed to steer funds to the right type of investment? Has growth of the public sector pre-empted development of our capacity to supply marketed goods? Are we still paying the price of our early industrial start, now reflected in our commitment to old industries and old technologies? There are no complete answers to these questions, though we consider some relevant evidence in later sections.

II   AGRICULTURAL DEVELOPMENT AND POLICY

As in other developed countries, UK agricultural production has been maintained and developed since the war at a higher level than would otherwise be the case, given the costs of domestic production and world price levels for agricultural products. Different methods of agricultural support were in force before and after Britain's entry into the EEC in 1973. It is primarily for this reason that table 4.6

TABLE 4.6
Agricultural Development 1961–81

				Annual average growth (%)		
	1960/62	1972/4	1980/82	1961-73	1973-81	1961-81
Index of real output (1975 = 100)	79	110	133	2.8	2.4	2.6
Employment (000s)	666	403	335	−4.1	−2.3	−3.4
Capital stock (£bn at 1975 replacement cost)	5.5[1]	8.2	9.7	3.4[2]	2.1	2.9
Index of labour productivity (1975 = 100)	44.5	102.3	148.8	7.2	4.8	6.2

Source: *AAS* and *NIE*.

Notes: 1   Estimate.   2   1964–73.

shows agricultural developments separately for the two periods. Because agricultural harvests are subject to considerable annual fluctuation, the levels of output and inputs are shown as three-year averages centred on the years 1961, 1973 and 1981. The statistics show that production has risen somewhat faster in agriculture than in other production industries over the last twenty years. They also reveal a big increase in the mechanization of production and capital intensity over the period, with a halving of total employment and the capital stock growing by more than three-quarters. The resulting increase in labour productivity is much greater than in most other industries. However, the growth of output slowed after 1973, with almost exactly proportional changes in the trends in both employment and productivity. Expansion of the capital stock also slowed, but to a markedly lesser extent.

Under the pre-1973 system of agricultural support, farmers received assistance in two main ways: deficiency payments, and direct grants for capital investment and farm improvement. The deficiency-payments scheme operated as follows. Agricultural products sold in the UK at world price levels, with more or less free access to the UK market for foreign producers, and some preferential treatment for Commonwealth producers. Where these prices were below the level of a guaranteed price, set by the government to encourage a certain level of home production taking production costs and farm incomes into account, the deficiency payment received by farmers was equal to the difference.

Thus the UK maintained open markets to foreign producers, and consumers enjoyed the relatively low world food price levels. At the same time, home production was encouraged and farm incomes were stabilized and controlled. The cost to the Exchequer varied inversely with the level of world prices. Early experience of an open-ended support scheme, with no upper limit on quantities produced at home and hence on the liability of the Exchequer, led to the introduction of 'standard quantities' for most products in the early 1960s; thereafter the guaranteed price fell on a sliding scale as these were exceeded.

The farm capital grants scheme provided assistance for investment in buildings and machinery and also projects such as land drainage, hill-land improvements and remodelling works for farm amalgamations. The rates of grant-aid tended to differ among projects, although steps were taken in 1970 towards a comprehensive scheme with a basic rate of 30%. Some subsidies were also offered for current expenditures, for example those associated with the use of fertilizers and lime. The guaranteed prices, grants and subsidies were reviewed annually.

Through this policy the government was able not only to maintain domestic production at a higher level than would have been achieved without official support (assuming other countries continued to support their own farmers), but also to influence the composition of agriculture and the efficiency of the industry. Especially in the later years of the policy, guaranteed prices were manipulated to produce a *selective* rather than a general expansion. Similarly, grants and subsidies were used to bring about desired changes in the structure of the industry and to mechanize and modernize it. The developments shown in table 4.6 were thus very much influenced by government policy.

Since 1973 agricultural support has come under the Common Agricultural Policy (CAP) of the EEC. The objectives are in principle very similar to those which governed previous UK policy. Thus Article 39 of the Treaty of Rome speaks of securing increases in agricultural efficiency, stabilizing agricultural markets, guaranteeing regular supplies, and ensuring reasonable prices to consumers and fair living standards for the agricultural population. The two policies are also similar in that support to farmers comes partly in the form of price guarantees, and partly in capital and current grants or subsidies. There are two major differences, however. Under the CAP the food prices paid by consumers reflect not world prices but EEC production costs. In general these are very much higher: 50-60% higher in the production of pork, wheat and barley, for example; roughly twice as high in the case of beef, maize, olive oil and rape-seed; and around four times as high for butter and powdered-milk production.[1] Secondly, very little of the total support under CAP is devoted to improving efficiency rather than to maintaining prices: a mere 4.1% of total expenditure in 1983,[2] compared with 60% or so going on grants and subsidies under the old UK system. This represents a failure of the

---

1 Eurostat: *Yearbook of Agricultural Statistics*.

2 European Communities, *Seventeenth General Report*, 1983.

EEC to implement the *Mansholt Plan*, which as long ago as 1968 was designed to shift the emphasis of CAP away from price support and towards structural reform.

The CAP is administered by the European Agricultural Guidance and Guarantee Fund. Grant aid is supervised by the Guidance section, though grants are actually paid out on its behalf by each national government. Price support is managed by the Guarantee section of the EAGGF. The aim is to bring about free intra-Community trade in agricultural products, with uniform prices among the members and a common external tariff. 'Target prices' are negotiated for most products which make domestic production profitable. To maintain market prices at or close to this level, there is a system of variable levies on imports from the outside world, broadly designed to equalize the supply price of foreign products (including transport costs) and the target price. In addition, there is provision for support-buying of unsold produce when prices fall below an 'intervention-price' level. In some cases, such as grain, the intervention price is set close to the target price. In certain other cases, however, such as fruit and vegetables, prices can fall significantly before support-buying occurs.

Because of the differences in the pre-1973 and CAP systems, Britain experienced severe adjustment problems on joining the EEC. One arose from the need to raise consumer price levels from world to EEC levels. Food prices rose very rapidly after entry, at a rate of 19.5% per annum in the five years up to 1977, and nearly 20% more than other retail prices over the whole period. Subsequently the index of food prices has risen less than prices in general, suggesting that the once-for-all adjustment was by then complete. A second, continuing problem arises from the structure of UK agriculture. As we have seen, the pre-1973 system did not seek to bring about a high degree of self-sufficiency in agricultural products in the UK. Indeed it to some extent encouraged Britain's relatively large import trade with non-EEC countries, and left the UK with a small agricultural sector, by European standards. Under the CAP, the imports became subject to levies, while there was only a comparatively small agricultural sector to benefit from its provisions. Since 1973, UK self-sufficiency in food products has increased sharply in some areas (at the expense of some Commonwealth and Third World countries), but it remains much below the EEC average for butter, fresh fruit, sugar and cheese, and to a lesser extent meat, vegetables, wheat and rye (table 4.7), and there remains a very large deficit, from Britain's point of view, on the agricultural account, which is the overwhelming reason for our being, with Germany, the principal net contributors to the overall EEC budget. Since 1980 the British government has been pressing both for greater control over the rapidly escalating costs of the CAP, and for budgetary reforms to ensure a 'broad balance' between national in-payments and out-payments.

Both the CAP and its pre-1973 predecessor have involved major, long-term distortions in the prices of agricultural products paid to farmers, in land values and in farm incomes. They have consequently resulted in a much greater allocation of resources to agricultural production than would otherwise occur through an undistorted price mechanism, with further, indirect allocative effects on industries supplying agricultural inputs or using agricultural products. Permanent support of agricultural production at an artificially high level in this manner could in principle be in the public interest, but requires some welfare explanation. Vested interests and the farm vote apart, it is quite hard to find any explanation for the CAP's objective of European self-sufficiency in most foods, except perhaps in terms of defence strategy: an ability to feed the population in time of war.

TABLE 4.7

Degree of Self-Sufficiency in Agricultural Products in the UK and the EEC (value of domestic consumption as % of domestic production)

| | UK | | EUR-10[1] | |
	1975/6	1980/1	1975/6	1980/1
Wheat (soft)	54	89	101	126
Rye	27	80	92	104
Barley	105	126	103	113
Oats	93	100	95	99
Potatoes	83	96	98	101
Sugar	29	46	105	125
Vegetables	75	79	95	99
Fresh fruit	30	30	79	84
Skimmed milk	169	224	109	145
Cheese	61	71	101	107
Butter	20	49	107	114
Eggs	100	98	100	102
Meat	74	77	96	101

Source: Yearbook of Agricultural Statistics 1983, Eurostat.
Note: 1 EUR-9 in 1975/6.

However, the nature of modern warfare casts doubt on such an argument, so that in global terms European self-sufficiency represents a highly questionable international division of labour, and protective measures against non-Community produce impede Third World development.

There have also been substantial distributional consequences of agricultural support policies. In the UK, farmers' incomes have on average risen from about 80% of male manual workers earnings in 1938 to more than 200% by the mid 1970s,[1] and the inflation of land values has simultaneously made the owners of quite modest farm holdings extremely wealthy. Agricultural workers, it should be pointed out, have not done so well, their earnings rising only from 53% of male manual workers earnings in 1939 to 75% in the mid-1970s. Under the CAP, a second distributional effect occurs because of its high-consumer-price aspect (in contrast to the 'cheap food' policy up to 1973). This is because food expenditure accounts for a higher proportion of total expenditure among poorer families, so that the cost of agricultural support falls disproportionately on them.

The existence of large agricultural subsidies has also created an incentive for farmers to apply intensive cultivation methods, and these have raised doubts over possible environmental damage and loss of amenity to the public. Intensive farming encourages the heavy use of fertilisers and pesticides, which may be resulting in gradual but cumulative damage to the soil, river pollution and loss of wildlife. Similarly, high crop-prices make it attractive to farmers to plough up marginal land, remove hedgerows and drain wetlands, which can further endanger wildlife and also reduce the recreational, visual and leisure value of the country-side. Under the provisions of the 1981 *Wildlife and Countryside Act*, farmers may now be paid compensation not to do some of these things. While this may alleviate

1   J.K. Bowers and Paul Cheshire, *Agriculture, the Countryside and Land Use*, 1983.

the countryside and wildlife problem, it can also result in paying farmers not to produce crops which would be unprofitable but for CAP price-support, and in any case would only add to existing, embarrassing and costly surpluses of unsold produce.

The CAP has a built-in weakness in this respect. The regime of high consumer prices and support-buying arrangements stimulates production and removes the normal market sanction on over-supply (downward price adjustment), while simultaneously discouraging demand. In the absence of widespread, non-market production quotas, surpluses cannot be prevented. Table 4.7 shows some of the areas in which there is serious over-supply, in particular dairy produce, sugar, and some cereals. In fact, as well as the infamous European butter and beef 'mountains' and the 'wine lake', there have also at various times been major surpluses of grain, sugar, fruit and, recently, sultanas. Thus the CAP today suffers from the problem of open-ended financial support like that which, as we have seen, was largely dealt with by the introduction of 'standard quantities' twenty years ago under the pre-1973 UK system.

In 1983 the CAP cost 16.5bn ECU and accounted for 65.7% of the total EEC budget. Over the preceding two-year period, agricultural spending had risen by more than 30%. At the time of writing it is predicted that the CAP will exceed its available resources later in 1984. There is widespread recognition of the need to reform the CAP, but a long history of inability to reach an agreement due to differences in national interests. In financial terms Britain, Germany and to a much smaller extent Italy have in the past been net contributors to the budget, while other countries have either benefited or received roughly what they gave, and therefore do not have the same direct incentive to seek reform. Moreover, in terms of particular branches of agriculture, all countries have specific and often conflicting national interests to protect. However, the looming insolvency of the CAP did produce a first tentative step towards reform in April 1984, when production quotas were introduced to cut milk production by 7%, and most other agricultural products received a 1% price cut. While the changes themselves were modest (for example, leaving milk production still 14% above total consumption), they could be of long-term significance, insofar as they were the first recognition that demand considerations must play a part in determining the CAP, and could provide a precedent for more substantial real cuts in product prices in the future.

Meanwhile the UK government has recently removed an additional, comparatively small source of benefit to farmers over which, unlike the CAP, it can exercise control. Thus the 1984 Budget removed agriculture from the scope of the Business Expansion Scheme (see section VI). So far, however, the government has not touched other forms of benefit to farmers which are outside the CAP, such as the exemptions from liability to local authority general rates on agricultural land and buildings, and from excise duty on fuel for agricultural vehicles. Nor has it used its discretion to reduce large 'monetary compensation amounts' (MCAs) since the spring of 1980 which protect British farmers against a reduction in the sterling value of guaranteed EEC prices caused by a strong pound.

III   THE NATIONALIZED INDUSTRIES
III.1   Introduction

The nationalized industries are run by publicly owned undertakings, set up by government to supply marketed goods and services, as opposed to 'public goods' like defence and broadcasting or social services like health and education which are provided at prices unrelated to use. Table 4.11 lists in descending order of turnover the principal organisations classed as nationalized industries in the public enterprise division of the Treasury in 1981/2, plus BL and Rolls-Royce. The industries together employ 7.5% of the total working population, and account for approximately 11% of UK capital stock (excluding dwellings). Nearly two-thirds of nationalized-industry activities were concentrated in the energy sector and in transport and communications. A statistical outline of recent developments and trends in these sectors will be found in tables 4.8 to 4.10.

TABLE 4.8

GB Inland Passenger Mileage 1968–82[1] (000m passenger-kilometres)

Year	Air	Rail	Road		Total
			Public-service vehicles	Private transport	
1968	1.9 (0.5%)	33.4 (8.9%)	59.0 (15.7%)	280.0 (74.8%)	374.3 (100.0%)
1973	2.4 (0.5%)	35.1 (7.7%)	53.0 (11.6%)	364.0 (79.4%)	458.5[2] (100.0%)
1978	2.4 (0.5%)	35.2 (7.1%)	50.0 (10.1%)	403.0 (81.4%)	494.9[2] (100.0%)
1982	2.8 (0.5%)	31.3 (5.9%)	40.0 (7.5%)	452.0 (85.0%)	531.6[2] (100.0%)
% change 1968-82	+47.4	−6.3	−32.2	+61.4	+40.6

Source: *AAS.*

Notes: 1 % figures in brackets show respective contributions to the total in any one year.
2 Also includes pedal cycles.

TABLE 4.9

GB Inland Freight Transport 1968–82[1] (000m tonne-kilometres)

Year	Road	Rail	Inland waterways	Pipelines[2]	Total
1968	79.0 (74.8%)	24.0 (22.7%)	0.2 (0.2%)	2.3 (2.2%)	105.6 (100.0%)
1973	90.4 (74.6%)	25.5 (21.1%)	0.4 (0.3%)	4.8 (4.0%)	121.1 (100.0%)
1978	99.1 (76.6%)	20.0 (15.5%)	0.4 (0.3%)	9.8 (7.6%)	129.3 (100.0%)
1982	92.0 (78.2%)	15.9 (13.5%)	0.4 (0.3%)	9.3 (7.9%)	117.6 (100.0%)
% change 1968-82	+64.6	−66.3	+100.0	+204.3	+13.6

Source: *AAS.*

Notes: 1 % figures in brackets show respective contributions to the total in any one year.
2 Excludes movements of gases by pipeline.

TABLE 4.10

Total UK Inland Energy Consumption by Final Users 1968–82: Heat Supplied Basis
(bn therms)

Type of fuel	1968	%	1973	%	1978	%	1982	%	Total change 1968-82
Coal (direct use)	13.6	(24.6)	8.1	(13.3)	5.7	(9.6)	4.8	(8.8)	−64.7%
Gas	4.9	(8.9)	11.0	(18.0)	15.4	(26.0)	16.9	(31.1)	+224.9%
Electricity	5.8	(10.5)	7.5	(12.3)	7.7	(13.0)	7.4	(13.6)	+27.6%
Petroleum	24.1	(43.7)	29.6	(48.5)	27.1	(45.8)	22.8	(42.0)	−5.4%
Other fuels[1]	6.8	(12.3)	4.8	(7.9)	3.3	(5.6)	2.4	(4.4)	−64.7%
Total	55.2	(100.0)	61.0	(100.0)	59.2	(100.0)	54.3	(100.0)	−1.6%

Source: AAS.

Note: 1 Includes coke, breeze, solid and liquid fuels derived from coal.

The UK is not alone in having a substantial sector of industry under public
ownership. In the EEC, this is the norm for postal services and telecommunications,
electricity and gas distribution, the railways, parts of road transport and coalmining.
All major countries have national airlines, and the steel, aerospace and shipbuilding industries are usually subject to at least a degree of state participation.
Vehicles production is likewise carried on elsewhere than the UK in public or
mixed enterprises (i.e. under joint public and private ownership); while Britain has
BL, France has Renault, Italy has Fiat and Germany has VW. The public sector is
particularly large in France, and Italy has two giant state companies: IRI, a wide-
ranging holding company; and ENI, an oil and chemicals firm. There are also certain
state monopolies for taxation purposes; that is, the state retains a monopoly profit
as part of its fiscal revenue. The match industry (in France, West Germany and
Italy) and the tobacco industry (in France and Italy) are examples.

In the USA, on the other hand, public ownership is unusual, though for many
years a significant number of industries were subject to regulation of their tariffs,
profits and services, even though their assets remained in private hands. The list
of industries included railroads; motor and water carriers; airlines; electric, gas,
water and sanitary services; telephones, telegraph and broadcasting; and financial
institutions. Recently, however, there has been a substantial programme of
'deregulation'.

Most of the major nationalized industries in Britain were set up in the
immediate postwar period. In the three decades thereafter there was a broad
political acceptance of the mixed economy though the boundaries of the publicly
owned segment were prone to change somewhat, according to which party was in
power. (The steel industry, in particular, was first nationalized in 1951, denation-
alized in 1953, and returned to public ownership in 1967.) This political consensus
has now collapsed, and a Conservative government is at the time of writing
embarked on a programme aimed at returning some £10bn of nationalized-industry
assets to private ownership. Let us first consider the evolution of policies towards
the nationalized industries up to the present, and then turn to the issues raised by
'privatization' and the details of the government's programme.

TABLE 4.11

Nationalized Industries, UK, 1981/2

Name	Turnover (£m)	Capital employed (£m)	Workforce (ooos)
Electricity Industry	8,057	32,605	147
British Telecom	5,708	16,099	246
British Gas	5,235	10,955	105
National Coal Board	4,727	5,891	279
British Steel	3,443	2,502	104
BL	3,072	1,521	83
British Rail	2,899	2,746	227
Post Office	2,636	1,347	183
British Airways	2,241	1,338	43
Rolls-Royce	1,493	992	45
British Shipbuilders	1,026	655	67
S. Scotland Electricity Board	716	2,817	13
National Bus Company	618	508	53
British Airports Authority	277	852	7
N. Scotland Hydro Electric	270	1,981	4
Civil Aviation Authority	206	162	7
Scottish Transport Group	152	157	11
British Waterways Board	16	50	3
Total	42,792	83,178	1,627

Source: M. Beesley and S. Littlechild, 'Privatisation: Principles, Problems and Priorities', *LBR*, 149, July 1983.

III.2   Past and Present Policies towards the Nationalized Industries

The first phase of policy towards public enterprise was set down in the postwar nationalization Acts, which required the industries to break even, taking one year with another. This requirement did little to ensure efficiency in production or that a socially desirable level of output would be chosen, since it can be met by setting prices equal to average cost, at any level. In 1961 the financial responsibilities of the industries were tightened in a number of ways, and financial targets were introduced.[1] However, policy remained open to the earlier criticism until explicit pricing and investment procedures were adopted in 1967. An important White Paper of that year introduced marginal-cost pricing and net-present-value procedures for investment decisions.[2]

The rationale for marginal-cost pricing is as follows. On the one hand, the demand curve for a product tells us how much consumers will pay per unit for different quantities supplied; it represents consumers' marginal evaluation of the good or service as output is varied. On the other hand, the marginal-cost curve tells us the incremental cost of producing each unit. Provided the money costs

---

1   *The Financial and Economic Obligations of the Nationalised Industries*, Cmnd. 1337, HMSO, April 1961.

2   *Nationalised Industries: A Review of Economic and Financial Objectives*, Cmnd. 3437, HMSO, November 1967.

incurred in production reflect the true opportunity cost of diverting extra resources from alternative uses, the marginal-cost curve records consumers' evaluation of the alternative product forgone. Hence, if consumers value the good in question more than the alternative (demand price exceeds marginal cost), then welfare can be increased by diverting more resources to its production and increasing output, and vice versa. Hence, the optimal level of output is determined where price equals marginal cost.

There are difficulties and limitations, however, over and above those of simply identifying and measuring the marginal cost of individual goods and services provided by complex industries like electricity, railways, coal, etc. For example, departures from marginal-cost prices may be called for where prices elsewhere in the system are not equal to marginal cost, as they generally will not be since oligopoly rather than perfect competition is the rule in the private sector and only under perfect competition does profit-maximizing behaviour ensure that price equals marginal cost. Secondly, where there are 'externalities' such as pollution or other environmental damage or traffic congestion, account should be taken of these and prices set equal to marginal *social* cost, rather than the purely private costs entering the accounts of the undertaking in question. Thirdly, except under conditions of constant returns, marginal-cost pricing will not necessarily ensure total costs are recovered (since marginal and average costs are equal only where the latter are at a minimum, and price equals average revenue); so that a problem arises of financing deficits or disposing of surpluses. Finally, it has to be remembered that the marginal-cost-pricing rule takes no account of the interpersonal distribution of income in the economy. Strictly speaking, the rule is valid only for whatever distribution happens to exist, and if this is not regarded as fair and reasonable, nor are the marginal-cost prices which the rule produces.

The idea behind the net-present-value (NPV) rule in investment decisions is to relate the future streams of benefits and costs during the lifetime of a project to the period when the decision must be made. Thus we define

$$\text{NPV} = \sum_{t=1}^{n} \frac{B_t - C_t}{(1+r)^t} - I$$

where B_t, C_t are benefits and costs respectively in year t, r is the discount rate and I is the initial cost. The formula allows for the fact that net benefits in the *more* distant future are worth *less* in today's values (since £1 invested now would be worth more, with compound interest, as time elapses). Any project is worth investing in if its NPV is positive, and the relative returns from different projects may validly be compared by reference to their NPVs.

To preserve a correct balance in resource allocation the discount rate r used in evaluating public-sector projects should be comparable with that used elsewhere (and any allowance made for uncertainty should also be the same). The 1967 White Paper laid down a public-sector rate of 8%, which was later raised to 10%. These rates were expressly chosen to match the rate looked for by private industry on marginal, low-risk investment at the times in question. Because of differences in financing methods and tax liability, the equivalent private-sector rate will be higher than any given nationalized-industry rate; the original 8% was held to be equivalent to 15-16% in the private sector.

The 1967 White Paper retained the existing system of financial targets for nationalized industries, in order to provide measures of expected performance against which to compare actual achievements. This may be viewed as the government attempting to apply a sanction on the efficiency of the nationalized industries similar to that of the capital market on private firms. Finally, the White Paper recognized that nationalized industries may provide so-called 'non-economic services', by which is meant services which yield greater social benefits than their social costs but which can only be provided at a financial loss. Examples include certain postal, telephone and transport services in rural areas, and the free emergency telephone service. From 1967 the policy intention has been for the government to provide specific subsidies or grants for such non-commercial operations.

The 1967 policy sought to achieve optimal resource-allocation within nationalized industries by focusing on the pricing of individual goods and services and on individual investment projects. However, difficulties were encountered in practice and in 1978 a subsequent White Paper,[1] while retaining the objective of optimal resource-allocation, marginal-cost pricing and NPV methods, shifted the focus of policy towards the opportunity cost of capital in industry as a whole. A 'real rate of return on assets' (RRR) was defined, to be achieved by the industries on new investment. The RRR is related to the real rate of return in the private sector, taking into account questions of the cost of finance and of social time-preference. It was initially at 5%, and was to be reviewed every three to five years. The RRR is not the same as the financial target rate of return for each industry, which varies, and takes into account the earning power of existing assets, sectoral and social objectives, and so forth. Thus the main matters over which the government has sought to exercise control since 1978 are the RRR and the financial target together with the 'general level of prices'. Individual prices and investment priorities have been left largely to the industries themselves, subject to the vague instruction to 'pay attention to the structure of prices and its relation to the structure of costs' and to the need to consult sponsoring departments on certain major investment proposals.

Establishing an appropriate working relationship between the nationalized industries, Ministers and their departments, and Parliament has, however, proved difficult. The central problem is to ensure an adequate degree of public accountability without restricting unduly the day-to-day operations of the industries. The original intention was that Ministers should lay down broad principles but not intervene in management. However, in 1968 the Select Committee on the Nationalized Industries concluded that Ministers had tended to do the opposite of what Parliament intended, giving very little policy guidance but becoming closely involved in many aspects of management.[2] A 1976 NEDO report proposed various structural reforms to counteract these difficulties,[3] but these were rejected by the 1978 White Paper. However, the White Paper did propose that explicit ministerial directions should replace the existing system of informal persuasion, in order to clarify the extent of Ministers' responsibility for the industries' performance. It was also proposed that a civil servant be appointed to corporation boards, to improve the understanding of industry problems on the part of sponsoring departments.

---

1 *The Nationalised Industries*, Cmnd. 7131, HMSO, March 1978.

2 *Ministerial Control of the Nationalised Industries*, H. of C. 371-I, II and III, 1968.

3 *A Study of the UK Nationalised Industries: Their Role in the Economy and Control in the Future*, NEDO, November, 1976.

Particular difficulties have arisen over government 'interference' with nationalized industry policies in pursuit of macroeconomic objectives, e.g. imposing
public-sector price and/or earnings restraint as an anti-inflationary measure. For
example, severe price restraint was applied in the years up to 1974 and investment
programmes were cut, with damaging effects on the implementation of the 1967
White Paper's policy. More recently the government in early 1984 forced a 2%
increase in electricity prices on an unwilling electricity supply industry, in what
the House of Commons Select Committee on Energy saw as a 'largely fiscal policy',
i.e. a tax. Government interventions of this kind do not breach the letter of official
policy towards the nationalized industries, as the relevant White Papers reserve the
government's right to bring national economic considerations to bear. However,
they have at times frustrated attempts to achieve socially efficient resource-allocation decisions in the nationalized industries, and also have affected their reported
financial performance one way or the other.

The performances of the nationalized industries are often criticized,[1] but
accurate comparison is complicated by a number of factors. Firstly, public-enter-
prise surpluses and deficits do not correspond exactly with private profits and
losses; allowance must be made for differences in funding, tax liability and
accounting practice (e.g. certain items, including capital costs, being deducted as
costs which would be paid out of profits in private industry). Then, in interpreting
performance on any measure, account must be taken of governmental responsibility,
as above, and also of the declining markets and general unprofitability of certain
nationalized-industry activities throughout Western Europe (e.g. rail, coal, shipbuilding and steel). Moreover, since 1980 some notable efficiency increases have in
fact been achieved. For example, labour productivity in British Airways rose 15%
in 1982-3 and real unit costs fell by 1%, British Steel now uses 9.3 man-hours per
tonne of steel produced compared with 13.2 before the 1980–81 strike, and BL
now produces 14 cars per man-year compared with 5.9 in 1979. While it is true that
these changes have come about under the threat or spur of imminent privatization,
they have nevertheless actually been achieved by the managements and workforce
under public ownership, and it has also to be remembered that, for example, the
rescue of BL and Rolls-Royce under *public* ownership has been based on the input
of capital (and management) which the market mechanism was apparently
unwilling to provide.

The efficiency of the nationalized industries has been subject to a limited
amount of independent scrutiny since 1965, when their prices became subject to
review by the National Board for Prices and Incomes. This continued during the life
of the Price Commission. On its disbandment in 1980, responsibility for a vestige
of price control was transferred to the office of the Director General of Fair
Trading and at the same time the nationalized industries became liable to investigation by the Monopolies and Mergers Commission.[2] However, the reviews made
under the auspices of all three bodies have related to particular price increases or
specific monopoly situations, and do not amount to a regular system of internal
efficiency audits for which a case could be argued – though MMC enquiries come
much closer to such audits than did earlier investigations.

---

1 For an appraisal, see R. Pryke, *The Nationalised Industries: Policies and Performance
since 1968*, Martin Robertson, 1981.

2 See section IV.2 below.

EEC policy towards public enterprise has so far been concerned mainly with the use of subsidies. These could be contrary to the rules and spirit of the Community, if subsidization of loss-making industries in particular countries prevented the free play of competition within the Community-wide industry. However, a distinction should be drawn between subsidies granted to undertakings supplying strictly non-commercial services, and general revenue support for operating deficits. It is the latter which would be most likely to meet with disapproval, though it could be hard for the Community to apply meaningful sanctions. The emphasis of policy to date has been towards securing 'transparency' of financial arrangements for public enterprise; that is, as a first step the aim is to elicit information which would reveal what subsidies are in fact being given and their size.

III.3 Privatization

Principles: 'Privatization' is a vague term. It could include charging for services previously supplied at prices unrelated to use by government agencies, injecting private (non-voting) capital into the financial structure of nationalized undertakings, opening up their markets to competition from private-sector firms, or full-scale denationalization – setting up public limited companies in place of nationalized undertakings, with the sale of 51% or more of the shares in these companies by the government to private investors. It is privatization in the last sense on which we focus here.

The government's motive for disposing of large slices of the nationalized industries in this way could be a purely political one, reflecting a preference for private ownership *per se*. Implications for the PSBR could also be an attraction. The sales proceeds are expected to amount to £2bn in each of the next five years. If this is set off against equivalent amounts of public expenditure, the government's true fiscal deficit could then be perhaps 25% higher than otherwise, while still apparently meeting stated PSBR targets.[1] Thirdly, however, the motive for privatization could be to improve the efficiency of the industries concerned, based on a belief in the superiority of market forces over government organization for this purpose. Whatever the government's motive, it is this last issue on which we shall focus, considering the possible merits of privatization as an efficiency instrument.

Privatized firms would be exposed to direct market forces in both the product and capital markets. The pro-privatization argument is that product-market competition will make suppliers more responsive to consumers' preferences, providing goods and services of the quality and variety demanded at lower prices than would otherwise be charged, and adapting more quickly to changes in demand and in technical opportunities through greater innovation.[2] The profit motive provides the incentive to compete in this way, and is reinforced by the need to satisfy capital-market requirements for future borrowing, and by the ultimate threat of

---

1 The *Treasury and Civil Service Committee Report on the Government's Economic Policy: Autumn Statement*, HMSO, 1984, however, recommended treating assets sales as exceptional items or as an alternative method of financing PSBR.

2 See M. Beesley and S. Littlechild, 'Privatisation: Principles, Problems and Priorities', *LBR*, 149, July 1983, pp. 1-20.

bankruptcy or takeover. The privatized firms would be better able to adapt and grow than their state-owned predecessors, because of their greater freedom to change and diversify their activities, which is generally not permitted by statute for nationalized industries.

The pro-privatization argument takes an optimistic view of competition and the welfare gains we may expect of it. The competition in question is not the textbook variety; this would require an absence of market power and equality of price and marginal cost. In general this is thought to demand large numbers of sellers, each responding to impersonal market forces. Elegant and precise theorems exist which show that a general, competitive equilibrium of this kind leads to efficient resource-allocation throughout the system and a social welfare optimum in production and exchange (albeit under restrictive assumptions). But these standard theoretical results cannot be invoked in the case of privatization, which is highly unlikely to result in the large-numbers competition found in conventional theory. For most, if not all, the nationalized industries are 'natural monopolies' or 'natural oligopolies', that is, industries in which production by more than one supplier, or at most a small group, would involve wasteful duplication or production at too small a scale for potential scale economies to be reaped.

Natural monopolies are, for example, likely to be encountered where production depends on a network like the national electricity grid, gas distribution pipelines, and local telephone and rail systems. Technical economies of scale or scope in production are likely to result in very few firms being able to produce efficiently in electricity generation, gas exploration and extraction, steelmaking, shipbuilding, volume car production, airlines and airports, and so on. Some activities might well be too large or risky to attract private bidders at all, for example the nuclear power industry, with its heavy costs and risks associated with R and D, public opposition to the siting of nuclear power stations, and waste-disposal problems. And even where there are no substantial technical economies of scale, e.g. in bus services, the number of operators who can compete efficiently on a given route is still limited.

It has been suggested that the supply prospects in practice are as follows.[1] Single-seller industries are to be expected in electricity and gas distribution, local telecommunications, airports, rail, waterways and probably postal services. 'Multiple' supply would be in prospect for electricity generation and gas production, national telecommunications, coal, air transport, steel, shipbuilding and buses, together with BL and Rolls-Royce. (The authors also distinguish those industries with good demand prospects — electricity, gas, telecommunications and air transport — from the rest of the present nationalized sector, where prospects are deemed to be bad.) However, the likely number of firms in 'multiple-supply' industries is not discussed. In the light of the factors listed above, we might perhaps guess it to be between two or three, and at most eight or ten.

Typically, then, where privatization results in competition it will be between small numbers of firms. The essence of this kind of competition is market rivalry, both among existing suppliers and from new entrants or the threat of potential entry, and it is on the benefits of competition in this sense that the economic case for privatization rests. But market rivalry of this kind can take many forms, depending on the way in which firms anticipate and respond to each other's

---

1 Ibid.

strategies. Largely because of this, there are few unambiguous theoretical statements than can be made about the link between such competition and social welfare, and in the absence of such statements widely diverging views and expectations are held. Thus, whereas the protagonists of privatization take the optimistic views outlined above, others give more weight to the possibility of much less socially beneficial outcomes.

They recognize, for example, the difficulties in preventing overtly collusive behaviour, or 'tacit collusion' in the form of mutual forbearance to intrude on competitors' territory, when the number of sellers in a market is small. They take note of the arguments and evidence that in tight oligopolies competitive energy can be channelled into wasteful product-differentiation and sales promotion (e.g. via advertising), leading to finely differentiated brands of products offering little real variety or choice to consumers, and the manipulation of consumers' preferences. They consider the possibility that new entrants can be deterred by entry barriers which are either inherent (e.g. due to patents or exclusive access to specialized resources) or contrived by established sellers (e.g. through 'predation' – undercutting entrants' prices temporarily to force withdrawal – or the *threat* of predatory moves through investment in overcapacity). Or they may envisage rivalry leading to market instability, with periodic price wars, the collapse or exit of some competitors and periods of little or no competition at all.

The extent to which product-market competition would increase will, in any case, vary from industry to industry. In steel, shipbuilding and international airline operations, for example, there is already intense rivalry due to chronic world overcapacity. Changing the ownership of UK producers in these cases cannot be expected to have any significant effect on the level of product-market competition; the privatization case must rely entirely on stricter discipline coming from the profit motive, capital-market pressure and the ultimate threat of bankruptcy, than from government controls. But would a government, faced with the employment, regional and possible strategic consequences of the collapse of privatized firms in these industries, in fact allow them to go bankrupt? BL and Rolls-Royce were, after all, rescued from collapse under private ownership in the 1970s, and it only has to be believed that the government, not necessarily the present one, might intervene for the ultimate bankruptcy sanction to lose its edge. Moreover, the steel industry recently provided an example of greater adaptability and restructuring in the publicly owned UK industry than in its predominantly private, German counterpart. Whereas British Steel has cut back output and employment substantially in line with the quota requirements of an EEC rationalization plan for the European industry as a whole, the German government has been unable to implement a strategy involving mergers between independent steel companies, in particular Thyssen and Krupp.

Elsewhere in nationalized industry there has always been competition in the transport sector between the different inland-transport undertakings, private fleet operators, hauliers and private motoring. The Coal Board, on the other hand, has been a near-monopoly supplier to a protected domestic market, and sheltered from the competition of substitute fuels for many years by the government preference for coal in the commissioning of new power stations.[1] Likewise the electricity and gas industries are sole suppliers of their respective products. Yet

---

1 Coal purchases by the electricity industry rose from 26% of total tonnage in 1960 to 62% in 1982.

taking the energy market as a whole, there is keen competition between alternative fuels, especially in areas such as space-heating. Of all the nationalized industries, postal services and telecommunications have in the past probably faced least competition, except in the delivery of parcels and, to a limited extent, from each other. However, scope for further competition was introduced into these areas in 1980 (prior to British Telecom's becoming the first major candidate for privatization in 1983), when their legal monopolies in mail-carrying and the supply of telephone equipment and services were broken. Greater competition was similarly introduced into passenger transport in 1980, with the liberalization of licensing arrangements for express coach services. Moves such as these affecting the PO, BT and the National Bus Company can be seen as *alternatives* to privatization in increasing the constraints of product-market competition on nationalized under-takings.[1] To the extent that they are successful, they may be expected to reduce any further gains from selling off assets to the private sector, limiting these to whatever benefits may be forthcoming from capital-market sanctions, as previously discussed in relation to steel, shipbuilding and air transport.

In sum, the increase in competition that would come about from a wide-ranging denationalization programme would vary from industry to industry, according to demand and technological factors affecting the number of sellers and conditions of entry to the industry, the form of competitive rivalry which emerged, the amount of competition which already exists, and the effects of other policy measures affecting competition in particular markets or in general. In some if not all cases it seems very likely that competition alone would not be a sufficient safeguard of the public interest, and some form of continuing government controls or 'regulation' would be needed.

There is already some limited experience of regulation in the UK, for example from industries like contraceptives and breakfast cereals where MMC investigations have resulted in long-term price controls, and from franchising arrangements in independent television. However, most of what we know of regulation is based on American experience, and this has revealed a number of problems. One is 'regulatory capture' – a process whereby a regulatory agency intended to protect consumers gradually turns into the champion and defender of the industry it is supposed to control, because of lobbying by the industry, the agency's dependence on the industry for its information, and so forth. Price regulation has been found to give rise to problems over the quality and variety of service and disincentives to contain cost levels, while regulating the rate of return on capital has led to distortions in the use of factor inputs involving excessively capital-intensive techniques.[2] Franchising arrangements – involving competitive bids for monopoly positions of limited duration – have not proved a popular solution in the US, due to problems such as political lobbying and ensuring that there are appropriate incentives for investment by franchise-holders whose presence in the industry may be temporary.

---

1 Problems of 'cream-skimming' can arise, however, where entrants cream off only the most profitable business, to the detriment of existing suppliers of a full range of services.

2 Because the rate of return on capital is constrained, the effective or 'shadow' price of capital falls below its market price, causing undue substitution of capital for labour by regulated profit-maximizing firms.

The shape of likely forms of regulation in the UK in the event of privatization is beginning to emerge in proposals for the denationalization of BT. The suggestions include output-related profits control, and price control under an '(RPI–x) formula'.[1] Under the latter, consumers would be assured that prices would not rise after privatization by more than the general rise in prices less an amount, x, where x is determined by bargaining between BT and the government. The idea is that consumers would be protected while at the same time the industry would have an incentive to secure increased efficiency, since it would keep the benefits (over and above those necessary to comply with the formula). The control was proposed as a temporary measure, necessary only 'until competition arrives', and in the longer term it is competition which is looked to as the principal regulator. The 1983 *Telecommunications Bill* itself provides for a privatized BT to operate under licence, which would require published tariffs and prohibit predatory price discrimination. The Bill also supplements present monopoly controls with an *Office of Telecommunications*, which may well prove the first of many if privatization proceeds, since otherwise the resources of the OFT and MMC could become even more severely overstretched than they are at present. However, such industry-specific agencies seem much more prone to regulatory capture than an expanded OFT and MMC might be and, in general, the BT proposals do not show the government to be grasping its own, pro-competition logic. For example, it has made it clear that, for up to seven years, only one competitor to BT, i.e. Mercury, will be permitted, and other licence applications under the *1981 Telecommunications Act* have been rejected.

The government would retain a further, continuing responsibility towards privatized nationalized industries over the provision of non-commercial services. (These could be fewer or more numerous after privatization than under nationalization, according to whether efficiency increases or decreases.) The principle here is straightforward, and no different from that under nationalization. The government should decide the type and level of service to be provided on behalf of the community, and pay the privatized firms supplying it an explicit subsidy, thus ensuring 'transparency'. The subsidy would require periodic review and adjustment to take account of the cost of materials, technological advances and so on, and some monitoring of output and perhaps costs would be necessary. The relationship between the government and firms would in many ways resemble that which already exists under defence contracts. Where there is multiple-supply, competitive tendering might even be a possibility.

The proposed arrangements for BT are rather different, however. The proposal is that BT should charge an access fee to other telecommunications networks, to finance call-boxes, and emergency and certain rural services. How well this *ad hoc* compromise would work is anybody's guess. There clearly is a risk that the government would lose both control and sight of what services are being provided; social obligations would be paid for by other telecom users and operators rather than taxpayers at large; and the arrangement is clearly not 'transparent'.

Our discussion shows that denationalizing any industry is a major decision involving social benefits and costs that are likely to vary greatly from case to case. Each decision should therefore be preceded by an analysis of these benefits

---

1   See S. Littlechild, *Regulation of British Telecommunications' Profitability*, DTI, London, 1983.

and costs. The analysis should take account of consumers' gains (or losses) due to changes in prices, outputs, the quality and variety of services provided, and the rate of innovation. The effects on total employment, imports and exports, raw-material and component suppliers, regional development and taxpayers should be considered. The results of the analysis should then be made public.

How much the industry would sell for should not affect the privatization decision, which should depend solely on the existence of a net social benefit, larger than the transactions cost of effecting the change. However, the sale price is important from the point of view of fairness and the distribution of wealth, since it represents the payment for which ownership is transferred from taxpayers at large to a smaller group of private investors. The aim should therefore be to ensure the sale price reflects a true value of the assets, with no undue capital gains or losses to purchasers and underwriters. This could raise technical difficulties, because the sums involved are of orders of magnitude greater than those normally traded on the stock market, and the sales could therefore prove indigestible even on a large, efficient market like London. Moreover, the value of the assets is to an extent in the government's hands, because privatizing legislation would determine the structure and regulatory framework under which the industry would operate, and hence its future profitability. The greater the monopoly power which these permit, the higher would be the sale price of the assets, but the lower the net social benefit, and the government clearly faces a problem in balancing these conflicting interests.

The proposed programme: At the time of writing, the government has announced a five-year plan to dispose of £8–10bn of public assets. Table 4.12 gives details of sales already made and future plans. BT is the first case involving a major public utility, raising in an acute form the issues which have been discussed.

The aim of the government appears to have been to carry out its denationalization programme as rapidly as the capacity of the stock market will allow, and beginning with the most saleable cases. The ambitious target of around £2bn sales each year means relying heavily on institutional investors and in particular on the cash flow into pension funds and insurance companies, which dominate stock-market equity holdings. This in turn depends heavily on achieving a substantial economic recovery in the UK, though some foreign participation is also expected; Italy, for example, is rumoured to be interested in acquiring a stake in BT, which may eventually form part of a European-wide system, and it is expected that some issues may be made on the New York market. However, potential stock-market digestion problems have apparently been a factor delaying sale prospects for BA; led to an instalment-plan sale of BT (spreading cash calls for the 51 per cent offered over eighteen months and three financial years); and meanwhile accelerated the sale of Enterprise Oil (a company formed in 1983 to hold the former oil assets of British Gas). In timing individual sales and pitching their offer prices, the government will no doubt be anxious to avoid repetitions of earlier mishaps, such as the substantial underpricing of Amersham International, and the heavily undersubscribed sales of Britoil and the second instalment of Cable and Wireless. The principal factors affecting the rapid saleability of individual undertakings include their demand prospects and current profitability, their size (the smaller the better), and the complexity of the organizational changes and administrative and parliamentary procedures required before the sale.

TABLE 4.12

The Privatization Programme

Year	Sale	Amount (£m)
	SALES TO DATE	
1979–80	5% of BP	276
	25% of ICL	37
	Shares in Suez Finance Company and other miscellaneous	57
1980–81	50% of Ferranti	55
	100% of Fairey	22
	North Sea oil licences	195
	51% British Aerospace	43
	Miscellaneous and small NEB	91
1981–2	24% of British Sugar	44
	50% of Cable and Wireless	182
	100% of Amersham International	64
	100% of National Freight	5
	Miscellaneous plus Crown Agent and Forestry Commission land and property sales	199
1982–3	51% of Britoil (first cash call)	334
	49% of Associated British Ports	46
	Sale of oil licences, oil stockpiles and miscellaneous	108
1983–4	Second cash call Britoil	293
	General Election	
	7% of BP	565
	25% of Cable and Wireless	260
	FUTURE SALES	
1984–5	Enterprise Oil	400
	British Telecom (first of three cash calls)	1,300
	British Airways	800
1985–6	British Telecom (second call)	1,300
	British Airports	400
	11 Royal Ordnance factories	300
1985–6	British Telecom (third call)	1,300
1986–7[1]	Some parts gas, electricity, plus about £1bn of smaller enterprises including Sealink, National Bus, Jaguar, Land Rover, Rolls Royce, Unipart, British Steel profitable businesses, British Nuclear Fuels, Naval war shipbuilding yards.	4,700
	Further tranches of BP and BT might also be sold.	

Source: *Financial Times*. The figures in the bottom half of this table are working assumptions.

Note: 1   To general election.

Had the government's intention been to maximize the gain in net social benefit, its priorities would probably have been different. Taking into account demand conditions, the prospects for competition amongst suppliers, the scope for efficiency gains through reorganizations not already undertaken, possible alternative ways of increasing competitive pressure, and size (which is positively related to net social benefit insofar as, for example, a given percentage price-cut or resource-saving is worth more when spread over a larger output), and focusing on aggregate net benefits to consumers, it has been suggested that the prime candidates for privatization would be electricity supply (excluding the national grid and area distribution boards), telecommunications (excluding local) and the National Coal Board.[1] As table 4.12 shows, the coal industry does not feature at all in present plans, electricity is among a large number of cases at the bottom of the list for which no individual priority has yet been given, and while BT is an early candidate, no separation of national and local services is planned. The government itself has so far shown little intention of undertaking detailed, case-by-case analyses of social costs and benefits, though the Civil Aviation Authority has been asked to review the allocation of airline route licences with privatization in mind, and a pre-privatization review of the electricity-supply industry has been promised, perhaps to be published as a consultative Green Paper. This case apart, the privatization programme is going forward on a general belief in the superiority of competition as an efficiency instrument, rather than as a result of research into the likely consequences in particular circumstances.

Net proceeds from the sales will in some cases be substantially less than table 4.12 suggests. Firstly, it may be necessary to lift existing debt burdens before the undertakings can be sold on the terms the government seeks. For example, it is likely that all the £800m receipts for BA will be needed to lift bank debts which at the moment exceed this figure, and the National Bus Company also has accumulated debt problems. Secondly, the nationalized industries typically have pension-fund deficits and/or index-linked pension obligations which it is thought privatized firms will be unwilling to take on without compensation. For example, over 90% of the proceeds from National Freight were needed to pay off its pension-scheme deficit, and some £1bn of the anticipated £4bn price for BT will be needed for similar purposes.

In sum, it seems that the efficiency gains which may be expected from privatization are questionable and likely to vary from case to case, while the relief brought by asset sales to the PSBR will be much less than the £2bn per annum which the programme at first suggests. However, if the programme is carried out, the government will certainly have exercised its preference for private ownership *per se*.

IV   COMPETITION POLICY AND CONSUMER PROTECTION
IV.1   Competition, Market Power and Welfare

Efficient market co-ordination of economic activity depends on competition and on consumers exercising free and well-informed choices. If, on the other hand, there is market power or consumers have poor information, the 'invisible hand', which is supposed to reconcile individually self-interested behaviour with the communal good, falters or is overruled. Public policies in this area therefore seek to monitor market competitiveness and consumer interests, and apply remedies where these are infringed.

Pure monopoly is the clearest case of market power, where one firm is the sole supplier in a market. However, power is rarely absolute, and the monopolist faces competition from substitute products. The intensity of this competition depends

---

1   Beesley and Littlechild, op. cit.

on the closeness of the substitutes, and is reflected in the position and slope of the monopolist's demand curve. The monopolist may also face dynamic competition from new products or production methods, which can erode either the demand for his good or the basis of his monopoly position. Nevertheless, subject to these constraints, the monopolist is not a passive price-taker but has discretion over the price he charges, which is the essence of market power.

Where a group of firms in an industry collude to form a cartel, they can assume some or all of the market power of a monopolist. Collusive agreements have often been confined to fixing the level of price, but may also cover quantities and qualities supplied, share out markets on the basis of geographical area or type of product, or predetermine the outcome of tenders for contracts. While the monopoly profits from collusive action can be high, cartels have their problems. In particular, once a price-fixing agreement exists, participating firms have an incentive to undercut the agreed price secretly and so increase their market share. Thus tensions can arise within the group, with problems in maintaining allegiance and policing the agreement. The difficulties recently encountered by OPEC countries in maintaining discipline over world oil prices during a period of over-supply vividly illustrate these problems. Because of organizational problems, cartels are most likely to succeed where the number of participants is not large. Since they must also control all or most of market supply if they are to be effective, it follows that they are most likely to be found in oligopolistic, or 'highly-concentrated', markets, where a few large firms control the bulk of production.

Even where there is no explicit agreement, the kind of rivalry which is likely to occur in oligopolistic markets will not necessarily promote social welfare.[1] For example, there may be tacit collusion, with mutually accommodating behaviour on the part of sellers in accordance with an unspoken understanding between them. One particular form of tacit collusion is where competitive pressure is attenuated by mutual 'oligopolistic forbearance'; each firm hesitates to compete vigorously for fear of an inevitable and mutually damaging retaliation. Alternatively, competition may be intense, but take the form of product-differentiation and advertising. While enlarged consumer choice and knowledgeability can increase welfare up to a point, there seems to be no natural constraint in the system to prevent this being exceeded in oligopolistic markets, and a suspicion of 'wasteful' product competition and 'excessive' advertising enters. Finally, it can be shown that where certain forms of apparently innocuous, non-cooperative oligopolistic interaction occur, the results can resemble those of pure monopoly. Thus, where firms seek to maximize their market share, and a mutually compatible equilibrium is found, it can be shown that the outcome is identical with that of explicit collusion (joint profit-maximization), which is in turn formally equivalent to multi-plant monopoly.

Mergers between firms are a further area of concern for competition policy. On the one hand, it is argued that they can be desirable mechanisms for rationalizing production as circumstances change or for exploiting scale economies, and a means for good management to drive out bad, via the workings of the 'market for corporate control'. Beneficial effects like these are most likely to arise from horizontal mergers, between firms competing in the same industry. However, such mergers also increase seller concentration, other things being equal, with conse-

---

1 See also section III.3.

quential risk of reduced social welfare from the exercise of the now enlarged market power in the industry. Clearly, securing market power can also have been a contributing or even the only motive for merger; mergers are after all the ultimate collusive agreement. Thus horizontal mergers pose a trade-off problem for competition policy, offering potential benefits but also potential losses. Strictly the balance of advantages cannot be assessed *a priori* and must be determined through empirical study.

Vertical mergers between firms at different stages in the same production chain pose a similar policy dilemma. Again, they may permit efficiency gains either in production or via improved information exchange and co-ordination. But they can also raise antitrust issues, where, for instance, a manufacturer takes over the firm supplying raw material both to himself and to his competitors, and would be able to charge disadvantageous prices to them, or where a manufacturer secures control over the sales outlets for both his own and his competitors' products.

Conglomerate mergers are mergers between firms where there had previously been neither a horizontal nor a vertical link. They have been thought to raise less serious anti-competitive risks but also fewer potential efficiency gains. Thus neither scale economies in production nor gains from improved production scheduling are available, and seller concentration does not increase. However, firm-level scale economies may occur, for example in raising finance and planning investment. On the other side, competition policy concerns have arisen over conglomerate merger cases in two areas. One is associated with the ability of conglomerate concerns to cross-subsidize activities, which could be used to exclude a competitor in one industry by incurring temporary losses there. The other concerns the practice of 'reciprocal buying' between divisions of a conglomerate organization, which again can be used to weaken competition. Furthermore, conglomerate mergers may represent pursuit of purely managerial objectives, including growth of the firm *per se*, with few benefits to the community, while large economic power-blocs develop with potentially far-reaching socio-political as well as economic consequences.

Wherever there is market power, the general concern is that this will have adverse allocative and distributional effects. Price will tend to exceed marginal cost, so distorting the allocation of resources amongst alternative competing uses and reducing consumers' surplus. In addition, supernormal profit will be earned if price also exceeds average cost, so that income is redistributed in favour of producers. It is sometimes also argued that firms with market power will tend to be technically inefficient, costs being higher than they need because the presence of excess profits blunts the desire to seek out and apply cost-minimizing techniques. However, this argument implicitly assumes pursuit of some objective other than profit (e.g. leisure or managerial objectives), maximization of which, unlike profit, does not entail cost-minimization under all market conditions. Moreover, a counter argument has been vigorously put, suggesting a beneficial effect of market power on dynamic efficiency – the rate of innovation of new products and technologies. Thus, Schumpeter and Galbraith, in particular, have stressed that the profitability and relative market security under monopoly and oligopoly are important enabling conditions for firms to undertake risky and high-cost R and D expenditures. Others acknowledge the opportunity which is created but question the incentive to exploit it, if competition is lacking. Thus far there is little demonstrable proof either way, and the issue remains controversial.

Economists have recently carried out substantive research in two areas relevant to competition policy: the magnitude of monopoly welfare losses, and the determinants and effects of mergers. An original estimate put monopoly welfare loss in the interwar period in the USA at less than one-tenth of one per cent of GNP. More recent estimates take into account certain technical issues and adopt a broader view of the social costs of monopoly, including the costs of acquiring monopoly positions, existing or potential. These suggest much larger losses: 7-13% of gross corporate product in the USA and 3-7% in Britain. However, those who defend monopoly on arguments relating to dynamic competition remain unconvinced, and the controversy continues.[1]

Empirical work on mergers has not been able to identify a single, dominant motive for merger, which is perhaps not surprising since there are so many possible reasons why firms might wish to merge. Extensive studies of merger effects indicate a general absence of observable, post-merger efficiency gains.[2] Thus it appears that mergers are not a major force making for improved industrial performance. On the other hand there is fairly widespread, though not universal, agreement that they contribute significantly to increased market power, as measured by the extent to which economic activity is concentrated in the hands of relatively few producers. Thus the general conclusion from a substantial number of studies is that at least fifty per cent, and on some estimates a much greater percentage, of the change in concentration in recent decades can be attributed to mergers. Moreover, this applies both to *seller concentration* – the concentration of sales in the hands of relatively few sellers in individual industries or markets – and to *aggregate concentration* – the concentration of economic activity in the hands of giant firms in the economy as a whole. The level and recent trends in both types of concentration are discussed further in section IV.3 below.

Consumer protection is in a sense the underlying rationale of policies to control anti-competitive market structures and practices, since the exercise of market power is typically at the expense of the consumers' interests. This aspect apart, economic theory does not place much emphasis on the need for consumer protection. In the textbooks, consumers are assumed to have a complete ordering of their preferences for different goods and services based on full information about the characteristics of the commodities and the utility to be gained from consuming them. Consumers then attempt to maximize their utility, faced with their income and market-determined prices. Provided these prices (including the price of labour and hence income) are competitively determined, the theory implies that all is well with the consumer. In practice the consumer is not fully and costlessly informed, and may not be able to judge the utility he will derive from a certain good. He may not, for example, realize that a drug may be unsafe under certain conditions or that food may be too old for use, and he may be faced by confusing packaging or subject to misleading claims by advertisers or retailers. Furthermore, he may not be able to choose how much or how little service he obtains with a good, and his right of redress against suppliers of unsatisfactory goods or services may be either unclear or impractical to exercise via the courts.

---

1 See K.G. Cowling and D.C. Mueller, 'The Social Costs of Monopoly Power', *EJ*, 1978, and S.C. Littlechild, 'Misleading Calculations of the Social Costs of Monopoly Power', *EJ*, 1981.

2 See, e.g., G. Meeks, *Disappointing Marriage: A Study of the Gains from Merger*, CUP, 1977; D.C. Mueller (ed.), *Determinants and Effects of Mergers: An International Comparison*, Oelgeschlager, Gunn and Hain, 1980, and K.G. Cowling, *et al.*, *Mergers and Economic Performance*, CUP, 1980.

There is nothing to guarantee that it is in the manufacturers' best interests for consumers to exercise a totally free and informed choice. It is this potential divergence of interests which creates the need for policy measures.

IV.2   Policy Measures

Promoting competition is one of the central aspects of the 'supply-side' policies of the Conservative government re-elected in 1983, and a major review of competition policies is under way at the time of writing. The following account describes the situation prior to any changes to which this review may lead. The first policy measure (introduced by a Labour government) was the 1948 *Monopolies and Restrictive Practices Act*. Several further measures followed, until the 1973 *Fair Trading Act* consolidated the existing law and codified and extended legislative safeguards for consumers. It also provided for the appointment of a Director General of Fair Trading to centralize the application of competition and consumer law; previously this responsibility had been rather widely shared. The 1973 Act is now the basis of current policy, along with the subsequent *Restrictive Practices* and *Resale Price Maintenance Acts* of 1976 and the 1980 *Competition Act*. In competition policy there are two main strands, embodying different approaches to the control of monopolies and mergers and of restrictive agreements between firms.

Monopolies and mergers which meet certain criteria may be referred for investigation by an independent administrative tribunal, the Monopolies and Mergers Commission (MMC). The Commission's task is to determine whether the case in question is or is likely to be detrimental to the public interest, and make recommendations for corrective measures as appropriate. Responsibility for implementing recommendations lies with the appropriate Minister, and statutory orders may be made binding on the companies concerned, or a settlement reached in the form of voluntary undertakings.

Section 14 of the 1948 Act defined the public interest as 'production . . . by the most efficient and economical means . . . in such volume and at such prices as will best meet the requirements of home and overseas markets'; progressive increases in efficiency and the encouragement of new enterprise; 'the fullest use and best distribution of men, materials and industrial capacity . . .'; and '. . . the development of technical improvements and the expansion of existing markets and the opening up of new markets'. No subsequent attempt has been made to improve on this comprehensive but rather vague formulation. However, it at least allowed the MMC wide discretion in evolving practical criteria.

Monopoly references may be made either by Ministers or the Director General. The latter is expected to provide a broader-based view of the state of competition in the economy, and has a responsibility to collect data on market structure and the behaviour of firms on which the MMC may draw. An economic information system now operates in the Office of Fair Trading for this purpose. Merger references are the prerogative of the Secretary of State, acting on advice from a Merger Panel. The panel screens merger proposals falling within the scope of the law, to determine the economic significance of each case and priorities for investigation.

From 1948, a monopoly could be referred where one firm supplied one third or more of a total market. In 1973 this was reduced to 25%, which from then on could apply to sales in a particular locality, rather than the national market. Cases of 'complex monopoly' – in effect tight oligopolies – were also brought within the scope of the legislation. Mergers which would result in a monopoly were not covered until 1965. Thereafter they became liable either via the monopoly market-share test or if the gross assets involved exceeded a certain value: £5m initially and £30m from 1984. The 1980 *Competition Act* extended monopoly control to certain public-sector bodies. The Act defined these as corporate bodies supplying goods and services whose members are appointed by a Minister under legislation, plus public bus services and water undertakings, certain agricultural boards and others. A principal objective was to provide a mechanism for enquiring into the efficiency of nationalized industries. Previously this had been possible via the Price Commission and before that the National Board for Prices and Incomes, in the context of price and incomes policies. The 1980 Act abolished the Price Commission, but retained a last vestige of price control, authorizing the Secretary of State to refer 'any price' to the Director General of Fair Trading for investigation.

Restrictive-practice agreements were originally treated in the same way as monopolies, and occupied the MMC almost entirely in its first years after 1948. In 1956 a separate procedure was introduced. Agreements under which there were restrictions relating to the price of goods, conditions of supply, quantities or des-criptions, processes or areas and persons supplied were presumed illegal unless the parties could establish a case for exemption before a specially constituted Restrictive Practices Court. A register of agreements was set up, and a Registrar was appointed to bring cases to the Court. This has the status of a High Court and consists of five judges and ten lay members.

The basic procedure still applies, though the definitive law is now the 1976 *Restrictive Practices Act*, which consolidated previous legislation, and the role of the Registrar has been taken over by the Director General of Fair Trading. To be exempted, the agreement must pass through one or more of eight escape clauses or 'gateways'. Thus, paraphrasing the legislation slightly, it must be shown that the agreement is necessary:

(a) to protect the public against injury; or
(b) because its removal would deny to the public 'specific and substantial' benefits; or
(c) to counteract measures taken by others to restrict competition; or
(d) to enable the parties to negotiate 'fair terms' with others; or
(e) because its removal would have 'serious and persistent' adverse effects on unemployment; or
(f) because its removal would cause a 'substantial' reduction in exports; or
(g) to maintain another agreement, accepted by the Court as not contrary to the public interest on other grounds;

or, finally, it may be shown that, while not necessary, the agreement

(h) does not restrict or discourage competition to any material degree.

This last gateway was framed with 'information agreements' particularly in mind. Here no restrictions are accepted, but information concerning prices and so forth is exchanged. Information agreements were not covered by the legislation from the outset but were brought within its scope from 1968 onwards. Otherwise, it is gate-way (b) which has been most frequently argued in cases which came to court, either alone or in conjunction with other clauses. If an agreement passes through one or more of the gateways, there remains a further obstacle: the so-called 'tailpiece' requires the Court to be satisfied that, on balance, benefits to the public outweigh detriments.

Originally the restrictive-practice legislation applied only to the supply of goods, but was extended to services in 1976. There is a time-limit for the registration of agreements, with penalties for non-registration, and interim orders may be made while a final decision is being made. The Minister may exempt certain agreements which he deems to be in the national interest or intended to hold down prices.

'Resale price maintenance' is a particular type of restrictive practice which is now dealt with by the separate Resale Prices Act of 1976. Prior to 1964, when individual RPM was first controlled, it was a common manufacturers' practice to specify actual prices at which their product should be retailed, with sanctions for non-compliance. Procedure for controlling resale price maintenance is very similar to that for restrictive practices in general, involving a general prohibition and 'escape clauses'. Although resale price maintenance remains in a few trades, for instance in the supply of books, it has in many cases been superseded by the device of 'recommended' retail prices, which are in effect maximum prices. This device has been investigated by the MMC, which concluded that it operated with different effects in different industries, not always contrary to the public interest.

The 1973 *Fair Trading Act* also empowers the MMC to investigate uncompetitive practices in monopoly situations. The 1980 *Competition Act* added a further provision for control of anti-competitive practices. These may now be subject to a preliminary investigation by the Director General of Fair Trading, and subsequently referred to the MMC if satisfactory undertakings are not forthcoming after the preliminary report.

Finally, as a member of the EEC, Britain is covered by the regulation dealing with monopolies, mergers and restrictive practices in articles 85 and 86 of the Treaty of Rome. The European Commission is the body responsible for applying the policies and investigating breaches in them.

The most fully developed parts of the regulations are those relating to restrictive practices. These prohibit all agreements, such as price-fixing and market-sharing, which prevent, restrict or distort competition in the EEC and extend over more than one member country. As in the UK, however, exemption may be gained via a 'gateway' if the agreement improves production or distribution or promotes progress. There is also provision for block exemptions.

EEC monopoly regulations are less clear-cut since, although any abuse of dominant position within the EEC is prohibited if it affects trade between member countries, it is not clear as yet what sort of market-share criterion constitutes dominance, or what abuses will be covered by the regulations. EEC case-law on monopoly is virtually non-existent as yet. Even less clear up to 1971 was the position of mergers. Until the case of Continental Can (an American firm) in that year, it was unsettled whether articles 85 and 86 could be applied to merger cases. Although this particular merger was allowed on appeal to the European Court of Justice, the implicit extension of the legislation to mergers was accepted. Since then a proposed regulation concerning mergers has been approved by the European Parliament. As originally proposed, it would prohibit mergers involving firms above a specified size or market share, with provision for exemption in special circumstances, and compulsory advance clarification for very large mergers. However, there was very slow progress towards its implementation and late in 1981 The European Commission submitted an amendment to its original 1973 proposal with a view to reopening discussions. The amended proposal restricts control more

closely to mergers with a Community dimension and involves memb
closely in the decision-making process.

The concept of overall government responsibility for consumer pr
opposed to piecemeal responsibility) is relatively recent. Under the 19
Director General of Fair Trading was again assigned a key position. He
to collect and assess information about commercial activities, in order to seek out
trading practices which may affect consumers' economic interests. If he finds areas
in which there is cause for concern, he then has two options. The Director General
may either make recommendations to the relevant Minister as to action which
might be useful in altering the malpractice, whether it concerns consumers'
economic interest or their health, safety and so on. Or, presumably where more
severe action is demanded, he may set in motion a procedure which could lead to
the banning of a particular trade practice. To do this he makes a 'reference' along
with proposals for action to the Consumer Protection Advisory Committee
(CPAC), which considers whether his proposals are justified, and that the practice
is covered by the legislation. After taking evidence from interested parties, this
body reports to the relevant Minister, who may then make an Order, subject to
the agreement of Parliament.

Another of the Director General's main functions in the area of consumer
protection is to make sure that those who are persistently careless of their existing
legal obligations to consumers mend their ways, either by his seeking a written
assurance or, failing this, in the courts. Lastly, the Director General has obligations
to pursue an informal dialogue with industry; to publish information and advice
for consumers; and to encourage trade associations to use voluntary codes of
practice to protect consumers.

IV.3   Policy Appraisal

Competition policy in Britain has now undergone thirty-five years of development,
with modifications to remedy shortcomings and fill in gaps in earlier Acts. In the
last ten years it has been considerably extended in scope, with accompanying
administrative reforms. On paper, a comprehensive battery of investigative powers
now exists. But the underlying principle is one of case-by-case review, judging each
case according to its effects on the public interest, and while this has the advantage
of flexibility and being able to take account of any positive effects there might be
from restrictions on competition, the procedure can be cumbersome, slow and
costly; for example, each MMC investigation takes months and some have taken
years.

The alternative would be to proscribe certain situations and behaviour – e.g.
'monopoly' and 'monopolization' – *per se*, without reference to their effects in
individual cases. This approach, which is adopted in the USA, rides roughshod over
arguments in defence of monopoly. On the other hand it does tend to exert a
greater impact and also results in policy being relatively removed from the political
arena. By contrast, British policy is subject to influence by the government of the
day, since responsibility for implementing recommendations lies with the Minister.

By the end of 1982, the MMC had reported on rather more than forty monopoly-
supply situations, covering such diverse goods as beer, breakfast cereals, fertilizers,
cigarettes, colour film, soap and detergents, contraceptives, wallpaper, building
bricks and tampons, and a range of services including those supplied by architects,

ɔarristers and solicitors, veterinary surgeons, stockbrokers, surveyors, the cross-channel ferries and credit-card companies. Despite the variety of product, this is hardly a large number of investigated cases in relation to the total number of monopolies and oligopoly situations in existence. Moreover there have been criticisms of both the quality of the MMC's analysis of individual cases, and the government's unaggressive approach in applying remedial measures, which has relied heavily on informal undertakings from the firms concerned. More generally, the policy has not succeeded in establishing clear guidelines on the kinds of abuse of dominant market positions which should be controlled, with a predictable prospect of strong countermeasures being taken where such abuses can be proven. As a result it is questionable whether this strand of policy has had far-reaching effects on the firms actually investigated, or any strong deterrent effect on behaviour elsewhere.

It may be, however, that the best safeguard against monopoly is an effective control on mergers, insofar as it is easier to stop monopoly situations in the making than to break them up or control their behaviour once established. But if this is so, it is an indictment of UK policy that no merger controls at all existed until 1965, seventeen years after the first legislation, during which time seller-concentration increased substantially. Since 1965 many proposed mergers have been screened, though only a small proportion have been referred to the MMC. Thus between November 1973 (when the Fair Trading Act came into force) and the end of 1983, around 1,700 merger cases were reviewed, of which only 51 were referred. Of these, very few proposals were stopped, though several more were allowed to proceed only after certain assurances had been given. Once again, however, merger verdicts and reports have failed to evolve clear guidelines on permissible levels of market concentration in merger cases, or to establish uniform criteria for assessing barriers to entry of new competition, or substitutability by consumers of one product for another. As with monopoly policy, this has led to an unpredictability of outcome in merger cases, and probably militated against the policy's impact.

Again like monopoly policy, the numerical impact of merger policy can hardly be said to have been widespread. When a government review body was set up in 1977 to consider the effectiveness of competition policy, it was widely anticipated that the onus of proof would be shifted in merger cases, forcing the companies to demonstrate positive benefits. In the event this did not happen.[1] Had it occurred, there is little doubt merger activity would have been greatly reduced. The actual merger rate since 1970 is recorded in table 4.13, which shows both the general level of activity (the Business Monitor M7 series) and the incidence of mergers within the scope of the Act. On average these accounted for just under a quarter of the total (considering industrial and commercial mergers only), though this proportion has risen to nearly 30% since 1980. Since 1965 there has been little sign of secular decrease in merger activity that might be attributed to policy, and though the proportion of conglomerate mergers has increased markedly in recent years (table 4.14), this is as likely to reflect reduced opportunities for horizontal mergers (so many firms having been taken over already) as any influence of policy.

Whatever impact monopoly and merger policy may have had in individual cases, it has not prevented a strong trend towards increased seller concentration both in

---

1   See *A Review of Monopolies and Mergers Policy*, Cmnd. 7198, May 1978, and *A Review of Restrictive Trade Practices Policy*, Cmnd. 7512, March 1979.

TABLE 4.13

Merger Activity 1970–82 (all cases)

		Proposals covered by Fair Trading Act		*Business Monitor M7 series.Industrial and commercial: number*
	Numbers	*Assets acquired (£m)*	*Industrial and commercial: number*	
1970-74 (per annum)	116	4,074	92	919
1975-9 (per annum)	215	7,945	165	450
1980	182	22,289	141	469
1981	164	43,597	126	452
1982	190	25,939	144	463

Source: Director General of Fair Trading, *Annual Report*, HMSO, 1982.

TABLE 4.14

Percentage of Proposed Mergers by Number and Value of Assets Acquired, Classified by Type of Acquisition, 1965–82

	Horizontal		*Vertical*		*Diversified*	
	By no.	*By assets*	*By no.*	*By assets*	*By no.*	*By assets*
1965-69[1]	82	89	6	5	12	7
1970-74[1]	73	65	5	4	23	27
1975-79[1]	62	67	9	7	29	26
1980	65	68	4	1	31	31
1981	62	71	6	2	32	27
1982	65	64	5	4	30	32

Source: Director General of Fair Trading, *Annual Report*, HMSO, 1982.

Note: 1 Annual average.

individual markets and at the aggregate level (though this trend has decelerated since about 1968).[1] Concentration can be measured in several ways, of which the simplest and most commonly used is the 'concentration ratio': the combined market share of e.g. the top five firms (CR_5). The latest published statistics at both industry (MLH) and product-group level are for 1977. Table 4.15 gives a frequency distribution by class of concentration for 162 MLH industries and 817 product-groups respectively. Amongst other things, this underlines how the broader MLH data understate the true level of seller concentration at market level; thus in over half the product groups, CR_5 exceeded 70%, compared with just under 30% of MLH industries. Note that in nearly one in six product-groups five firms controlled 90% of the market or more. Overall, the statistics strongly suggest that oligopoly is the prevailing market structure.

Earlier data for 1963 suggested the UK level of market concentration was much

1 See L. Hannah and J. Kay, *Concentration in Modern Industry*, London, 1977, and P.E. Hart and R. Clarke, *Concentration in British Industry 1935-75*, CUP for NIESR, 1977.

TABLE 4.15

Seller Concentration, Selected UK Markets, 1977

Concentration class (range of five-firm concentration ratio, %)	Number of markets in class			
	Product group basis[2]		MLH basis	
	No.[1]	%	No.	%
0–9	0	0.0	0	0.0
10–19	6	0.1	6	3.7
20–29	25	3.1	15	9.3
30–39	37	4.5	21	13.0
40–49	102	12.5	34	21.0
50–59	101	12.4	22	13.6
60–69	124	15.2	16	9.9
70–79	145	17.7	15	9.3
80–89	140	17.1	18	11.1
90–100	137	16.8	15	9.3
Total	817	100.0	162	100.0

Source: Business Monitor (PO 1006): Statistics of Product Concentration of UK Manufacturing.

Notes: 1 The meaning of this column is that there is no product-group in which the largest five firms account for less than 10% of total sales, six in which they account for 10–19%, and so on.

2 The markets included are sub-Minimum List Heading product-groups in mining and manufacturing, for which five-firm concentration ratios are available.

higher than in France and Italy, and much the same as in Belgium and the Netherlands.[1] Strictly comparable data for West Germany is not available, but the data which does exist suggests a pattern similar to that in the UK (cf. the last two columns of tables 4.16 and 4.15).

TABLE 4.16

Seller Concentration in West Germany, 1977

Concentration class (range of concentration) ratio, %)	Three-firm CR		Six-firm CR	
	No. of industries	%	No. of industries	%
0–9	13	8.2	5	3.8
10–29	58	36.9	29	22.1
30–59	57	36.3	55	42.0
60–100	29	18.5	42	32.1
Total	157	100.0	131	100.0

Source: Monopolkommission, Hauptgutachten III, 1978/79, *Fusionskontrolle bleibt vorrangig*, Nomos Verlagsgesellschaft, Baden-Baden, 1980.

1 See M.C. Sawyer, 'Concentration in British Manufacturing Industry', *OEP*, November 1971, and Louis Philips, *Effects of Industrial Concentration: A Cross Section Analysis for the Common Market*, North Holland, 1971.

Alongside the trend towards a higher degree of seller concentration in individual markets there has been a similar, accelerating increase in overall concentration, as measured by the share in net output of the 100 largest firms in the economy. Before World War I this was less than 20%, rising to 33% in 1958. Over the next twelve years the rate of increase roughly trebled, and in 1970 the largest 100 firms accounted for nearly 50% of net output.[1] The precise connection between overall concentration and seller concentration in individual markets is not well documented. But of the largest 100 manufacturing companies between 1968 and 1974, approximately half were known to have two or more 'monopolies' (25% shares in particular markets), and, of these, twenty companies had five or more monopolies.

In purely numerical terms, restrictive-practice control appears to have been more successful than monopoly and merger policy. By the end of 1982 there were 4,780 registered agreements (including 775 relating to services), of which 2,323 had been abandoned (118 relating to services) and a further 1,093 had had all restrictions removed. Not all these cases were heard by the Court; since 1956 only 658 goods agreements have been referred. Most abandoned agreements were either terminated voluntarily after the results of key cases became known, or simply left to expire. Undoubtedly, a great mass of overt price-fixing that had existed before 1956 no longer exists, and by the mid-1970s the DGFT was able to say that no more significant, known cases remained to be dealt with (though this was before the extension of the legislation to cover services agreements).

However, both the escape clauses in the 1956 Act and the quality of the Court's reasoning and decisions have been adversely criticized. Indeed, doubts have been expressed over the suitability of judicial practices for resolving complex economic issues. Thus it is not clear whether the right decisions have been taken. Moreover, it is questionable how far the abandonment of restrictive practices has actually affected behaviour in the markets concerned. As we have seen, cartel arrangements are most likely in fairly concentrated, oligopolistic markets, where they may merely formalize the mutually accommodating behaviour which would in any case occur. Removal of an agreement in these circumstances would not touch the underlying, structural cause of this behaviour. Moreover where restrictive agreements have been abandoned firms may have been able to substitute alternative arrangements. The extension of the law to embrace information agreements in 1968 was in response to such a development. It is also possible that the introduction of restrictive-practice control in 1956 may have intensified merger activity. Very few studies have been undertaken into the consequences of restrictive-practice abandonment, and it would be a useful extension of present policy to require the MMC to undertake such follow-up studies.

On the consumer protection side, a number of references have been made to the CPAC. By the end of 1982, twenty voluntary codes of practice had been introduced covering, amongst others, package holidays, new and used car sales, shoe sales and repairs, funeral services, mail-order trading, laundering and dry-cleaning. Various other practices have been investigated, including advertising, bargain-offer claims, party-plan and door-to-door selling, as has the conduct of a large number of individual firms. The 1968 Trades Description Act has been

---

1 S.J. Prais, *The Evolution of Giant Firms in Great Britain: A Study of Concentration in Manufacturing Industry in Britain 1909-70*, CUP, 1976.

reviewed, and the 1974 Consumer Credit Act implemented (under which the OFT is responsible for licensing traders). A working party on advertising reported in 1980, and a wide range of leaflets has been published containing various kinds of consumer information.

The variety and detail of the consumer protection activities undertaken since 1973 is in some ways impressive. As expected, the overwhelming emphasis has been on voluntary solutions: negotiated codes, assurances and the like. The advantages of this approach, its flexibility, cost-effectiveness and constructiveness, are heavily stressed by the Director General of Fair Trading in his *Annual Reports*. Its main drawback is perhaps that voluntary co-operation is most likely to be forthcoming where it is least needed.

Under the Conservative governments in power in the early 1980s, there appears to have been a considerable shift of emphasis in competition policy. Although it has been declared government policy to promote competition, the OFT is reported to have been under ministerial pressure over merger and restrictive-practice referrals, and some of its recommendations have been overruled. On the other hand, the government has somewhat unexpectedly moved rapidly in announcing measures to end the 180-year-old legal monopoly on house conveyancing held by solicitors (though in this case action was prompted by a Labour MP's Private Member's Bill); to permit advertising by opticians and remove their monopoly in the supply of spectacles (though not eye-testing); and to liberalize competition on the Stock Exchange, in particular by removing the minimum commission on share dealings and allowing participation by outsiders (such as banks) in Stock Exchange firms. Meanwhile the activities of the MMC have been heavily committed to its role as monitor of nationalized industries, acquired under the 1980 Act. Public-sector investigations under way or completed have included London commuter services (British Rail), domestic gas appliances (British Gas), the CEGB, Yorkshire Electricity and other parts of the electricity supply industry, the Severn-Trent and Yorkshire Water Authorities, the NCB, the Civil Aviation Authority, counter services of the PO and the BR Property Board.

The awaited official review of competition policies is expected to reiterate the emphasis on competition. If it is to have any influence, however, it will need to do more than state the obvious, and set out clear guidelines on what form competition should take, and equally clear, predictable penalties for its infringement.

V   REGIONAL POLICY
V.1   Introduction

Regional policies seek to reduce or eliminate disparities in incomes, industrial growth, migration and, above all, unemployment between different geographical areas of the country. If markets operated in a smooth frictionless fashion there would be no need for such policies, since the disparities would be self-eliminating. In particular, regional unemployment would signal labour-market disequilibrium with excess supply of labour at the ruling wage levels, to which the market would respond with lower real wages and product prices. In practice, however, there are market frictions due to downward rigidities in nationally determined wages and prices, and to the immobility of capital and labour (the latter on account of such factors as rehousing problems, imperfect knowledge of job opportunities elsewhere, and social ties).

Moreover, government intervention would be justified even with frictionless markets if private and social costs and benefits diverge. Thus a firm might choose a location in the south-east of England on the basis of the costs actually entering its accounts. But the socially optimum location could be elsewhere, e.g. in Wales, Scotland or the North, when account is taken of social costs such as traffic congestion, the availability of social overheads like schools, hospitals, etc., as well as less tangible benefits such as the preservation of existing community life in areas which might otherwise become depopulated.

If the firm's private production costs are higher at the socially optimum location, there is a real resource cost in diverting it there, and also a subsidy may be required. However, welfare is raised and policy intervention remains justified as long as the benefits exceed the costs. In practice, UK policy has been based on a premise that location does not significantly affect costs, at least for much of manufacturing.

For the purposes of regional policy the UK is divided into eleven standard regions: Northern, Yorkshire and Humberside, East Midlands, East Anglia, South East, South West, Wales, West Midlands, North West, Scotland and Northern Ireland. The imbalances between the regions which policy seeks to redress originate from complex geographical, technological and historical causes. In the UK, falling employment in agriculture and the decline of the former staple industries, especially coal, cotton-textiles, steel and shipbuilding, have been major influences since the mid 1950s. In the earlier phases of industrialization in Britain, these had located close to sources of power and raw materials in the North, Scotland and Wales. More modern industries, particularly those using electrical power, have developed elsewhere. Thus structural developments in the economy create tendencies for centres of economic activity to shift, while demographic developments remain largely shaped by the past, and it is against these tendencies that regional policies must pull. However, the UK regions are nearly all mixed urban-rural areas with a fair spread of activities, and the imbalance between them is not as severe as in some other countries, e.g. Italy, where there are extreme differences between the industrialized north and the largely agricultural south of the country.

Until recently UK regional policy has not sought to address the problem of declining employment and population in inner cities. Indeed, central and local government policies to relieve congestion and assist urban renewal in large conurbations have encouraged an exodus to the suburbs and new towns. Under the New Towns Act 1946 and the Town Development Act 1952, more than twenty new towns have been established, and rather more enlarged. This policy may have conflicted with regional policies, since the new towns have by no means all been in development areas, and may have been a counter-attraction to firms which otherwise might have responded to regional incentives. However, the existence of serious problems in inner cities is now recognized and this is reflected in recent regional policy developments, including the creation of 'Enterprise Zones' in 1980, and the designation of free ports in 1984.

Like Britain, the EEC also has a number of regional problems in older industrial areas developed around iron-ore and coal. These include the Ruhr, Saar and Lorraine. A further, serious EEC regional problem stems from the existence of low-income agricultural areas to which industrialization has never come. Originally these were mainly in parts of France and, especially, the south of Italy (where gross value added was under half the national average in 1980 and only a quarter of that in Hamburg, the richest part of the EEC). With the expansion of the Community, this aspect of the EEC regional problem has already been intensified by the addition of the Irish Republic and Greece, and will be further increased by the admission of Spain and Portugal. The flourishing industrial centres of the EEC, on the other hand, lie mainly along the Rhine–Rhone valleys, from the Netherlands to Northern Italy. These are estimated to have accounted for some 60% of the Gross Product of the EEC before its enlargement in 1973. Some commentators now speak of a 'golden triangle' in Europe, lying roughly between Hamburg, London and Milan.

At the time of writing the government has published an assessment of regional policy and invited comments on a number of specific issues.[1] Legislation to reshape existing policies is expected to be put before Parliament some time in 1984. The next two sections discuss the present provisions and the impact of policy to date, and section V.4 then briefly considers likely future directions.

V.2   Policy Measures

The strategy of regional policy has been to identify specific areas requiring assistance, primarily on the basis of above-average unemployment rates. Firms located in or moving to these areas have then been offered various financial incentives, while administrative controls have been placed on industrial expansion elsewhere. Both the qualifying areas and the type and value of financial incentives have been changed frequently in the last twenty years, and the degree of control on industrial development outside the assisted areas has also fluctuated. Policy measures were first introduced in the prewar Special Areas Act of 1934. Postwar policy has been implemented through the Distribution of Industry Acts since 1945, the Local Employment Acts from 1960, and various Finance Acts, but present policy is based mainly on the 1972 Industry Act.

Four main types of area receive special treatment at present. These are *Development Areas*, each covering the whole or most of one of the standard regions of the UK; *Special Development Areas*, which were first created in 1967 to deal with problems caused by colliery closures, but later broadened to include other areas; *Intermediate Areas*, which are the so-called 'grey areas' lying outside development areas, but suffering similar problems; and *Enterprise Zones*, which are very small districts (averaging only around 500 acres) primarily in older urban areas. In addition there are special provisions for Northern Ireland, and the government has recently designated six 'free ports' (in Belfast, Cardiff, Prestwick, Liverpool, Birmingham and Southampton), which are areas to which goods can be imported free of customs duties and other levies, provided they are sent abroad again after processing.

At one time the assisted areas contained about 47% of the working population. However, since the map was last redrawn in 1979 this figure has fallen to 27.6%. At present, Special Development Areas cover 7% of the workforce in England, 5% in Scotland and 1.1% in Wales. For Development Areas the corresponding figures are 4.5%, 1.6% and 2.7%, and for Intermediate Areas 4.5%, 0.4% and 0.7%.

Many different types of regional assistance have been given since 1945. The main forms of financial aid presently on offer are *regional development grants* and

---

1   *Regional Industrial Development*, Cmnd. 9111, HMSO, December 1983.

regiónal selective assistance. Grants cover 22% of the cost of buildings, works, plant and machinery in Special Development Areas, and 15% in Development Areas. Selective assistance is usually by a further, discretionary grant towards capital and training costs for projects meeting job-creating criteria. Table 4.17 shows that total spending on regional aid, which grew rapidly up to 1982/3 but has since declined sharply, has been predominantly on the automatically available regional grants rather than the discretionary selective assistance. Other forms of UK assistance include exchange-loss guarantees for certain EEC loans and rent subsidies on government-provided workshops and advance factories. Higher levels of support are given in Northern Ireland, including industrial development grants of 30–50% of fixed investment costs, rent-free factories, and 40–50% R and D grants.

TABLE 4.17
Regional Industrial Assistance 1977/8–1982/3, GB (£m at out-turn prices)

	77/8	78/9	79/80	80/81	81/2	82/3	83/4[1]
Regional development grants	393	417	331[2]	491	617	690[2]	440
Regional selective assistance	44	104	78	74	76	90	98
Land and factories	52	85	110	141	161	137	105
Total	489	606	519	706	854	917	543

Source: FT.

Notes: 1 Estimated.
2 From June 1979 to November 1982 there was a four-month deferment of grant on approved applications. This reduced the 1979/80 figure by about £110m and raised the 1982/3 figure by up to £150m.

Administrative control over industrial expansion outside the assisted areas has been exercised mainly via *Industrial Development Certificates* (IDCs) relating to new factory buildings or extensions. Up to 1972 they were required in all areas for projects above a certain minimum size, and after 1966 their issue was strictly controlled in the Midlands and South East. From 1972 IDCs have not been required in Development Areas, and since 1974 a three-tier system has applied to the rest of the country although, in the continuing recession which followed, IDC control has apparently not been applied strictly. Office development has been subject to similar controls, though this has never been regarded as a major policy instrument for dispersing jobs to the regions.

Enterprise Zones are a recent addition to regional policy which reflect an underlying belief of the Conservative government that private initiatives can be stifled by excessive public-authority involvement and government rules and regulations. Therefore in addition to financial benefits (100% capital allowances and exemption from both general rates on industrial and commercial property and development land tax), firms are intended to benefit from simplified government procedures and speedier administration of controls over development. For example, firms in the Enterprise Zones designated from 1980 onwards are excluded from the scope of Industrial Training Boards, exempted from any remaining IDC requirement, promised speedier processing of requests for customs warehousing etc. and receive minimal requests to supply statistics to government.

EEC regional policy came into operation with the establishment of a European Regional Development Fund in 1975. The fund originally worked solely on a national quota basis, within which the fund could contribute up to 20% towards job-creation schemes and 50% towards infrastructural development under the national policies of member states. Since 1979, however, a small proportion of the fund has been earmarked for 'non-quota' purposes. This was intended to provide finance for projects negotiated between member governments and the European Commission (EC), which would direct funds towards the most pressing problems and at the same time permit a more integrated, Community-wide policy to emerge. Between 1975 and 1982 the non-quota section took just over 10% of the total 7.3bn ECU allocated from the fund.

The ERDF now accounts for around 8% of the Community budget. This is of course very much less than the 63% spent on agriculture, and also represents only about 5% of total spending on regional support policies by member states. Nevertheless the UK has been a substantial beneficiary, receiving 1.75bn ECU up to 1982 (only Italy has received more, with 2.78bn ECU). However, the EEC funds have not resulted in assistance to firms over and above that discussed under the UK policy heading since receipts from the fund go to the government rather than to the promoters of individual projects. In principle the EEC funds are intended to be additional to government spending in the regions, but in 1980 there was some dispute between Britain and the EC as to whether this had actually been the case.

In 1981 the EC put forward radical proposals for revision of the ERDF. These reflected concern that regional disparities within the Community had widened over the preceding ten years, sought to focus policy more sharply on the most serious problems, and emphasized the need to knit regional policy and other Community programmes more closely together. The main proposals were to abolish national quotas and focus attention on specific regions (including Northern Ireland, parts of Scotland and Wales, and the North and North West of England) and to raise the non-quota section of the fund to 20%, thereby increasing the influence of the EC over the national policies of member states. Studies of the regional impacts of all major Community programmes were also proposed, in particular of agricultural support under the CAP and assistance for the restructuring of coal and steel production under the ECSC Treaty.

However, these proposals met with considerable resistance from member states unwilling to relinquish their quotas and control over national policies. As a result, revised proposals emerged in 1983. National quotas were now retained, but in the form of upper and lower bounds on a given country's share, giving more flexibility in the allocation of funds, and providing the EC with some scope for a *de facto* increase in the non-quota section.

The non-quota part of the fund's activities would focus on 'Community programmes' of co-ordinated longer-term measures, over which the EC would take the initiative. The clear intention is that these would in effect become the core of a central Community-wide policy, and the EC proposed that these programmes would occupy 30% of the fund after three years of revised operation and 40% after four. However, there seems little prospect at the time of writing that the issues raised by these proposals will be tackled seriously until problems of agricultural and budgetary reform have been dealt with, though in early 1984 a package of 710m ECU was agreed under this heading to help economic regeneration in areas hit by closures in the steel, shipbuilding and textile industries of the Community.

V.3   Regional Policy Impact

It is officially accepted that regional policies had created around half a million jobs in the assisted areas by the end of the 1970s.[1] This estimate is based on academic research which suggests a range of 350,000–650,000 jobs, after allowance for local multiplier effects. The cost of each job created during the 1970s is put at £35,000 in 1982 prices. The rate of job-creation was much lower in the late 1970s than in the late 1960s, when it reached a peak of about 25,000 a year.

Since the objective of policy is to mitigate regional disparities, its impact should ultimately register on regional indicators of industrial output, incomes and especially unemployment. Table 4.18 shows regional unemployment for 1983, the latest data available at the time of writing, and comparative figures for 1966 and 1975 (when major phases of regional policy began). While unemployment has increased dramatically in all regions over the period, the dispersion of regional unemployment rates has in general declined, though the overall level has of course increased.

TABLE 4.18

Regional Unemployment and Redundancy Rates

	Unemployment (%)			No. of redundancies per 1,000 employees[1]	
	1966	1975	1983[2]	Average 1977–9	Average 1980–82
N. Ireland	5.3	7.9	21.0	n.a.	n.a.
Scotland	2.7	5.2	15.0	33.8	77.5
North	2.5	5.9	17.3	28.6	76.4
North West	1.4	5.3	15.7	25.5	77.1
Wales	2.8	5.6	16.1	29.8	104.2
West Midlands	0.8	4.1	15.7	10.6	57.2
Yorks & Humberside	1.1	4.0	14.1	17.5	74.9
East Anglia	1.4	3.4	10.6	12.9	37.6
South West	1.7	4.7	11.3	12.8	51.3
East Midlands	1.0	3.6	11.7	8.6	53.4
South East	0.9	2.8	9.5	9.0	34.2
UK	1.4	4.1	13.0	GB 16.9	58.8

Source: *DEG/AAS.*

Notes: 1   In manufacturing.
           2   Estimate.

In interpreting these trends it must be recalled that there are two forces at work: structural factors and policy. Recent research suggests that up to 1966 structural factors were operating very strongly against the most depressed regions

---

1   *Regional Industrial Policy: Some Economic Issues*, DTI, 1983.

(Northern Ireland, Scotland, the North and the North-West).[1] However, policy
exerted a beneficial effect in each case. In the period 1966–75, the adverse
structural effects were less adverse (and in fact became favourable in the case of the
Northern region), while policy, as we have seen, was at its height. In general, we
may conclude that policy contributed substantially to the narrowing of differentials
up to 1975, especially after 1966. Since 1975, as we have seen, the strength of
regional policy was very much reduced, and the continued narrowing of
differentials around a much higher average figure may be seen as largely due to the
spread of very deep recession to previously more prosperous industries and regions.
The regional incidence of redundancies in manufacturing industries is shown in
table 4.18, the most dramatic change in fortunes of any region being experienced
by the West Midlands. Whereas this region once had the lowest unemployment rate
in the whole country, it has now slipped well into the ranks of the problem regions,
on a par with Scotland, the North West and Wales. The principal factor in this
transformation has been the decline of car production and associated engineering
trades. By contrast, East Anglia (within the European 'golden triangle') has been
the most dynamic of the regions, with a substantial growth in employment relative
to the national average.

While the effectiveness of regional policy must ultimately register in regional
statistics of the kind just considered, questions may also be asked about the nature
of the policy instruments used and their cost-effectiveness. Statistical analysis
indicates that all three major types of policy instrument – IDCs, capital subsidies of
one kind or another, and contributions towards operating costs – have exerted a
separate, significant influence.[2] A number of criticisms have nevertheless been
made.

First, most of the financial incentives have related to capital expenditures,
imparting a capital bias to the policy as a whole. Thus the firms most likely to be
attracted to assisted areas are those with highly capital-intensive technologies, offering
relatively few new jobs for a given total expenditure. Moreover, the distortion of
relative prices for labour and capital in the assisted regions will encourage all firms
in them, including those not attracted by regional policies, to substitute capital for
labour so far as technological constraints will permit. Significantly, the highest job-
creation rates of regional policies occurred, as we have seen, in the late 1960s and
early 1970s when the capital bias of the policy was offset by the Regional Employment Premium, a labour subsidy paid to manufacturing firms in Development
Areas, in addition to capital subsidies, from 1967 to 1976.

Secondly it has been argued that the use of *automatic* financial incentives (like
cash grants, tax allowances and REP), as opposed to *discretionary* regional grants
tied to specific programmes of job-creation, has reduced the cost-effectiveness of
regional support, since aid is given to firms already in Development Areas, as well as
to those moving in or setting up. Thirdly, the use of cash grants as opposed to
incentives in the form of reduced tax liability has been criticized on grounds that

---

1 *Cambridge Economic Policy Review*, Vol. 6, No. 2, July 1980. See also Vol. 8, No. 2,
December 1982, for a further analysis of employment problems in the cities and regions of
the UK, and prospects for the 1980s.

2 See B. Moore and J. Rhodes, 'Evaluating the Effects of British Regional Policy', *EJ*, Vol.
83, 1973, pp. 87–110; 'Regional Economic Policy and the Movement of Manufacturing Firms
to Development Areas', *Economica*, 43, pp. 17–31, February 1976; and *Methods of Evaluating
the Effects of Regional Policy*, Paris, OECD, 1977.

it does not differentiate between efficient and inefficient firms (i.e. those making profits and others). On the other hand, industrialists argue that cash grants have more influence over firms' decisions, because their size is known and the monies are recoverable at or soon after capital expenditures, whereas the magnitude and timing of future tax remissions is much more uncertain.

These criticisms of regional policy measures also apply to the financial incentives in Enterprise Zones, which resemble those of regional policy proper. According to an independent report,[1] some 10,700 jobs have been generated in just over one thousand companies since the first zones were designated in 1981, at a cost of around £16,500 per job. However, most of the jobs are in companies transferring from locations nearby. Thus 75% of companies opening in a zone came from the same county and at least 85% originated within the region; only 14 companies had moved between regions. So far, it seems, 'enterprise' has been mostly on the part of firms responding to the lure of, in particular, a 10-year rates 'holiday' by moving down the road, rather than on the part of new firms setting up and creating jobs which did not exist before.

V.4   Future Policy Directions

The latest (December 1983) White Paper[2] contains the government's assessment of existing policy and regional needs and suggestions for future policy, and invites comment on a range of specific questions. The aim appears to be to reduce regional policy costs, but to seek greater cost-effectiveness and to emphasize job-creation. The emphasis is to move away from automatic subsidies towards greater 'selectivity', focusing on the encouragement of new, indigenous development in assisted areas, as opposed to simply transferring jobs from elsewhere. It is proposed to correct a perceived bias towards manufacturing industry by placing greater emphasis on service industries.

Regional development grants are to be retained, but awarded to approved projects rather than qualifying premises, judged on criteria of capital expenditure *or* job-creation, and subject to a cost-per-job ceiling. An increased share of expenditure will in future go on regional selective assistance. The map of assisted areas will be redrawn, probably on the basis of smaller units than at present. It is not yet clear whether there will be two main categories of assisted areas or three, and what change in the geographic spread of the policy there will be, though it is widely expected that the West Midlands will be among any new areas qualifying for assistance in future.

VI   INDUSTRIAL POLICY
VI.1   The Nature of Industrial Policy

Defining the boundaries of industrial policy is difficult because most government policy decisions touch on industrial production in some way. Fiscal and monetary policies are obvious examples. Pay and price controls likewise impinge on industries

---

1   Roger Tim and Partners, *Monitoring Enterprise Zones: Year Three Report*, 25 Craven Street, WC2.

2   Cmnd. 9111.

at the micro-level in different ways, as do regional and competition policies. Defence and social policies like housing affect the composition of final demand and hence relative industry outputs, and so on. However, the principal objectives of all these policies are either macroeconomic or are concerned with raising welfare where there is market failure of some sort. Their effects on industry are mostly incidental, often unintended and sometimes conflicting. These effects complicate the formulation of industrial policy in a narrower sense—i.e. policies which explicitly seek either the achievement of particular production targets or industrial structures, or to promote growth, investment and technical progress in individual firms and industries.

Several strands of industrial policy in this narrower sense have developed in a rather piecemeal fashion in the postwar period. The government has supported R & D and innovation both financially and via the National Research and Development Corporation (NRDC) and other means. Recently it has taken measures to promote new enterprises, for example giving assistance to small new firms, and to promote the service and information technology industries. Large sums have been spent on structural reorganization in declining industries, where the government has come to the aid of ailing firms either through specific industry schemes (as in cotton textiles, aircraft and shipbuilding) or more generally via the former Industrial Reorganisation Corporation (IRC) and National Enterprise Board (NEB). Tax incentives for investment have been in force throughout the period, and public money has also been made available to firms for general investment. Finally, there have been some attempts at strategic planning. These began with the establishment of the National Economic Development Council (NEDC) in 1962, culminated in the National Plan of 1965 and continued, in a much watered-down form, through the Industrial Strategy of 1975 to the work of the individual Economic Development Councils (EDCs) and Sector Working Parties (SWPs) at industry level. The system of investment incentives is discussed in chapter 2. We review each of the other main strands of policy in more detail in the following paragraphs, and conclude by considering the argument for a more coherent policy, perhaps drawing on experience from other countries.

VI.2   R & D, Hi-tech and Information Technology

Although the emphasis of government policy on the high-technology electronics and telecommunications industries as vehicles for economic recovery is quite recent, there is a longer-standing history of support for R & D and industrial innovation in Britain, as in other industrialized countries. The basic rationale is that the social rate of return from innovation exceeds the private benefits, because the innovator will not be able to appropriate all the returns from his innovation; even when he has the protection of patents, others may benefit in ways that are not reflected in his returns. Thus if R & D and other innovative effort is left entirely to market forces, too little will be undertaken. Early US case-studies suggested a social rate of return of 56% compared with a private return of only 25%.[1] The analysis also highlighted the large variations in private returns and showed that in

---

1 See E. Mansfield, 'Measuring the Social and Private Rates of Return on Innovation' in *Economic Effects of Space and Other Advanced Technologies*, Strasbourg, Council of Europe, 1980.

nearly one third of cases it would not have been rational for firms to invest in the projects if the returns had been known in advance with certainty; yet in nearly all these cases the social return was positive. Similarly large gaps between social and private returns have been found in subsequent studies, and influence current thinking on innovation policy. This has a number of strands, including financial subsidies, institutional measures, and specific provisions for certain hi-tech industries.

Total R & D spending in Britain amounts to about 2.4% of GDP, and compares with 2.3% in the US, 2.0% in Japan and 1.9% in the EEC.[1] The government meets nearly half the total cost in Britain, about the same as in the US and EEC, and rather more than in Japan. However, more than half UK government R & D is on defence, compared with only a quarter in the EEC as a whole, and none at all in Japan. Hence the comparison based on civil projects is less favourable. On this basis the UK expenditure is some 1.8% of GDP, slightly more than the US and EEC (1.7%) but less than in Japan, Germany and France. Moreover, we must remember when interpreting these figures that GDP per head is relatively low in the UK. Recognizing that by international standards UK spending on civil R & D is low, the government plans to increase its level of support to £269m in 1984-5, compared with £231m in 1983-4 and only £86m in 1979-80.

One of the criticisms of UK R & D effort in the past has been its heavy concentration in certain narrow fields, notably aerospace and the nuclear programme. Moreover the social value of highly expensive programmes like Concorde has been widely doubted, while much of the value of past research on the British, gas-cooled nuclear reactor may now become wasted if future nuclear power stations are equipped with the American, pressurized-water system. However, the latest statistics show a substantial fall in the proportion of industrial R & D in aerospace, from 21.6% in 1975 to 18.2% in 1978, while there has been a rapid growth in electronic components (16.9% to 22.4%) and also computers (3.8% to 5.3%). Even so, R & D spending remains much less evenly spread than in most other countries, including Japan.

Institutional measures to encourage technical progress in Britain began with the establishment of the NRDC in 1948, to finance the development of inventions made in universities, government laboratories and by private individuals where this was in the public interest. The total resources at its disposal were, however, not large, some £15m a year towards the end of its existence, when it also undertook some manufacturing. In 1982 the NRDC was merged with what remained of the NEB, to form the British Technology Group (BTG).[2] The government also sponsors work on behalf of industry in its own research establishments, funds research in universities and through various Research Councils, and supports co-operative research associations in a number of industries.

In the field of information technology, the government has taken steps to preserve independent British manufacture of mainframe computers and microchips. (One suspects this reflects an underlying element of defence-strategy thinking, over and above any considerations of industrial development and employment.) ICL, the mainframe computer manufacturer, has received financial support and also benefited from preferential treatment in public-sector computer procure-

---

1 Source: *AAS*, *ET* and Eurostat, *Government Financing of Research and Development*, 1981.

2 See also section VI.3.

ment. More recently, INMOS, which manufactures semi-conductors, has received a total government investment of £65m (and loan guarantees of a further £40m), resulting in a 75% shareholding by the BTG. At the time of writing, INMOS appears to have overcome early production problems and financial losses, and is beginning to achieve volume production of 'standard' microchips in the mainstream market dominated by US and Japanese manufacturers such as Motorola, Texas Instruments, NEC and Hitachi. Its production activities are located in South Wales and Colorado, and INMOS is the only British contender in the mainstream market, other British companies like GEC, Plessey and Ferranti producing specialized components rather than chips mass-produced to a fixed pattern. However, there are some doubts over the future of INMOS. In 1983 the government of the day made it clear that all future capital should come from private sources, and it is understood that a £20m private share placing is being sought. But it would be consistent with government policy to privatize its present stake in the company, except that the most likely purchasers are foreign and this would mean abandoning the original policy objective to preserve an independent UK supply. One bid from the American AT and T company has been rejected, though it is not clear whether this was on grounds of principle or because the £45m bid was too far below the company's estimated worth of £200m.

As a further part of its information technology policy, the government has appointed a Minister with specific responsibilities over the area. Under a Microprocessor Application Project it has provided programmes to increase awareness and training at senior levels in industry, the trade unions and public-sector bodies, as well as financial contributions towards firms' costs in commissioning consultants and developing specific microprocessor applications. These increased activities will doubtless lead to further growth of total R & D expenditure in this area, beyond that recorded up to 1978. In the university sector, the government has encouraged the provision of postgraduate 'conversion' courses in electronics to help ease a growing shortage of skilled staff for hardware and software development, systems analysis, computer-aided design and telecom management, and earmarked a significant number of new university posts, in a declining system, for information technology purposes.

A recent development has also occurred at EEC level, in the form of a European Strategic Programme for R & D in Information Technology (ESPRIT). Once again the intention is to counteract US and Japanese domination of information technology industries. ESPRIT provides for 1.4bn ECU to be spent between 1984 and 1988 to encourage co-operative research projects across national boundaries in the EEC. These will be initiated and carried out by private-sector firms, within a framework determined by the European Commission, with ESPRIT meeting half the total cost.

VI.3   Structural Reorganization

Under this heading we are concerned both with government assistance to declining industries and failing firms, and with intervention to promote growth, exploit scale economies and encourage the birth and development of small new enterprises. In textbook models these adjustments come about naturally via the long-run competitive process of entry and exit, merger and internal growth. However, in practice capital-market sanctions can be slow to operate, financial institutions may not be responsive to the needs of companies at all stages of their growth and development, and the private and social costs of redeploying inputs (e.g. due to the duration of unemployment) may be greater through widespread bankruptcy and subsequent market responses than under a more gradual, government-assisted process. Where the government acts merely as a catalyst, aiding adjustment that would ultimately occur through the operation of market forces, its actions may be considered uncontroversial. If, however, the end result is to maintain industries permanently at an artificial level of production, other considerations of resource allocation arise, like those concerning agriculture (see section II).

The government has been directly involved with the major contraction or expansion of several public-sector industries, especially coal, rail, steel, telecommunications and gas. Action in the private sector was initially undertaken by means of schemes for specific industries facing changed trading conditions, intensive foreign competition and decline. Thus the 1959 *Cotton Industry Act* provided for government contributions to encourage contraction and rationalization of the industry, hit by competition from the Far East. In the case of the *aircraft industry*, the government used its position as the industry's dominant consumer to force a reorganization of nineteen companies into five groups in the 1960s. Assistance to the *shipbuilding industry* also began in the early 1960s, with credit subsidies, and continued with a £68m reorganization of 27 major yards into large regional units in a three-year period after 1967. In both the aircraft and shipbuilding cases, government Committees of Inquiry had concluded there was no case for maintaining production at artificially high levels, for reasons concerning the balance of payments, unemployment or defence. Both industries ultimately passed into public ownership in 1977.

Government intervention across private industry as a whole was facilitated by the establishment of the Industrial Reorganisation Corporation (IRC) in 1966 and by the 1968 Industrial Expansion Act. The IRC was intended to seek out opportunities for rationalization in private industry, and in these cases to initiate and finance mergers which might not otherwise occur. During its existence the IRC was associated with some spectacular mergers (including Leyland–BMC and GEC–AEI–English Electric) but it was quickly abolished by the Conservative government in 1971. The Industrial Expansion Act permitted government support for schemes to improve efficiency which would benefit the economy but required financial backing. There was some scope for helping rationalization, but the aim was to extend and amplify the work of the IRC, rather than overlap with it.

Under the 1970–74 Conservative government the emphasis swung away from 'structural' solutions and towards greater reliance on the pressure of competition as a stimulus to reorganization and greater efficiency. The first expression of this was a declared intention to allow market forces to put down 'lame duck' firms, but this was soon modified when concern about the social and national implications of the failure of Rolls-Royce and Upper Clyde Shipbuilders led the government to intervene in early 1971.

Measures to help small firms, implementing the recommendations of the Bolton Committee,[1] were also presented as a means of fostering new competition. The small firms policy began with the establishment of a small firms division within the (then) Department of Trade and Industry, to safeguard their interests, and local

---

1 *Report on the Committee of Inquiry on Small Firms*, Cmnd. 4811, HMSO, 1971.

advisory centres were subsequently set up and various financial reliefs given. However, powers to grant selective financial assistance to industry contained in the 1972 Industry Act were less pro-competitive, and more in the spirit of the earlier Industrial Expansion Act. The 1972 Act also provided for grants in exchange for state shareholdings in the companies concerned. This was not used by the Conservative government, but was subsequently implemented by its Labour successor, in particular during its rescue of British Leyland in 1975.

The emphasis on extending state ownership in the provision of assistance to industry appeared to have been greatly extended by the Labour government when it set up the National Enterprise Board (NEB), also in 1975. In some ways a successor to the IRC, the NEB had an initial finance of £1,000m to assist firms and promote industrial reorganization. At the time there were some expectations that the NEB would lead to a major extension of public ownership, to include at first 100 and then 25 of the largest UK companies. But this did not materialize and in practice the NEB was mostly occupied in dealing with the securities and other property in public ownership which had been transferred to it, including Alfred Herbert, Ferranti, Rolls-Royce and BL. The return of a Conservative government in 1979 heralded the end of the NEB in its original form. The 1980 Industry Act ended its function to extend public ownership, promote industrial reorganization and encourage industrial democracy, and the Secretary of State for Industry subsequently took over its responsibility for Rolls-Royce (after the resignation of the entire NEB) and later BL. What remained of the NEB was ultimately merged with the NRDC to form the British Technology Group, its focus thus shifting to new ventures, including the previously mentioned INMOS project.

The Conservative government has predictably returned to the policy of encouraging enterprise and small firms. In fact it introduced no less than 108 different measures affecting small companies between 1979 and 1984. Many were seldom used, and the sheer numbers were thought to create such confusion that a DTI review was set in train in 1984 with a view towards producing a simplified programme of assistance, the details of which are still awaited at the time of writing.

Many of the measures involved some form of tax relief, including a preferential 'small companies' rate of corporation tax, tax relief for pre-trading expenditure by new companies, and income-tax relief on up to £40,000 of shares subscribed to unquoted companies by individuals under a Business Expansion Scheme (originally set up in 1981 as a Business Start-Up Scheme and confined to new companies). Other kinds of measure included arrangements to encourage profit-sharing and employee share-option schemes, and a Loan Guarantee Scheme, to permit government underwriting of small-company borrowing from banks.

The current emphasis in government policy on small business is not confined to Britain, and various schemes for its encouragement and assistance are in force throughout Europe. According to a recent independent study,[1] Britain has the most favourable climate for small business in only one respect, namely taxation. When other factors are taken into account, including labour conditions, the cost of premises and (lack of) discriminatory legislation, Britain ranked in ninth place overall in a league of ten European countries, surpassing only Italy, and with West Germany, France and Greece in the top three places.

---

1 Economist Intelligence Unit, *The European Climate for Small Business : A Ten Country Study*, EIU, 1983.

When attempting to assess any of the foregoing policies for structural reorganization, it is important to see them in the context of the existing distributions of firm and plant size. These are highly skewed; the great majority of plants and firms are small, but output is heavily concentrated in a comparatively tiny number of very large units (table 4.19). Thus in 1980 90% of manufacturing plants employed less than one hundred employees (and over half in fact had no more than ten workers), but contributed only a fifth of total net output. At the other end of the scale, just over 500 plants with more than 1,500 employees were responsible for no less than a third of net output. A similar pattern can be seen in the case of firms. The average number of plants per firm is only 1.2, and the vast majority of firms are small, single-plant enterprises, while a few very large firms have many plants.

TABLE 4.19

Distribution of Plants and Firms by Employment Size, Production Industries Excluding Energy, 1980

Employment size-category	No. of Units	(%)	Total employment 000s	(%)	Total net output £m	(%)
(a) Establishments[1]						
1–99	98,879	(90.8)	1,391	(21.6)	14,099	(20.6)
100–499	7,777	(7.1)	1,670	(25.9)	16,890	(24.7)
500–1499	1,651	(1.5)	1,338	(20.8)	14,572	(21.3)
1500 and over	578	(0.5)	2,038	(31.7)	22,914	(33.5)
Total	108,885	(100.0)	6,437	(100.0)	68,475	(100.0)
(b) Enterprises[2]						
1–99	84,944	(94.2)	1,146	(18.8)	10,788	(16.6)
100–499	3,916	(4.3)	795	(13.0)	7,717	(11.9)
500–1499	812	(0.9)	677	(11.1)	7,055	(10.8)
1500 and over	491	(0.5)	3,486	(57.1)	39,534	(60.7)
Total	90,163	(100.0)	6,104	(100.0)	65,094	(100.0)

Source: Business Monitor PA 1002, Report on the Census of Production, 1980.

Notes: 1 An establishment is the smallest unit capable of supplying census information, usually a factory or plant at a single site or address.
2 An enterprise means one or more establishments under common ownership or control.

Over time, there has been a long-term trend towards large-scale production. Plants with more than 1,500 workers accounted for some 15% of total employment in private-sector manufacturing industry in 1935, but for over 30% in 1980; those with under 100 employees accounted for 26% in 1935 and for 21% in 1980. During the 1970s, however, there was also a very large increase in the total number of firms and plants; after remaining static in the 1960s, the number of manufacturing establishments rose from around 70,000 in 1968 to 75,000 in 1972 and then to the figure shown in table 4.19. All of this increase occurred in the smaller size-categories, the number of plants with more than a hundred workers actually falling over the period. Despite this, the change in the shares in total output of the different size-categories has not changed dramatically. Thus while it may be that there are ICIs and Unilevers of the future among the small firms of today, it should be borne in mind that the present policies encouraging small enterprise affect only a small proportion of existing production activity.

VI.4   Industrial Strategy

British industrial policy has never adopted an industrial strategy in the sense of binding sectoral output targets, or even a coherent list of priority industries towards which the government would assist the mobilization of resources. The nearest approach to such a strategy was the National Plan of 1965.[1] The plan was the culmination of a strand of development influenced by the contemporary French system of 'indicative planning'. This had seen earlier expression in the establishment of the National Economic Development Council (NEDC) in 1962. This is a tripartite body representing employers, trade unions and government at a very senior level, supported by a permanent staff. It remains in being at the time of writing, though a shadow has recently been cast on its future by TUC abstention from meetings as a protest against government policy. Some twenty-one EDCs for individual industries were also set up on a similar basis. The general hope was for a consensus approach in analysing and helping overcome impediments to faster growth, at both the national and the industry level.

The National Plan itself was not a plan in any *dirigiste* sense, but a set of industry-by-industry projections of the implications of an assumed growth of the economy at 4% a year from 1964 to 1970. Though it followed a NEDC report on the obstacles to faster growth, the plan was the work of the newly created Department of Economic Affairs, set up in an aura of enthusiasm for the age of the 'white-hot technological revolution' following the election of a Labour government in 1964.

In the event the planning exercise was short-lived, brought to an end by the national economic crisis measures of 1966. The plan's 1969 successor, entitled *The Task Ahead*,[2] was originally to have been the Second Plan, but turned out to be a much less detailed and ambitious document, merely discussing the possible use of resources under alternative growth rates. However, the institutional structure of the NEDC and EDCs survived. During the Conservative government of 1970–74 the focus of their activities shifted towards more low-key activity concerning problems of growth and efficiency at industry level. A wide range of analyses was carried out, and the results were disseminated within industries via newsletters and reports, with some inter-industry exchanges.

The industrial strategy concept was revived in 1974, with Labour once again in power. This time the strategy was launched by the NEDC.[3] Once again the first stage was to analyse the short-term difficulties facing individual sectors and

1   Department of Economic Affairs, *The National Plan*, Cmnd. 2764, HMSO, 1965.

2   Department of Economic Affairs, *The Task Ahead: Economic Assessment to 1972*, HMSO, 1969.

3   See *The Regeneration of British Industry*, Cmnd. 5710, HMSO, 1974, and *An Approach to Industrial Strategy*, Cmnd. 6315, HMSO, 1975.

recommend ways of overcoming them. The emphasis then was to turn to analysing performance and agreeing on medium-term programmes of action to improve competitive performance. A further set of tripartite bodies was set up for this purpose, the Sector Working Parties (SWPs). In selecting the sectors, the governing idea was 'picking winners', i.e. industries which were 'intrinsically likely to be successful' or potential growth centres. By 1979, 40 SWPs had been created, covering about 40% of manufacturing output, and including eleven remaining EDCs which had taken over the role of SWPs.

The work of the SWPs has, like that of the EDCs, been very varied, involving studies and recommendations on things like investment and productivity, manpower and training, product design, development and standardization, the identification of markets, marketing techniques and export finance. Management and union representatives are intended to see that the programmes are practically viable, and government representatives to see that the programmes are harmonized nationally. Under the 1975 Industrial Strategy, the government was also committed to take steps in support of the sector programmes, such as providing extra financial assistance for investment (as in the case of microelectronics), for entry into export markets and for industry training schemes. The government also undertook to 'identify the industrial implications of the whole range of government policies' and give more weight to the needs of industry in shaping them.

The value of the work undertaken by the SWPs and EDCs and co-ordinated under NEDC is hard to judge. Jointly they provide a forum for dialogue between government and industry, and this could result in the government discovering more about the micro implications of its macro policies, so avoiding some of the adverse effects of unduly sharp and frequent changes in economic regulations, pre-emption of resources for the public sector and personal consumption, and intervention in the nationalized industries. At industry level many topics have been discussed and many reports issued dealing with specific problems affecting performance. There is, however, a doubt about the effectiveness of the tripartite, consensus line of attack in the UK, which may be quite good at diagnosing the causes of poor performance, but much less able to agree on remedies and go on to implement them.

The current (Conservative) government's approach to industrial policy is one of deep scepticism towards the value of planning and government interference, and of greater confidence in market forces to reveal growth potential and solve co-ordination problems. As a result, institutions like the NEDC and SWP tend to occupy a less prominent position in government policy, which instead focuses on liberating the 'supply side' of the economy by breaking up restrictive practices, liberalizing the labour market, making training and education more responsive to industrial needs, curbing inflation, restoring incentives and profitability, and reducing the public sector.

VI.5 Lessons from Abroad[1]

It is sometimes suggested that the UK could learn from the experience of other countries' industrial policies and in particular from France and Japan. The French

---

1 For a further discussion, see C.J.F. Brown, 'Industrial Policy and Economic Planning in Japan and France', *NIER*, August 1980.

reputation is for 'indicative planning', wherein much of the value it is believed lay in the consultation process leading to sectoral projections, rather than in the execution of plans as such. But as we have seen, this has already been tried in the UK; the National Plan of 1965 was an attempt to import this system, and the consultative machinery still remains. The discredit into which planning somewhat undeservedly fell in the UK after the crisis measures of 1966 has tended to impede further attempts. In any case, planning has been much less effective in France itself since the late 1960s, when politically stronger governments have placed more emphasis on macroeconomic and social policy.

The Japanese strategy has been to identify a number of priority industries and concentrate effort and resources in these. This has been achieved without central direction, within a market economy, but utilizing certain institutional features not present in the UK: strong government influence (via the banks) over the supply of corporate investment funds; control over access to foreign exchange in an economic system which has until recently been highly protected; and a commitment to the 'consensus approach' to decision-making which is part of Japanese culture. It has also been achieved largely at the expense of competition policies and the provision of social services, which raises questions about the kind of society being aimed at.

While there are few readily importable features of French and Japanese experience at the level of practical policy, there are perhaps two more general lessons. The first is the importance of clearly articulated goals, and the second is the need to take the long-run view. Both have been conspicuously absent in the UK. As we have seen, Conservative strategy relies heavily on market co-ordination, and seeks to encourage the independence of firms and to create a favourable environment for private initiatives. When Labour has been in office the emphasis has tended more towards large-scale organization and supplementing market processes with some form of information exchange or planning. While it is possible to dispute which is the superior approach, there may be an argument that either would be better than a policy which vacillates between them, as governments change. Certainly it must be bewildering to industry to see both 'bigness' and 'smallness' in fashion at different times, institutions like IRC and NEB come and go, and the frequent changes that have occurred in the value and types of financial assistance on offer. Greater continuity of policy, of whatever kind, would at least provide a more stable context for the planning of investment and longer-term development.

REFERENCES AND FURTHER READING
General Texts

D.A. Hay and D.J. Morris, *Industrial Economics, Theory and Evidence*, OUP, 1979.
F.M. Scherer, *Industrial Market Structure and Economic Performance*, 2nd edition, Rand McNally, 1980.

Current Developments

National Institute Economic Review (especially February issues each year, and the regular statistical section and calendar of economic events) and
Economic Progress Reports (published monthly by the Information Division of the Treasury).
Financial Times

Industrial Performance

S.J. Prais, *Productivity and Industrial Structure*, CUP, 1983.
M. Panic (ed.), *The UK and German Manufacturing Industries*, NEDC, 1976.

Agriculture

J.K. Bowers and Paul Cheshire, *Agriculture, the Countryside and Land Use*, Methuen, 1983.
D. Swann, *The Common Market*, 5th edition, Penguin, 1984.
European Commission, *The Common Agricultural Policy*, revised edition, 1981.

Nationalized Industries

R. Rees, *Public Enterprise Economics*, 2nd edition, Weidenfeld and Nicolson, 1984.
R. Pryke, *The Nationalised Industries : Policies and Performance since 1968*, Martin Robertson, 1981.
NEDO, *A Study of the UK Nationalised Industries : Their Role in the Economy and Control in Future*, 1976.
J.A. Kay and Z.A. Silberston, 'The New Industrial Policy—Privatisation and Competition', *MBR*, Spring 1984.
Symposium on 'Privatisation and After', *Fiscal Studies*, Vol. 5, No. 1, Feb. 1984.

Competition Policy

E. Mansfield, *Monopoly Power and Economic Performance*, Norton, 1968.
K.G. Cowling *et al.*, *Mergers and Economic Performance*, CUP, 1980.
G. Meeks, *Disappointing Marriage: A Study of the Gains from Merger*, CUP, 1977.
D.C. Mueller (ed.), *Determinants and Effects of Mergers : An International Comparison*, Oelgeschlager, Gunn and Hain, 1980.
L. Hannah and J. Kay, *Concentration in Modern Industry*, London, 1977.
P.E. Hart and R. Clarke, *Concentration in British Industry 1935–75*, CUP, 1980.
S.J. Prais, *The Evolution of Giant Firms in Great Britain*, CUP, 1976.
European Commission, *Competition Law in the EEC and ECSC*, 1981.
W.J. Hopper and T.A.E. Sharpe, 'Competition Policies in the European Community', *TBR*, December 1983.

Regional Policy

H. Armstrong and J. Taylor, *Regional Economic Policy*, Philip Allan, 1978.
B. Moore and J. Rhodes, *Methods of Evaluating the Effects of Regional Policy*, Philip Allan, 1978.
Cambridge Economic Policy Review, Vol. 6, No. 2, July 1980, and Vol. 8, No. 2, December 1982.

Industrial Policy

C.F. Carter (ed.) *Industrial Policy and Innovation*, Heinemann, 1981.

F.M. Scherer, *The Economics of Multi-Plant Operation*, Harvard Univ. Press, 1975.

C.F. Pratten, *Economies of Scale in Manufacturing Industry*, CUP, 1971.

NEDC, *Industrial Performance : Trade Performance and Marketing*, 1981.

NEDC, *Industrial Policies in Europe*, 1981.

NEDC, *Industrial Policy in the UK*, 1982.

A.K. Cairncross, P.D. Henderson and Z.A. Silberston, 'Problems of Industrial Recovery', R.C.O. Matthews and J.R. Sargent (eds.), *Contemporary Problems of Economic Policy*, Methuen, 1983.

A.K. Cairncross, J.A. Kay and Z.A. Silberston, 'The Regeneration of Manufacturing', R.C.O. Matthews and J.R. Sargent (eds.), *Contemporary Problems of Economic Policy*, Methuen, 1983.

5

Labour

David Metcalf and Ray Richardson

I   EMPLOYMENT
I.1   The Working Population

The working population in the UK in September 1983 was officially estimated at 27 million people. This total was composed of 21.2m employees in employment, 2.3m employers and self-employed, 325,000 members of HM Forces and 3.2m unemployed.[1]

The working population is not fixed in size. During the 1970s, for example, it grew on average by about 130,000 (or about ½%) a year, and there were considerable fluctuations from year to year. These changes reflect the operation of two factors. First, there are changes in the size of the population of working age, i.e. demographic factors. Secondly, there are variations in activity, or labour-force participation, rates, i.e. the proportion, for any age or sex group, of working to total population.

In recent years, the population of working age has been expanding quite fast. This has been a consequence of relatively small numbers of people reaching retirement age, a reflection of low birth rates in the First World War, and of a sharp rise in the number of teenagers, a reflection of the very high birth rates of the 1960s. These trends will become much less pronounced during the 1980s, but the population of working age will continue to rise. In the first half of the 1990s, however, it is officially estimated to fall, particularly for males.[2]

Activity-rate analysis is a good deal more complex and speculative. Activity rates differ sharply between demographic groups, and, for some groups, vary substantially over time. Thus, females generally have relatively low but rising activity rates, while younger and older males have relatively low and falling activity rates.

The standard economic analysis of male activity rates sees them as being affected by earnings in real terms, non-wage income and educational opportunities. For example, long-run economic growth tends to reduce male activity rates. In particular, younger males stay in the educational system longer and older males retire earlier, especially when growth is accompanied by improved retirement pensions. Between 1961 and 1982 the proportion of boys who stayed on in school rose from 23% to 50% for 16-year-olds and from 13% to 22% for 17-year-olds.[3] In addition, the number of males attending universities approximately doubled over the same period. For older men, the reported activity rates have fallen in each successive Census of Population; for example, the activity rate of 65–69-year-olds fell from

---

1   *DEG*, March 1984, p. 57.

2   *DEG*, 'Labour Force Outlook for Great Britain', February 1984, pp. 56–64.

3   *AAS*, 1971, p. 106, and *AAS*, 1984, p. 91.

48% to 31% between 1951 and 1971, and fell again to only 16% by 1981. It is officially projected to fall to 8% by 1991. In part, these long-run changes reflect the fruits of economic growth, both directly through increased incomes and indirectly through greater government support to education and retirement pensions.

Superimposed on the inverse relation between long-run growth and male activity rates is a complex, and not necessarily stable, reaction to fluctuations in growth. The dominant postwar reaction of the male working population to fluctuations in growth has been that it has tended to contract (or grow less rapidly) during economic recessions and grow (or contract less rapidly) during periods of economic expansion. The recession which started in 1974 was an exception to this general pattern, for it witnessed a 300,000 rise in the number of male employees (i.e. those in employment plus the unemployed). But after 1979 the normal pattern was re-established. Between September 1979 and September 1983, male unemployment rose by about 1.3m, male employment fell by about 1.5m and the total of male employees consequently fell.

It was suggested above that the typical response to long-run growth is that the male working population contracts, while the typical response to short-run growth is that it expands. These two responses, the negative and the positive, are not contradictory, as they might seem at first sight. The first concerns people's response to a permanent increase in wealth levels; the second concerns their response to what is presumed to be a temporary rise in employment prospects. This is an application of the fundamental notions in economics of income and substitution effects. If a worker is not planning to supply the maximum amount of labour at all times, he can choose the most advantageous periods when the supply is to be offered. On many calculations the most advantageous periods occur when wages are high and jobs are easy to find; that is, in expansionary conditions. Consequently, a recession is a period during which there is less point in offering one's services. This view therefore predicts that over the business cycle the size of the working population will be positively related to the state of the economy. It is usually termed the 'discouraged worker effect', meaning that as the economy contracts, the number of people in employment falls by more than the increase in the number counted as unemployed.

There is an alternative and opposite view to the one just described, labelled the 'added worker effect'. It suggests that as 'primary' (i.e. permanent) members of the working population are made unemployed in recessions, 'secondary' (i.e. temporary) workers are drawn into the workforce so as to provide an additional source of income for the family; the result is that the number of unemployed rises more than the number disemployed. This view obviously has some validity but it is basically a qualification to the 'discouraged worker' hypothesis. It stresses that many households plan imprecisely, that unpredicted events are important and force changes even in carefully laid plans, and that savings, credit and social welfare payments may be inadequate to maintain family living standards for more than a relatively short period. These and other factors are all of obvious practical importance, but they should not be taken to imply that the 'discouraged worker' hypothesis, with its emphasis on rational calculation, is thereby unrealistic and likely to be misleading.

Whereas male activity rates have declined over the long run, female activity rates have increased very sharply. Ignoring the self-employed and HM Forces, females accounted for nearly 42% of the labour force in 1983, as compared with just over

30% in 1950. In discussing long-run changes, however, a distinction should be made between married and non-married females. The activity rates for young non-married females have fallen, while those for older non-married females have risen; for example, between 1951 and 1981 they are estimated to have fallen for 20–24-year-olds from 91% to 78%, and to have risen for 45–59-year-olds from 61% to 77%.[1]

The reasons for the distinctive pattern for young non-marrieds are not clear, but they are probably connected with (a) the rise in the extent of girls and young women staying on at school and attending universities, and (b) the rise in the number of one-parent families financially supported either by the state or by alimony or by other family resources.

For married women the picture is unambiguously one of increased activity rates, albeit at different rates for the different age-groups. Table 5.1 shows the striking changes that are officially estimated to have taken place.

TABLE 5.1
Wives' Activity Rates (%) by Age, Great Britain, 1951, 1971 and 1981

Age-Group	1951	1971	1981
16–19	38	42	49
20–24	37	46	57
25–44	25	46	59
45–59	22	57	67
60+	5	14	12
All ages	22	42	50

Source: *ST*, 1979, p. 84 and *ST*, 1984, p. 58.

The importance of these changes can hardly be overstated, and their implications extend far beyond the labour market. What is of immediate importance here is to consider the reasons for the rise. One possibility is that there has been a widespread reduction in the extent of sex discrimination in the labour market. For this to have happened, however, there would have been either a consistent rise in the wages of females relative to those of males or a significant shift in the employment structure, with large numbers of females joining the better-paid and more attractive occupations. Neither of these developments seems to have taken place, certainly not on a major scale, in the first 35 years after the Second World War. Whether or not sex discrimination, however defined, has been extensive, there have been no conclusive studies demonstrating changes in its extent.[2]

Turning to influences primarily affecting married women, we can point first to the fact that the average number of children per family has fallen over time. Whether this is a cause or effect of higher participation is not known. What is known is that activity rates have risen for younger wives as well as for older wives, and that activity rates have also risen for married women with young children. This

---

1 *ST*, 1979, p. 84 and *ST*, 1984, p. 58.

2 For an analysis that suggests that there have only been small changes in the extent of occupational segregation by sex, see C. Hakim, 'Sexual Divisions Within the Labour Force', *DEG*, November 1978, pp. 1,264–8, and C. Hakim, 'Job Segregation Trends in the 1970s', *DEG*, November 1981, pp. 521–9.

suggests that declining family size is, at most, a partial explanation of rising activity rates.

A second possibility is that, due to the introduction of new products, there has been a rise in the productivity of the housewife, effectively allowing her to produce the same amount of services as before but in less time. By itself, this improved productivity does not necessarily make for greater participation by the wife in the labour force because, at the same time, everyone's income has risen. With the rise in income one might expect both the family's demand for housewifely services and the housewife's demand for personal leisure to increase, thereby decreasing the incentive to join the labour market. Only if the domestic-productivity effect is strong will the net effect be to release housewives for market work.

A third possible explanation of the rise in activity rates for married women is that social attitudes have become increasingly tolerant of wives, and even of mothers, working. This explanation is probably the most popular of all and there is certainly no doubt that attitudes have changed. Again, however, there is the difficulty of deciding the extent to which changes in attitudes were an independent cause or were themselves a response to changes in practice. It does seem plausible that the two world wars were very influential in this matter. They were, as far as the labour market was concerned, exogenous events inducing many women to join the market for the first time. This process surely changed social attitudes, encouraging working wives. It is also notable that over the last twenty years the largest increases in activity rates for married women are associated with older women, who experienced to the full the turmoil of wartime. However, one note of caution is worth sounding about the impact of wartime exigencies. The available data are very sketchy, but they suggest that the increase in the proportion of wives who work in the market is very much an international phenomenon, extending even to countries where the direct impact of the war was quite modest.

The above explanations all run in terms of supply influences, implying that progressively more married women are willing to work in the market. Demand influences may also have been important. One possibility is that the growing similarity of regional employment structures, in part perhaps a result of the attempts by successive governments to induce greater regional evenness of employment, have been successful in bringing work to women who previously had very limited job opportunities. It is certainly the case that female activity rates have tended to rise more rapidly in those regions where they were historically low.

But there has not been merely a geographical redistribution of jobs. For most of the period since the end of the 1930s the UK economy has generally been run at unprecedented and persistent tightness. This must explain a major part of the rise in the female working population.

A second, structural, argument relating to demand influences can be made. Female activity rates might have risen because expansion has been particularly marked in industries employing a high ratio of female to male workers. On the other hand, these sectors are not inherently female-intensive and, in the absence of full employment, they might well have used significantly more male labour over the years. Again, it seems reasonable to put the major emphasis on the general expansion of the economy when considering demand influences which account for the long-established rise of female participation in the labour market. Essentially, what has been happening here has been the tapping of a labour reserve.

It has not been easy for economists to do convincing empirical work explaining the patterns of wives' activity rates over time, because suitable data have not been readily available. One recent study found that the growth in real wages had played a part in attracting more women into the labour market, but they found the evidence to be suggestive rather than conclusive.[1]

In addition to this time-series work, there have been studies looking at cross-sectional patterns, i.e. patterns at a point in time, which can be translated into explanations of the time-series developments. One study investigated the variation in married females' activity rates between towns and cities in Great Britain. It was shown that wives' activity rates were greater, the higher were female wage rates and the lower were male wage rates; wives' activity rates were also higher for the foreign-born, for those who lived in the larger cities and for those who lived in towns with low male unemployment rates.[2]

Some of these results were confirmed in a study using survey data on nearly 4,000 wives. It was shown that wives were more likely to be in the labour force if their own potential wage was high, if their husband's wage was low, if they did not have young children, if they were West Indian or Irish born and if their husband was in employment.[3]

As with males, there have been considerable fluctuations in the female labour force superimposed on the longer-run trends. Again, the usual pattern has been for the female working population to expand most rapidly when the economy is growing fast, and to expand slowly or even to contract when the economy moves into recession.

I.2 Aggregate Employment Patterns

Between 1950 and 1965 the number of male employees in employment in the UK followed an upward trend, from 13.6m to 14.9m. Since 1965 there has been a trend in the reverse direction, so that by June 1983 the number was down to about 11.9m. Within the latter period, the rate of decline has varied substantially. It was fairly rapid up to 1972, much slower between 1973 and 1978, and exceedingly fast thereafter. In the period from December 1978 to September 1983, the number of male employees in employment fell by about 1.5m, or nearly 80,000 per quarter. Such a sustained and substantial fall is without precedent in the postwar period.

In contrast to the pattern for males, female employment continued to rise until 1979. Between 1959 and 1979 there was a 25% increase in the number of females in work and only three years during which female employment fell. From September 1979, however, the latter fell in each quarter until mid-1983, from a total of 9.7m to one of about 9.0m.

One of the important differences between the male and female labour forces is the degree to which they work on a part-time basis. In 1981, more than 40% of the female labour force worked only part-time (i.e. normally worked for less than 30 hours per week), as against only 5% of men. Part-time work has also been on the increase.

---

1 H. Joshi, R. Layard and S. Owen, 'Why Are More Women Working in Britain', Centre for Labour Economics, *Discussion Paper No. 162*, LSE, June 1983.

2 C. Greenhalgh, 'Labour Supply Functions for Married Women in GB', *EC*, August 1977. Somewhat similar, but not identical results can be found in R. McNabb, 'The Labour Force Participation of Married Women', *MS*, September 1977.

3 R. Layard *et al.*, 'Married Women's Participation and Hours', *EC*, February 1980.

I.3   Employment by Industry and Occupation

In September 1983 the manufacturing sector of the British economy employed
fewer than 27% of all employees at work. Adding the number of employees in
agriculture, mining, construction, gas, electricity and water, we still get less
than 36% of all employees, implying that the service sector now accounts for well
over half of the employment in the country. The recent tendency for the service-
sector labour force to grow relative to the whole labour force began in the mid-
1950s, when the manufacturing and service sectors each employed about 42.5%
of the total number of employees. The marked absolute decline in manufacturing
employment began in 1966. In that year, manufacturing employment stood at
8.4m; subsequently it has fallen in nearly every year (1969, 1973, 1974 and 1977
are the exceptions) and in nearly every individual manufacturing grouping, so that
in January 1984 there were only 5.4m workers employed in manufacturing.

Within the service sector the main growth areas have been professional and
scientific services, particularly in education and medical and dental services. In the
fourteen years to June 1983, the numbers employed in professional and scientific
services rose by nearly three-quarters of a million. Some service sectors have
become smaller over this period, for example transport and communications (due
mainly to the rapid decline in railway employment), but the general long-run
tendency has been one of growth.

The principal reasons for these employment shifts are the differences between
the sectors in their rates of growth (a) of final, including foreign, demands and (b)
of labour productivity. There are changes in the final demand for an industry's
products as a result of movements in the income and wealth of the economy as a
whole, the structure of prices and the appearance of substitute products, particularly of rival products produced abroad. Thus, in conditions of generalized
recession and an unusually high exchange rate, employment in manufacturing fell
with unprecedented rapidity, between December 1979 and December 1981, by
17% or nearly 1,200,000 workers.

In addition to changes in final demand, changes in labour productivity can also
affect the structure of employment. Over the long run it is clear that labour
productivity has grown faster in manufacturing than in most of the service trades
and that this has resulted in a contraction in the relative demand for labour in
manufacturing. It also seems to be the case that labour productivity has very
recently been increasing at an unusually rapid rate in British manufacturing. What is
said to be happening is that, in order to survive extreme recessionary pressures,
many employers are able to or are being forced to reorganize work practices and
introduce new standards of efficiency. Whatever the reason, there does seem to
have been a sharp increase in labour productivity relative to trend. Whether this
relative productivity gain will survive a return to more prosperous and easygoing
conditions is not clear.

Another way of examining the composition of the labour force is to examine
the division between the private and the public sectors. Over the period 1961 to
1980, there was an increase in the proportion of the employed labour force working in the public sector, from 24% to nearly 30%. The rate of increase was most
rapid in the years 1966-7, 1969-70 and 1974-5, when the level of private employment fell sharply and public employment was fairly stable. After 1980, however,

the relative size of the public sector as a whole began to fall.[1]

Within the public sector, local authority employment rose very sharply, by more than 60%, in the 1960s and 1970s. Between 1980 and 1983 it fell by about 80,000, or about 3%. Central government employment also grew fast in the 1960s and 1970s, by 30%, mainly because of growth in the National Health Service. Subsequently it has changed hardly at all. Finally, employment in the public corporations (i.e. roughly the nationalized industries) was fairly constant for many years, despite an increase in the number of corporations. Since 1980, however, there has been a nearly 20% fall in public corporation employment, in part because of privatization and in part because there have been substantial run-downs in certain industries.

These structural changes are also reflected in the relative growth of female employment, referred to above, because much of the service sector has made intensive use of female labour. Thus, approximately 68% of the employees in professional and scientific services are female, as against 24% in agriculture, only 4% in mining and 7% in shipbuilding. It is true that the textile and clothing industries are also female-intensive, but their decline has not been great in comparison to the expansion of the service sector. It is also worth emphasizing again that a significant number of females, particularly in the rapidly expanding service sectors, work only part-time. Thus 55% of the females working in education and 40% of those in medical and dental services are part-time workers. This compares with less than 25% for manufacturing, and it may suggest that some of the sectoral shifts that have occurred are not a purposeful move away from manufacturing but the use of a previously unused labour reserve that would not be available for full-time work, or perhaps even for part-time work in other sectors.

I.4   Hours Worked

To clarify discussion of work, one should distinguish between normal basic hours, normal hours and actual hours of work. The first term relates to the number of hours a person is expected to work at basic rates of pay; the second includes any guaranteed overtime paid at premium rates; the third, and for most purposes much the most interesting notion, includes all overtime, guaranteed or not. Actual hours are typically in excess of normal hours, but by including absenteeism and sick days in the picture the situation may be reversed.

As with activity rates, two lines of enquiry can be distinguished for hours worked by the labour force as a whole. First, one wants to explain the trend; second, one wants to explain temporary variations around it. Further, it is revealing to examine the structure of hours worked, e.g. by occupation or wage level.

Over a long period, average actual hours of work have fallen, from around sixty hours per week in the early part of the century to around forty hours now. Initially, the fall was in hours per day; subsequent reductions have been first in days worked per week and second in weeks per year. There is therefore a clear tendency for extra leisure to be bunched, there being 'economies of scale' in leisure activities.

---

1 The most detailed discussion of public-sector employment trends is to be found in M. Semple, 'Employment in the Public and Private Sectors, 1961-78', *ET*, November 1979, pp. 99-108. More recent figures are to be found in S. Briscoe, 'Employment in the Public and Private Sectors, 1975-1981', *ET*, December 1981, pp. 94-102 and E. Doggett, 'Employment in the Public and Private Sectors', *ET*, March 1984, pp. 96-104.

For many years, normal hours fell more rapidly than actual hours, implying an increase in the number of overtime hours. Thus, between 1948 and 1968 normal weekly hours of male manual workers fell from 44.5 to 40.1. Actual hours in the same period tended to rise until the mid-1950s and fall thereafter. Since the late 1960s, however, normal hours have been relatively constant but actual hours have tended to fall.

Hours of work fluctuate a good deal from year to year. The changing tempo of the economy is the principal explanation of these variations, with the length of work-weeks falling in recessions and rising in expansions. Thus, the proportion of operatives in manufacturing industry who worked any overtime fell from just under 35% in 1978 to under 27% in 1981; subsequently, as the economy began to expand somewhat, it rose above 32%.

There are wide variations between industries in actual hours worked. In 1978 the average annual hours worked per manual employee in Great Britain was 2,144 in construction, as against 1,655 in mining and quarrying. Within manufacturing, the range was from 1,992 in the timber and furniture sector, to 1,694 in clothing and footwear.

Some of the variation observed in such a cross-section is due to different industries being at different stages in their own business cycle. Additionally, some industries have relatively old labour forces whose work-weeks are naturally shorter. Nevertheless, there are persistent real variations across industries and occupations in hours worked, and these certainly affect the attractiveness of the different jobs. Some research work has shown that for a sample of ninety-six industries in Britain the number of hours offered by the average manual male worker was positively affected by the hourly wage rate and low skill levels, and negatively affected by the number of fellow workers employed in the factory, residence in the South East and Midlands, and residence in conurbations. Further, the number of work-hours demanded from the male worker was greater when the worker was more skilled, aged between 25 and 54, and working in industries that were fast-growing or highly concentrated; fewer hours were demanded from young males and from those who tended to work alongside females.[1]

I.5   The Quality of the Working Population

As time goes on, the average skill level of members of the labour force rises. This is one component of the increased quality of the working population, implying that, from a given number of workers and a given quantity of supporting factors of production, potential output grows over time. Other important sources of higher quality are better health levels, an improved spatial distribution of employment and, up to a point, shorter working weeks. In quantitative terms the increase in skill levels has had much the largest impact on productivity of any of these sources.

There is no precise, independent measure of the increase in average skill level in the UK over any period and no comprehensive indication of the allocative efficiency of labour between various skill levels. In recent years, however, a number of studies have been made, mainly of the educational system. The formal education sector is not the only source of skill augmentation but the model testing its efficiency has

---

1   D. Metcalf, S. Nickell and R. Richardson, 'The Structure of Hours and Earnings in British Manufacturing Industry', *OEP*, July 1976.

general applicability. The problem at issue may be described as follows. If the sector is organized efficiently, the net social value of a pound of expenditure will be the same at the margin for all types and levels of education. What we must do, therefore, is to equalize the social profit on all educational activities.

The terminology employed here may be disagreeable to some people. However, as long as account is taken of all sources of cost and benefit, whether they be material or psychic, there can be no real objection. It is true that some sources may not be measurable in practice and that others may be measured only imperfectly. These defects do not suggest that no measurement should take place, merely that decisions and judgements should not be based solely on what is measurable.

In fact the measurement of the profitability of education and training programmes is decidedly imperfect. The usual measure of benefits is some estimate of the expected increase in monetary earnings enjoyed by the trainee, i.e. his expected full earnings minus the earnings he would otherwise expect were he not to undertake the training under consideration. To take a concrete example, in estimating the profitability of a university degree a comparison is made between the observed earnings of people already graduated and those of people who stopped just short of going to university. This provides an earnings differential for each age-group, which stands for the earnings increase expected by the current trainee at each stage of his working life.

This estimate is extremely crude, and a number of adjustments can be made to improve on it. For example, not all of the crude differential can be attributed to education, because ability and motivation levels differ between the two groups from which data are drawn. Consequently, an effort should be made to estimate the independent effect of ability differences.

Once the estimate of benefits has been obtained, it is necessary to estimate the costs of the training. The principal cost is the output that could have been produced by the trainee had he been in full-time work. Its value is usually measured by the monetary earnings he forgoes while being trained or educated. Added to the forgone earnings are the direct costs of instruction, represented by salaries of teachers, cost of buildings, etc.

Two early research efforts for the UK were by Blaug and by Morris and Ziderman, and both contain a clear account of the procedures and difficulties involved. The latter was more comprehensive and among its conclusions were (1) that postgraduate qualifications were not very profitable for society, and (2) that higher national certificates were very profitable indeed. If these calculations were correct, they suggest that the UK educational system was inefficiently structured and was turning out the wrong mix of graduates.[1]

Many workers receive considerable amounts of training after they leave school, and successive governments, particularly during the last twenty years, have attempted to influence the provision of such training. Prior to 1964, the great bulk of industrial training was provided on the initiative of individual employers, often within a context of industry-wide understandings between trade unions and

---

1 M. Blaug, 'The Rate of Return on Investment in Education in Great Britain', *MS*, September 1965; V. Morris and A. Ziderman, 'The Economic Return on Investment in Higher Education in England and Wales', *ET*, May 1971. For a useful, though complex, survey of the relevant work on Britain, see G. Psacharopoulos and R. Layard, 'Human Capital and Earnings', *RES*, July 1979. See also the interesting article by A. Dolphin, 'The Demand for Higher Education', *DEG*, July 1981.

employers' organizations. This voluntary system was widely believed to be defective. In particular, it was said to lead to inadequate provision of training, especially for certain highly skilled manual trades. The principal argument here was that many firms who would otherwise be willing to provide training did not do so on a sufficient scale because they could not be sure of retaining the skilled labour after training had finished. This argument carries with it some implicit assumptions concerning who pays for the training (as opposed to who provides it or makes it available) but it was nevertheless influential in leading to the 1964 Industrial Training Act.

The 1964 Act created a system of Industrial Training Boards (ITBs). By 1969 there were 27 ITBs, of widely differing size, which together covered about 65% of the working population. The principal function of the Boards was to improve the quantity and quality of training provided in industry, and their principal mechanism was a system of levies and grants. Each Board imposed a levy, essentially a payroll tax, on all but the smallest firms in their industry. The revenue raised was then returned to those firms in the industry which ran approved training schemes. The intention was to make all potential users of the skilled labour contribute to the costs of training.[1]

Certain adjustments were made to this system under the 1973 Employment and Training Act, but more radical changes were introduced with the 1981 Employment and Training Act. Using the powers given to him under this Act, the Secretary of State for Employment announced in November 1981 that he had decided to abolish all but seven of the ITBs. Elsewhere, he indicated that he was satisfied that 'the training requirements of the sector concerned can be effectively met on a voluntary basis with less cost and bureaucracy'. It is too early to judge whether this assessment was well founded. At the same time, the government introduced what was advertised as 'the most far-reaching and ambitious set of proposals for industrial training ever put before Parliament'. The scheme was complex, and its centrepiece was the youth training scheme, discussed below in section II.3. Again it is too soon to arrive at a judgement on the success of these new arrangements.

II   UNEMPLOYMENT

If unemployment is to be cut to 2m by 1990, we need to create over the six years 1984-9 at least 1,200 net new jobs every day. Every month for those six years, extra jobs equivalent to the 37,000 people employed by British Petroleum or Whitbread's must be created. Unemployment is truly the problem of our time. In this section we first describe the composition of the unemployed. Then we analyse why unemployment is so high. Finally we consider the prospects for lowering unemployment.

---

1 For a good discussion of the issues involved in training, see A. Ziderman, *Manpower Training: Theory and Policy*, Macmillan, 1978; see also B. Showler, *The Public Employment Service*, Longman, 1976, especially chapter 5.

II.1   Composition of the Unemployed

Stocks, flows and durations[1] : In 1983 unemployment in the UK averaged 3.1m, equivalent to 13% of the labour force. Males accounted for over two-thirds of the total. Published unemployment figures substantially understate actual unemployment. The unemployment statistics need the following corrections to present a true picture of unemployment:

	Numbers (m)
1983 unemployment (average)	3.1
Add unregistered unemployment	0.7
Subtract claimants not actively seeking work	−0.4
TOTAL	3.4

Unregistered unemployed people are those identified in surveys as unemployed but who do not appear in the monthly count. The 0.7m figure consists of the authoritative DE estimate for 1981 (0.45m), plus extra unregistered unemployed as a consequence of the changed method of counting introduced in 1982 (0.15m), plus the withdrawal of some men aged over 60 from the labour force (0.1m). Men aged 60 and over no longer have to register to secure national insurance credits: this makes the unemployment data more accurate because they were mainly occupational pensioners who were not available for work, so nothing is added to the unemployment total on this count. But, in addition, men aged 60 and over are eligible for a higher rate of supplementary benefit than other unemployed people if they leave the labour force, and we should add 0.1m to the unemployment figure on this score. On the other hand, the DE estimates that some 0.4m registered claimants are not actively seeking work and these people should be deducted from the total. When these modifications are made, the truer unemployment total in 1983 was around 3.4m. In addition a further 0.5m individuals were kept out of unemployment via the special employment measures.

In 1983 the inflow of individuals into unemployment in GB was 4.4m and an almost identical number (4.3m) left unemployment. These flows do not all refer to separate people because some individuals have more than one spell of unemployment. The average duration of each completed spell of unemployment was over two-thirds of a year (3.0m stock/4.4m inflow) or 35 weeks.

This average-spell duration is an important statistic, because the main reason the stock of unemployed people rises is that the average duration of unemployment rises and not that more people become unemployed. For example in 1955 when unemployment was at an all-time (peacetime) low of 1.1%, the average duration of each spell of unemployment was only 3½ weeks. Since 1966 flows into unemployment have been remarkably stable at around 4m per year, so the higher unemployment rates primarily reflect longer-spell durations.

The incidence of unemployment among people is very unequal. With 4m registrations a year and a labour force of 27m, in nearly 7 years the number of registrations equals the size of the labour force. Therefore if a person is in the labour force for 49 years he would, if unemployment were distributed equally, expect to have 7 spells of unemployment during his lifetime. Yet we know many

---

1   The sources of information for this section include OPCS, *General Household Survey* (GHS) (annual); *Labour Force Survey*, 1979, 1981; DE *Gazette*, especially June 1983.

people never suffer a single spell of unemployment. Indeed, in any year some 3% of the labour force account for 70% of the total weeks of unemployment. Clearly a fraction of our labour force must be constantly at risk of long-term unemployment and/or recurrent spells of unemployment. Unfortunately the group who bear the burden of unemployment are concurrently towards the bottom of the pay distribution, work in the most risky occupations, and are those who also suffer a high incidence of ill-health – i.e. labour-market disadvantage is cumulative.

Demographic and occupational characteristics[1] : In October 1983 unemployment rates by age had the following pattern (DE *Gazette*, December 1983, table 2.15):

	under 25	25-54	55-59	All ages
Males %	26	13	16	15
Females %	20	6	7	10

Prime-age men and women have lower unemployment rates than younger and older groups (changes in coverage of unemployment statistics for men aged 60-64 have rendered their unemployment statistics meaningless). Young workers have high unemployment rates because they have a high propensity to become unemployed and many have recurrent spells of unemployment: the inflow to unemployment of the under-25s is treble that of the prime-age group, but their unemployment spells are of similar duration to the 25-54-year-olds. By contrast, older workers are less likely than prime-age groups to become unemployed, but once unemployed they have very long spell durations – they remain unemployed for a long time.

There is no doubt that youth employment prospects have worsened in the last decade or so. In 1973 males under 20 had an identical unemployment rate to the all-male rate (3.5%), but now their rate is double the all-male rate. There are two main reasons. First, young workers are harder hit in recession than adult workers and, conversely, their employment prospects pick up faster when the economy improves. Firms economize on labour in a recession and they reduce recruitment. This hits young workers because of their higher turnover rates and lack of labour-market experience. Second, the cost of employing young workers has risen relative to the cost of employing adults. These cyclical and cost effects have a stronger impact on the employment of males aged under 18 than on other teenagers. It can be calculated from Wells' thorough study of the youth labour market that a rise of 3% in the relative cost of employing males aged under 18 is associated with a fall of around 60,000 in their employment. Of this 60,000 figure, 15,000 represents a loss in aggregate employment but the remaining 45,000 is made good in the form of an increase in adult male employment and female employment as employers substitute adult for teenage employment because the adults have become cheaper relative to the teenagers.

The higher unemployment experienced by older workers partly reflects the fact that the structure of jobs and wages within the firm makes it difficult to allow for

1 See in particular W. Wells, *The relative pay and employment of young people*, DE Research Paper 42, 1983 and L. Lynch and R. Richardson, 'Unemployment of young workers in Britain', *BJIR* November 1982.

the waning productivity of older workers, who are therefore specially prone to redundancy. And once older workers become unemployed, they suffer long spells because firms tend to prefer younger workers. A quarter of all vacancies and a third of labouring vacancies have an explicit upper age-limit of 50. The higher unemployment of older workers also reflects their higher incidence of illness and disability.

Single men experience unemployment rates double those of married men of the same age and socio-economic group. It is not clear whether this reflects the institution of marriage – single men have less pressure to take up another job – or whether married men are simply higher quality than single men and so are desired both by women and by employers. The fact that unmarried men are more likely to suffer from mental instability and alcoholism than their married counterparts hints that the labour-quality point is important.

Once men are married their incidence of unemployment increases with the number of their dependent children. In 1980 the following male unemployment rates were extracted from the *General Household Survey* (*GHS*) for married men:

Number of dependent children	0	1	2	3	4+
Unemployment rate (%)	4	5	4	6	12

There are many reasons. First, the level of family support for those in work is substantially below that for those out of work. In 1984 a working head of household with a 3-child family received £19.50 a week child benefit, but (if we assume the children to be aged 9, 11 and 13) got nearly twice that amount (£36.55) if on Supplementary Benefit. Second, families with a large number of dependent children are less mobile. Third, lower-skilled groups – those most at risk of unemployment – have slightly larger families, but the positive relation between family size and unemployment also holds for particular skill groups. Fourth, sociological literature suggests that groups who are alienated from society and who suffer a feeling of powerlessness are prone to both higher fertility and higher unemployment.

There are also marked disparities in the incidence of unemployment by occupation. The 1977 *GHS* (the last date for which such information is available) indicates that over the three years 1975–7 the following proportions of men experienced one or more spells of unemployment:

Socio-economic group	%
Professional workers, employers, managers	4
Intermediate and junior non-manual	8
Skilled manual and own account non-professional	10
Semi-skilled and unskilled manual and personal service	19

Thus the likelihood of a spell of unemployment for manual workers is well over twice that for non-manual workers. Further, people classified by the Employment Service as general labourers account for around a third of the unemployed. Their lack of training causes unskilled workers to bear the brunt of macroeconomic fluctuations and firms' expansions and contractions. The persistently low level of the vacancy to unemployment ratio also reflects lack of demand for these workers, which prolongs their unemployment spells. For example, in June 1982 there was one registered vacancy to every 200 unemployed general labourers – our economic system puts the least skilled at most risk of unemployment.

Geographical structure[1] : During the half century to 1975 the main geographical focus was 'the regional problem'. Although this had a number of dimensions, it was encapsulated in the variation in unemployment rates by region. For much of the postwar period Scotland, Wales and Northern England had unemployment rates some three times as large as those in the Midlands and the South East. More recently, regional differences in unemployment relativities have become much less severe. The coefficient of variation (standard deviation/mean) of unemployment rates across the 10 British regions fell from .42 in 1966 to .21 in 1983. The five regions with the highest unemployment rate in 1983 – North, Wales, West Midlands, North West, Scotland – had an average rate of 16%, only half as high again as the average 11% rate in the remaining regions.

One reason for the narrowing in unemployment rates is the impact of regional policy. In 1981 employment in the Assisted Areas was around 0.5m higher than it would have been without the array of capital and labour subsidies operating over the period 1960-80. Most of these 0.5m jobs were diverted from the rest of Britain. Even so, unemployment remains stubbornly high, relative to the rest of Britain, in Scotland, Wales and the North. The recent DTI report suggested this is because, as compared with the South East, these areas have 'an industrial milieu less favourable to successful entrepreneurship; a somewhat unfavourable rate of product innovation; a relatively low level of employment in the business services sector; an occupational structure characterized by a low proportion of managerial and professional jobs; a high level of dependence for manufacturing employment on branch plants owned by national or international companies whose UK head offices are concentrated in the South East'.

Perhaps because the regional disparity of unemployment is now less, the focus of attention has shifted towards local labour markets, urban-rural movements and the decaying cores of our inner cities. Within each region the three local labour markets with the highest unemployment rates have treble the amount of unemployment experienced by the three local labour markets with the lowest rates. Thus in 1983 the fun palaces of Margate, Sheerness and Clacton had an unemployment rate of 19% while salubrious, boring Guildford, Hertford and Alton had rates of under 6%.

An important spatial employment trend in the last two decades is the net shift of manufacturing employment out of the major conurbations into small towns and rural areas. Thus between 1960 and 1978 London lost 43% of its manufacturing employment and the other conurbations lost more than a quarter of theirs. By contrast, manufacturing employment rose by more than a quarter in small towns and rural areas. This trend happened in every region.

The most pressing spatial unemployment problem now is the high rates of unemployment in the cores of our great towns and cities. The male unemployment rates (%) given by the 1981 Census for the inner areas (containing one third of the relevant population) and outer areas of four major towns were:

	Inner area	Outer area
Birmingham	25	17
Liverpool	31	21
London	14	8
Manchester	28	18

1 The facts in this section are taken from Department of Trade and Industry, *Regional Industrial Policy: Some Economic Issues*, 1983.

In all major towns the inner area rate is typically half as large again as the outer area rate. This reflects the residential concentration of groups of the population least able to compete for available jobs within the wider labour-market area of which they form a part.

II.2   Why has Unemployment Risen?[1]

Recorded UK unemployment is now some ten times as large as it was in the 1950s:

Average of the year	Male unemployment %
1951–55	1.3
1956–60	1.8
1961–65	2.1
1966–70	2.9
1971–75	4.4
1976–80	7.3
1981–83	14.7

Two sets of factors account for the higher unemployment. First, the long-run rate of unemployment has risen. Second, there are fluctuations around this long-run unemployment rate and in the 1980s the actual rate has exceeded the long-run rate. Fear of inflation and balance-of-payments deficits has inhibited policies to reduce the actual rate to nearer the long-run rate.

The long-run rate of unemployment is sometimes called the natural rate, the equilibrium rate or the NAIRU—the non-accelerating inflation rate of unemployment. It is important to understand that there is nothing 'natural' about it. It is *not*, as is sometimes believed, the rate that would hold in perfect competition. On the contrary, if union monopoly power increases and real wages are bid up, this is likely to increase the long-run rate, so a reduction in union power would, by implication, cut it. Probably the best way of thinking about the long-run rate is in terms of the NAIRU. Have certain things changed—union power or unemployment benefits for example—such that the government now needs a higher or a lower level of unemployment to control inflation? We shall discuss a number of changes which have taken place in the labour market which might have raised the NAIRU. From the supply side, we examine the growth and composition of the labour force and changes in unemployment benefits. On the demand side, we consider changes in the structure of employment and the role of real wages. In 1966–70 the actual rate of unemployment was about equal to the long-run rate. We are essentially posing the question: what part of the rise in actual male unemployment from 3% in 1965–70 to 15% in 1981–3 is attributable to the rise in the long-run rate? (It is sometimes helpful to focus on the male unemployment rate because coverage and registration behaviour among females causes the female rate to be understated.)

The size and composition of the labour force changed substantially in the decade 1974–84 and this may, temporarily, have raised the long-run rate of unemployment. The civilian labour force grew by 1.2m, from 25.2m in 1974 to 26.4m in

---

1   For a fuller discussion see C. Greenhalgh, R. Layard and A. Oswald (eds.), *The Causes of Unemployment*, Clarendon Press, Oxford, 1983. See in particular articles by Minford and Andrews and Nickell on the impact of benefits and of unions on unemployment, and Dilnot and Morris on the course of the benefit to wage ratio.

1984. It may simply be difficult for the economy to absorb an extra 2,400 people a week into jobs. However, this argument should not be pushed too hard: in the decade 1950-60, for example, the working population rose by 1.5m but unemployment remained below 0.5m. Nevertheless it is possible that the labour market has become less flexible and adaptable between the 1950s and the 1970s/1980s, and it is now more difficult to absorb a growing labour force into jobs.

Younger workers now account for a higher fraction of the labour force than previously. Youths aged 16-24 comprised 19% of the labour force in 1974 but 23% ten years later. As youths have an unemployment rate around double that of prime-age (25-54) workers, this composition effect might also have raised the long run rate of unemployment. However, this effect is partially offset by the fact that older workers, who also have relatively high unemployment rates, account for a smaller fraction of the labour force: those aged 55 and over comprised 18% of the workforce in 1974 but only 15% in 1984. Further, women—who have a somewhat lower unemployment rate than men—increased their share of the labour force from 39% to 40% over the decade.

The most contentious issue on the supply side concerns unemployment benefits. Changes in the level of unemployment and supplementary benefits relative to income from working, and changes in the administration of benefits, might both influence the long-run rate of unemployment. The effect of the level of benefits works through two channels. First, if the benefit-to-pay ratio rises, this could cause workers to substitute unemployment for work, either by becoming unemployed or, more likely, by prolonging unemployment. It is this channel that is considered here. Second, benefits may set a floor to real wages, with the resulting level of real wages making it uneconomic to hire unproductive workers. This scale effect is considered below under the real wage discussion.

The benefit-to-wage ratio is called the replacement rate (RR). The expected income out of work to expected net income if in work for a sample of family units where the head is in full-time employment in each year's Family Expenditure Survey is given in table 5.2. The average replacement rate measures the incentive which an individual has to take or retain a job rather than contemplate a 13-week spell of unemployment. The marginal replacement rate measures the incentive

TABLE 5.2

Development of Replacement Rates over Time

	13-week average rate			53rd week marginal rate		
	Average (mean)	% with >0.9 average rate	% with <0.5 average rate	Average (mean)	% with >0.9 marginal rate	% with <0.5 marginal rate
1968	0.75	15	4	0.46	5	57
1975	0.75	19	7	0.58	3	33
1978	0.81	27	4	0.62	5	23
1980	0.73	12	8	0.50	2	48
1983	0.60	3	21	0.50	2	53

Source: A. Dilnot and C. Morris, 'Private costs and benefits of unemployment', in C. Greenhalgh et al. (eds.), The Causes of Unemployment, Clarendon Press, Oxford, 1983, tables 5 and 6.

which he will have, after a year of unemployment, to take work rather than remain unemployed for an additional week. The RR rose in the decade 1968–78, and by 1978 over a quarter of the working population had an average potential RR of over 90% for a 13-week spell of unemployment, although only 5% had such a high RR for the marginal week after a year of unemployment. However, since 1978 the RR has fallen substantially. This reflects the combined influence of the axeing of the earnings-related supplement to unemployment benefit, the taxation of benefits and the fall in the real value of unemployment benefit. In addition more people *in* work receive housing benefits. Those who asserted that the rise in benefits was an important contributory factor in the rise in unemployment in the 1970s will presumably now be arguing that the fall in the RR over 1978–83 should have cut unemployment. In 1978 unemployment was 1.4m. In table 5.2 we see that the RR has fallen 26%. Assuming, conservatively, an elasticity of unemployment with respect to benefits of 0.6, the reduction in the RR would be associated with a fall in unemployment of 0.22m (1.4m x 0.26 x 0.6). Certainly the tendency for benefits to lead to substitution of unemployment for work is unlikely to have contributed to any rise in the long-run rate of unemployment in the 1980s. Anyway, when there are few vacancies, if one person is deterred by benefits from taking a job someone else will snap it up, so it is hard to see how benefits increase or decrease aggregate unemployment via this substitution mechanism.

It is possible that changes in the administration of benefits are associated with changes in unemployment. The divorce in the 1970s of the job-finding and benefit-paying functions of employment exchanges may, for example, have reduced pressure on unemployed people to seek work and reduced the resources devoted to helping longer-term unemployed individuals into work.

The long-run unemployment rate will rise if the mismatch between unemployment and vacancies worsens. There is no evidence that this has happened by region or by occupation. However, the industrial structure of the economy has changed substantially in the last two decades, and particularly since 1979. In 1966 half the employed labour force was in the index of production industries (mining, manufacturing, construction, utilities), but by 1983 this production sector only accounted for a third of employment. And between 1979 and 1983 2m jobs were lost in this sector. The larger switch out of production industries worsened the industrial matching of vacancies and employment and so raised the long-run rate of unemployment.

It is often argued that technical change causes unemployment. In the context of our question 'Has the long-run rate of unemployment risen?' it would be necessary to show that the rate of technical progress was faster in the 1970s and 1980s than in the 1950s and 1960s. This seems unlikely. Anyway, there is a weak *positive* association across industries between labour productivity and employment growth: sectors where technical progress is most rapid appear to have the largest rise or smallest fall in employment, quite the reverse of what would be expected if technical change is a major factor in determining unemployment.

The NAIRU is partly determined by those factors which influence the achievable real wage, namely productivity and the terms of trade. So we must now analyse real wages, non-wage labour costs, labour productivity and the price of imported materials.

The ratio of real labour costs (pay plus non-pay items deflated by the wholesale price index) to labour productivity is termed the real product wage. It may be thought of as the share of labour in value added. If the manufacturing real product wage is set at 1969 = 100, since then the index has never fallen below 100 and in 1975 it was as high as 115. Labour costs rose more rapidly in the 1970s than previously while labour productivity grew more slowly.

Union power is one factor in the rise in real wages. This is a slippery concept, but we know that in the 1970s a higher fraction of the labour force was unionized than in the 1950s, and that the mark-up union members receive over non-union members also rose substantially. Econometric evidence suggests that since the 1950s the increase in union power has reduced employment by around 400,000 and raised the NAIRU by 1-2% points.

Non-wage labour costs have also risen. In 1984/5 there is an employers social security payroll tax of 10.45% on earnings up to £250 a week. (For employees contracted-out of the state earnings-related pension scheme the firm pays 10.45% on earnings up to £34 and 6.35% between £34 and £250.) In addition, from 1977 to 1984 there was a surcharge on this payroll tax of between 1% and 3.5% which went direct to the Exchequer rather than to finance national insurance benefits. These payroll tax rates are considerably larger than the insurance contributions paid by firms up to 1975. (Note, however, that for a given revenue total employment is hit less by a payroll tax than a per capita tax.)

Various strands of employment protection legislation passed in the 1970s also raised the cost of employing labour. Increased notice periods, unfair dismissal provisions and strengthened maternity rights, all made it more difficult to shed labour. Further, where a dismissed worker qualifies for a redundancy payment the firm's share of that payment rose from 30% in 1969 to 59% in 1984. These legislative changes can be thought of as an extra tax on employment. They resulted in firms screening potential new recruits more carefully because it is now more costly than it was before to shed labour.

Real unit labour costs also rose because the growth rate of labour productivity fell. Between 1963 and 1973 output per person employed grew on average by 2.7% a year in the whole British economy and by 3.8% in manufacturing. But between 1974 and 1980 these increases slowed to 0.3% a year each. There was a once-and-for-all rise in (cyclically corrected) labour productivity between the first quarters of 1980 and 1981. This was a batting-average effect associated with the shedding of plant, labour and management which on average tended to be less productive than the surviving parts of manufacturing industry. Since the first quarter of 1981 the underlying trend of manufacturing productivity is *below* the 2.2% a year experienced in the 1970s. A substantial recovery in investment is required to raise productivity to the trend of the 1970s.

Any adverse effect of the rise in real unit labour costs on employment was compounded by the rise in the price of imported materials, which increased faster than wholesale prices, squeezing manufacturers' profit margins. The index of real import costs (defined as import unit values deflated by the wholesale price index, 1969 = 100) rose by half between 1972 and 1974 (90 in 1972 to 135 in 1974), and in 1983 the index stood at 122. To maintain employment in the face of these pressures on industrial costs, the real product wage should have fallen, but in fact it rose.

It is hard to put a precise number on the long-run rate of unemployment. Nickell suggests that in 1979 the male rate was around 5%-6%, the rise from 3% in 1966-70 to 6% being accounted for by larger shifts of labour among industrial sectors, employment protection legislation, a higher RR and an increase in union power. Minford puts the 1980 natural rate (male plus female) somewhat higher at around

7%. He argues that the natural rate would be lowered substantially by measures to reduce real benefits and union monopoly power because this, in turn, would reduce real wages and boost employment. Both these things have happened. The average 13-week RR fell from 0.73 to 0.60 between 1980 and 1983, the proportion of the labour force unionized also fell, the closed shop was loosened-up and secondary picketing outlawed. So 7% is surely a ceiling on the long-run unemployment rate. As unemployment in 1983 and 1984 was 13%, nearly double this long-run rate, we can be optimistic that a judicious use of macroeconomic policy could cut unemployment substantially, to around half its present level. However, the authorities are wary of an expansionary macroeconomic policy because they fear it might feed into prices and money wages rather than output and jobs.

II.3   Moderating Unemployment

If unemployment (on current definitions) is to be cut to 2m over the six-year period to 1990, at least 2.7m extra jobs must be created by 1990:

		(m)
1.	Current unemployment (Feb. 1984)	3.2
2.	Aim: 1990 unemployment	2.0
	Jobs needed	
3.	To absorb the increase in the labour force	0.7
4.	To make the simple cut in unemployment (2–1)	1.2
	SUB-TOTAL	1.9
5.	Encouraged-worker effect, ratio 1.4 : 1	0.8
	TOTAL	2.7

DE data indicate that the labour force will grow by 0.7m during this period. Add to this the simple cut from 3.2m to 2.0m in unemployment. So far 1.9m jobs are needed. But expansionary policy results in employment rising by more than registered unemployment falls. If we assume, conservatively, that this 'encouraged-worker effect' results in 14 extra jobs needed for every 10 cut in unemployment, this gives us a net job-creation effort of 2.7m. Recall from section II.1 that with a stock of unemployment of 2.0m there would also be some unregistered unemployed and some of the 2.0m would not be seeking work. Further some 0.2m adults are at present being kept off the unemployment register by special employment measures (see below). The 2.7m figure is equivalent to over 1,200 jobs a day, half as much again as the previous six-year fastest postwar growth rate, when employment grew between 1959 and 1965 by 740 extra jobs a day. But we must not be too pessimistic: between 1933 and 1937 employment rose by 2m, and in the USA employment rose from 70m in 1960 to 108m in 1984.

Reductions in income tax are an expensive way of generating extra employment, with each extra job having a gross annual cost of over £30,000 (1982/3 prices). By comparison, even when British Leyland was getting substantial assistance from public funds the annual gross cost per job supported was under £4,000 a year. So reflation via tax cuts would certainly not boost employment sufficiently and anyway is ruled out because of the inflationary consequences. This is why successive administrations have turned to special employment measures (SEM) in an attempt to buy more employment per £. In this section we first examine these SEM. Then we consider briefly industrial assistance and the debate on 'where the new jobs are coming from', paying special attention to the role of manufacturing industry.

Special employment measures[1] : In January 1984, 660,000 people were covered by SEM. The DE calculate that, but for these SEM, unemployment would be 465,000 higher. Public spending on these measures is around £1.5bn in 1984/5. The main schemes can be divided as follows:

	Nos. covered, Feb. 1984
Job creation etc.	
Community Programme	112,000
Enterprise Allowance	23,000
Schemes to cut labour supply	
Job Release Scheme	90,000
Temporary Short Time Working Compensation Scheme	14,000
Youth measures	
Youth Training Scheme	305,000
Young Workers Scheme	105,000

In deciding whether to establish, expand or contract a particular measure, Whitehall compares it with what would happen if the same money were used for income-tax cuts. The criteria on which such comparisons are based include the impact of the measure on employment, unemployment, the balance of payments, the inflation rate, and the level and distribution of output. The main criterion from this list is unemployment. Here there are two basic steps used by the DE. First, a register effect is calculated. Next, the net cost per person off the register is estimated.

The register effect of a SEM is usually less than the number of participants. This may be due to:

(a) deadweight: windfall payments for actions consistent with a scheme, which would have occurred in its absence (e.g. Job Release payments in respect of employees who would have retired anyway);

(b) substitution: where employees or trainees covered by a scheme take the place of ineligible employees;

(c) displacement: where the output subsidized by the SEMs competes with the output of unsubsidized firms, so that their demand for labour is reduced.

The next step in the evaluation procedure is to estimate the net Exchequer cost of the measure: that is, its gross cost less savings on benefit payments and additions to revenue ('flowbacks') which accrue to the government as a result of the measure.

---

1 For a fuller discussion see D. Metcalf, 'Special employment measures: an analysis of wage subsidies, youth schemes and worksharing', *Midland Bank Review*, Autumn/Winter 1982, pp. 9–21, and House of Commons, Fourth Report of Public Accounts Committee 1983–1984, *Special Employment Measures*, HC 104, November 1983.

This net cost of the SEM may in turn be compared with the average net cost per unemployed person, estimated to be at least £5,000 by the Treasury in 1982/3.

The Community Programme (CP) can be thought of as a 100% wage subsidy to certain public-sector employment. The priority groups of the CP are adults aged 25 and over unemployed over 12 months, and youths aged 18–24 unemployed over 6 months. In October 1983 there were 1.3m such people, so the CP does not make much of a dent in this long-term unemployment—it covers under 1 in 10 in the priority group. The net cost per person taken off the register by the CP was around £2,000 a year in 1982/3.

A previous measure, the Temporary Employment Scheme (TES), provided wage subsidies mainly to private-sector employment. This paid £20 a week for up to a year to firms for each employee kept on who otherwise would have been made redundant. The evaluations generally suggest that this was a successful measure with low net Exchequer costs and very favourable balance-of-payments effects. The TES was a scheme which subsidized *marginal* employment, and there is evidence that such schemes have a bigger employment effect per £ of subsidy than alternative uses of the money which cut average labour costs. Given the enormous job-creation task, an incremental employment subsidy has been suggested. This is also a marginal scheme, to subsidize *extra* employment. Estimates suggest that if firms were paid £70 a week for each employee on their books over and above a previous benchmark level of employment, some 250,000 jobs could be created at an annual Exchequer cost of £0.5bn or only £2,000 per job per year.

The second set of SEM concentrate on reducing the labour supply. This can be achieved either by reducing labour-force participation rates, e.g. by early retirement, or by worksharing. The Job Release Scheme (JRS) is a selective early-retirement scheme which aims to encourage older workers who are close to pensionable age to leave employment and thereby release jobs for younger unemployed people. Applicants receive an allowance till they reach the state retirement age. For each applicant employers must undertake to recruit one additional worker who is unemployed and who would not otherwise have been hired. The DE calculate that in October 1982 the net cost per person off the register via the JRS was £1,800.

Under the Temporary Short Time Working Compensation Scheme (TSTWCS) firms were encouraged to adopt short-time working instead of making redundancies. Firms were eligible for support for six months at the subsidy rate of half the normal earnings for workless days. In early 1981 almost one million individuals ('sharers') were covered by this scheme, equivalent to nearly a quarter of a million jobs supported. As output recovered the scheme declined so that by February 1984 only 14,000 people were covered by it, and the scheme closed in 1984. TSTWCS aimed to prevent jobs which were thought to have a long-term future from being lost through short-term difficulties. At its peak in February 1981 the DE believe that it reduced registered unemployment by 165,000 at a net cost of around £1,000 per person off the register. Although this is a very economic way of spreading unemployment around, it seems that many, possibly most, of the jobs supported by the scheme eventually disappeared—it generally only postponed redundancies rather than averted them.

These labour-supply-reducing SEMs are very cost-effective. But it should not be concluded that worksharing is therefore generally desirable. First, worksharing involves income sharing. Indeed the debate on how to combat unemployment would be improved if worksharing were called income sharing. If annual or weekly pay is cut in line with the cut in weekly or annual hours, then worksharing has considerable potential for lowering unemployment. But if, as unions demand, weekly pay remains constant in the face of a cut in hours, unit labour costs rise, which is either purely inflationary or, to the extent that firms feel unable to pass on higher unit costs fully into prices, is more likely to cause a fall rather than a rise in employment. Second, the present government may well believe that with present trade-union attitudes heavy unemployment is necessary to maintain single-digit inflation. So in its eyes reducing the labour force would not help at all because the same amount of unemployment would still be needed. Third, it is not clear how hours 'saved' by worksharing can be parcelled-up into full-time equivalent jobs. For example, the production line process may require fixed manning levels. And the structure of employment is different from the skill and area composition of the unemployed.

The DE has calculated that if normal weekly hours were cut from 40 to 35 without any corresponding loss in nominal weekly pay and if the potential loss of output was accounted for as follows:

	%
increased employment	35
higher output per man	20
more overtime	35
lower output	10

then registered unemployment would be reduced by 350,000 while labour costs would rise by 8.5%. The PSBR would fall by around £2bn (1984/5 prices). This all looks quite attractive, but it is very important to understand that it is solely a first-round estimate. The rise in unit labour costs will, in time, cause employment to fall back and unemployment to rise again. *Work-sharing is also real income sharing.* Unless individuals are prepared to sacrifice some real income there is little scope for permanently reducing unemployment by this route.

The biggest SEM in 1984 was the Youth Training Scheme (YTS). All 16-year-olds who did not remain in full-time education were offered a year-long foundation programme of training, further education and work experience. The YTS had places for around 400,000 young people, two-thirds of whom were in schemes sponsored by private and public employers and voluntary agencies, and the remaining third in schemes arranged directly by the MSC. Sponsoring organizations were paid £1,850 a year per trainee, out of which they paid a training allowance of £1,300. If YTS is really about raising the quality of the labour force, rather than keeping a cohort of unemployed teenagers from appearing in the unemployment statistics, it could be introduced at 15 rather than 16. YTS includes a 13-week minimum off-the-job training component. But a more comprehensive levy/grant system, coupled with compulsory day release, is required if the aim is really to improve the quality of training.

Under YTS the firm gets the teenage labour at no cost to itself. Therefore to maintain some hirings through orthodox channels, the Young Workers Scheme (YWS) provides a subsidy to firms who recruit youngsters. The scheme is aimed at young people aged between 16 and 18 in their first year of employment. The government believes that one reason why teenage unemployment is so high is because the cost of teenage labour is too high relative to its productivity. Therefore the YWS is *inversely* related to earnings. It pays £15 a week where the wage is under £40 and £7.50 a week where the wage is between £40 and £45. In April 1983 around a quarter of 16 and 17-year-old employees had earnings below the £45 limit. Most of the YWS payments are deadweight, a windfall to firms who would have hired the teenagers anyway: under a fifth of the youngsters covered represents net new jobs.

Special employment measures started in 1975. A decade or so of experience suggests they are a cost-effective way of reducing unemployment. The average net cost per person off the register in 1982/3 was £2,000 a year, under half the average cost imposed on the Exchequer by an unemployed person. Unemployment, alas, seems unlikely to drop much in the 1980s so these SEM will probably continue, in one form or another, for some years to come.

Selective industrial assistance: The National Economic Development Office has calculated that in the early 1980s assistance to industry was running at £20bn a year. This figure included tax expenditures (i.e. capital allowances and stock appreciation relief), research and development subsidies, and state handouts to BL, BSC, British Aerospace, British Shipbuilders, National Coal Board and British Rail. The lion's share of this industrial assistance went to manufacturing industry, yet manufacturing is a small sector of the economy – it only accounts for around a quarter of output and employment. This raises two questions. First, why is the manufacturing sector deemed so worthy of support? Second, to the extent that employment considerations figure in the allocation of support, which manufacturing sectors should receive support and which should not?

Three reasons are advanced for the importance of manufacturing. First, manufacturing is often held to be the engine-room of the growth process. Manufacturing output (at constant prices) grew at 3.4% a year between 1948 and 1973 (faster than any other sector) and GDP rose at 2.8% a year; by contrast, between 1973 and 1981 manufacturing output fell by 2.5% a year (a bigger fall than any other sector) and GDP only rose by 0.1% a year. Proponents of the view that a fast-growing manufacturing sector generates a fast-growing economy argue that manufacturing is technologically progressive and is a source of scale economics. But others question this: there are many examples of technological progressiveness outside manufacturing – telecommunications and health care, for example, and scale economics are likely to be as important in distribution as in manufacturing. Second, manufacturing is also held to be important because much service employment 'depends' on it, but this argument can also be inverted – buses are surely only desired for the journeys they permit. Probably the third argument, concerning trade flows, is the most valid: manufacturing is more export-oriented than services.

Within manufacturing there is a weak positive correlation across industries between the change in employment and the rate of growth of labour productivity. *If* this association is *causal*, it has a clear message for industrial assistance: support should be directed to the growing sectors because then we get a faster rate of productivity growth and we *also* get more employment. In the past much industrial assistance went to sectors where productivity growth was below average – cars, motorcycles, planes, ships and steel. Would we be better served, in terms of both output and employment, if that support went instead to sectors like chemicals, instrument engineering and electrical engineering, where labour productivity growth is so much higher?

Regional assistance is one strand of industrial support. In 1981 employment in the Assisted Areas was around half a million higher than it would have been without the regional subsidies (and employment in the rest of Britain was correspondingly lower). The average cost of this job-diversion exercise is around £40,000 per job, which may be a reasonable price to pay to make more equal the chance of getting a job in northern and southern Britain. But the industrial distribution of this spending is bizarre. Over the period 1966 to 1976 chemical companies received £1.46bn, mainly capital subsidies, yet actually reduced employment. They were paid over £64,000 in regional assistance for each job they destroyed. And the cost per diverted job in metal manufacturing and mechanical engineering was over £250,000. Sensibly the government has decided (Cmnd. 9111, December 1983) to put a limit on the subsidy per job and to extend the subsidies to services.

Prospects[1] : In late 1983 there was a debate among the Chancellor, TUC and CBI at the National Economic Development Council on 'where the new jobs are coming from'. The Treasury essentially writes manufacturing off as a net source of future jobs. It identifies some sectors where manufacturing employment grew by more than 10,000 in the last decade — computers, petroleum and natural gas, radio, radar and electronic goods — but the Chancellor does not believe we should look to the manufacturing sector to provide many extra jobs in the future. This is also the view of outside forecasters. Both the Cambridge Economic Policy Group and the Institute for Employment Research at Warwick predict further falls in manufacturing employment by 1990. Therefore some of the £20bn in industrial assistance will have to be switched to services to generate jobs and reduce unemployment. As this government is unlikely to want to increase employment in public services, the burden of the job-creation effort will fall on private services.

III   INCOME AND EARNINGS

The distribution of income is described first. Pay is the most important income source so we then turn to discuss the forces generating the distribution of earnings among individuals. Particular aspects of the pay structure — by occupation, industry, sex and race — are examined next. We conclude with an analysis of the twin problems of income support provided by social security and low pay.

III.1   Distribution of Income[2]

The *composition* of personal incomes in the UK in 1982 was:

---

1   See National Economic Development Council papers NEDC (83)58 by the Chancellor and NEDC (83)59 by the TUC on the question 'where will the new jobs be?'

2   Information in this section is from *ST,* 1984, No. 14, chapter 5.

Source	%
Pay	62
Income from self-employment	7
Rent, dividends and interest	8
Private pensions, annuities etc.	7
Social security benefits	13
Other current transfers	3
Total: (£218bn)	100

Pay accounts for a little over three-fifths of household income, some 7 percentage points lower than its 69% share in 1975. This partly reflects the growth of unemployment, which is also a major reason for the growing importance of social security benefits.

The *distribution* of personal incomes in 1980–81 is outlined in table 5.3.

TABLE 5.3

Distribution of Total Income before and after Income Tax, UK, 1980–81

	Average income		Percentage of income paid in tax
	Before tax (£s)	After tax (£s)	
Top 1%	31,200	20,000	36
2–5%	15,100	11,700	23
6–10%	11,300	9,010	20
Top 10%	14,800	11,200	25
11–20%	8,700	7,080	19
21–30%	6,970	5,720	18
31–40%	5,700	4,710	17
41–50%	4,520	3,800	16
51–60%	3,480	3,010	14
61–70%	2,480	2,260	8
71–75%	1,660	1,600	3
Bottom 25%	NA	NA	NA

Source: *ST*, 1984, table 5.14.

Note: Data refer to tax units, i.e. generally treat a married couple as one unit. No data are available for the 7.4m tax units (bottom 25%) whose income is not subject to tax.

The median pre-tax income was around £4,000, so those in the top 10% of the distribution had well over treble the average income. Many of those in the top decile of the *income* distribution will derive a substantial fraction of their income flow from their stock of *wealth* (e.g. dwellings, stocks and shares). The most wealthy 10% of the population owned 60% of marketable wealth in 1981 (when total marketable wealth was £535bn).

Half the units had income under £4,000, and the average income of those in the top 10% is under £15,000. The fact that there are relatively few people with high incomes makes the redistribution of income and greater provision of desirable health and education services difficult. While it may be possible to squeeze many thousands of pounds out of a rich individual, there are not many of them, so that the extra revenue raised by squeezing them harder is quite small. It should also be borne in mind that these figures refer to the distribution at one specific point in time; many of those in the bottom half of the distribution in 1980–81, like pensioners and students, will be in the top half at other points in their life. The inequality in lifetime incomes is less than the inequality of the income distribution observed at any particular point in time.

Some of the inequality is redressed via taxes on incomes and benefits in the form of cash and services. It can be seen from table 5.3 that income tax makes the distribution more equal because the percentage of income tax paid rises with income. Further, poorer families receive *proportionately* more (though *absolutely* less) than richer families from state spending on education, health, and housing and transport subsidies. The extent of income redistribution from taxes and state spending can be seen from the following figures for 1981:

All households	Original income, %	Final income, %
Bottom fifth	1	7
Next fifth	8	12
Middle fifth	18	18
Next fifth	27	24
Top fifth	46	39
TOTAL	100	100

Final income is defined as original income less income and other taxes plus state spending on social security benefits and other things like education. The share of the top 20% of the income distribution fell from 46% of original income to 39% of final income, while the share of the bottom 20%, many of whom had no original income, rose from 1% to 7%. Nevertheless, the final income of the top fifth is still over five times greater than the final income of the bottom fifth.

III.2   Distribution of Earnings

The distribution of earnings, like the distribution of income, is positively skewed (median earnings are less than mean earnings). However, the earnings distribution is more equal than the distribution of income because the latter includes a return on wealth which is more concentrated.

The dispersion of earnings in April 1983 (full-time workers, men aged twenty-one and over, women aged eighteen and over, whose pay for the survey week was not affected by absence) is set out in the following table.[1] Both men and women at the lowest 10% point earned around two-thirds of median pay, while the best-paid 10% earned over two-thirds more than the corresponding median.

---

1   DE, *New Earnings Survey*, 1983, Part A, table 1. The data in this section refer to individuals, not families or Inland Revenue income units. Many people only work part-time or part of the year, and therefore the distribution of annual earnings of those who worked at any time during the year is different from the distribution above, because the annual earnings distribution has a concentration of people in the lower tail. A full discussion of the evidence on the distribution of earnings and evaluation of theories seeking to explain this distribution is contained in A.R. Thatcher, 'The New Earnings Survey and the Distribution of Earnings', in A. Atkinson (ed.), *The Personal Distribution of Incomes*, Allen and Unwin, 1975. E.H. Phelps Brown, *The Inequality of Pay*, OUP, 1977, also contains much evidence on this topic.

	Median earnings per week (£s)	Lowest decile	As a % of median		
			Lower quartile	Upper quartile	Highest decile
Men	150	64	79	130	170
Women	99	66	80	130	168

There are two particularly important and interesting facts concerning the distribution of gross weekly earnings of male *manual* workers. First, the dispersion of the distribution has been quite stable for almost a century:

Distribution of weekly earnings, manual men (% of median)		
	1886	1983
Lowest decile	69	68
Lower quartile	83	82
Median	100	100
Upper quartile	122	123
Highest decile	143	152

This stability suggests that we might seek to explain the distribution of earnings by factors such as differences in ability, motivation and luck, which might be expected to remain fairly stable from one generation to the next, rather than by appeal to institutional factors such as the growth of unions, or social forces such as the extension of public intervention, which have changed dramatically in the last century.

Second, the position an individual occupies in the distribution changes from year to year. Evidence on the gross weekly earnings of all full-time adults who were in the New Earnings Surveys in 1970 to 1974 (*DEG*, January 1977) indicates that the lowest-paid workers received by far the largest percentage increase in earnings between one survey and the next, while the higher-paid workers tended to experience much smaller percentage increases. Such movements are known as 'regression towards the mean'. Between 1970 and 1974 21% of male manual workers were in the lowest-paid tenth in at least one of the five surveys, but only 3% were in this tenth in all of the surveys. These movements refer to weekly earnings of full-time workers and therefore reflect the variable nature of many components of manual workers' earnings (e.g. overtime, short-time, bonuses, piecework), the effects of job changes and the incidence of wage settlements. Movements in individuals' hourly earnings, which may more nearly reflect skill and motivation, or in annual earnings, which may reflect the incidence of unemployment, could be more or less pronounced than the fluctuations in weekly earnings.

One important explanation of the positive skew in the earnings distribution relates to the coupling of natural ability and training. In a smoothly functioning, competitive labour market, earnings will reflect productivity at the margin. Among all the determinants of marginal productivity we may concentrate here on a worker's 'natural ability' and training. If, for a given level of formal training, a man comes to the labour market with relatively great motivation, ability and drive he will tend to earn more than the average worker. Further, it is established that on average the more naturally gifted man tends to undertake more than average amounts of training. An unskewed distribution of ability combined with a skewed distribution of training produces a skewed distribution of productivity. The last, in an approximately competitive market, produces a skewed earnings distribution.

This simple picture is only a partial explanation of the actual earnings distribution. First, not everyone has equal access to the educational and training sectors, even where natural ability is the same for all. One implication is that relatively bright working-class children have difficulty in getting sufficient secondary and advanced education. This means that ability is not properly harnessed with education, thereby reducing the degree of earnings inequality.

Second, in some activities, including many of the professions, free entry of labour is restricted and earnings are pushed above the competitive level by union activity. The impact of such behaviour on the distribution of pay depends on (i) the numbers affected, and (ii) the size of the union mark-up. Union activity among male manual workers probably reduces inequality because even though a similar proportion of skilled and unskilled workers are covered by union agreements, the pay premium associated with union coverage is higher for unskilled workers than for the skilled.

Third, luck plays a significant part in determining earnings, particularly in any one year. The last qualification is important because the discounted sum of lifetime earnings is a more valid measure of material well-being than current earnings.

If a man is lucky one year but unlucky the next we would have a misleading view of his well-being by looking at either year in isolation. Similarly, if a man is receiving a low wage currently because he is training, but expected to do well when he is trained, it would be mistaken to view him as a poverty case. The same may apply to people approaching retirement.

The *General Household Survey* (*GHS*) provides, each year, information on individual earnings and related individual characteristics such as age, schooling, work experience, race and family background. The 1975 *GHS* has been extensively analysed.[1] Let us consider the factors which generated the distribution of pay among the 5,000 or so full-time male employees in the sample.

Consider first the distribution of hourly earnings. Years of full-time education have a substantial effect on hourly earnings. Holding constant father's occupation, work experience, ethnic background, health and marital status, each additional year of education raises pay by between 5% and 10%. Does this mean education is a good weapon against poverty? The trouble with ordinary education is that while a person is being educated one does not know whether or not he is going to end up poor. In any case there is such a spread of earnings for people with a given level of education that even if all education disparities were eliminated the remaining inequality would be still over 93% of what it is now.

One could go further than eliminating educational disparity. Positive discrimination could be practised whereby those who had low earnings potential would be given *more* education than others. But this implies the ability to spot low earners while they are still being educated and it is doubtful whether this is

---

1   R. Layard, D. Piachaud, M. Stewart, *The Causes of Poverty*, Royal Commission on Distribution of Income and Wealth (Diamond Commission), *Background Paper*, No. 5 (to *Report No. 6, Lower Incomes*), HMSO, 1978, especially chapter 4. This is the best discussion on the factors generating the distribution of pay in Britain. The remainder of this section draws freely on this source.

practicable. It could, however, be done for adult training—by then people have shown what they can and cannot earn—and there is evidence that short periods of vocational training can improve a person's position in the occupational hierarchy.

Pay is influenced by work experience. On average an individual with between 30-40 years of work experience earns, *ceteris paribus*, twice as much as a person with 5-10 years' experience. But the individual stuck in a particular manual job has little prospect of a real wage increase (other than from general economic growth) after the first 10 years.

Family background, measured by father's occupation, influences hourly earnings directly and also indirectly via education levels. An individual with a non-manual father had in 1975, *ceteris paribus*, hourly earnings 12% higher than those with unskilled fathers.

Marriage is also associated with higher pay. After controlling for other factors, married men had hourly pay 14% greater than single men. This may be because marriage puts pressure on individuals to work harder or may simply reflect the fact that better-quality men are more likely to get married.

The factors above account for around a third of the variance of *annual* earnings. Another third is explained by differences in the number of weeks worked in the year by each individual. This is itself influenced by human capital factors. Individuals with relatively high hourly earnings work more weeks—it is the unskilled who bear the burden of unemployment and, to a lesser extent, sickness.

We now turn to examine some more narrowly defined aspects of the distribution of earnings. In the next section the pay structure by occupation and industry is examined. This is followed by a discussion of labour-market discrimination against women and non-whites. The lower tail of the distribution is studied in the final section on low pay.

III.3 Wage Structure by Occupation and Industry

Wage structure by occupation: The foundations of wage theory are contained in two famous principles. First, Adam Smith's principle of net advantage states that when competition exists in the labour market the 'whole of the advantages and disadvantages' of different occupations will continually tend towards equality. Note that this principle does not imply that wages will tend towards equality, but that (suitably discounted) lifetime returns to one occupation will tend to equal those in another occupation. The returns that make an occupation attractive or unattractive are both pecuniary and non-pecuniary. Second, we have the principle of non-competing groups, which evolved from the work of John Stuart Mill and Cairnes: this states (broadly) that certain non-competitive factors may inhibit the tendency towards equality in net advantages.

Linked to these two principles are two sets of reasons for the existence of occupational wage differentials: compensatory wage differentials and non-compensatory wage differentials.

Compensatory wage differentials are those which are consistent with competition in the labour market. If individuals were not compensated for the factors listed below (in the form of higher wages when at work), then the supply of labour to those occupations would tend to be deficient. All other things being equal, individuals will tend, for example, to be compensated in the form of higher wages

for entering occupations that (1) require long periods of education and/or training, (2) are dangerous or dirty, (3) are subject to lay-offs or have a relatively
short working life. (4) Also if they are risk-averters, they will desire to be compensated by higher mean earnings in the occupation if the dispersion of the
earnings around the mean is very large. (5) Differentials will also accrue to wholly
exceptional workers, such as professional sportsmen and entertainers, this being
an example of economic rent applied to the labour market.

Non-compensating occupational wage differentials are different. They occur
where economic or institutional reasons inhibit competition in the labour market.
For example, closed-shop agreements protect union members from non-union
competition. Legal restrictions boost solicitors' pay for conveyancing work. And
minimum-wage legislation might raise the pay of those at the bottom of the earnings distribution above the competitive level.

Earnings by broad occupational groups are presented in table 5.4. It will be seen
that earnings of non-manual workers are greater than those of manual workers. This
reflects in some large part the relative education/training intensities of the two
groups. There is also evidence of other compensating differentials. Bricklayers (in
group 16) earn 310p per hour, while general labourers (in group 18) earn 273p: the
bricklayers are being compensated for their relatively low earnings while
apprenticed. Within group 9, firemen earn 375p per hour while security guards
earn 306p. The firemen are being compensated because their job is more dangerous
and requires more training.

There is also evidence of individuals being compensated for being more able, or
having more alternative job opportunities, or undertaking a more skilled task, even
though the length of education and training is similar to that of their less-skilled
colleagues. In group 3, for example, teachers in further education earn £34 a week
more than secondary-school teachers. Within group 17, the earnings of a lorry
driver are positively related to the size of vehicle: drivers of heavy-goods vehicles
(over 3 tons) earn 31p per hour more than other goods drivers.

Trade unions are able to influence the occupational earnings structure if the
demand for labour is inelastic and/or if they can control the labour supply. For
example, miners (in group 16) earn 500p per hour, which is 63% more than
postmen (in group 7) earn. This reflects, in part, the strength of the National Union
of Mineworkers, conferred by the inelastic demand for domestic coal which results
from the currently used methods of electricity generation, together with limitations
on coal imports. In contrast the lengthy postmen's strike of 1971 certainly did not
bring the country to a halt, partly because telephonists and other postal workers
continued working and tolerable substitutes were therefore available for the postal
workers' services.

Wage structure by industry[1] : There are a number of reasons for studying the
industrial wage structure. First, it is important to know whether labour can be
allocated among industries independently of wages, or whether expanding (con-

---

1   The most substantial recent work on this issue is R. Wragg and J. Robertson, *Post-War
Trends in Employment, Output, Labour Costs and Prices by Industry in the UK*, Research
Paper No. 3, DE, June 1978.

TABLE 5.4

Earnings by Occupation: Full-Time Adult Men, April 1983

	Average gross weekly earnings (£)	*Average gross hourly earnings (p)*
Non-manual		
2 Professional and related management and administration	231	—
3 Professional and related in education, welfare and health	198	—
4 Literary, artistic, sports	208	—
5 Professional and related in science, engineering and technology	201	—
6 Managerial	195	—
7 Clerical and related	142	353
8 Selling	152	373
9 Security and protective service	191	435
Manual		
10 Catering, cleaning, hairdressing	120	265
11 Farming, fishing and related	110	244
12 Materials processing (excluding metal)	145	316
13 Making and repairing (excluding metal and electrical)	145	332
14 Processing, making, repairing (metal and electrical)	154	348
15 Painting, repetitive assembling, product inspection	136	318
16 Construction, mining	144	329
17 Transport operating	141	302
18 Miscellaneous	139	311
Total: Manual	195	503
Total: Non-manual	144	319
Total: All occupations	168	398

Source: DE, *New Earnings Survey*, 1983, Part D, table 86.

Note: Both sets of figures exclude those whose pay was affected by absence. The gross hourly earnings figure excludes the effect of overtime.

tracting) industries must pay higher (lower) wages to get the labour they require. Such information is useful in designing a pay policy. Second, how are the gains in labour productivity distributed? They can go to labour in the form of higher wages, or firms in the form of higher profits or consumers in the form of lower prices. Analysis of the industrial wage structure provides evidence on the topic. Third, it is important to know whether, independent of the characteristics of the individuals working in the industry, highly concentrated industries or industries with large plants pay higher wages; such data would be useful in, for example, designing our monopoly legislation.

Price theory implies that in the long run, given competitive conditions, each industry will, *ceteris paribus*, pay for a given grade of labour a wage identical to that paid by other industries. The *ceteris paribus* assumption implies that there are no differences in the non-pecuniary attractions of different industries or location or in the cost of living by location. In the long run, therefore, the growth in industry wage levels should not be correlated with the growth in the amount of labour employed. In the short run an industry which expands its demand for labour will tend to have to raise the wages it pays because of short-run inelasticities in labour supply. Therefore the theory predicts a positive association in the short run between changes in employment by industry and changes in wages by industry.

It is clear that in the long run there is no relationship between changes in pay and changes in employment. Wragg and Robertson studied 82 manufacturing industries over the period 1954–73. The pay changes in each industry were very similar but employment experience was very different. Indeed, the weaving industry suffered a loss of employment of 6.2% p.a. yet had a higher-than-average increase in earnings. In the long run, therefore, expanding industries do not have to increase their pay at a rate above the average to meet their labour requirements, and industries where employment is contracting still give around average pay rises. This reflects the continual churning which goes on in the labour market – 10m job-changes a year, and around 0.75m new entrants to the labour force and individuals retiring from it – which allows the labour force to adjust to the changing requirements imposed by the economy.

But what of the short run? It appears that there is a positive association between earnings changes and employment changes. This upward-sloping short-run market-labour supply curve implies that to avoid labour shortages developing a pay policy might need to permit such shortage sectors to pay above the norm.

An industry may react to an increase in physical productivity by lowering its relative product price or raising the relative wages it pays. If wage changes among industries are significantly (positively) related to movements in value productivity (i.e. variations in physical productivity and product prices taken together), this implies that non-competitive forces, such as ability to pay, determine the wage structure. In contrast, if the differential wage changes are unrelated to changes in value productivity by industry, this implies that competitive forces dominate in the explanation of wages. We anticipate such forces will be important because there is no reason, on equity or efficiency grounds, to expect that sectors with high labour productivity or growth in labour productivity will, *ceteris paribus,* pay high wages; working with bigger machines, if the intensity of work is unchanged, is no reason for higher pay.

The statistical associations found for 1954–73 for 82 manufacturing industries by Wragg and Robertson among the growth rates of output per head (i.e. labour productivity), earnings, unit labour costs and prices, were clear and unambiguous. Earnings changes were very similar across the 82 industries while labour productivity changes differed markedly. In turn, there was a negative association between labour productivity changes and movements in unit labour costs and, finally, a negative relation between labour productivity changes and price rises. This suggests that workers who cannot increase their productivity easily (such as musicians or nurses) do not find their relative position in the pay structure worsening persistently. Further, after allowing for general inflation, the gains from increased labour productivity flow mainly to consumers.

III.4   Wage Structure by Sex and Race

Evidence: Females account for 44% of employment in Britain, yet among full-time workers in 1983 men were 6 times more likely than women to be earning over £200 a week and 13 times more likely to be earning over £300 a week. Females earn less than males in each broad occupational and industrial group: the data in table 5.5 show that the hourly earnings of full-time female adult workers were, on average,

TABLE 5.5

Male–Female Hourly Earnings, Full-Time Workers, April 1983

	Female (p)	Male (p)	Female/Male (%)
Total manual	222	319	70
Total non-manual	309	503	61
Total	288	398	72
Occupations: manual			
Catering, cleaning, hairdressing	216	334	65
Materials processing (excluding metals)	215	316	68
Making and repairing (excluding metal & electrical)	215	332	65
Processing, making, repairing (metal & electrical)	240	348	69
Repetitive assembling, etc.	229	317	72
Transport, etc.	237	302	78
Occupations: non-manual			
Clerical	275	353	78
Selling	211	373	57
Security	411	435	94

Source: DE, *New Earnings Survey*, 1983, Part D, tables 86, 87.

Note:　　Data refer to adult workers whose pay in the survey week was not affected by absence and excludes the effect of overtime.

72% of male hourly earnings, and that the percentage differential between male and female pay is higher for non-manual workers than for manual workers.

There are two broad reasons why average male pay exceeds average female pay. First, and most important, women are crowded into the low-paying occupations and industries. Second, within occupational groups women tend to be paid less than men. In education, for example, women are disproportionately represented in the relatively low-paying primary segment, and within primary-school teaching women earn 15% less than men. It must be noted, however, that even within primary teaching the main reason for the differential is not that women are paid less than men for doing the same job but rather that women are under-represented in the higher-paying headship and deputy headship jobs. This example could be repeated for other occupations and industries.

Reasons why women earn less than men: A major reason why women earn less than men is that their attachment to the labour force is weaker than that of men. On average, each year of labour-force experience raises the pay of both men and women by around 3%. But, when women drop out of the labour force their pay potential *drops* 3% for each year of home time. So, essentially, if a man and woman enter the labour force with equal potential and the woman works for 10 years and then drops out of the labour force for 10 years by the time she re-enters work she is 20 years 'behind' the man—it is as if she is entering the labour force 20 years later. This relatively weak female attachment is in large part because it is widely believed that it is the role of women rather than men to drop out of the labour force to care for young children.

Attitudes on the roles of the two sexes can certainly be influenced by economic factors; for example the two world wars, which caused the demand for female labour to rise substantially, were particularly important in raising the labour-force status of women. This suggests that the respective roles of men and women are thus amenable to change via economic and other influences. The observed weaker labour-force attachment shows up in differences between men and women in turn-over rates, qualifications, size of local labour markets and the industries worked in.

Labour turnover is a little higher for women than for men. Such turnover imposes costs on the employer; at a minimum these costs will be the costs incurred when replacing employees. For example, in manufacturing the separation rate of women is two-thirds higher than the male rate. It is often argued that these figures reflect a composition effect, i.e. that females are disproportionately represented in industries and occupations which themselves have high turnover. This appears not to be true: in almost every industry and every occupation, female turnover is greater than male turnover. An alternative possibility, however, concerns the age composition of the labour force. Young workers have dramatically higher turnover rates than prime-age and older workers. Therefore some of the observed higher female labour turnover may occur because younger workers account for a higher fraction of the female labour force than the male labour force.

Because women have higher turnover rates than men, employers have less incentive to pay for female training. A profit-maximizing employer will be willing to pay for his employees' training if he can get a return on his investment by paying the trainee less than the value of his services when the training is completed. Given that women are more likely to quit or to be absent from a firm than men, employers will prefer to train men. This is compounded by hours legislation pro-hibiting women from working over a certain number of hours per week or at certain times.

Similarly, girls have less incentive to finance their own education and training. Staying on at school or university or taking a computer-programming course entails costs, for example tuition costs or forgone earnings (i.e. earnings that would have been received if working). If a woman has children this will involve a period out of the labour force; further, women retire at a younger age than men. The time over which she will receive benefits in the form of higher earnings from the training is less than for a man. Thus, among those aged 16–29 in 1981 only 10% of females held a post-school qualification below degree standard (e.g. apprenticeship, teaching qualification, nursing qualification) but 30% of men held such qualifications. In contrast, women in this age-group are far more likely to hold CSE or O-Level qualifications, a preparation for their segmentation into clerical occupations. The contrast is also clear if we consider highly qualified people (i.e. those holding an academic or professional qualification of degree standard). In 1981 10% of men but only 4% of women in the working population held such qualifications.

Females will also tend to be paid less than men if the firm draws them from a limited geographical area: they will incur lower transport costs on average than men. Also, women may tend to work in more pleasant conditions. The structure of the industries in which females work is a further element in the explanation of the sex differential. Females are disproportionately represented in small plants and atomistic industries, which tend to pay less and offer poorer career prospects than larger plants and concentrated industries; also a relatively low proportion of the female labour force is unionized, which reflects in part the higher costs of organiz-ing in industries consisting of small plants.

Equal Pay Act and Sex Discrimination Act:[1] The Equal Pay Act requires that a woman is to receive equal treatment to a man within the same firm when she is employed (a) on work of the same or broadly similar nature to that of men; (b) in a job which, though different from those of men, is of equal value. It was passed in 1970 but its full application was delayed until the end of 1975 to allow employers time to adjust to the new set of conditions on pay. The end of 1975 was also the time when the Sex Discrimination Act, requiring equal opportunities for men and women, became law.

The course of movements in relative female/male pay and female/male employment is outlined in table 5.6. Among full-time workers the hourly minimum wage rates set out in collective agreements had reached equality by 1976, and the hourly earnings of females rose from 64% of the male figure in 1973 to 73% in 1976, an enormous increase in such a short period. Simultaneously the relative employment of females was rising.

TABLE 5.6
Relative Female/Male Pay and Employment Movements 1970–80 (%)

| *April* | *Full-time workers* | | | *Part-time females, full-time males* | |
	Hourly wage rates W_f/W_m	*Hourly earnings* W_f/W_m	*Employment* F/M	*Hourly earnings* W_f/W_m	*Employment* F/M
1970	83	64	40	–	–
1973	87	64	41	51	10
1976	100	73	42	59	11
1980	100	71	46	57	12

Source: Z. Tzannatos and A. Zabalza, 'The anatomy of the rise of British female relative wages in the 1970s: evidence from the New Earnings Survey', *BJIR*, 1984, tables 1, 2 and 7.

Note: W_f is wage or earnings of female: W_m is wage or earnings of male; F and M are, respectively, employment of females and males. The hourly wage rate data refer to the weighted average of minimum rates of manual workers laid down in collective agreements.

The changes in female relative pay 1973–6 are coincident with the implementation of the Equal Pay Act. It is sometimes held that the Equal Pay Act is likely to be ineffective in improving the relative pay of part-time female workers because many work in segregated jobs which do not afford easy comparison with similar tasks done by men. But note that the relative hourly earnings of part-time females to full-time males also rose substantially between 1973 and 1976, from 51% to 59%.

Before jumping to the conclusion that the Equal Pay Act was responsible for the

---

1 This section draws on A. Zabalza and Z. Tzannatos, 'The effect of Britain's anti-discrimination legislation on relative pay and employment', Centre for Labour Economics, LSE, *Discussion Paper 155*, May 1983, and 'The anatomy of the rise of British female relative wages in the 1970s: evidence from the new Earnings Survey', *British Journal of Industrial Relations*, 1984.

large rise in female relative earnings in the mid-1970s, let us examine some possible alternative explanations. First, theory and evidence suggest that relative pay gets compressed during a cyclical upswing. This cannot account for the rise in female relative pay because real GDP *fell* between 1973 and 1975. Second, was there an autonomous decrease in the supply of female labour? On the contrary, we see from table 5.6 that female employment *rose* from 40% of the male figure in 1970 to 46% in 1980, a rise of 15% over the decade.

A third possibility concerns composition effects. Female relative pay can rise if females are now paid more in all sectors or (although pay in male and female jobs stays the same) because females have moved into higher-paying industries and occupations. It turns out that almost all the rise in the relative pay of females is because of the rise *within* occupations and industries. Such a uniformity in the behaviour of relative pay among quite different sectors must surely have been the consequence of a common cause – like the Equal Pay Act – and it is not attributable to the particular fortunes of each of the sectors. Indeed, the importance of the Equal Pay legislation is confirmed by Public Administration, the only sector where female relative pay did not rise during 1970–80. This is consistent with the fact that for the majority of workers in this sector – the non-manual employees – equal-pay principles were already in force before 1970.

Fourth, the letter of the Act, if not its aim, could be met by reducing men's pay. In sectors where there are many females employed, the equality of female and male pay might be achieved by lowering male pay in that sector relative to average male pay. This did not happen. For example, male pay (relative to average male pay) rose in both the Wage Board sector and among NHS Ancillaries, two sectors where female employment is substantial.

A final alternative explanation for the rise in female relative pay concerns the role of incomes policy. Many of the incomes policies of the 1970s were wholly or partially flat-rate (e.g. £1 + 4% or £6 a week) and a flat-rate rise gives equal cash amounts to all employees, so narrowing percentage differentials. In fact, there is strong evidence that the egalitarian aims of these incomes policies were not achieved and the pay structure among individuals or across industry and occupations did not narrow. Further, statistical estimates suggest that well under a fifth of the rise in female relative pay was due to the independent effect of incomes policy norms.

So we are left with one major explanation – the Equal Pay Act. There are two main channels through which the Equal Pay Act might have worked to raise female relative pay – collective agreements or the process of law. It seems clear that the major impact of the Act was via collective bargaining. The system of setting basic wage rates is centralized in Britain, and a small number of collective agreements determine the wage rates of a large number of workers. In the early 1970s, the 15 largest national agreements covered around 5.5 million workers, a quarter of all employees, and the number of workers covered by collective agreements or minimum Wage Orders was 14m, or nearly two-thirds of all employees. Over the period 1950–70 the weighted average of the minimum female hourly wage rate to the minimum male rate remained constant at around 82%. But, as the Equal Pay Act came gradually into force, it reached 87% by 1973 and then 100% by the time the Act was fully implemented in 1976 (table 5.6). Further, it is clear from the table that the rise in the female relative minimum wage rates was simultaneously translated into a rise in relative earnings, of workers both covered and uncovered by collective agreements.

The other channel through which the Equal Pay Act might have worked is via the legal machinery. If a woman (or man) believes she has been treated unfairly by her firm under the Act she can apply to an industrial tribunal (a court dealing with labour laws). There have been few such applications. In 1976, the first year of the operation of the Act, there were 1,742 applications but by 1982 the number had fallen to 39. Most applications are settled by conciliation and of those that reach the tribunal, only a small minority are decided in favour of the applicant. It is clear that, so far, the legal process has very much taken second place to collective bargaining as the vehicle for implementing the Act. However, an important change in the Act was implemented in 1984 to bring Britain into line with European practice. Previously, the 'work of equal value' dimension of the Act required a job-evaluation exercise. But from 1984 that is no longer so. It is to be expected that many individuals will feel that, inside a given firm, they do work of equal value to a colleague even though the job is not the same. Such individuals are now likely to apply to an industrial tribunal to get equal pay. It is fair to predict that the demand for lawyers, and hence lawyers' pay, will rise as a consequence of this amendment.

Did employers respond to the large rise in the cost of female labour by hiring less of it? It seems not from table 5.6—in the 1970s relative female employment rose by 15%. However, the issue is more complicated than it appears at first sight. Much of the expansion in female relative employment occurred because of the expansion of the public sector and, more generally, it was the female-intensive industries in both the public and private sectors which expanded in the 1970s. When we control for the effect of industrial structure on female employment, we find a *negative* association between female relative pay and female relative employment. This is probably the reason why, between 1976 and 1978—the first three years of the operation of the Act—female unemployment rose by a half while male unemployment fell.

Studies show that in 1970 the hourly earnings of men were around 30% higher than those of women with similar education, experience and father's occupation.[1] By 1975 the corresponding differential had fallen to between 12% and 15%. So the Equal Pay Act achieved over half of the total relative-pay gains needed to eliminate labour-market discrimination completely.

It is unlikely that there is now much unequal pay for equal work. For example in 1983 male sales assistants were paid 289p an hour while female sales assistants were paid 191p an hour. Obviously, if the men and women were perfect substitutes the females would soon replace the males. Rather, remaining labour-market discrimination mainly concerns access to the higher-paying occupations. It is here that the Sex Discrimination Act comes in as a potentially important channel in overcoming the current under-representation of women in high-paying sectors. It covers

---

1 Calculated from A. Zabalza and J. Arrafut, 'Wage differentials between married men and women in Great Britain: the depreciation effect of non-participations, *Review of Economic Studies*, 1984. See also R. Layard *et al., The Causes of Poverty*, Background Paper No. 5, Royal Commission on the Distribution of Income and Wealth, HMSO, 1978, pp. 52–6, and Christine Greenhalgh, 'Male-Female Wage Differentials in Great Britain', *EJ*, December 1980. Broadly, these estimates are derived by computing separate earnings-functions for men and women. Then an estimated female wage is calculated by assuming that a female of particular characteristics is paid according to the male wage structure. The difference between the estimated female wage and the actual female wage is termed 'discrimination'. Such calculations are, as the authors recognize, very difficult to undertake accurately.

education and the supply of goods and services as well as employment. The act states that women must be given equal treatment in the arrangements for selecting a candidate for a job, in the terms on which a job is offered, on access to promotion, transfer and training or any other aspects of the job and on dismissal. The Act established the Equal Opportunities Commission with fairly wide powers: it can help individuals to bring cases if it considers them of wider interest; it can conduct formal investigations compelling people to give evidence; it can serve non-discrimination notices and seek injunctions against persistent discriminators. Unfortunately the EOC has so far done little to raise the status of women. Indeed; since this hapless organization was established male-female differentials have widened!

In 1983 the hourly earnings of full-time women were 72% of those of full-time men. The evidence above suggests that approximately half of the difference is because men and women have on average different characteristics. Women have, for example, less labour-force experience and education than men. The other half is discrimination, not in the sense of unequal pay for equal work but because, for given characteristics, women do not rise so high in the hierarchy of occupations. Although a better use of the Sex Discrimination Act could help with both these factors, a surer way to eliminate the remaining pay differential, if it is held desirable to do so, would be to strengthen the attachment of women to the labour market.

The government could consider a number of alternative methods to improve the labour-force status of women. First, it might encourage them to join unions: the male-female wage differential is, *ceteris paribus*, smaller in those industries which are highly unionized. Second, more girls could be encouraged to take apprentice-ship or college training by providing them with differentially large training grants. Third, female quotas, especially in the higher occupational grades, could be enforced. Finally, women's pay could be forced up relative to men's pay by sub-sidizing women's employment.

Race:[1] There is clear evidence that non-whites suffer discrimination in employ-ment. Other things being equal (i.e. holding constant age, experience, weeks worked, years of schooling, marital status etc.) non-white males earn around 17% less than equivalent whites. The extent of this discrimination is greater for those of Asian ethnic origin than men of West Indian origin. The bulk of this discrimination is not attributable to unequal pay for equal work, rather the problem is that black and brown workers seem not to be able to gain access to the higher-paying occupations. Thus while 58% of Pakistani males and 32% of West Indian males working in Britain are unskilled or semi-skilled, the corresponding figure for whites is 18%. Further, almost no whites with degree-level qualifications do manual work but around one-fifth of such men from minorities do manual work and members of ethnic minorities are much less likely than whites to be in professional and management occupations.

Another way of describing this discrimination is to say that non-whites have, on

---

1   Evidence in this section is taken from R. Layard *et al., The Causes of Poverty*, op. cit.; M. Stewart, 'Racial discrimination and occupational attainment in Britain', *Economic Journal*, September 1983; DE *Gazette*, October 1983, pp. 424–30; J. Smith, *Labour Supply and Employment Duration at London Transport*, Greater London Paper, No. 15, 1976.

average, flat experience-earnings profiles, while for whites the earnings profile rises with labour-market experience. This has a particularly important consequence for the returns to education for non-whites and whites. Non-whites born outside the UK do no worse in terms of occupational attainment than equivalent whites providing they left school at age 15 or below. But those non-whites who left full-time education at 16 or over suffer substantial discrimination: they simply do not rise up the hierarchy of occupations in the same way as white workers. Thus the returns to extra education are substantially lower for non-whites than for whites.

Although the majority of the non-white labour force was born outside the UK there is evidence that the vicious circle of non-whites crowding into lower-level occupations—hence flat experience-earnings profiles and lower returns to extra education—is continuing among non-whites born in the UK. For such people in the age-group 16–29 in Great Britain in 1981, the percentages with post O-Level qualifications were:

	Male	*Female*
White	45	23
Non-white	25	13

These post O-Level qualifications include degrees, HNC/HND, teaching and nursing qualifications, apprenticeships, City and Guilds and A-Levels. It is rather worrying that whites are almost twice as likely to possess such a qualification as non-whites. Indeed, in the case of degree or equivalent qualifications, white men are six times more likely to possess the qualification than non-whites. A plausible explanation for the discrepancy is that British-born non-whites observe the relative occupational attainments of whites and non-whites in the labour force and conclude there is not much point in pursuing the extra education.

A further problem is that the occupational status of non-whites may lead employers to conclude that, in some cases, they have a more relaxed attitude to work than whites. In fact, a higher average turnover rate or absenteeism rate is likely to be a characteristic of their occupations and industries rather than an inherent racial characteristic. For example a study of labour turnover at London Transport showed that, other things being equal, blacks had a longer duration of employment than whites. Although non-white immigrants to Britain may have been content with lower average occupational status than the indigenous population, the same is unlikely of their sons and daughters. The relative educational and occupational achievements of young British-born whites and non-whites are a cause for concern.

III.5 Social Security

One aspect of income distribution which causes widespread concern is the problem of poverty. Low earnings from work are only part of the problem (and are discussed in the next section). Others at the lower end of the income distribution include old people, the sick and disabled, large families or families with lone parents, and the unemployed. In this section we discuss how to measure poverty, the current social security system and suggested reforms.[1]

Measurement: Poverty can be defined as an absolute or relative standard. Absolute standards are based on consumption of necessities. Relative standards are normally related to some measure of income in the general population. Thus, the amount of supplementary benefit (SB) payments, which is often taken as defining the level below which poverty may be said to exist, would reflect an absolute concept if, over a long period of time, it was geared exclusively to prices and it would reflect a relative concept if it were geared to average earnings. Over most of the postwar period the poverty line as defined by supplementary benefits was being determined by relative rather than absolute standards: the real value of benefits has more than doubled since 1948.

At the end of 1981 the numbers of families and people living (a) below the poverty line or (b) on it were:

		Families	*People*
(a)	Numbers with incomes below SB level	1.8m	2.8m
(b)	Numbers receiving SB	3.0m	4.8m

Nearly 2m families and 3m people lived *below* the supplementary benefit level. Around half these people are unemployed or are in work. The other half are sick, disabled or pensioners. There has been a substantial rise in the numbers living below the poverty line since 1977, when the corresponding number of people was 1.9m. Presumably the main reason why people live below the poverty line is that although eligible for SB or Family Income Supplement (FIS, see below, the corresponding benefit for those in work) they do not claim it. The number of families (3.0m) and people (4.8m) in families in receipt of supplementary benefit have also risen in recent years. Two-fifths of these SB recipients are pensioners.

There are other ways of measuring poverty than counting heads. One way is to calculate a 'poverty gap' in money terms. The poverty gap is simply the amount by which income falls short of the official poverty line. In 1975 before social security benefits were paid the gap was 6% of GDP, but after social security benefits were paid the gap was only 0.25% of GDP. When put like this the performance of the social security system is impressive, though this is not to deny that families who are falling below the poverty line face real hardship or that the official poverty line itself may be inadequate.

Social security system: The social security system provides income in two main ways. First, contributory benefits are based on national insurance contributions

---

1 For more information see Treasury and Civil Service Committee (Chairman: M. Meacher), *The Structure of Personal Income Taxation and Income Support*, HC 386, HMSO, May 1983. This document is particularly clear on the vexed issues of the poverty trap and unemployment trap discussed in the next section. It also contains a concise description of the negative income tax scheme and social dividend scheme, and that description is replicated here. See also W. Beckerman, 'The impact of income maintenance payment on poverty in Britain', *EJ*, June 1979.

and paid from the National Insurance Fund.[1] In 1983-4 retirement pensions
accounted for £16bn out of the £20bn total spending on contributory benefits.
Second, disability benefits, supplementary benefit, family benefits and housing
benefits are paid direct from the Exchequer. Over half of the total non-
contributory benefits of £13bn consists of means-tested supplementary benefit
and housing benefit. The other major non-contributory item is child benefit.
Total social security spending of £34bn represented 29% of public expenditure
in 1983-4.

Social security has undergone important changes in the last decade. First,
national insurance contributions are earnings-related and there is an earnings-
related component to the state pension scheme which, when fully mature later
in the century, will eliminate the need for older people to have recourse to supplementary benefit. However, the reverse has happened with unemployment and sickness benefit where the earnings-related component has been axed, causing many
more among the sick and unemployed to need supplementary benefit. Second,
unemployment benefit is now taxable. Third, child benefit (£6.85 a week for each
child in 1985) is a cash benefit paid to the mother. Previously the main family
support was given via the tax system to the father. Fourth, an array of new benefits for disabled people has been introduced. Fifth, the employer is now responsible for paying the first eight weeks of statutory sick pay (SSP) in any one year.
For those earning £68 a week or more the SSP is £42.24 a week. The employer
then claims the money back from the National Insurance Fund.

Despite these changes, there are real faults in the system. First, nearly 3m people
are living below the poverty line, which shows that the benefits are simply not
getting to people in need. Second, another 5m people have to rely on SB, which
shows that other anti-poverty measures are not working properly. Third, the
income-related nature of many benefits discourages full take-up and also results in
high implicit marginal tax rates (this poverty-trap problem is discussed, together
with the unemployment trap, in the next section). Fourth, certain groups — particularly the disabled and lone parents — fit uneasily into the current system and this
makes it difficult to apply a coherent benefit structure to them.

Reform: There have been three main sets of suggestions concerning the future
direction of reform: a 'new Beveridge plan', a negative (or reverse) income tax and a
social dividend scheme. They have a superficial similarity, in that under each
scheme individuals will be guaranteed a minimum income at around supplementary
benefit level and the need for means-testing would be much reduced or abolished.
In fact, however, the three schemes are very different from each other.

Under the original Beveridge proposals it was proposed that social *insurance*
should guarantee everyone a minimum standard of living. This subsistence income
was to be provided as a right, without a means test: the part played by SB was to

---

1 In 1984-5 employers pay 10.45% on earnings up to a ceiling of £250 per week for employees
who are not contracted-out of the earnings-related state pension scheme. For contracted-out
employees, they pay 10.45% on earnings up to £34 and 6.35% between £34 and £250.
Employees who are not contracted-out pay 9% on earnings up to £250. If contracted-out
they will pay 9% on earnings up to £34 and 6.85% between £34 and £250. These contributions
raise £23bn, over two-thirds as much as is raised from income tax.

be virtually phased out. In the postwar period, however, National Insurance benefits have usually been below the prescribed minima laid down by supplementary benefits. The suggestion is therefore to implement fully the original Beveridge proposals. One of the aims of the current pension scheme is to ensure pension benefits of sufficient size to virtually eliminate the need for pensioners to turn to supplementary benefits to augment their income. Higher child benefits are also important. Advocates of this universalistic approach to curing poverty generally qualify it by suggesting that the benefits from raising social-security payments could be taxed and thereby directed towards those with lower incomes. This policy would obviously be successful in raising the incomes of non-employed disadvantaged individuals. It does not involve high marginal tax rates at low incomes and is therefore less likely to have disincentive effects on working harder. Further it would not involve any major administrative headaches. But it does have two problems. First, it would cost an additional 4–7p on the basic rate of income tax (quite apart from the tax clawed-back from benefits). However, this is merely another way of stating the seriousness of the poverty problem. Second, the problem of the employed with low incomes remains.

The negative (or reverse) income tax (NIT) and social dividend (SD) schemes assume a minimum income guarantee (the poverty line), which is a cash benefit varying according to the circumstances of a family. This cash benefit is paid in full to those without any other income and so it supplants those social security benefits which are at present paid to those without any work.

It is for those in work that these NIT and SD schemes differ in their mode of operation. Under the NIT, the minimum income guarantee is withdrawn as quickly as possible as earnings rise, until a level of income is reached (the break-even point) where the guarantee payment disappears and tax starts to be paid. Typically the withdrawal rate below the break-even point might be 70% and the tax rate above around 30%. Unless the minimum income guarantee is kept very low—below present levels of social security—even a withdrawal rate of 70% puts the break-even point above the present tax thresholds. So a substantial minority of the population faces a 70% marginal rate and some of the characteristics of the present poverty trap are reproduced.

Under a social dividend scheme, the minimum income guarantee is paid to every individual either as a cash benefit or as a credit against tax. There is no withdrawal of benefit as such. Nevertheless, because tax is charged on all income other than guaranteed income, there comes a point at which tax liability equals benefit (or credit) received. This is the tax break-even point. So the high withdrawal rate on low incomes is avoided, but the tax above the break-even point is higher than under NIT. The break-even point is significantly higher than under NIT.

Assume the poverty line (guaranteed payment) for a married couple with two children is £70 a week. A typical NIT might have a withdrawal rate of 70%, giving a break-even gross income of £100 (£70/0.7), and a tax rate of 32% above £100. The typical social dividend scheme might have a constant tax rate of 43%, giving a break-even point at a gross income of £163 (£70/0.43). It is unlikely that the Chancellor of the Exchequer would be content with such high break-even income levels.

III.6   Low Pay[1]

Low pay is one part of the poverty problem. Industries which are at the bottom of the earnings structure tend to be characterized by high proportions of small plants, of women workers, of unskilled workers and of falling demand for labour. It is also clear that low-paid workers are disproportionately represented in the service sector.

Low pay is also related to age and skill. Teenagers, workers in their early twenties and workers over fifty are disproportionately represented. Older and unskilled workers not only tend to have relatively low earnings, but also to suffer higher rates of unemployment. Unemployment rates referring specifically to unskilled workers are at least three times the national average unemployment rate. The annual earnings differential between them and other workers is therefore greater than is apparent from a comparison of the earnings of those who are in work.

Two important features of the structure of the low-pay problem are worth noting. First, if the low-paid are described as those in the lowest tenth of the distribution of manual earnings, we observe considerable movement across the boundary of this lowest tenth. 21% of manual men were in the lowest tenth at least once in the five years 1970 to 1974, but only 3% were in this tenth in each of the years. Second, low pay must be seen as part of a general problem of labour-market disadvantages in that it is associated with high incidence of job instability, ill-health and lack of fringe benefits. The low-paid worker is more vulnerable to the interruption of earnings power, cannot save for old age or emergencies, and can only borrow at very high interest rates such as through HP. Thus low pay is an important element in the cycle of poverty.

The interaction of low pay, social security benefits and income tax generates the poverty trap and the unemployment trap. The *poverty trap* results from increased reliance on income-related benefits and causes high marginal tax rates on additional earnings faced by people on such means-tested benefits. It is the spread of housing benefits coupled with the decline in the tax threshold (rather than Family Income Supplement, see below) which has been the main factor leading to families facing marginal tax rates of 60% or more. DHSS calculations suggest that it is low-income married couples with children that are caught in the poverty trap. For example, for a married couple living in local authority housing with 4 dependent children in April 1983 an increase in the husband's gross weekly earnings from £54 to £116 brought no improvement in living standards because net weekly spending power remained at £100, i.e. he suffered a marginal tax rate of 100%.

The poverty trap is real, but the number of families it affects depends on one's assumptions. Starting with actual take-up of means-tested benefits, and assuming all benefits to have been adjusted immediately on receipt of a pay rise in 1979, about 1½% of all working families — 270,000 — would have gained less than 50p per week from an increase of £1 in gross earnings. However, if we assume full take-up

---

1   For fuller discussion, see Chris Pond, 'Wage Councils, the Unorganised and the Low Paid', ch. 8 in G.S. Bain (ed.), *Industrial Relations in Britain*, Basil Blackwell, 1983; D. Metcalf, *Low Pay, Occupational Mobility and Minimum Wage Policy in Britain*, American Enterprise Institute, 1981; *Social Trends*, 1984, ch. 5.

of means-tested benefits, the number of families facing a 50p in the £ marginal-tax rate rises to 700,000. In fact FIS and its associated benefits (like free school meals) are awarded for 52 weeks at a time, so the number of families who in practice would have suffered from the worst effects of the poverty trap would have been much smaller. Of the 270,000 above, about 30,000 families with children might have received no increase in net income from a £1 rise in earnings.

There is no real evidence that the poverty trap has undermined work incentives. Some decisions—such as whether or not the wife works—are not subject to the same high tax rates. But, as the Meacher Report noted: 'It is impossible to believe that there is not widespread resentment, confusion, frustration and cynicism.'

The other incentive issue is the *unemployment trap*—the possibility that incomes out of work may be little different from those in work. Supplementary benefit is the relevant out-of-work income measure. Of 2.1m male unemployed claimants in November 1982 (the latest available data), only 21% were receiving unemployment benefit alone, 52% were receiving only supplementary benefit, 11% were having their unemployment benefit topped-up by supplementary benefit and 15% were receiving no benefit. For a family where the married man is in full-time work, with two children aged 2 and 4, supplementary benefit in November 1982 was 64% of average net earnings (gross earnings plus child benefit, less tax and national insurance contributions).

However, this average figure conceals a lot and government officials clearly do not believe that there is much of an incentive problem. The memorandum from the Treasury, DHSS and Inland Revenue to the Meacher Committee quoted results from a study of unemployed men which showed that only 9% had higher incomes when they were out of work, whereas for 35% income when unemployed was less than half that in their last job.

The Meacher Committee concluded that the poverty-trap and unemployment trap can be moderated by a rise in income-tax thresholds or a rise in child benefit. Since those with children are more at risk from the two traps than those without, they favoured increasing child benefit. One option considered superior to the present tax-benefit system was to raise child benefit to £15 a week for the first child and £10 for subsequent children. This permits abolition of FIS and the child needs allowance for rent and rate rebates. It would be paid for by reducing the income-tax allowance of a married man to that of a single person.

In Britain we approach the problem of low pay in two main ways. First, the FIS is a form of negative income tax. Second, the wages councils provide a form of minimum-wage legislation.

FIS was introduced in 1971 to help mitigate poverty caused by low pay. When family income falls short of a prescribed level (from November 1983 £85.50 per week for a one-child family plus £9.50 for each additional child), the family is paid a benefit equal to one half of the difference between its total gross income and the prescribed level (with a maximum supplement of £22 for a one-child family and £2 for each additional child). This is a potentially powerful policy to raise the welfare of the low-paid, but unfortunately only half those who would benefit take up FIS. On average, the 150,000 families on FIS got around £12 a week in 1983. Families who receive FIS are also automatically entitled to certain other benefits, including free school meals, free milk and vitamins for expectant mothers and children under school age, and exemption from NHS charges for prescriptions, glasses and dental treatment. FIS has the considerable merit of attacking *family* poverty. This is important because the bulk of low-paid people are young workers and married women, and most such workers do not live in the poorest families.

Elements of a minimum-wage policy exist via the wages councils, which set minimum rates in certain industries. This direct state intervention in fixing minimum wages first occurred in 1909 with the Trade Boards Act. In 1945 trade boards were renamed wage councils. There are 27 wage councils covering 2.75m workers in around half a million establishments. Three councils cover over a million workers in hotels, clubs, pubs, cafes and restaurants, and two more cover a million shopworkers. There are also two wage boards covering 275,000 farm-workers. Wage councils are generally believed to be rather ineffective in helping low-paid workers and are thought to inhibit the development of voluntary collective bargaining arrangements.

A national minimum wage is advocated by those who do not like FIS because it is an income-related benefit and who believe that wage councils have been in-effective. If the minimum wage was set at around two-thirds of median male earnings its cost would be equivalent to around 5% of the total wage bill (1.5% for men and 15% for women). Although a national minimum wage is, at first sight, an attractive proposition it is not without drawbacks. First, many low-paid people are single people and married women. They typically live in families with more than one earner. So a national minimum wage would leave much family poverty untouched: it would not help the family just above the minimum wage but with needs greater than income, perhaps because the family is large. Second, unless other workers are content to see their pay differentials eroded, a national minimum wage is simply inflationary—it pushes the whole distribution of money wages to the right, leaving the lowest-paid no better off, in either relative or real terms, than before. Third, the minimum wage implies an increase in unit labour costs and is likely to result in lower employment. Recall that the young and old and unskilled—those the minimum wage is designed to help most—already have the highest unemploy-ment rates. It is sometimes said, however, that the minimum-wage legislation will have a 'shock effect' and thereby raise productivity without any loss in employ-ment. This is unlikely to be widespread in that it implies that firms currently have a careless attitude towards profits. Further, many of the low-paying industries are competitive and are therefore unlikely to need a national minimum wage as a spur to efficiency.

This suggests that provision of more training facilities, better information about wages and opportunities both locally and nationally, inducements to labour mobility, wage subsidies, and running the economy with lower, more evenly distributed unemployment levels, are likely to be more effective solutions to the problem of low pay than is a national minimum wage.

IV TRADE UNIONS, INDUSTRIAL RELATIONS AND WAGE INFLATION
IV.1 Trade Unions

Trade-union membership in the UK is falling rapidly. Between 1979 and 1982, the last year for which the Department of Employment has published estimates, membership fell by 14%, from 13.3m to 11.4m. It is probable that there was a further substantial decline in 1983. This is in sharp contrast to the 1970s, a period in which membership grew very quickly by historical standards. In the ten years to end 1979, union membership rose by 28%, more than three times faster than in the 1960s.[1]

The major immediate reason for the turn-around in union membership growth is the fall in the number of people in work. Employment in the heavily unionized manufacturing sector, for example, has been cut by nearly 1.5m since 1979. Union membership, however, is now falling faster than employment, at least for the economy as a whole. Expressed as a percentage of all employees in employment, trade-union membership reached 58% in 1980; by 1982 it had fallen to 54%.

Recent empirical work suggests that, over a fairly extended period, changes in trade-union membership in the economy as a whole have been systematically associated with certain economic developments. Membership has tended to fall when unemployment has grown, and to have increased when price inflation has risen, when average money wages have been rising fast and when the labour force has been expanding quickly. These associations are now reasonably well established but their interpretation is not straightforward. It could be, for example, that more rapidly rising wages encourage workers to join trade unions; equally, however, more workers joining trade unions could lead to more rapidly rising wages. What does seem plausible is that, in addition to these aggregate associations, certain structural changes have influenced trade-union growth. The changing industrial and occupational composition of the labour force, the great rise in the number of women in work, and the changing boundaries between the public and private sectors are all likely to have had an effect on union membership. Union membership rates among women, for example, are still significantly below those for men, even though the gap is closing.[2]

It should be stressed that the direct impact of unions extends far beyond its members. The *New Earnings Survey* for 1973 and 1977 gave estimates of the number of workers whose pay was affected by various kinds of collective agreements, whether they were union members or not. Only 17% of full-time male workers and 28% of full-time female workers were found not to have had their pay covered by collective bargaining; i.e. the influence of unions was far more pervasive than their membership figures might imply.

Union membership is particularly extensive among male workers, manual workers and workers in the manufacturing and public sectors. There are no absolutely reliable figures on union membership by industry, because even the unions involved do not always know how many of their members work in each industry. The most authoritative study, however, estimated that union density in 1979 ranged from 7% in the very large miscellaneous services industry, which includes accounting services, legal services, hotel and catering etc., to over 95% in such industries as cotton textiles, coal mining, the public utilities and much of the transport industry.[3]

There is a substantial body of empirical research seeking to explain the

---

1   *DEG*, January 1984, pp. 18–20.

2   G. Bain and F. Elsheikh, *Union Growth and the Business Cycle*, Basil Blackwell, 1976. See also the review by R. Richardson in *BJIR*, July 1977, and A. Booth, 'A Reconsideration of Trade Union Growth in the U.K.', *BJIR*, November 1983.

3   R. Price and G. Bain, 'Union Growth in Britain: Retrospect and Prospect', *BJIR*, March 1983.

variations in trade-union membership between industries and occupations. Two broad classes of reasons have been suggested. The first refers to the workforce and suggests that some types of workers believe that unions offer little of value. A study of workers' voting behaviour in union representation elections in the US, for example, showed that workers were more likely to want a union if they earned relatively low wages within the firm, felt that they had a poor chance of promotion, felt that they suffered from arbitrary behaviour by their supervisors or had experienced racial discrimination. The higher wage earners, and those who were optimistic about promotion or had good relations with their supervisors, tended to see much less attraction in union representation and voted against it.[1]

The second set of reasons refers not so much to the workers as to the kind of situation they find themselves in at work. A recent survey of over 2,000 British establishments, covering all sectors of the economy, stressed the importance of the workplace context. It concluded that the chief reasons for the different patterns of union recognition and density were the type of ownership, the size of establishments, the size of enterprises and workforce composition. Unions were more likely to be found in the public sector, in large plants, in large organizations and in establishments where male workers predominated. Unions were also more likely to be found, other things being equal, in multi-establishment than in single establishment firms. Overall, the authors of the study concluded, their results were consistent with the view that union recognition and density patterns were mainly the result of government and management policies and practices, especially in relation to the implications of managing large numbers of people. The authors felt that the inclinations and wishes of individual workers were of relatively minor significance in determining union density.[2]

This conclusion ties in with some related work on the closed shop, i.e. on the arrangements that make union membership a condition of employment. There are both pre-entry shops, where membership is required before a worker can be hired, and post-entry shops, where a worker must join on being hired. Post-entry closed shops are the much more common form. The incidence of closed shops in Great Britain has grown strongly in the last 15 years. One estimate is that they now cover at least 5.2m workers, nearly 25% of all employees. They are estimated to be particularly common in mining, in gas, electricity and water, in printing, in transport and communications, and in shipbuilding. They are rare in agriculture, in professional and scientific services, and in insurance, banking and business finance. Although closed shops quite properly arouse strong emotions, it should be recalled that in most cases their existence has been preceded by very high levels of union densities. A closed shop, or union-membership agreement, is nearly always a formal recognition of extensive unionization. On many occasions, managements appear to have seen them not so much as leading to a significant increase in union power but as a potential force for making industrial relations more orderly. Whether they were correct in taking this position remains an open question, but there can be little doubt that some of the surge in the extent of the closed shop during the 1970s was due to at least tacit management approval.[3]

1 H. Farber and D. Saks, 'Why Workers Want Unions', *JPE*, April 1980.

2 W. Daniel and N. Millward, *Workplace Industrial Relations in Britain*, 1983, Chapter II.

3 J. Gennard, S. Dunn and M. Wright, 'The Extent of Closed Shop Arrangements in British Industry', *DEG*, January 1980, pp. 16–22. See also Daniel and Millward, op. cit.

Finally, something should be said about the number and size-distribution of trade unions. The number of unions has been tending to fall for many years, both as a result of trade-union mergers and because some unions simply cease to function. By the end of 1982, the Department of Employment estimated that there were 401 trade unions, down from 470 in 1975. The recent rapid fall in union membership has meant that the average number of members per union is now falling. The number of very small unions is increasing; in 1982, there were no less than 78 unions with fewer than 100 members. At the other end of the scale, the number of unions who reported having at least 100,000 members (the level which now gives automatic membership on the General Council of the TUC) fell from 27 in 1979 to 22 in 1982.

In addition to those in independent trade unions, many workers belong to other staff associations that engage in collective discussions or negotiations on terms and conditions of employment. Still other workers are in industries or occupations that have wages councils, public bodies that are designed to reproduce some of the features of collective bargaining where trade-union growth is thought to be inherently difficult. About 3 million workers are in this last category, and it is of some importance that a minister has announced that the government will shortly be looking at the effects of wages councils 'with a most searching eye' to see whether their modification, or even abolition, would reduce unemployment. A recent investigation of the consequences of abolishing six of the wages councils concluded that, after abolition, there was a deterioration in pay and conditions for a minority of workers and that normal collective bargaining by no means fully replaced the wages councils.[1]

IV.2   Economic Analysis of Unions

The existence and activities of trade unions raise very large questions in the fields of politics, sociology and law. On a somewhat narrower and more practical front, trade unions have had a considerable influence on the operation of work rules, consultation procedures and worker representation. Economists, however, have tended to concentrate on the impact of trade unions on wages and resource allocation.

The theoretical analysis of union behaviour by economists is not very satisfactory. At its simplest, the union is often assumed to have organized all the relevant workers and to be facing a set of unorganized employers. In many respects, the analysis is analogous to the standard treatment of monopolies in product markets. In this context, the decision that the union has to make is to trade off jobs for higher wages.

The union is seen to face a given demand curve for its members' services. Higher wages mean fewer jobs (a) because they tend to raise product prices and reduce product demand, and (b) because they are liable to raise the price of labour relative to other factors of production and encourage factor substitution. In this model, therefore, it is the prospect of reduced employment possibilities that disciplines the union wage claims. In order to predict what a union will decide to press

---

1   C. Craig, J. Rubery, R. Tarling and F. Wilkinson, *Labour Market Structure, Industrial Organisation and Low Pay*, Cambridge UP, 1982.

for, it is necessary to know both the elasticity of the demand facing it and the relative value placed by the union on job opportunities and wages. In order to know the latter it is necessary, in the spirit of this model, to know something about how decisions are arrived at within the union.

Economists frequently ignore some of these qualifications and simply predict that unions will secure a greater wage where they face relatively inelastic demand conditions. As a corollary of this prediction, it is also suggested that in situations where demand elasticities are high,a union may have nothing to offer its potential members and may therefore not exist. If we add to this some consideration of the costs of successful organization, we have at least an embryo theory of union-density patterns. It is usually said that such costs are low when the workforce in question is (a) stable and so not subject to high rates of quits or lay-offs, (b) concentrated among relatively few employers, (c) concentrated geographically, and (d) has certain attitudes, e.g. group loyalties.

The simple theory of union behaviour sketched above is greatly weakened by the assumption that employers are not organized but act atomistically. When they too are organized, as they usually are in the UK, we enter the world of bargaining and bilateral monopoly. The theories relating to such a world are often elegant and are sometimes entertaining but they are rarely fruitful. Certainly they have not yet produced operational models that have been widely accepted by those who wish to understand the real world. This failure is not confined to the analysis of union behaviour but appears throughout economics whenever strategic, or 'game', situations are central. We therefore have in this area a fragile theoretical platform from which to survey and analyse the real world.

Turning now to empirical work, it is possible to investigate the impact of unions on (a) relative average wages between trades, (b) the dispersion of wages within trades, and (c) average real wages. Most of the recent research has been concerned with the first of these three dimensions. The standard approach is to use multiple regression analysis to isolate and measure the impact of unions on relative wages once other possible influences have been taken into account. A great variety of 'other possible influences' have been considered and different authors have investigated different wage structures. Attention has most commonly been focused on average wages by manufacturing industry for manual male workers.

The early research in this area concluded that unions had a very powerful effect on relative wages. Estimates of the union mark-up – i.e. the difference in average wages, other things equal, between a wholly unionized industry and one where unions were completely absent – were of the order of 20-30%.[1] More recent estimates have been much lower. These have come from enquiries using the same general procedure but different kinds of data. In particular, the data have referred to individual workers or individual establishments rather than to broad industry averages. For various technical reasons these newer estimates are likely to be more accurate. For example, it is probable that they can more accurately take into account the fact that the unionized and non-unionized are dissimilar types of workers and should not be compared without careful qualification.

The newer studies suggest that the average union mark-up tends to be 10% or less.[2] This seems a much more plausible number than the earlier estimates. If

---

1 D. Metcalf, 'Unions, Incomes Policy and Relative Wages in G.B.', *BJIR*, July 1977.

2 M. Stewart, 'Relative Earnings and Individual Union Membership in the U.K.', *EC*, May 1983.

unions really did raise relative wages by an average of 30% it would be difficult to understand why the whole labour force was not unionized. Even the newer mark-up estimates are not beyond criticism, however, and future research might well reach significantly different conclusions. Thus, if the standard approach were applied to non-manual workers it would probably find that the mark-up was negative. The best interpretation of this finding would not be that unions reduced the earnings of their non-manual members, but that union membership tends to be high among low-wage non-manuals and low among those towards the top of hierarchies. In other words, union-density patterns may be both a consequence and a determinant of relative wages.

Apart from having a significant effect on relative average earnings between industries, unions also tend to compress the distribution of earnings within industries and occupations. An emphasis on 'the rate for the job' is a frequent and explicit union goal. It is seen to increase group cohesiveness, solidarity and determination, fundamental requisites of successful trade unions.

Finally, there is the impact of unions on real wages. The theoretical analysis on this question is complex, and the empirical work is very scanty. Real wages are a reflection of (a) labour productivity and (b) the bargaining power of labour over the division of total output. It is obviously likely that unions tend to increase labour's bargaining power, at least for a period. It may of course be the case that in the very long run most, or even all, groups of workers face highly elastic demand conditions for their services and enjoy no permanent bargaining power. Over a period of many decades, however, large numbers of workers can clearly gain significant bargaining power through collective action. The degree and duration will clearly vary from case to case. The impact of unions on labour productivity, however, is very much less clear.

The traditional view is that the impact of unions on their members' productivity should be broken down into a number of steps. First, any rise in wages that a union secures for its members is very likely to raise the capital/labour ratio, as factor substitution takes place. This will, in turn, raise labour productivity in the unionized sector (the capital/labour ratio, and hence labour productivity, in the non-unionized sector might fall or rise). A second consequence of the higher wage is that more productive workers might be encouraged to move to the unionized sector. This would also raise labour productivity there but would clearly reduce it in the sectors which the more productive workers left.

Over and above these effects, the standard analysis of union behaviour suggests that unions will tend to be responsible for a lowering of labour productivity. They are widely believed, and in some cases known, to institute and consolidate a large variety of restrictive labour practices, in the form of manning rules, job demarcation rules, etc. They are also believed to resist the rapid introduction of technological changes. In some cases this might be root-and-branch opposition, while more commonly it is associated with extensive and detailed consultation, as well as extra compensation. One study claimed that a very significant part of the difference in productivity between comparable British and foreign plants could be attributed to restrictive practices.[1]

There is, however, an alternative view that has begun to be investigated with some seriousness, so far exclusively in the US. This view does not deny that unions

1 C.F. Pratten, *Labour Productivity Differentials within International Companies,* Cambridge UP, 1976.

may be instrumental in promoting restrictive labour practices, but it suggests that these should be set against a second set of factors. A non-unionized workforce, it is claimed, may have a range of discontents and grievances which are not being effectively communicated to management. As a result, it is argued, workers will have poor motivation, low performance levels, high absenteeism and high voluntary turnover, all of which raise costs and reduce productivity. Finally, it is claimed, unionization may ameliorate these problems by forcing management to consider and perhaps deal with the workers' discontents. This could raise performance, reduce absenteeism and turnover, make training more profitable than it would otherwise be and raise labour productivity. The empirical work explicitly considering these possibilities in the US has concluded that on balance unions raise labour productivity, i.e. that the advantages via better communications are greater than the disadvantages from restrictive practices.[1]

As might be expected, this recent work has generated substantial controversy and disagreement.[2] To some it seemed that the estimated increases in productivity were so large that we should expect to see managements encouraging unions to organize their workers. This does not, of course, follow. Any increase in productivity would have to be set against wage increases and there is no presumption that the net effect would be to lower costs. The other criticisms of the new work are fairly technical, some of them revolving around severe measurement problems. There is, however, another interpretation of the statistical findings. If labour productivity is relatively high in unionized firms, it does not follow that unions have been responsible for raising productivity over what it would otherwise have been. It may merely be that unions tend to be found in plants where labour productivity is high for other reasons, for example in large plants with high capital/labour ratios and a degree of monopoly power in the product market. It is perfectly possible that unions could be reducing labour productivity through restrictive practices but still leaving it higher than in non-unionized plants or industries.

The last point to be considered is at whose expense, if anybody's, these various union effects are made. If unions secure higher wages for their members, who loses? If unions really do raise labour productivity, it could be that no one loses, that the gain is an uncovenanted benefit. For the other effects, however, a loss could fall (a) on the employer, in the form of lower profits, (b) on consumers, in the form of higher prices, (c) on workers who are not union members, in the form of lower wages elsewhere and reduced job opportunities in the unionized sectors, or (d) on taxpayers, in the form of higher taxes to pay for larger industrial subsidies, e.g. to nationalized industries. Examples can be found of each of those groups having been adversely affected by particular union activities, but it is not possible to say where, on average, any burden does fall.

IV.3   Strikes

The significance of strikes can be measured by the number of stoppages that occur, by the number of workers involved in the stoppages and by the number of working

---

1   R. Freeman and J. Medoff, 'The Two Faces of Unionism', *Public Interest*, Fall 1979.

2   J. Addison and A. Barnett, 'The Impact of Unions on Productivity', *BJIR*, July 1982.

days lost through stoppages. The official estimates of all of these measures are known to be something of an understatement because they exclude most of the stoppages which last for less than one day, as well as those which involve fewer than ten workers. Further, the official figures include only those stoppages deemed to result from industrial disputes over terms and conditions of employment. Those deemed to be 'political' are excluded. Finally, there is no obligation on the parties to report stoppages, and many that take place may not be picked up.

The most volatile of the three measures is the series on working days lost. In recent years it has ranged from a peak of nearly 29m in 1979 down to 3.6m in 1983. The number of stoppages has also fallen, down to about 1,250 in 1983, as against more than double that figure in most of the 1960s and 1970s. These figures put the strike problem into context. 3.6m working days lost among over 20m employees implies that the average UK employee loses about 1½ hours a year by striking! For the economy as a whole the economic significance of strikes can easily be exaggerated.[1]

Although the UK has a rather poor international reputation for strikes, its performance, as measured by working days lost per thousand employees, is not unusual for a developed economy. During the last decade the UK has usually lost many fewer days than Spain, Italy or Eire, and significantly fewer than Canada, Finland and Australia; however, the record is much poorer when compared with Holland, Japan, Western Germany and France.

The incidence of strikes is very unevenly distributed across workers, firms, industries and occupations. Industries that typically lose a relatively high number of days per worker through strikes include drink, many of the engineering industries, especially motor vehicles, printing and some of the transport industries. Other industries, for example agriculture, clothing, textiles, gas, electricity and water, and most of the private-sector service industries, tend to lose very few days through strikes.

It is important to note that the very great majority of workplaces experience no strikes at all in any one year. This is clearly evident in the official figures and is confirmed in a number of large-scale surveys. The latest of these, relating to the year up to mid-1980, a year of relatively high strike incidence, produced some very interesting but complex results. First it confirmed that strikes are but one form of industrial action, and not necessarily the one to which workers usually have recourse. Thus, for manual workers as a whole, the strike was only marginally more frequent than were all other forms, including overtime bans, working-to-rule, go-slows or blacking of work. For non-manual workers, these other forms of industrial action were more common than strikes.

The study also sought to shed fresh light on what factors were associated with the taking of industrial action in one form or another. It concluded, first, that size of establishment was strongly associated with strike activity. More precisely, manuals (and non-manuals) were more likely to take industrial action in plants with large numbers of fellow manual (non-manual) workers. In addition to plant size, industrial action among manual workers was also found to be higher where union density was high, where the proportion of male workers was high, where there was collective bargaining at establishment level, and where there was extensive

---

1 *DEG*, November 1983, pp. 475–80.

piece-rate bargaining. Many of these associations were also found for non-manuals.[1]

An important public policy issue of recent years concerns the payment of supplementary benefit (SB) to strikers' families. It is certainly true that state support to strikers' families increased in the 1970s compared with the earlier post-war period. This increase was associated, in part, with a change in the pattern of strikes, in particular with an increase in the number of longer, official strikes, particularly in the public sector (e.g. postmen 1971, miners 1974, firemen 1977, and steelworkers 1980). But the proportion of those eligible who actually received supplementary benefit was, at most, around one-third. Further, SB seems to have played only a minor role in the budgets of those on strike. Only 15% of the postmen's income while on strike came from the state. Strikers and their families relied far more on running down their savings, deferring HP and rent and mortgage payments, living off wives' pay and back-pay, and tax rebates. Gennard provided persuasive evidence that state income support did not cause or prolong strikes; he also suggested that modifications in the availability of SB to strikers' families would, in some cases, cause hardship and would possibly sour industrial relations.[2] In spite of this, the present government decided to change the rules governing transfer payments to the families of strikers. When, early in March 1984, coal-miners started to go on strike, after months of an overtime ban, they discovered that the SB to which their families would otherwise have been entitled had been reduced by £15 a week to reflect the strike pay which they were 'deemed' to be receiving. The fact that they were not receiving any strike pay was irrelevant. They also discovered that any SB received would subsequently be taxable and that they were not entitled to receive any tax rebates due until the end of the strike.

Whether these entitlement changes have in any significant way affected strike patterns in the last few years is by no means clearly established. It is true that the number of strikes and working days lost have fallen substantially, but that is to be expected at a time when unemployment is high and rising, inflation is falling and real earnings beginning to increase.

IV.4   Industrial Relations

Strike activity is the most heavily publicized aspect of industrial relations but is by no means the most important one. It arouses considerable public comment and often provides dramatic situations with great political significance but, in so doing, it tends to obscure other aspects of the relationships between employer and employee which make up industrial relations. For a number of reasons, the British 'system' of industrial relations has been the subject of much analysis and debate, particularly since the mid-1960s.

Initially many observers were disturbed by the UK's slow rate of growth in comparison to that of the rest of Europe. It was felt by many that our complex, old-fashioned and rather ramshackle industrial relations arrangements had a lot to do with this. It was also widely felt that unions, or, more even-handedly, our particular system of collective bargaining, either caused or exacerbated inflation. To these largely economic issues were added related social, legal and political matters.

1   Daniel and Millward, op. cit., Chapter IX.

2   J. Gennard, *Financing Strikes*, Macmillan, 1977; see also J. Gennard, 'The Effects of Strike Activity on Households', *BJIR*, November 1981 and 'The Financial Costs and Returns of Strikes', *BJIR*, July 1982.

There has been, for example, a long-standing debate as to the tactics that are proper in the pursuit of wage claims. There has also been a debate on the question of the closed shop, the circumstances in which it should be allowed, and the rights and position of individual workers who do not wish to be union members.

Most generally, there has been a growing unease over the power that trade unions are thought to be acquiring. Whether they have grown in power and in what respects this might have happened, and in what ways any such changes might affect behaviour or events, are all questions whose answers are by no means easy to establish. But if opinion polls are to be believed, there is a considerable body of opinion in the country which holds that in a variety of ways unions are too powerful.

These and other questions have prompted a spate of industrial relations legislation since 1971. Following the Donovan Commission Report of 1968, the then Labour government proposed reforms but withdrew them in the face of strong union and backbench opposition. It was left to the Conservatives to legislate substantial reform but their Industrial Relations Act (1971) had a stormy history, arousing bitter hostility in the trade-union leadership, before it was repealed in an early action by the Labour government of 1974. That action, the Trade Union and Labour Relations Act, together with the associated Trade Union and Labour Relations (Amendment) Act (1976), in many ways restored the pre-1971 situation, but in some respects the position of trade unions was further strengthened.

Additional industrial relations legislation was also introduced. The Employment Protection Act (1975) encouraged constructive union activity. Employers were, for example, required to disclose certain information judged to be relevant to collective bargaining, consult with unions on the handling of redundancies, and face more pressure to recognize independent trade unions when their employees wished to be represented. The legislation also gave powers to the Advisory, Conciliation and Arbitration Service and extended the legal rights of individual employees, for example in maternity pay and leave provision. The position of unions was also strengthened by the passing of the Health and Safety at Work Act (1975) and the Industry Act (1975).

Since its return to power in 1979, the Conservative government has adopted a new strategy. Instead of attempting root-and-branch structural reform, in the manner of the 1971 Act, the present government has introduced, step by step, a series of relatively limited measures designed, in the words of Sir Geoffrey Howe, 'to create a more reasonable balance of bargaining power between the partners in industry'. The first set of measures formed the 1980 Employment Act, which proposed, first, that closed-shop agreements should become more difficult to enter into, and that individuals who suffer damage from the operations of a closed-shop agreement should have some additional legal redress. Second, the Act made provision for public money to encourage the taking of secret ballots on certain questions such as union elections and strike calls. Third, it redefined the limits of lawful picketing so as to seek to influence who may picket and where picketing may take place. The Act also amended certain parts of the Employment Protection Act relating, for example, to trade-union recognition, unfair dismissal provisions and maternity provisions. Finally, it changed the immunity which the law provided for so-called 'secondary' industrial action, such as blacking and strikes.

The second set of measures formed the Employment Act 1982. This was a somewhat eclectic set of proposals, *inter alia* (i) giving substantially greater compensation for those unfairly dismissed when a closed-shop agreement is enforced,

(ii) making it more likely that the trade union involved will make a contribution to such enhanced compensation, (iii) making provision for periodic review of existing closed shops, (iv) making unlawful certain practices which require, or put pressure on, contractors to use only union labour, (v) making trade unions liable to be sued in certain circumstances, i.e. modifying the legal immunities that trade unions previously enjoyed, and (vi) restricting the definition of what constitutes a trade dispute, implying in turn a restriction of the legal immunities of those who organize industrial action.

The third set of measures appeared in 1983 as the Trade Union Bill and is still being considered by Parliament at the time of writing (April 1984). The Bill contains a series of proposals designed to change the governmental structure and decision-making processes within trade unions. Its main features are that it (1) requires the principal executive committee of a union to be elected by secret ballot of the union's members, (2) removes immunity from legal action in cases where unions do not hold an appropriate ballot before authorizing or endorsing a call for a strike, and (3) requires unions to ballot their members at least every ten years if they wish to spend money on political activities. In addition, the TUC has agreed with the government a voluntary scheme making it easier for union members to contract out of paying the political levy, i.e. that part of their dues which goes to support political activity. The government has, however, explicitly reserved its freedom to legislate on this matter if the voluntary scheme is found to be working inadequately.

These three pieces of legislation are not the only actions of the present government designed directly to affect industrial relations. Thus, in 1982 it announced the abolition of the Fair Wages Resolution, which had required employers with government contracts to pay wages and offer conditions in line with those in their industry locally. Again, in 1984 the government declared that no worker employed at certain government establishments could henceforth be a union member; a sum of £1,000 per worker was paid to compensate for the loss of previous rights. Finally, the government has announced plans to issue a discussion paper, and perhaps introduce legislation, on the subject of outlawing or inhibiting strikes in certain 'essential' public services.

This battery of legislation is certainly having an effect, although its impact is very difficult to disentangle from that of the very slack labour market in which it is operating. Some of the legislation has clearly affected developments in particular situations. For example, a union has already been 'joined' in an unfair dismissal case being heard before an industrial tribunal on a closed-shop issue. In another very well publicized case, the National Graphical Association fell foul of the secondary picketing clauses of the 1980 Act, had consequently to pay large fines and damages, and lost in the industrial dispute. In many other cases, however, the new laws have not actively been used and their impact can only have been as a background threat.

IV.5   Wage Inflation and Incomes Policies[1]

Of all the areas of controversy and disagreement in economics, the one that is most confused and least resolved is probably that of inflation, particularly its causes and

---

1   See also Chapter 1, Section IV.

cures. It is widely agreed that the most important immediate determinant of price inflation is changes in money wages. This is because wages are the major component of production costs and, as a matter of fact, the prices of finished goods usually change only after costs have changed. There are, of course, other components of costs, and changes in these may also affect prices. Thus, the rate of price inflation is additionally affected by changes in (a) non-wage labour costs, e.g. training costs or National Insurance costs, (b) productivity, (c) taxes or subsidies on goods and services, (d) the foreigh currency price of imported goods, (e) the exchange rate, and (f) profit margins. In the recent past, each of these has had an influence on the price level for a time but changes in wages have been even more important.

The determinants of at least some of these non-wage-cost components are not a matter of very great controversy, though they are often very difficult to forecast at any given time. However, there is very little agreement as to what determines the course of wage costs, and correspondingly little agreement on how that course might be changed by policy.

There are, however, many observers who believe that wage inflation is the result of the configuration of unions or of collective bargaining structures. Such analysts have also tended to believe that the course of wage inflation is largely uninfluenced by the unemployment rate, except for relatively brief periods, i.e. they tend to stress the importance of rates of change in unemployment rather than levels of unemployment.

A relatively early expression of this diverse group is to be found in the work of Hines, who attributed wage inflation to trade-union pushfulness. Hines set out an index of trade-union pushfulness $\Delta T = T_t - T_{t-1}$ (where T_t denotes the proportion of the workforce unionized, or union density, in year t). His thesis was that ΔT is a measure of union activity which manifests itself simultaneously both in increased union membership and density and in pressure on money wage rates. He tested this hypothesis with aggregate data from 1893 to 1961 and found, broadly, that through time excess demand for labour had become less important as a cause of inflation and that in the postwar period wage pushfulness was a key factor in the explanation of inflation.[1]

Given the controversial nature of this topic and the originality of Hines' contribution, it is not surprising that the latter has been subjected to careful scrutiny. The most wide-ranging critique was that of Purdy and Zis,[2] who examined Hines' theory, data, estimation technique and interpretation, and re-estimated his model to take account of their various criticisms. When this was done, the impact of ΔT on wage changes, although still positive, was much reduced. This was confirmed by Wilkinson and Burkitt, who used carefully constructed data on unionization by industry and found that ΔT was significantly associated with changes in only one industry, textiles, out of the eleven they studied.[3]

Statistical studies have neither confirmed nor rejected the central place of unions in the inflationary process and, in consequence, the debate concerning the underlying causes of inflation continues unabated. It is generally agreed that a cor-

1   A. Hines, 'Trade Unions and Wage Inflation in the UK 1893–1961', *RES*, 1964, and A. Hines 'Wage Inflation in the UK 1948–62: A Disaggregated Study', *EJ*, 1969, pp. 66–89.

2   D. Purdy and G. Zis, 'Trade Unions and Wage Inflation in the UK', in D. Laidler and D. Purdy (eds), *Inflation and Labour Markets*, Manchester UP, 1974.

3   R. Wilkinson and B. Burkitt, 'Wage Determination and Trade Unions, *SJPE*, June 1973.

relation exists between the growth in the money supply and the rate of inflation, and that this correlation is stronger in the long run than in the short run. What is in dispute is whether inflation is caused by excessive growth in the money supply, or whether union power or some other social force causes money wages to rise which in turn induces the authorities to expand the money supply in order that unemployment does not result.

In response to the problem of wage inflation, there have been many attempts since the 1960s to run incomes policies. These have taken a very wide variety of forms. For example, they have differed as to whether they were voluntary or compulsory, as to whether they had a flat-rate norm (i.e. so many pounds per week) or a percentage norm, and as to whether they permitted exceptions or not. The key question for these experiments is whether they were effective. More precisely, any incomes policy is likely to lead to some loss of allocative efficiency in the economy, by inhibiting changes in relative wages. Does it provide some compensating benefits by slowing down the rate of wage and price inflation below what they would otherwise have been?

The accumulated evidence on the effect on wage inflation of incomes policies as they have been applied in the UK suggests very strongly that they have generally been ineffective. Earnings increases are usually reduced below what they would otherwise have been in the early stages of the policy; but increasingly, and most notably when a government is compelled to dismantle the policy, earnings rise again to reach a level very close to that which they would have reached had no such policy ever existed.

For example, a Department of Employment Working Party estimated that over the years 1965, 1966 and 1967 earnings rose about 4% less than they otherwise would have done without a policy, whilst in 1968 and 1969 earnings rose 4% more than they would have done had there never been a policy. The total impact of the policy was nil.[1] This raises the question, why are incomes policies taken off? Presumably the answer is that, at least as they have been applied in the UK, they become politically or economically unsustainable after a while.

This is also the conclusion reached by two extremely thorough studies of the effect of incomes policies over the whole postwar period. In one study the authors summarize all the recent literature and conclude 'incomes policy apparently has little effect either on the wage determination process or on the average rate of wage inflation'.[2]

In the other study, a careful and subtle statistical analysis, the conclusion was that wage increases in the period immediately following the ending of the various policy experiments matched any reductions gained during their operation.[3]

One reason for these findings is that incomes policies have often been introduced while the economy was being expanded. This was notably the case with the policies of the Conservative government in 1972 and 1973. It is precisely in such circumstances that one might expect least success because tight labour markets lead both workers and employers to try to circumvent the policy, the former because they

1 DE, *Prices and Earnings in 1951-69*, HMSO, 1971, para. 57.

2 M. Parkin *et al.*, 'The Impact of Incomes Policy on the Rate of Wage Change', in M. Parkin and M. Sumner (eds), *Incomes Policy and Inflation*, Manchester UP, 1972.

3 S. Henry and P. Ormerod, 'Incomes Policy and Wage Inflation', *NIER*, August 1978, pp. 31-9.

want higher wages and the latter because they want more labour. Arguably
one of the few incomes policy successes was with Stage 1 of the Labour government's policy in 1975. At the time, unemployment was rising rapidly and output
was stagnant or falling, so that macroeconomic policy and the incomes policy were
working in harmony against inflation. It could be argued that in these circumstances the incomes policy contributed nothing, that the success in reducing
inflation should be ascribed to macroeconomic or monetary policy alone. However, most observers agree that the incomes policy at least caused the reduction in
wage inflation to come earlier than it would otherwise have done.

Another strand of thinking on incomes policies is that in some circumstances
they might raise the rate of wage inflation. This view is based on the proposition
that the policy norm might become a floor rather than a ceiling—the norm might
be seen as a minimum entitlement. This view probably influenced the Labour
government in 1978 when it pitched the norm quite low, at 5%, and hoped that
any excess, or drift, would still keep wage inflation in bounds. In the event, the
tactic was transparent and the experiment backfired. 5% was judged to be far too
low in comparison with most workers' expectations and any small chance that the
continuation of the policy might secure official union support disappeared.

In spite of the fact that they are widely judged to have had only a temporary
success in reducing the rate of wage inflation, while at the same time frequently
giving rise to political embarrassments, incomes policies have always retained their
advocates. These usually become more numerous with the passage of time after
any previous incomes policy experiment has been scrapped, because the costs of
alternative policies then become more clearly revealed. The principal anti-inflation
alternative to incomes policy has been economic contraction, either passively
tolerated or actively engineered. The deeper that alternative has bitten and the
higher the unemployment rate has climbed, the more people have tended to turn
back to incomes policies in the hope that they might offer a more sensible and
rational way of conducting our economic affairs. In such a context, the failures of
previous incomes policies are attributed to errors in their form or design rather than
to generic defects.

The most recent revival of interest in incomes policies appeared after about 2½
years of seeking to manage the economy without one. During that time, unemployment soared to another postwar record but wage inflation came down only to
around 10%. Their advocates began to stress the possibility that incomes policies
can increase employment without raising inflation. It was admitted that all incomes
policies are likely to generate economic costs; for example, they might make the
structure of wages more rigid than it would otherwise be, thereby adversely affecting the efficiency with which labour and other resources are allocated. It was
claimed, however, that the size of any such costs was likely to be greatly exceeded
by the benefits of a successful incomes policy, in particular by the increase in
employment which it would bring about. If this were true, the only problem
would be to design a successful policy. In attempting this, some economists have
begun to advocate a form of incomes policy that was originally designed some years
ago but never put into practice. Its principal mechanism is a tax levied on
employers who grant wage increases in excess of the government's norm.[1]

---

1   The idea seems originally to have been proposed by H. Wallich and S. Weintraub, 'A Tax-
based Incomes Policy', *Journal of Economic Issues*, June 1971. It has been revived more
recently by R. Jackman and R. Layard; see, for example, R. Layard, 'Is Incomes Policy the
Answer to Unemployment?', *EC*, August 1982.

The main reason for reviving this particular incomes policy variant is the belief that previous policies in the UK have not provided sufficient incentives for wage bargainers to comply with their terms. Even when incomes policies have been statutory in form, their penalties for non-compliance have not usually been clear or believable, particularly to those engaged in wage negotiations. A tax on excess settlements, however, is likely to be clear to everyone, even if some of its implications are in doubt.[1]

Whatever its particular form, the tax is held to give an important additional incentive to employers to resist above-norm settlements; further, any net tax payments would increase total costs of production and thereby threaten employment, so that it might also give trade unions an additional reason not to push as hard for 'excessive' wage increases. Both sides of the labour market, therefore, are said to be given a clear reason to moderate their wage settlements.

The discussion surrounding this device is necessarily speculative, because it has not so far been tried in practice. However, many observers doubt that it would work effectively for more than a relatively brief period. They look at what has happened in labour markets since 1970 and note that many firms have been under immense and sustained economic pressures. During that time, wage settlements have nearly always greatly outstripped productivity increases, even when firms generally have been facing profits difficulties, liquidity crises, loss of markets and problems of mass redundancies. The picture has been similar on the workers' side. The rapid rise in unemployment has certainly attenuated, but not eliminated, wage inflation. Worse, at the time of writing (April 1984), it is becoming clear that the downward trend in wage settlements is ending, and may even be starting to reverse, even though well over 3 million workers are unemployed. The inflationary impact of this is substantially offset by the fact that labour productivity continues to rise very fast, particularly in manufacturing.

If productivity increases were to start slowing down, however, and many believe this is likely, a continuation of relatively high wage settlements would begin to make some form of incomes policy increasingly attractive to many people.

REFERENCES AND FURTHER READING

A. B. Atkinson, *Economics of Inequality*, second edition, Clarendon Press, 1983.
G. Bain (ed.), *Industrial Relations in Britain*, Blackwell, 1981.
British Journal of Industrial Relations, July 1977, Symposium of Labour
    Economics and Industrial Relations.
Department of Employment, *British Labour Statistics: Historical Abstract 1886-1968*, HMSO, 1971.
C. Greenhalgh, R. Layard and A. Oswald (eds.), *The Causes of Unemployment*,
    Clarendon Press, 1983.
E. Hobsbawm, *Labouring Men*, Weidenfeld and Nicolson, 1968.

---

1 It should be stressed that different writers favour different taxes, even when they are all sympathetic to the same broad ideas; thus, for example, some would advocate seeking to tax all excess settlements while others, for reasons of administration, would confine the tax to large employers. A complete discussion of the available permutations would take many pages and would be out of place here.

W.J. McCarthy (ed.), *Trade Unions*, Penguin, 1972.

E.H. Phelps Brown, *The Inequality of Pay*, Oxford UP, 1977.

Royal Commission on the Distribution of Income and Wealth, *An A to Z of Income and Wealth*, HMSO, 1980.

Statistical Appendix

TABLE A-1
UK Gross Domestic Product, Expenditure (at 1980 prices), 1971-83 (£m)

Year	Consumers' Expenditure Durable Goods	Consumers' Expenditure Non-Durable Goods and Services	General Government Final Consumption	Gross Domestic Capital Formation Excluding Dwellings	Gross Domestic Capital Formation Dwellings	Value of Physical Increase in Stocks and Work in Progress	Exports of Goods and Services	Total Final Expenditure at Market Prices[2]	Imports of Goods and Services	Adjustment to Factor Cost[1]	Gross Domestic Product at Factor Cost[2]
1971	9,593	105,126	39,264	31,258	8,316	533	43,789	237,498	−42,838	−24,580	170,096
1972	11,636	109,883	40,885	30,838	8,670	−22	44,302	246,055	−47,101	−26,464	172,199
1973	12,263	115,471	42,814	33,716	8,082	5,047	49,451	266,716	−52,693	−28,208	185,538
1974	10,731	114,821	43,465	33,250	7,389	2,860	53,072	265,498	−53,350	−27,279	184,279
1975	10,816	114,008	45,814	32,281	8,016	−2,901	51,657	259,499	−49,576	−26,863	182,858
1976	11,367	113,730	46,249	32,632	8,224	1,081	56,282	269,425	−51,641	−27,783	189,743
1977	10,654	113,992	45,734	32,314	7,537	2,638	59,913	272,734	−52,251	−27,763	192,371
1978	12,109	119,376	46,728	33,476	7,734	2,090	61,024	282,537	−54,267	−30,270	198,000
1979	13,930	124,074	47,683	34,277	7,134	2,490	63,268	292,856	−59,908	−31,492	201,456
1980	13,019	124,305	48,387	32,899	6,342	−3,236	63,209	284,925	−57,429	−30,854	196,642
1981	13,415	124,144	48,250	30,833	4,828	−2,655	61,932	280,747	−55,462	−30,039	195,246
1982	13,483	125,907	48,938	32,598	5,286	−1,030	62,663	287,845	−57,564	−30,907	199,374
1983	16,875	127,937	50,473	33,610	6,053	748	63,190	298,886	−60,433	−31,979	206,474

Sources: *NIE*, 1983; *ET(AS)*, 1984; *ET*, April 1984.

Notes: 1 This represents taxes on expenditure less subsidies valued at constant prices.
2 For the years before 1978, totals differ from the sum of their components.

TABLE A-2

UK Prices, Wages, Earnings and Productivity, 1971-83: Index Numbers (1980 = 100)

Year	Retail Prices (All Items)	Weekly Wage Rates	Hourly Earnings (manufacturing)	Average Weekly Earnings (GB)	Average Earnings Non-manual Employees (GB)	Output per Person Employed (GDP)	Output per Person-Hour Worked (manufacturing)
	1	2	3	4	5	6	7
1971	30.3	25.3	25.7	26.4	26.6	90.4	82.8
1972	32.5	28.8	27.5	29.7	29.6	92.6	87.9
1973	35.5	32.7	31.2	33.8	32.8	96.1	94.1
1974	41.2	39.2	38.2	39.8	37.3	94.3	94.7
1975	51.1	50.8	48.5	50.4	48.2	93.0	93.0
1976	59.6	60.6	56.5	58.2	58.1	95.4	97.8
1977	69.0	64.6	61.9	63.5	63.5	97.8	98.7
1978	74.7	73.7	71.7	71.7	71.3	100.2	99.7
1979	84.8	84.7	83.0	82.9	79.9	102.6	101.3
1980	100.0	100.0	100.0	100.0	100.0	100.0	100.0
1981	111.9	110.2	114.2	112.9	115.9	101.5	104.3
1982	121.5	117.8	125.0	123.5	126.7	104.7	109.0
1983	127.1	124.4	136.2	133.9	138.3	107.8	115.3

Sources: Column 1: *ET(AS)*, 1984 and *ET*, May 1984. These figures have been recalculated to give 1980 = 100.

Columns 2, 3, 4: *NIER*, May 1984 and previous issues. Column 2 relates to manual workers only. Column 3 relates to manual and non-manual workers and is based on *NIER* estimates. Column 4 covers workers in all industries.

Column 5: *DEG*, January 1984 and previous issues. This series relates to GB and covers workers in all industries. The series is compiled on the basis of surveys for April of each year with a base year April 1970 = 100. For this Table, the figures have been recalculated to give 1980 = 100.

Columns 6, 7: *ET(AS)*, 1984 and *ET*, May 1984.

TABLE A-3

UK Personal Income, Expenditure and Saving 1971–83 (£m)

	PERSONAL INCOME BEFORE TAX							
Year	Wages and Salaries	Forces Pay	Employers' Contributions	Current Grants from Public Authorities	Other Personal Income	Total[1]	Transfers Abroad (Net)	UK Taxes on Income (Payments)
	1	2	3	4	5	6	7	8
1971	29,644	758	3,079	4,780	9,540	47,801	−12	6,515
1972	33,308	862	3,662	5,845	11,153	54,830	34	6,629
1973	38,443	925	4,418	6,420	13,515	63,721	78	7,726
1974	45,510	1,071	5,714	7,876	15,688	75,859	97	10,419
1975	59,010	1,283	8,097	10,284	17,985	96,659	110	15,042
1976	66,148	1,474	10,178	12,765	21,069	111,634	−28	17,422
1977	73,235	1,506	11,468	15,092	23,275	124,576	–	18,149
1978	83,821	1,645	12,971	17,871	26,693	143,001	74	19,501
1979	97,839	2,020	14,906	20,939	33,627	169,331	207	21,668
1980	115,714	2,436	17,752	25,458	39,280	200,640	256	25,851
1981	124,052	2,708	20,005	31,173	41,663	219,601	278	29,147
1982	132,661	2,904	20,714	36,309	46,445	239,033	268	32,304
1983	145,006		22,117	39,693	49,046	255,862	253	33,527

Sources: *NIE*, 1982, 1983; *ET*, April 1984.

Notes: 1 Before providing for depreciation and stock appreciation.
2 Before providing for depreciation, stock appreciation and additions to tax reserves.
Column 6 = 1 + 2 + 3 + 4 + 5
Column 10 = 6 − 7 − 8 − 9
Column 13 = 14 − 11
Column 15 = 10 − 14

National Insurance and Health Contributions	Total Personal Disposable Income[2]	CONSUMERS' EXPENDITURE				PERSONAL SAVINGS		
		Durable	Goods	Other				
		Amount (£m)	As % of PDI	Amount (£m)	Total	Amount[2] (£m)	As % of PDI	Year
9	10	11	12	13	14	15	16	
2,826	38,472	3,074	8.0	32,525	35,599	2,873	7.5	1971
3,337	44,830	4,119	9.2	36,381	40,500	4,330	9.7	1972
3,937	51,980	4,520	8.7	41,630	46,150	5,830	11.2	1973
5,000	60,343	4,575	7.6	48,512	53,087	7,256	12.0	1974
6,848	74,659	5,714	7.7	59,625	65,339	9,320	12.5	1975
8,426	85,814	6,798	7.9	68,994	75,792	10,022	11.7	1976
9,508	96,919	7,602	7.8	79,110	86,712	10,207	10.5	1977
10,107	113,319	9,762	8.6	89,834	99,596	13,723	12.1	1978
11,531	135,925	12,677	9.1	105,826	118,503	17,422	12.8	1979
13,944	160,589	13,019	8.1	124,305	137,324	23,265	14.5	1980
15,918	174,258	13,820	7.9	139,274	153,079	21,159	12.1	1981
18,139	188,322	15,511	8.2	152,879	168,390	19,932	10.6	1982
20,649	201,433	18,801	9.3	165,655	184,456	16,977	8.4	1983

TABLE A-4

UK Population, Working Population, Unemployment and Vacancies, 1971–83 (thousands)

Year	Total Population (Mid-year estimate)	Working Population[1,2]	Unemployed including school-leavers[1]	Unemployed excluding school-leavers (Monthly average)	Unemployment Rate (%)[3]	Vacancies (Monthly average)[4]
	1	2	3	4	5	6
1971	55,907	25,207	696	776	3.4	131
1972	56,082	25,267	778	855	3.7	147
1973	56,218	25,614	557	611	2.6	307
1974	56,231	25,658	528	611	2.6	297
1975	56,213	25,878	838	923	3.9	154
1976	56,202	26,093	1,265	1,249	5.2	122
1977	56,173	26,209	1,359	1,333	5.6	155
1978	56,160	26,342	1,343	1,319	5.5	210
1979	56,218	26,610	1,235	1,242	5.1	241
1980	56,303	26,819	1,513	1,561	6.4	143
1981	56,348	26,718	2,395	2,413	10.0	97
1982	56,335	26,730	2,770	2,793	11.7	111
1983[5]	n.a.	26,705	2,984	2,970	12.4	145

Sources: Column 1: *MDS*, May 1984; Columns 2 and 3: *ET(AS)*, 1984, and *MDS*, May 1984; Columns 4 and 5: *MDS*, May 1984; Column 6: *ET*, December 1983 and earlier issues; Column 6: *ET*, May 1984 and earlier issues.

Notes:

1 Estimates are for June of each year.

2 The Working Population includes employees in employment, self-employed persons, HM Forces and the unemployed (including school-leavers). Numbers in the sub-aggregates not given here may be found in the listed sources.

3 The unemployment rate is obtained by dividing the monthly average unemployment figure by the relevant figure for total employees (including unemployed) for June of that year. Self-employed and HM Forces are excluded from the figure for total employees.

4 Figures for 1974, 1975, 1976 and 1977 are based on estimates for some of the months.

5 The estimate for Column 1 for 1983 is not available.

TABLE A-5
UK General Government: Current Account, 1970–82 (£m)

	1970	1971	1972	1973	1974	1975	1976	1977	1978	1979	1980	1981	1982
RECEIPTS													
Taxes on income	7,388	8,003	8,100	9,164	12,589	16,646	18,846	20,333	22,449	25,032	30,740	35,789	40,300
Taxes on expenditure	8,417	8,740	9,255	10,124	11,453	14,136	16,456	20,028	22,956	29,755	36,157	42,090	47,082
National Insurance, etc. contributions	2,655	2,826	3,337	3,937	5,000	6,848	8,426	9,508	10,107	11,531	13,944	15,911	18,069
Gross trading surplus	152	177	146	139	148	162	149	188	205	190	189	199	124
Rent, etc.[1]	703	785	782	937	1,268	1,534	1,932	2,248	2,471	3,158	4,219	4,636	4,867
Interest and dividends, etc.	899	1,030	1,171	1,374	1,775	2,027	2,363	2,710	2,922	3,402	3,895	4,374	5,361
Imputed charge for consumption of non-trading capital	301	349	402	497	599	763	908	1,029	1,167	1,395	1,756	2,018	2,205
Total	20,515	21,910	23,193	26,172	32,832	42,116	49,080	56,044	62,277	74,463	90,900	105,017	118,008
EXPENDITURE													
Current expenditure on goods and services	8,690	9,901	11,273	12,875	16,029	22,193	25,833	28,233	31,904	36,966	46,663	52,520	57,877
Non-trading capital consumption	301	349	402	497	599	763	908	1,029	1,167	1,395	1,756	2,018	2,205
Subsidies	884	939	1,153	1,443	3,004	3,690	3,476	3,307	3,661	4,446	5,303	5,785	5,452
Grants to personal sector	4,330	4,780	5,845	6,420	7,876	10,284	12,765	15,092	17,871	20,957	25,484	31,173	36,169
Current grants abroad (net)	177	205	234	358	320	358	803	1,116	1,703	2,058	1,823	1,689	1,844
Debt interest	2,025	2,089	2,286	2,738	3,607	4,211	5,394	6,367	7,207	8,961	11,363	13,218	14,265
Total current expenditure	16,407	18,263	21,193	24,331	31,435	41,499	49,179	55,144	63,513	74,783	92,392	106,403	117,812
Balance: current surplus[2]	4,108	3,647	2,000	1,841	1,397	617	−99	900	−1,236	−320	−1,492	−1,386	196
Total	20,515	21,910	23,193	26,172	32,832	42,116	49,080	56,044	62,277	74,463	90,900	105,017	118,008

Sources: *NIE*, 1981, 1982, 1983.

Notes: 1 Includes royalties and license fees on oil and gas production.
      2 Before providing for depreciation and stock appreciation.

TABLE A-6

UK Money Stock, Domestic Credit Expansion, Public Sector Borrowing Requirement (£m), Interest Rates and Exchange Rate 1971-83

Year	Money Stock[1,4] (M₁)	Money Stock[2,4] (Sterling M₃)	Money Stock[3,4] (M₃)	Change in Money Stock[5] (Sterling M₃)	Domestic Credit Expansion[6]	Public Sector Borrowing Requirement[7]	Yield on UK Treasury Bills (%)	Yield on 2½% Consols (%)	Sterling Effective Exchange Rate[8]
	1	2	3	4	5	6	7	8	9
1971	11,088	20,111	20,541	2,459	1,177	1,364	4.46	9.05	133.1
1972	12,657	25,443	26,245	4,927	6,691	2,055	8.48	9.11	128.3
1973	13,303	32,046	33,478	6,702	8,066	4,200	12.82	10.85	116.3
1974	14,739	36,300	37,698	3,255	6,926	6,370	11.30	14.95	112.7
1975	17,483	37,595	40,573	2,331	4,466	10,501	10.93	14.66	104.1
1976	19,467	41,160	45,129	3,565	7,461	9,149	13.98	14.25	89.2
1977	23,523	45,154	49,429	4,130	701	5,988	6.39	12.31	84.5
1978	27,364	51,891	56,792	6,737	8,022	8,351	11.91	11.92	84.8
1979	29,856	58,487	63,806	6,596	10,329	12,638	16.49	11.38	90.8
1980	31,044	69,405	75,748	10,933	15,219	12,173	13.58	11.86	100.0
1981	34,452	78,784	88,854	9,379	13,908	10,730	15.39	12.99	99.2
	36,533	86,322	96,373						
1982	40,668	94,312	107,215	7,984	16,092	5,448	9.96	11.91	94.4
1983	45,230	104,120	120,721	9,577	n.a.	11,662	9.04	10.24	86.7

Sources: Columns 1–3: AAS, 1983, 1984 and FS, April 1984; Column 4: AAS, 1983, 1984, and FS, April 1984; Column 5: ET(AS), 1984, with revised figures kindly supplied by Bank of England; Column 6: AAS, 1984 and FS, April 1984; Column 7: ET(AS), 1984 and ET, April 1984; Column 8: AAS, 1984 and FS, April 1984; Column 9: ET(AS), 1984 and ET, April 1984. Columns 1–6 are all based on seasonally unadjusted data. Columns 1–3 refer to amounts outstanding at the year end.

Notes:

1 M_1 consists of notes and coins in circulation plus sterling sight deposits held by the private sector.

2 Sterling M_3 is a wide definition of the money stock. It includes notes and coins, together with all sterling deposits (including certificates of deposit) held by residents in the private and public sectors. See also Note 9 below.

3 This is column 2 plus all deposits held by UK residents in other countries. See also Note 9 below.

4 The money stock series contain a number of breaks caused by changes in the method of compilation of the series and, in particular, a major break at the end of 1981, for which two figures are shown above. The figures given here should be used with caution and reference should be made to the listed official publications for details of the statistical changes and the quantitative significance of the breaks.

5 For various reasons, partly covered in Note 4, the annual change given in column 4 is not necessarily equal to the first difference of column 2. See also Note 9 below.

6 DCE is the increase in the domestic money stock (£M_3) after adjustment for any change in money balances caused by external transactions. See chapter 2 and *BEQB*, March 1977. This series is now discontinued for reasons explained in *BEQB*, June 1983, p. 172. The entry for 1983 is not available.

7 The public sector includes the central government, the local authorities and public corporations. The borrowing requirement is discussed in chapter 2. See also Note 9 below.

8 This is a trade-weighted index of the foreign-exchange value of sterling. The official index is based on 1975 = 100, but for this Table the figures have been recalculated to give 1980 = 100. A decline in the index indicates an overall depreciation of sterling.

9 Series for columns 2, 3, 4 and 6 are based on the old definitions because revised figures for the full period covered by the Table were not available in time for publication. For a discussion of the new definitions, see *FS*, May 1984, p. 144, *ET*, February 1984, and chapter 2, section III.8. Revised data for more recent years were first presented in *FS*, May 1984.

TABLE A-7

UK Balance of Payments, 1971–83 (£m)

CURRENT ACCOUNT[1]

	Visible Trade			Invisibles			
Year	Exports (f.o.b.)	Imports (f.o.b.)	Visible Balance	Government Services and Transfers (net)	Private Services and Transfers (net)	Interest, Profits and Dividends (net)	Invisible Balance
	1	2	3	4	5	6	7
1971	9,043	−8,853	190	−520	952	502	934
1972	9,437	−10,185	−748	−585	1,018	538	971
1973	11,937	−14,523	−2,586	−767	1,117	1,257	1,607
1974	16,394	−21,745	−5,351	−839	1,497	1,415	2,073
1975	19,330	−22,663	−3,333	−928	1,975	773	1,820
1976	25,191	−29,120	−3,929	− 1,455	3,183	1,365	3,093
1977	31,728	−34,012	−2,284	− 1,815	4,037	116	2,338
1978	35,063	−36,605	−1,542	− 2,371	4,410	661	2,700
1979	40,687	−44,136	−3,449	− 2,800	4,606	1,090	2,896
1980	47,422	−45,909	1,513	− 2,456	4,644	−51	2,137
1981	50,977	−47,325	3,652	− 2,215	4,497	1,338	3,620
1982	55,565	−53,181	2,384	− 2,642	4,407	1,402	3,167
1983	60,658	−61,158	−500	− 2,901	4,970	480	2,549

Sources: *ET(AS)*, 1984; *ET*, March 1984.

Notes: 1   All items listed represent a positive flow if unsigned. Negative flows are indicated by a − sign preceding the figure. For capital-account items, a positive flow represents an increase in liabilities or a reduction in assets, whilst a negative flow indicates an increase in assets or a reduction in liabilities.

          2   Includes Capital Transfers for 1972 (−£59m) and 1974 (−£75m).

          3   The sum of Columns 8, 13 and 14 is defined in official sources as 'Balance for Official Financing'. The balance is normally the negative of the item shown in Column 15. For certain years this relationship is disturbed by special items which should be added to the sum of Columns 8, 13 and 14 in order to get the appropriate figure for Column 15. The special items during the period covered by this Table relate to various allocations of SDRs as follows: 1971, +125; 1972, +124; 1979, +195; 1980, +180; 1981, +158.

INVESTMENT AND OTHER CAPITAL TRANSACTIONS[1]

Current Balance	Official Long-term Capital	Overseas Long-term Investment in UK Private & Public Sectors	UK Private Long-term Investment Overseas	Other Capital Flows Mainly Short-term	Total Investment and Other Capital Transactions[2]	Balancing Item	Total Official Financing[3]
8	9	10	11	12	13	14	15
1,124	−274	1,015	−860	1,911	1,792	230	−3,271
223	−254	772	−1,402	211	−673	−815	1,141
−979	−255	1,497	−1,760	696	119	89	771
−3,278	−287	2,204	−1,148	833	1,527	105	1,646
−1,513	−291	1,514	−1,367	298	154	−106	1,465
−836	−161	2,091	−2,269	−2,636	−2,975	183	3,628
54	−303	4,399	−2,334	2,404	4,166	3,141	−7,361
1,158	−336	1,877	−4,604	−1,200	−4,263	1,979	1,126
−553	−401	4,283	−6,802	4,755	1,835	428	−1,905
3,650	−91	5,208	−8,033	1,461	−1,455	−1,003	−1,372
7,272	−336	3,458	−10,670	196	−7,352	−765	687
5,551	−337	3,609	−10,872	4,342	−3,258	−3,577	1,284
2,049	−562	6,405	−10,895	3,008	−2,044	−821	816

Index

inflation (*continued*)
  employment rates and, 8, 117
  excess demand and, 38-9, 42-6, 49,
    50
  exchange rates and, 41, 42, 47, 157-8,
    168
  and floating exchange rate, 157-8
  high demand and, 32
  high employment and, 25
  hyperinflation, 41
  and import prices, 47
  imported, 34, 38, 41-2, 47, 48, 50
  incomes policies and, 48-9, 297-301
  indexes, 37-8
  Keynesian view of, 63
  monetarist view of, 49-50, 58
  and money supply, 40, 41, 47, 49-50,
    57, 67, 299
  1960-83, 47
  PSBR and, 119-20, 121-2
  and purchasing-power parity, 158
  recent trends, 55, 56-7, 122, 124
  savings and, 12-13
  short-term capital flow and, 168
  since 1970, 48-9
  as a tax, 108, 120
  and trade unions, 39, 40, 46, 48, 49,
    50-1
  and unemployment, 34-5, 42-6, 50, 58,
    60, 64, 257, 298, 300
  and union membership, 288
  wages and, 34, 39, 40-1, 46-8, 50-1,
    297-301
information technology, 233-4
infrastructure, investment, 165
initial allowances, 111, 112
inland freight transport, 199
Inland Revenue, 6, 97, 288
  see also taxation
INMOS, 234, 236
innovation, 53, 54, 146-7, 148, 232-4
input, intermediate, 6
Institute for Employment Research, 266
insurance companies, 83, 96, 97
Insurance Companies Act 1974, 96
inter-bank market, 80
interest rates, 15
  building society, 95-6
  and capital inflow, 127
  and consumer expenditure, 28
  demand and, 62
  determination, 91
  and excess demand for money, 41
  and hire-purchase borrowing, 13
  and inflow of capital, 131
  in inter-bank market, 80
  investment and, 28
  minimum lending rate, 87, 118
  money supply and, 36, 41, 91
  mortgages, 95-6
  and multiplier process, 24

1971-83, 310
  North Sea oil and, 165
  profits and dividends (IPD), 171
  and public borrowing, 28, 36
  retail banks, 82
  and short-term capital flow, 169-70
intermediate development areas, 226
intermediate input, 5
International Monetary Fund (IMF), 66,
    130, 131, 136, 151, 156, 160, 166,
    177, 179-85, 188
  Jamaica Agreement, 185n
  Second Amendment, 182, 183-5
  Special Drawing Rights, 130-1, 180,
    181-3, 184
  Substitution Account, 183
  Supplementary Financing Facility, 184
  Trust Fund, 185n
intra-industry trade, 145-6
investment:
  acceleration principle, 15
  agriculture, 194, 195
  capital gains tax and, 108-9
  corporation tax and, 110
  currency, 169
  finance for industry, 232, 233-4, 240
  floating exchange rates and, 156
  forecasting, 29, 34
  foreign, 125, 130, 169, 170-1, 313
  grants, 112
  gross, 3, 4
  import controls and, 166
  income, 106
  and interest rates, 28, 62
  management, 83
  and net-present-value (NPV) rule, 202,
    203
  North Sea oil and, 165
  and output, 10, 16-17
  overseas, 97, 160
  pension funds, 97
  public-sector, 18
  and quality of capital stock, 53-4
  retail banks, 82
  taxation and, 99
  trusts, 83, 97, 108
  and UK external account, 127-9, 130
  see also fixed investment
IRC, *see* Industrial Reorganization
    Corporation
Ireland, Republic of:
  EEC regional policies and, 224
  strikes, 294
IRI, 200
Irving, R.W., 174n
Ishiyama, U., 177n
Isle of Man:
  accepting houses, 83
  banks, 77n
  financial institutions, 69
  overseas banks, 85